The Making of Lawyers' Careers

The Chicago Series in Law and Society
Edited by John M. Conley, Charles Epp, and Lynn Mather

ALSO IN THE SERIES:

The Crucible of Desegregation: The Uncertain Search for Educational Equality
by R. Shep Melnick

Cooperation without Submission: Indigenous Jurisdictions in Native Nation–US Engagements
by Justin B. Richland

BigLaw: Money and Meaning in the Modern Law Firm
by Mitt Regan and Lisa H. Rohrer

Union by Law: Filipino American Labor Activists, Rights Radicalism, and Racial Capitalism
by Michael W. McCann with George I. Lovell

Speaking for the Dying: Life-and-Death Decisions in Intensive Care
by Susan P. Shapiro

Just Words: Law, Language, and Power, Third Edition
by John M. Conley, William M. O'Barr, and Robin Conley Riner

Islands of Sovereignty: Haitian Migration and the Borders of Empire
by Jeffrey S. Kahn

Building the Prison State: Race and the Politics of Mass Incarceration
by Heather Schoenfeld

Navigating Conflict: How Youth Handle Trouble in a High-Poverty School
by Calvin Morrill and Michael Musheno

The Sit-Ins: Protest and Legal Change in the Civil Rights Era
by Christopher W. Schmidt

Working Law: Courts, Corporations, and Symbolic Civil Rights
by Lauren B. Edelman

The Myth of the Litigious Society: Why We Don't Sue
by David M. Engel

Policing Immigrants: Local Law Enforcement on the Front Lines
by Doris Marie Provine, Monica W. Varsanyi, Paul G. Lewis, and Scott H. Decker

The Seductions of Quantification: Measuring Human Rights, Gender Violence, and Sex Trafficking
by Sally Engle Merry

Invitation to Law and Society: An Introduction to the Study of Real Law, Second Edition
by Kitty Calavita

Pulled Over: How Police Stops Define Race and Citizenship
by Charles R. Epp, Steven Maynard-Moody, and Donald P. Haider-Markel

Additional series titles follow the index.

The Making of Lawyers' Careers

Inequality and Opportunity in the American Legal Profession

ROBERT L. NELSON, RONIT DINOVITZER,
BRYANT G. GARTH, JOYCE S. STERLING,
DAVID B. WILKINS, MEGHAN DAWE,
AND ETHAN MICHELSON

The University of Chicago Press
Chicago and London

The University of Chicago Press, Chicago 60637
The University of Chicago Press, Ltd., London
© 2023 by The University of Chicago
Published 2023
Printed in the United States of America

32 31 30 29 28 27 26 25 24 23   1 2 3 4 5

ISBN-13: 978-0-226-82890-9 (cloth)
ISBN-13: 978-0-226-82892-3 (paper)
ISBN-13: 978-0-226-82891-6 (e-book)
DOI: https://doi.org/10.7208/chicago/9780226828916.001.0001

Library of Congress Cataloging-in-Publication Data

Names: Nelson, Robert L., 1952– author. | Dinovitzer, Ronit, 1971– author. |
    Garth, Bryant G., author. | Sterling, Joyce Sheila, 1945– author. |
    Wilkins, David B., author. | Dawe, Meghan, author. | Michelson, Ethan, author.
Title: The making of lawyers' careers : inequality and opportunity in the American
    legal profession / Robert L. Nelson, Ronit Dinovitzer, Bryant G. Garth, Joyce S.
    Sterling, David B: Wilkins, Meghan Dawe, and Ethan Michelson.
Other titles: Chicago series in law and society.
Description: Chicago ; London : The University of Chicago Press, 2023. |
    Series: Chicago series in law and society | Includes bibliographical
    references and index.
Identifiers: LCCN 2023016561 | ISBN 9780226828909 (cloth) |
    ISBN 9780226828923 (paperback) | ISBN 9780226828916 (ebook)
Subjects: LCSH: Lawyers—United States. | Lawyers—United States—Social conditions. |
    Law—Vocational guidance—United States. | Practice of law—United States. |
    Equality before the law—United States. | Discrimination in employment—
    Law and legislation—United States.
Classification: LCC KF297 .N45 2023 | DDC 340.023/73—dc23/eng/20230508
LC record available at https://lccn.loc.gov/2023016561

To John P. Heinz:
teacher, mentor, role model, scholar, writer, and friend

Contents

Note on Authorship ix

PART 1 Introduction

1 Introduction: The Making of Lawyers' Careers   3

2 From the Golden Age to the Age of Disruption:
   Setting the Context for Lawyers' Careers in the New Millennium   27

PART 2 The Structure of Lawyers' Careers

3 Change and Continuity in the Legal Field: From Walled-Off
   Hemispheres to More or Less Mixed Hierarchical Sequences   49

4 Race, Class, and Gender in the Structuring of Lawyers' Early Careers   79

5 Two Hemispheres Revisited: Fields of Law, Practice Settings,
   and Client Types   99

PART 3 The Narratives of Lawyers' Careers

6 Moving Up and Moving On: Careers in Law Firms   131

7 Rethinking the Solo Practitioner   165

8 Moving Inside: Practicing Law in Business Organizations   197

9 Commitment, Careerism, and Stratification: Careers in
   Government, Nonprofits, and Public Interest Organizations   215

PART 4 Inequalities of Race and Gender

10 White Spaces: The Enduring Racialization of American Law Firms   243
   With Vitor M. Dias

11 Student Debt and Cumulative (Dis)Advantage in Lawyers' Careers   260

12 Hegemonic Masculinity, Parenthood, and Gender Inequality   278
   With Andreea Mogosanu

PART 5 Public Roles and Private Lives

13 Dualities of Politics, Public Service, and Pro Bono in Lawyers' Careers   303
    With Ioana Sendroiu

14 Lawyers' Satisfaction and the Making of Lawyers' Careers   325
    With Ioana Sendroiu

PART 6 Conclusion

15 Conclusion: Structure and Agency in the Making of Lawyers' Careers   351

Acknowledgments 367
Notes 369
References 375
Index 395

An online appendix can be found at https://themakingoflawyerscareers.org.

Note on Authorship

This book is the culmination of more than 20 years of collaboration by some of the authors. The authorship listed in the table of contents reflects a combination of the long-term contributions of authors and more recent efforts to analyze and write up the findings. Scholars who primarily worked on specific chapters—Vitor Dias, Andreea Mogosanu, and Ioana Sendroiu—are listed as *with* for those chapters.

While all the authors contributed and commented on the entire manuscript, some are primarily responsible for certain parts of the book. The introduction and conclusion—chapters 1 and 15—were coauthored by Robert Nelson, David Wilkins, Bryant Garth, Ronit Dinovitzer, and Meghan Dawe. David Wilkins took the lead on chapter 2. Ronit Dinovitzer, in addition to playing a leading role in all phases of data collection and the maintenance of longitudinal files, coauthored chapter 3 with Bryant Garth, chapter 12 with Andreea Mogosanu, and chapter 14 with Robert Nelson, Ioana Sendroiu, and Meghan Dawe. Joyce Sterling and Bryant Garth conducted most of the in-depth interviews presented throughout the book and featured in part 3 and were the lead coauthors of part 3. Meghan Dawe and Robert Nelson were the primary authors of chapters 4 and 5, collaborated on the analysis and writing of the narrative chapters, and were coauthors of chapters 13 and 14. Meghan Dawe was the sole author of chapter 11, was the main data analyst for the most recent phase of the After the JD (AJD) Project, and was the executive editor for the overall manuscript. Ethan Michelson was the main author of chapter 10.

PART 1

Introduction

Introduction:
The Making of Lawyers' Careers

Five Lawyers' Careers

Alicia, Paula, James, Lynden, and Constance are lawyers. Though all spent part of their careers in a business-oriented law firm with more than 100 attorneys, they have followed distinctive career trajectories. Alicia, a White woman, attended a lesser-ranked urban law school and started in a litigation defense firm. Paula, a Latina, attended an elite law school and, like most of her classmates, initially worked in a prestigious corporate law firm. James, a White man, graduated from an even *more* elite law school (consistently ranked in the top 6), held two federal clerkships, and joined a prestigious law firm known for high-profile criminal defense work. Lynden, an African American man, graduated from a top-20 law school and became an associate in a leading DC litigation law firm. And Constance, also a Latina,[1] attended law school at night while working as a full-time social worker in child protective services (CPS), where she impressed a district attorney who offered her an internship in another unit and hired her as a staff attorney on graduation.

Comparing these five divergent career trajectories reveals important truths about the legal profession's early twenty-first-century structure of opportunity and the strategies individual lawyers employ to navigate its possibilities and constraints. We start with Alicia.

Alicia   With an LLM in international business, Alicia originally set her sights on a large, major-market firm. "When people say, 'You're from one of those firms,' they're impressed," Alicia said, noting their "great resources," "incredible reputations," and "considerably better" pay. We do not know whether she had access to such jobs, but she ultimately decided those firms were a poor fit for her goals: "I really wanted somewhere . . . that was a family orientated firm, that if something happened, they understood. That I could have a weekend life, I had a social life." Thus, she was pleased to begin her career at a midsize law firm with more than 100 lawyers. Primarily an insurance defense firm, it tended to hire graduates from tier 3 schools like Alicia's and paid beginning associates just over half the largest firms' starting salaries. Her hire may have been facilitated by a family connection, though Alicia avoided mentioning it while interviewing—she told us she wanted to get the job on her own merit.

In our first interview with Alicia, she was three years into her career and exuded personal and professional confidence. She observed that she was out-performing other associates, gaining significant responsibility on trial mat-ters, and on the partner track: "I know I definitely, within five years, will be married and will have at least one child . . . and most likely two. And I know that my goal is to be partner within five years from now." By the second inter-view, six years later, her narrative was less optimistic, peppered with warning signs about her future at the law firm. For instance, she said when she started at the firm it took "approximately six to eight years" to make partner but that now it was more like eight to ten years: "I'm hitting that nine-year mark. I was up [for partner] last year, and obviously I didn't get it. I'll probably be up again this year." Putting in close to twelve-hour days and using the weekends to "catch up," she was beginning to see her firm as "somewhat discriminatory," suggesting that "some of the other gentlemen who've made partner just from [her] group" were not working as hard or as productively as she was. Just as she had reassessed her goal to work in a large corporate law firm, she was now reassessing her goal of making partner at this smaller insurance defense firm.

Describing it as an "epiphany," Alicia nonetheless seemed to be trying to justify her assertion that she did not "need the title *partner* to be a good law-yer": "At this stage, I don't need to be partner. I don't need the title. Would I like it? Yes, but I don't need it. If I don't make it this year, that's fine. If I don't make it ever, that's fine. It doesn't change my work quality; it doesn't change who I am; it doesn't change anything about me at all. . . . It's an honor, but it's not a necessity." She also reported some personal disappointments—a breakup and the vagaries of the dating scene—but, when we asked where we would find her in three or four years, she still answered "probably right here."

In our third interview with Alicia, she was 12 years into her career. She had been passed up for partner again, a senior male partner intimating that the decision had been closely contested but that, ultimately, he suspected that some partners deemed her "not pretty enough," and Alicia noted that she had failed to land corporate clients. She struggled for another year at the firm before securing an inside counsel position in a large financial company in the same city on the strength of her wide-ranging litigation experience and abil-ity to think strategically.

Reflecting on her job change, Alicia conceded that being passed over for partner had been "very painful" yet ultimately positive. Moving to the bank position "changed [her] way of thinking about the law": "It changed my way of thinking about me.... The past two years have been amazing. I work really hard, yes, but me as a human I'm happier." She did not mention marriage or children, and she was working roughly similar hours for slightly less pay, but she was "back . . . to feeling excited about being a lawyer." She had adapted her practice, spoke in glowing terms about the diversity of her corporate law department, and appreciated that her coworkers accepted her bold style (including choosing to wear brightly colored hair and drive a sports car). As of 2021, her LinkedIn page shows her in the same city, holding an even more senior inside counsel position at another financial institution.

Paula The daughter of Mexican immigrants, Paula followed her older sister out of the family's working-class roots and into a law career. She attended a top public university, graduated from an elite law school, and began in corporate practice with a leading national law firm where she had spent her first summer as an intern. She started in a relatively small office in a major legal market. She was interested in partnership but reckoned chances were slim "because the corporate practice at that time had one, two, three partners and . . . maybe about five associates": "I didn't see there was a way." During her early years at the firm, Paula considered herself fortunate to gain informal mentorship from a female equity partner: "She was good in the sense that some of the practices she taught me I still have to this day." Still, she never felt that the partner would really go to bat for her: "I don't think that she was . . . the sort to, like, 'I'm going to adopt you, and I'm going to make sure you make it, too.' "

After a few years, Paula married and moved to a new city so that her husband could be closer to his ailing father. The firm transferred her to an office there, and she hoped it would provide a "fresh start." Unfortunately, it became apparent that it was "pretty tough as a woman" in the new environment, an "old boys' kind of club." After her father-in-law died, Paula and her family decided to move back to their original city.

With her education credentials and experience, Paula found it easy to move to another prestigious firm. The new job, however, proved short-lived. After just a year and a half, she left, explaining:

> I think at that point, I just really was frustrated . . . with practice in a big law firm; by that point it wasn't what I really wanted anymore. . . . In a way, it was lack of fit, too. . . . I did have a very good mentor at [the second firm], but

he wasn't in general corporate practice. He was not in my practice group. . . .
And he was very honest and . . . told me what he thought it took to become a
partner, . . . but I saw what it took from his side, and . . . he worked all the time.
Networked all the time.

Noting that this mentor had a stay-at-home wife, she recalled: "And so at that
point I think it was more a decision about 'what kind of lifestyle do I want?'
Do I want [work and networking] to be my primary focus in my life? Or do I
want to—and I was married . . . but I did not have children . . .—have more of
a balanced lifestyle?" With the help of a headhunting firm, she hit the market
again.

Today, Paula is the deputy general counsel at a Spanish-language media
company. She has been there for 15 years and hopes one day to become general counsel (whether with this company or another). She speaks Spanish at
work, she is satisfied with her position, and she is pleased that "the hours here
at work are very nice" because she now has three children. Conceding that
motherhood has involved opting out of networking opportunities, she does
note that a significant career shift could be tough: "I think I've missed out,
probably a lot, by not going to all these networking events. [These events can
make] a connection for another job. I mean, I'm not there to meet people."

James   James's story helps illustrate the operation of large law firms' fast
track to partnership. At his first interview, James had been working in his
firm for six years. Though he did not come from privilege, his father was
a respected professional, and he went to a top-10 undergraduate institution
and a top-10 law school. After clerking for two federal judges, he essentially
had his pick of jobs. He received an offer from the Justice Department Honors Program, which he believed would give him "a lot of opportunities to do
things as a young lawyer." One of his coclerks, however, had an offer from a
prestigious national law firm and suggested James might find it attractive. Indeed, he did. At his interview, James remembered, he liked everyone he met
and thought the work was "very interesting." When he accepted the position,
he was not gunning for partnership:

> I never really thought that I would be the big firm lawyer for a long time. I
> think coming in from the outside I sort of expected that going to a big, known
> firm, that it would be insurmountable hours and I would burn out relatively
> quickly. And I came in thinking, "I'll just see how it goes," . . . and nothing
> has driven me away. I mean I've had a good experience, and so . . . I wouldn't
> have told you coming in that this is something I was looking for, but I've been
> happy while I've been here.

The mentorship environment—particularly informal mentorship, which helped him learn "things [he] should be trying to do" and "people to work with or avoid"—facilitated his success, and he was grateful to "have had people look out for me in terms of getting the breadth of experience" he needed. For him, it fit with the firm's emphasis on building relationships rather than simply generating business. "While I'm sure no one would look down their nose at you if you were out there trying to gather business, it's not something that is stressed," he said.

Unsurprisingly, in our wave 2 interview, James had been elevated to his firm's single tier of equity partners. He remained modest, saying: "It certainly was not my dream all along to be a partner at a big law firm, but the fact was I enjoyed what I was doing and sort of kept checking in every couple of years and realizing things seemed to be going well." Making partner simply felt like a good fit: "So . . . if it's possible, I guess I feel more included than before." He made clear, however, that becoming partner was based on doing excellent work. His work straddles the line between civil and criminal practice, which is a hallmark of his law firm. He has gained more responsibility, but his has been a gradual process of accumulating more stature in the firm.

When we asked during his wave 3 interview what it took to become a partner, James responded that partners must have a "broad range of skills" and "fit the culture." He also conceded that these criteria are "easy to say and . . . harder to identify": "But that is it. I mean, you're looking for . . . the next generation of people we think are stars." One must fit within the firm and possess some quality that the existing partners recognize but cannot define. With respect to diversity, James felt that his firm was more committed to diversity than most large firms, but he flagged the often-mentioned problem of attrition among minorities.

As for work/life balance, James noted in his third interview that, "selfishly, [he didn't] know how [they] would have made it through" a particularly time-consuming trial if his wife were not currently a stay-at-home parent to their two children. When the couple met, both worked as lawyers at the same firm; when they married, she moved to a government position. By the wave 3 interview, James reported that she "didn't go back [to work]" after their second child and was "trying to decide what she's going to do next": "And it's driving her crazy. She wants to be back at work, yes. . . . She was never the, she will tell you, the 'stay-at-home mom.'"

Lynden   Lynden is an African American lawyer who was pushed out of a large law firm and typifies the fate of many African American lawyers in law firms. Raised by a single mother who worked as a maid, he had overcome those disadvantages to attend an elite undergraduate school and after graduation land a science-oriented position with the federal government. He then attended a top-20 law school and became an associate in a prestigious DC law firm. Seeking a litigation practice, he moved to another well-regarded DC law firm that focused on litigation. From the beginning he felt like an outsider and worried that he was perceived as lacking the requisite "businessperson type of personality" that would make him partnership material. At our first interview, he had not yet been considered for promotion to partner. He had two children, and his wife essentially stayed at home, allowing him to throw himself into the partnership tournament.

But, at the wave 2 interview, Lynden had been turned down for partnership, had been given notice of his termination, and was trying to figure out his next move. In discussing what went wrong, he suspected he was left out of practice groups on account of his race—which kept him from being able to bond with partners. He did not find powerful mentors who might help him take care of "what would be necessary" for him to make partner. Worse, when the practice groups began to splinter from the law firm in the recession, groupless Lynden was simply terminated. No one in the firm protected him. No one led him to another opportunity. Reflecting back on his experience, he recognized that he had never made it into a "silo" within which he could prosper. That left him "bouncing around the outside." He was grateful to fall in with others "who were not in a silo": "And those people were very nice to me, gave me great advice, but they can't help me maneuver, so I was on the outside bouncing around, . . . and they were bouncing with me." Prompted to discuss why he thought he was a perpetual outsider at the firm, he said: "Well, you know, this is not completely unrelated to race and background and things like that. It's part of what world you grow up in . . . it's . . . the comfort level in networking . . . in an all-White, mostly all-White world. . . . Seems like . . . but I'm not sure it's race." Could it also be related to social class—the "background" he mentioned? Lynden conceded that he had lacked common cultural capital with the partners: "Right, I've been asked if I could be a fourth for some golfing, and I've never . . . I've never even been on a green."

By the third After the JD (AJD) Project interview, Lynden had returned to working in the federal government, this time as a lawyer for a regulatory agency. Unlike in the law firm, in his new job he had the opportunity to appear regularly in court to represent his agency.

Constance Constance started her career very differently than did Alicia, Paula, or James. She worked full-time as a CPS social worker while attending the night program at a midtier law school. On one of her CPS cases, her hard

work and intelligence impressed the district attorney. This led to an internship during her last year of law school and, eventually, a job in the district
attorney's office on graduation. After starting her career in the domestic violence unit, she was promoted to felony assaults, then gang prosecutions. It
was considered a plum assignment, though she said it prompted "really good
advice" from a lawyer who had left the district attorney's office: "Try your
first murder case, and get out. . . . You've got everything you are going to get
out of the office from a training perspective, and then they're going to suck
you dry." Constance took the advice to heart. She tried her first murder case
while pregnant with her second child, then took advantage of a serendipitous
relationship.

As it happened, Constance had prosecuted a criminal defense attorney
for engaging in a conspiracy to bribe a witness. The expert witness she hired
to testify on the legal obligations of the defense lawyer was impressed by her
work and told her he would be happy to hire her when she was ready to leave
the district attorney's office. Later, when she completed that first murder trial,
she accepted the offer. Constance and her mentor now working alongside
each other in a small branch office of a large law firm, the two were building a practice advising and representing lawyers on ethical issues. Through
extensive publications and speaking engagements, they grew their practice
and attracted attention. An even larger and more national law firm recruited
them both to join as lateral partners, bringing their whole group with them.

Constance became a nationally recognized expert in the niche practice
area of advising and defending lawyers on ethical issues. In our last interview,
she spoke of her satisfaction with her somewhat unanticipated career trajectory: "I don't think anybody in law school knows that this is a thing . . . that
you can have a very successful national practice based entirely on representing lawyers and law firms and it's really, really fun." Not only is she professionally prominent and well compensated, but she also has considerable flexibility
in her work schedule: "Nobody knows where I am. So I work at home a lot.
I'm on the road. So I don't think I have a typical day. I'm a single parent, so I
have a lot of here and there obligations. . . . I'm usually out of [the office] by
3:30 or 4:00 P.M. . . . Last night I took my daughter to practice . . . drop her
off, and then go to like a Starbucks or a place nearby and work for two hours
while she's in practice, and go back and get her." Nevertheless, Constance
mused that she might consider changing practice areas within her firm once
her children graduated from college. LinkedIn shows that she subsequently
moved to a partnership position in a large international law firm in the same
city before relocating to a national legal market where she now works as a
partner and deputy general counsel for a large global law firm. The average

partner compensation at her firm—including both equity and nonequity partners—is reportedly $1.25 million per year.

Inequality and Opportunity: Connecting Agency and Social Structure

These five stories are rooted in and take meaning from the structures of the American legal profession. They also reveal the role of personal agency in the making of lawyers' careers. Large-scale social structures—hierarchies such as gender, race, class, law school status, and macroeconomic conditions—all shape lawyers' career prospects, yet they are not necessarily determinative. Social hierarchies structure the careers of lawyers. They do not function as a caste system, yet they also do not disappear just because someone has achieved success by beating the odds to obtain a certain position.

Keying into personal narratives allows us to see that social and professional hierarchies hold contingent power: sometimes they are background conditions, and other times they emerge as dynamic factors. Paula drew on her elite credentials (as well as her Spanish-language proficiency) to move in-house, a shift that reflects the changing organization of corporate legal services. Constance worked her way up from the ground level, from night school to a local government job, a boutique law practice in a satellite office of a regional firm, a partnership in a national law firm, a partnership in an international law firm, and, finally, a partnership and a deputy general counsel position in a global firm (a new kind of position that underscores the importance of her emerging specialty, representing lawyers). With her credentials, it is unlikely Constance could have obtained an entry-level position in her current firm; instead, at each stage, she impressed powerful mentors who facilitated her upward movement. In fact, as Paula's story showed, it is even less likely that Constance could have risen through the ranks to equity partnership—the old-boy network remains pervasive in many firms, just one of many structural obstacles for those outside majority power broker groups. Paula saw the limitations of mentorship when she realized her mentor was not willing to push for her success, and Alicia, who appeared on the cusp of partnership after nine years in her firm, found sexism prevented her advancement. Both were still able to convert their experience into successful careers outside corporate law firms. Lynden experienced how largely White law firms may hire African American attorneys who then still may feel as if they are social class outsiders. Without powerful mentors, they will bounce around the power centers of the firm and get fired when the economy sours. After this disappointment, Lynden followed a track that many African American attorneys take—moving into a government position.

Parenting and partnerships also arose as important to success. Certainly, Constance's career narrative is one among many proving that female attorneys *are* able to parent while maintaining high-powered professional careers. Yet part of Constance's strategy involves full-time domestic help; another is her ability to work on the move, unconfined at this point by an office schedule. Interviews reveal that this is not a viable strategy for many other women, who joke about their need to have a wife who can take care of childcare and domestic responsibilities. Men typically do not face the same trade-offs of career and family, nor do they equally share homemaking with their wives (Bianchi et al. 2000; Kan et al. 2011; Offer and Schneider 2011). James attributed his own success in part to his wife's decision to put her career as a lawyer on hold in order to look after their children even though she had never aspired to do so and appeared eager to get back to work. Paul noted that her husband works from home and that, at the time of our third interview, the family had a nanny. Still, she suggested that to accommodate her family she had not done the kind of networking she thought might help her realize her ambition to become a general counsel.

These individual narratives are framed by the deep structures of the American legal profession, structures conditioned by the market and by enduring legal and professional hierarchies. Through historical processes of iterative social construction, the market and the hierarchies are racialized and gendered and classed. Despite considerable change, inequalities remain inextricable from the operation of the market and the professional opportunities that are open or closed to individual lawyers—or perceived as such.

In these five stories, for instance, we can see the division between public sector law and private sector law and their correlated inequalities—the higher pay and status afforded the private bar vs. government and public interest practice and how stepping into one track or the other can have career-long impacts on mobility and earnings. All five lawyers introduced thus far came to ply their professional skills in private practice in the service of resource-rich business and professional clients (two-thirds of the lawyers in our study were, by the time they entered the profession, dedicated to serving business clients, from small to large businesses). The career opportunities and rewards of the public sector are dwarfed by those of private practice, particularly for those representing business clients. Those lawyers who begin their careers in the public sector frequently receive the advice Constance was given: to convert public sector capital into private sector opportunity as soon as possible. It is not entirely unusual for lawyers like her to cross this structural boundary, though her story is exceptional in that she moved from state prosecutor to partner in a large corporate law firm. Paula, meanwhile, represents what is becoming a well-trod elite path from a top-tier law school to a large law firm to a well-paid and increasingly prestigious in-house counsel position. This path provides, as we will see, an outlet for the many lawyers who will never make partner at the law firms they initially join—a reality particularly significant for women, who have flocked to in-house counsel positions in recent years.

Indeed, the experiences of these three women stand in sharp contrast to the narrative shared by James. A White man with elite education credentials, he began as an associate in a large law firm, was nurtured and coached, and seamlessly transitioned to equity partner, all while feeling right at home. In a profession dominated by elite White men, his is the traditional path, flowing from first year to partnership. Although Paula and Constance underscore that women—including some Latinx, African American, Asian American, and Native American lawyers—are key players at the country's top law firms, their career trajectories are nonetheless nontraditional for the structure of their profession. James was obviously devoted to his wife (formerly a fellow lawyer at his firm) and spoke warmly of her interest in returning to practice, perhaps in a public sector or nonprofit organization, though he noted frankly that her decision to leave the labor market facilitated his high-level litigation practice. He had also imbibed the firm's common sense regarding diversity (that it was desirable but hard to achieve because minority lawyers rarely stayed long) and continued to judge potential partners on the subjective standard of fit. Lynden exemplifies how lawyers of color from disadvantaged backgrounds do not achieve fit and may be characterized by firm leaders as an example of the difficulty of retaining attorneys of color when in fact they were left unprotected in the law firm and pushed out.

This book is based on the AJD Project, a unique longitudinal study on which five of the coauthors have worked for over two decades. The project has followed more than 5,000 lawyers who began practice in the year 2000 and were selected as a representative national sample of new lawyers. Its unprecedented data set includes over 10,000 survey responses and 219 in-depth interviews, allowing us to investigate lawyers' careers from many angles. For instance, we can tease out the role of social hierarchies of race, ethnicity, and gender as well as hierarchies of prestige like those associated with law school selectivity and more or less esteemed legal specialties. We can consider how education debt affects the lives and careers of law school graduates. Putting these data in conversation with a robust social scientific literature clarifies the contours of the legal field at a moment when many commentators— even a fair number of lawyers—suggest the legal profession is undergoing a significant transition, perhaps even a crisis (Barton 2015; Campos 2012; Garth 2017; Monahan and Swanson 2019; Tamanaha 2012; Yoon 2014).

A good portion of the scholarly literature, for instance, documents and laments the disproportionate exodus of women and minorities from law firms prior to partnership consideration. When questioned, the firms posit that women usually leave because of lifestyle and family commitments and that minorities leave for other opportunities, pursuing work in politics or government. Our study suggests, instead, that law firms have been built on a specifically White and masculine structure that has begun to take up the rhetoric of diversity but changed only slightly in relation to external pressure. All women—even those who do not have children—are penalized in the profession and may leave when they believe they have maxed out their advancement potential, while people of color (especially African Americans and Native Americans) are not primarily lured away by other opportunities but pushed out by discrimination, alienation, and a lack of supportive, effective mentorship.

There are many versions of the perpetual literature on the downside and limits of lawyers' careers. We address many of the themes in these introductory chapters and in chapter 14. One strand reasons that, because of the high debt that most law school graduates incur, individuals should not attend law school unless they are reasonably sure that they can secure the high starting salaries of corporate law firms. By extension, one should not attend lower-ranked law schools since their students are seldom granted access to corporate positions. We find, however, that the vast majority who graduate from law schools across the rankings find ways to succeed that lead them to value their law degree and their decision to attend law school. There are many stories of upward mobility.

One way the upward mobility story is told in the legal profession is expressed in the statement that, once a lawyer begins to practice, law school pedigree no longer matters. What matters is the quality of the lawyer's work. Although graduates from almost all law schools are found in almost all legal positions, we find that the advantages associated with law school prestige—which include entrée to corporate law firms and then to a host of other positions that are most available to those who began in corporate positions—accumulate and over time widen the gap between those who graduate from highly ranked law schools and those who graduate from lower-ranked schools. We see this in income, in the ability to repay debt, and in the status of the positions attained. That these elite law school graduates are also more likely to come from privileged social backgrounds underscores the degree to which our study shows how opportunity and upward mobility exist in a market that is overwhelmingly characterized by the reproduction of advantage in school attended, race, gender, ethnicity, and social class.

This book's combination of quantitative, qualitative, and public records data provides a unique lens through which to consider the American legal profession. We are able, in these chapters, to address the ways structural stasis and change interact with individual agentic strategies to shape lawyers' careers and to consider the evidence for some of the most common, often contradictory critiques of the profession. As scholars write about the crisis of American law, many charge that it has become too commercialized, abandoning a traditional commitment to public service and reasoned deliberation in the pursuit of profit (Glendon 1996; Kronman 1993; Linowitz 1994). The fact that most Americans have virtually no access to legal services stands as the most potent and visible manifestation of this critique (Hadfield 2016; Sandefur 2014). Further, the rewards of a legal career are not equally attainable, and scholars rightly underscore disparities in the incomes and opportunities available to women and minorities—particularly in elite settings—as evidence of ongoing discrimination (Epstein et al. 1995; Sterling and Reichman 2016; Wilkins and Gulati 1996). Others argue, instead, that a growing professional instability (venerated firms failing, incomes slipping against the cost of living, widespread layoffs) has made legal careers less desirable. In other words, a law degree is no longer considered a ticket to a secure and lucrative career (Merritt 2015; Susskind 2013). From blogs to the legal press, stories in this vein abound: a rewarding legal career is all but out of reach amid grinding hours, crushing education debt, and a lack of meaningful work (see the references in Monahan and Swanson 2019). The 2008 global financial crisis accentuated these concerns. Suddenly, fewer than 60% of law school graduates were able to find a job requiring a JD, leading law schools saw their enrollments plummet from historic highs, and a few closed their doors for good (American Bar Association 2016; Leipold and Collins 2016; Merritt 2015; Rampell 2013; Tamanaha 2012). With law firms shuttering (Yoon 2014) and disruptions in the form of legal process outsourcing, paraprofessionals, and alternative legal service providers proliferating in other arenas, from technology companies to the Big Four accounting firms (Wilkins and Esteban Ferrer 2018), commentators have speculated about "the death of big law" (Ribstein 2010) and "the end of lawyers" (Susskind 2008).

To be sure, the crisis commentary is neither new (Garth 2013; Solomon 1992) nor generally based in valid research methods (Monahan and Swanson 2019). It may simply reflect the positions of elites and/or those critics who benefit from participating in public debate (Garth 2013). Still, these widely shared critiques are influential in public and professional conceptions of the legal profession, so they merit serious consideration. Our sociological inquiry also recognizes that the recurring but evolving crisis rhetoric is itself part of the process of professional change and reproduction. The crises are evoked as entrepreneurs/brokers argue that their suggestions and corrections—more use of technology, more diversity, more family-friendly workplaces, larger intellectual property departments, better compliance with professional standards—are essential to the legitimacy and/or survival of the profession. So, too, are the rebuttals, in which hierarchies are reiterated and professional ideologies clarified in recommitments to public service and meritocratic standards.

Theoretical Perspectives

Our analysis in this book draws on the Bourdieusian categories of the legal field (more on this momentarily) and three general theoretical perspectives that have shaped the sociology of the legal profession. The book is, of course, a collaborative project, so as authors we vary in our theoretical orientations. For example, some of us see the crisis literature in Bourdieusian terms as jousting for symbolic power among actors in the legal system, while some of us take the crisis critique on its own terms.

Before we can move forward, readers may appreciate a brief overview of the three interconnected, coconstituted theoretical perspectives most common to the sociology of the legal profession: the hemispheres thesis, social capital theory (and the profession-specific interplay between social and other forms of human capital), and a range of political economy theories that situate the legal profession in the broader economic, social, and political contexts in which lawyers and clients live and work. Again, though we outline these perspectives separately and in terms of their differing orientations and research agendas, each is significantly connected to and informed by the other.

HEMISPHERES

We begin, as has almost every other account of the American legal profession in the past 40 years, with the foundational work of John Heinz and Edward Laumann on lawyers in Chicago. Working under the auspices of the American Bar Foundation, in 1975 Heinz and Laumann conducted one of the first comprehensive studies of lawyers in a single jurisdiction, surveying 777 randomly selected lawyers from every sector of the Chicago bar. In the resulting *Chicago Lawyers* (Heinz and Laumann 1982), they argued against

standard orthodoxy, regarding lawyers neither as members of a single uni-
fied profession nor as representatives of distinct subprofessions based on
legal specialty or expertise. Instead, the lawyers in their sample were most
usefully divided into two hemispheres by clientele: the *personal plight sector*
(those who served individuals and small businesses) and the *corporate sector* (those who served businesses and other large organizations). By way of
demonstration, they showed that many other apparent distinctions could be
explained by this fundamental divide. Lawyers in the corporate hemisphere,
for instance, occupied the socially and economically desirable end of other
divides; they hailed from elite social backgrounds, attended top law schools,
worked in larger law firms, did prestigious legal work, and earned high incomes. Jews, Catholics, and other ethnoreligious minorities, on the other
hand, were largely excluded from the corporate hemisphere and concentrated
in the personal plight sector. They tended to graduate from local law schools,
work in state and local government or in solo or small-firm practice, handle
less prestigious work (like criminal defense and personal injury), and make
far more modest incomes. At the time of this initial study, these two sectors
of the bar were roughly equal in size—hence the designation *hemispheres*—
and largely distinct, with few lawyers moving from one hemisphere to the
other. Heinz and Laumann conclude: "Though there are certainly distinctions among lawyers that cut across the line between the two broad classes of
clients, this fundamental difference in the nature of the client served appears
to be the principal factor that structures the social differentiation of the profession" (1982, 320).

    In 1995, Heinz and Laumann, joined by Robert Nelson and Rebecca
Sandefur, reprised the 1975 survey of the Chicago bar to determine what—if
anything—had changed over the intervening two decades, publishing the results as *Urban Lawyers* (Heinz et al. 2005). Most notably, the changes they
documented highlighted the inclusion of women and racial minorities (who
were nearly absent from the original study), a near doubling in the size of the
profession, and a distinct turn toward bureaucratization. Though the profession had become segmented in ways that could not fully be captured in
a binary of hemispheres, their results continued to support the notion of a
fundamental cleavage between corporate and personal client lawyers.

    There were, however, two important changes in the relative composition
and importance of the two hemispheres. First, some of the factors that had
been closely correlated with client type in the original study had significantly
eroded. Specifically, the stark ethnoreligious segregation between business
and personal client practitioners had largely disappeared by 1995, with Jewish and Catholic lawyers represented in elite law schools and large law firms

in numbers that matched—and sometimes exceeded—their representation in the general population. Similarly, by 1995 elite corporate law firms had expanded into fields such as criminal defense (adding what was called the *white-collar defense* of corporate officers, directors, and other wealthy individuals) and proxy fights (now called *mergers and acquisitions*), which were previously the province of the personal plight hemisphere. Second, the relative size of the two sectors of the bar had shifted dramatically over 20 years. In 1975, the individual and corporate hemispheres were roughly equal in size in terms of lawyers' total effort; by 1995, the corporate sector consumed almost two-thirds of lawyers' work. This shift in relative size was echoed in a widening pay gap, with corporate sector lawyers' earnings rising dramatically and individual sector lawyers' earnings declining slightly.

The orientation and findings reported in Heinz and Laumann (1982) help us assess how much change has taken place in the US legal profession since the late 1970s.

SOCIAL CAPITAL, INTERNAL LABOR MARKETS, AND ORGANIZATIONAL THEORY

The French sociologist Pierre Bourdieu pioneered what is called *field theory*, a sort of extended metaphor that shows how individual actions are contextually structured. In this book, we imagine the legal field as a semiautonomous space of struggle—an arena marked by common rules for game play that can also be contested (see Bourdieu and Wacquant 1992).[2] Actors internalize and naturalize the rules, then adopt strategies to maximize their chances of field-specific success. In general, this involves actors building up the sort of capital that is valued in the field or finding ways to get the field to value alternative capital they already possess.

Rivera (2016)—a study of hiring practices at investment banks, management consulting firms, and elite law firms—is a beautiful example of this kind of approach. Rivera finds that hiring partners tend to look for qualities that are similar to their own—that is, they assign higher value to job candidates who not only have elite education degrees (i.e., types of human capital) but also play the right kinds of sports and take the right kinds of vacations (i.e., types of social capital). In other words, they prefer to hire those who fit with current corporate culture. Similarly, Neely (2022) finds that hedge fund managers protect their interests by building dense networks of Wall Street elites who look and act like them. The social capital perspective recognizes the socially constructed nature of the credentials and status that make up the hierarchies of law.

Because the actors in the field of law often believe in markers of status and accomplishment, these forms of social capital have real consequences. A social capital perspective also accounts for the dynamics of struggle and competition within the field. The kinds of social capital a field values—that can give an actor a leg up in the competition—are contested and change when, for instance, the stature and resources attached to inside corporate counsel become more powerful or external demands raise the desirability of greater diversity in law firms. By the same token, this perspective reminds us that changes in the legal field do not necessarily topple its existing value structures, although they may temper them.

Our data are uniquely compatible with a social capital perspective on lawyers' careers, because the AJD Project makes it possible to follow individual careers over time. In both the questionnaires and the in-depth interviews, we inquired about many forms of capital that might play a role in the evolution of a lawyer's career.

Paula's experience is helpful here. Taking a social capital approach, we can better see why—the significant increase in the number of women and people of color who begin their careers in large law firms notwithstanding—the institutions' fundamental structure and hierarchy remain unchanged. Like other graduates from her elite law school, Paula had no trouble obtaining an entry-level position in a large law firm even though she is both female and the daughter of Mexican immigrants. That would have been unthinkable during the 1960s "golden age," when expressly discriminatory policies kept even top-of-their-class, elite pedigreed people like future the Supreme Court justices Ruth Bader Ginsburg and Sandra Day O'Connor from being hired. By the mid-1980s, virtually all law firms had responded to changing social norms, demographics, and professional needs by abandoning such policies. Women constituted 40% or more of elite law schools' graduating classes, it was increasingly socially unacceptable (and sometimes illegal) to deny gender equality, and legal firms needed warm bodies if they were to keep operating within an economic model that depended on multiplying the number of timekeepers at the bottom to produce higher profits for those at the top. By the time Paula and her AJD Project classmates entered the bar in 2000, any firm hoping to recruit the best needed to implement gender parity in entry-level hiring and engage in affirmative outreach to Latinas like Paula and other people of color (a norm backed up by the National Association of Law Placement and its annual directory, which published every law firm's hiring record broken down by gender and race and reported the formal antidiscrimination policies adopted by law school placement offices).

Yet these changes have not disrupted the partner-level social structure of elite law firms. Her social capital had gained value in that it afforded Paula a way in, but, after trying the partnership track in several sites and finding no true sponsors willing to push toward and advocate for her inclusion in equity partnership, she opted to take the off-ramp to a successful career as an in-house counsel. As we indicated above, this relatively recently developed track sees many elite-credentialed women, including minority women, given the opportunity to start in large law firms, but promotional constraints push them to leave for in-house legal departments that value their large-firm experience and sidestep the partner cliff. It is a great strategy for individuals dealing with structural constraints, but it does not break down the structures. It allows corporate law firms to be more open to hiring women (and minorities in similar, but different ways) without disrupting the dominance of lawyers like James at the top of the pyramid. White men with elite credentials and wives at home continue to have a much greater chance at equity partnership.

Indeed, this innovation allows firms to point to their assiduously diverse recruitment efforts, then blame women and minorities for "choosing" to chase other opportunities or prioritize personal lives for the continued homogeneity of the partnership ranks. As Padavic et al. (2020) point out, these scripts are based on assumptions (not data) and on social defenses that divert attention from untenable working demands and the paucity of women in leadership roles (Ely et al. 2014). Meanwhile, the inside counsel revolution has resulted in a corporate consolidation of female and minority talent: 140 of the general counsels of Fortune 500 companies are female (28%), compared to 15%–20% of equity partners and less than 5% of managing partners in top law firms, and 9% are minority identified. They are leading the charge when it comes to pressuring law firms to improve their chronic diversity problems (Wilkins and Kim 2016); where direct calls to action have had limited impact, the very fact of tremendous growth in the size and sophistication of corporate legal departments has been indirectly critical in restructuring the policies and practices of large law firms. Ironically, this includes the acceleration of the 24-7 work culture that pushes many talented lawyers out of large law firms and into in-house legal departments (Heineman 2016).

Social capital theory extends the more orthodox human capital theory famously developed by the economist Gary Becker (1957) to account for patterns of inequality more robustly. In human capital theory, individuals strategically invest in education and other types of training expected to yield economic returns in the marketplace. Employers reward workers according to these investments and other aspects of effort that yield a marginal return.

The result is (or purports to be) an economically efficient, rational, and meritocratic income determination system. Human capital theory would, for one, attribute racial and gender gaps in earnings to differences in individual human capital investments. Becker allows that discrimination *may* occur in labor markets but should be driven from markets over time because group-level discrimination produces less efficient outcomes for employers.

A pure human capital analysis cannot account for the observable outcomes of law firms' partnership tournaments. Because law firms continue to hire associates on the basis of their pedigree, they have an incentive to protect their investment by giving the best-pedigreed associates preferred access to good work assignments and training opportunities (Wilkins and Gulati 1996), an initial seeding that's self-evidently self-reinforcing. These selected incoming lawyers are more likely than are their peers to develop and to be seen as possessing the kinds of skills and dispositions prized by senior lawyers and clients (Wilkins and Gulati 1998). Partners invest in prized associates on the training track as the others are relegated to less supported, less meaningful, less visible, and less desirable work—and eventually no work at all. One's stock of capital is only as good as its highly contingent, field-specific valuation or exchange rate. However committed to the goal of diversity, corporate law firms were constructed around and continue to reinforce an embedded ideal of a White, male, elite-educated upper echelon.

The structures of opportunity in corporate law firms and in other legal practices are revealed both in quantitative and in qualitative data. The well-worn career paths and strategies—which in Bourdieusian terminology we can refer to as *habitus*—are internalized by actors who implicitly or explicitly recognize their natural fit with particular tracks; the elite track into corporate law firms has widened, but equity partnership tracks within those firms are narrower. Fewer people can successfully take on and leverage that habitus credibly. Others will languish or change tack, destined for in-house positions, boutique firms of corporate expatriates, and the federal government. Other well-worn and internalized habitus are found among the graduates of low-ranked schools, concentrated in the world of solo and small firms and state government.[3]

Our data also help us understand how fields and strategies are nested. The semiautonomous social field of the legal profession fits within the broader social, economic, and political world in which lawyers and clients live and work. The legal profession operates within a context of existing hierarchies, resulting in corporate lawyers in the United States gaining advantage via their proximity to economic power and state power (owing to their historic importance in this specific national context). The theories that help us map this contested terrain illuminate and are illuminated by observed patterns in lawyers' careers and lawyers' career narratives.

POLITICAL ECONOMY

Lawyers work at the intersection of the market and the state. Scholarly theories about this relationship range from the classic professions model, in which the state grants professionals monopolies in exchange for self-regulation and an ethical commitment to public values (Carr-Saunders and Wilson 1933; Goode 1957; Paterson 1982; but see Nelson and Trubek 1992), to critical examinations of monopoly as a strategy of self-interest (Freidson 1970) and market control (Abel 1982; Larson 1977). In *The System of Professions* (1988), Abbott asserts that professions should be seen in relation to each other, as a system of professions competing for control over jurisdictions by seeking to valorize their knowledge bases.

Wilkins et al. (2019) expand this focus by proposing an ecosystem metaphor, developed through their studies of corporate legal professions in China and other emerging economies. Within this theoretical model, the legal field's micro-level components—law firms, clients, and legal education—act as gears. Changes to one component produce changes in the structure and functioning of the other gears. The macro-level political economy involves the state, the market, and the bar, which control the legal field. Sharing elements with Bourdieusian structural sociology, this theory holds that the legal field is deeply connected to political and economic power; law and lawyers support existing power structures and provide them legitimacy by ostensibly constraining the powerful to the confines of the law. The position of serving but remaining relatively autonomous from external power also extends power to the legal profession and its hierarchies. The relative autonomy built into professional ideology suggests that lawyers are not just hired guns (Dezalay and Garth 2008; Gordon 1984), though the relational dependence on economic, political, and social power is essential if the profession is to thrive and attract ambitious and well-connected aspirants.

This truism means that, when economic, political, and social power change, such as from the welfare state to the much more competitive neoliberal economy or via societal shifts granting or recognizing more power to women and minorities, the legal field must respond and adapt (Ballakrishnen 2021; Dezalay and Garth 2021). Otherwise, it might lose status and leave its internal structures in disarray. Stories of change and continuity reflect the mix of a changing political economy and the slowly adapting, path-dependent structures of the legal profession. The cries of crisis are commonly employed both to slow transformation and to criticize resistance to change.

Constance's career narrative is useful for seeing how, as Wilkins et al. (2019) argue, the micro-level shift in power between clients and law firms is the product of macro-level changes in the relationship between the state, the market, and the bar. Moving from a regional to a national and then global law firm, Constance has carved out a lucrative career advising and defending lawyers on ethical issues. Her niche has boomed in recent years as the rapidly expanding number of statutes, administrative regulations, and common law duties have come to govern legal professionals—and leave them open to lawsuits and criminal prosecutions previously rare to the traditional professional model, in which lawyers were trusted to self-regulate under professionally generated ethical rules rarely enforced by disciplinary authorities (and particularly rarely against corporate lawyers [Steele and Nimmer 1976; Wilkins 1992]).

Since the 1970s, state officials at every level of US government (and, increasingly, other national governments) have shed their traditional deference to bar authorities. Today, they have taken aggressive civil and criminal actions against lawyers and firms. At the same time, dramatic expansions in the size and geographic scope of law firms, the lateral mobility of lawyers like Constance (Galanter and Henderson 2008), and the incidence of business-to-business litigation as a tool of global "lawfare" (Galanter 1986) have swamped even elite firms in disqualification motions, malpractice claims, and other civil liability lawsuits. In attempting to retain legitimacy and relevance, bar authorities have revised the rules of professional conduct to focus on preventing and rectifying financial fraud, but it is clear that the macro-level forces of state actions and the erosion of gentlemanly market norms preventing businesses from settling their disputes through the legal system (Macaulay 1963) are driving the micro-level dynamics of Constance's practice and, therefore, her career.

Another aspect of the political economy of American lawyers is the relationship between lawyers' private practices and their public roles. In a Bourdieusian perspective, lawyers may use or gain power in the legal field from participation in public service and pro bono legal projects that help gain respect (Dinovitzer and Garth 2009). At the profession level, this respect can take the form of legitimating lawyers' professional monopoly and serve as symbolic redress for the vast, persistent inequalities in access to legal services. Individual attorneys may find such public service a means for establishing a reputation by which they gain clients seeking to bolster their own credibility by employing lawyers with good public service reputations (Wilkins 2004a).

High-profile service may also operate as a marker of social status within the profession, given its cultural orientations; large law firms have institutionalized pro bono activities, and the American Bar Association (ABA) recommends that all lawyers perform 50 hours of pro bono work a year, indicating that public service is a key reputational ideal (Adediran 2020; Bosvieux-Onyekwelu 2018; Cummings 2004).

The political orientations of lawyers are another useful target for theoretical inquiry. Scholars have asked, for example, how individual politics affects lawyers' professional work, whether political party affiliations or economic and social ideologies shape career choices, whether professional practice instead shapes politics, and whether, perhaps, politics and practice are actually decoupled for most lawyers. Heinz and Laumann (1982) and Heinz et al. (2005) found that the Chicago bar was politically fragmented along the lines of client interests but that many corporate practitioners identified as Democrats and expressed liberal economic and social values. Bonica et al. (2016), investigating political orientations through lawyers' campaign contributions, similarly found that attorneys generally lean to the liberal end of the ideological spectrum, compared to other educated professionals, though there is considerable ideological heterogeneity that can be parsed by practice setting, size of law firm, law school attended, field of practice, and geographic location. On the whole, the fact that corporate lawyers tend to share the moderately reformist politics and neoliberal economic values of the educated elites who primarily govern the state and economy indicates the tight coupling of the legal establishment with existing power bases.

Once again, the AJD Project's longitudinal research design gives its data clarifying power. In each wave, the survey collected data on pro bono work, participation in community activities, political party affiliation, and economic and social liberalism. These data reveal the shifting linkages between lawyers' private practices and public roles over the course of their careers.

Research Design and Data

The data analyzed in this book are by far the most comprehensive collected on the careers of lawyers—on the careers of any occupational group, perhaps. In contrast to studies more narrowly focused on the graduates of specific law schools (see Aiken and Regan 2016; Dau-Schmidt et al. 2009; Dau-Schmidt and Mukhopadhaya 2021; Lempert et al. 2001; Monahan and Swanson 2019; and Wilkins et al. 2015) or cross-sectional studies of lawyers in specific cities (Hagan and Kay 1995; Heinz and Laumann 1982; Heinz et al. 2005), this project has produced a nationally representative longitudinal data set for an entire cohort of lawyers with three waves of surveys (2002–3, 2007, and 2012) and career mobility tracking through 2019.

We selected the sample in a two-stage process. In the first stage, we divided the nation into strata by region and size of the population of new lawyers in 2000. From these, we selected all four major legal markets (those with more than 2,000 new lawyers: Chicago, Los Angeles, New York City, and Washington, DC), five of nine large markets (those with 750–2,000 new lawyers: Boston, Atlanta, Houston, Minneapolis, and the San Francisco Bay Area), and nine smaller markets (those with fewer than 750 new lawyers; New Jersey outside Newark, Connecticut, Florida outside Miami, Tennessee, Oklahoma, Utah, Oregon, St. Louis, and Indiana). In the second stage, we used state bar records to select lawyers who, when combined, would be statistically representative of the national population of lawyers admitted to the bar in 2000. With the assistance of the Law School Admissions Council, we oversampled for race and ethnicity.[4]

The longitudinal survey started with a wave 1 sample of 8,225 lawyers across the 18 sampling areas. With 4,538 respondents, the response rate was 56%. In wave 2, 70% of wave 1 respondents responded again, and 26.9% of wave 1 nonrespondents responded, for an overall response rate of 50.6%. Owing to cost considerations, wave 3 surveys were sent to only those who had responded in a previous wave; we received 2,984 responses, for a response rate of 53%. Ultimately, 2,035 respondents answered all three survey waves. Although by contemporary standards these are high response rates, we conducted web searches to compare wave 3 respondents to nonrespondent members of the initial sampling frame. We found no significant differences in bar status or employment setting. The surveys elicited detailed data on social background, education, employment, earnings, networks, community and professional activities, and job satisfaction.[5]

Figure 1.1 displays the national scope of the sample, with wave 3 respondents' geographic distribution illustrated by the relative size of the circles. Some respondents moved from their wave 1 location, yet the largest groupings of respondents still correspond to the four major legal market cities.

AJD Project principals supplemented these sizable survey data sets by conducting 219 in-depth interviews with survey respondents. Interview respondents were selected from the survey sample to overrepresent lawyers of color, public interest lawyers, and lawyers in small firms and solo practice (Dinovitzer and Garth 2020). Of the 146 interviewees, 47 were interviewed twice, and 26 were interviewed three times. The interviews were recorded, transcribed, and then analyzed using software including ATLAS.ti.

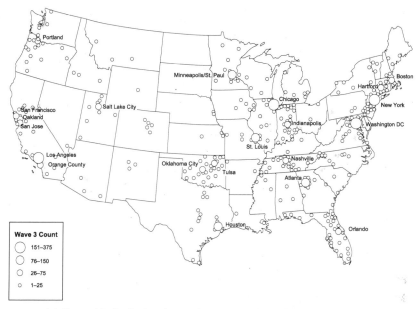

Wave 3 Count
○ 151–375
○ 76–150
○ 26–75
o 1–25

FIGURE 1.1. Geographic distribution of respondents at wave 3

Plan of the Book

We present our analysis of agency and structure in the making of lawyers' careers in five parts. Along with this introduction, part 1 sets the historical context of the AJD Project cohort's careers. In part 2, chapter 3 analyzes the structure of lawyers' careers through the survey data, revealing a series of sequences (or pathways) along which the diversity of lawyers' careers commonly fall. These are assigned to four higher-level categories—those who start in large law firms, those who start in small and midsize law firms, those who work in business (as inside counsel or businesspeople), and those in government and public sector jobs—that tell us a great deal about the structure of the profession. In particular, chapter 4 examines how social background predicts law school status, which in turn shapes career moves, and chapter 5 revisits the measures of specialization by fields of law and client type that laid the basis for the two hemispheres thesis.

Part 3 presents the narratives of lawyers from all four sectors of practice to bring the social capital approach to life. Working from in-depth interview data, we consider the strategies lawyers pursue as they develop their careers and try to navigate and find meaning through their families, relationships, and community engagements. The strategies they employ are molded by class, gender, and race, though they affirm lawyers' agency in career-based decision-making. Interview data also grant new insights into the sector-specific operation of status hierarchies, suggesting revisions to some previous literature.

Inequalities of race and gender are the focus of part 4. We begin with an analysis of the enduring racialization of law firms. Racial disparities in exits and promotions to equity partnership leave law firms "White spaces." We then examine education debt over the course of careers and find another form of racialization: the accumulating disadvantage affecting African American lawyers, whose debt levels rise from early to midcareer and outstrip all other racial and ethnic groups' debt levels. We turn to an analysis of the diverging career paths of men and women, in which we see the gendered character of marriage and family and gender inequality in the earnings of lawyers. These patterns can be aptly described as evidence of hegemonic masculinity. Men build their careers and families through the support of women. And men— particularly fathers—earn more in law practice, whereas women, including women without children, earn substantially less across the earnings distribution and despite controls for relevant determinants of earnings.

Part 5 turns to the evolution of lawyers' public roles and personal career satisfaction over the course of their careers. We examine their political orientations, participation in community organizations, and pro bono legal service contributions in order better to understand how their public activities relate to their professional work. We find a dualism in which relatively politically liberal lawyers predominantly serve business interests. We also find a dualism in the ways lawyers pay lip service to the importance of pro bono projects but largely fail individually and collectively to provide significant levels of pro bono representation. Our analysis of career and job satisfaction data belies the contention that lawyers are unsatisfied and suffering from a wide range of physical and psychological maladies. Most lawyers express high levels of career satisfaction. Women and people of color, who face manifold disadvantages over the course of their careers, report satisfaction levels equal to or exceeding those of their peers. This is one of the great ironies of inequality and opportunity in the American legal profession.

We conclude, in part 6, by returning to the relationship between agency and structure in lawyers' careers in light of the uniquely rich data yielded by the AJD Project.

From the Golden Age to the Age of Disruption: Setting the Context for Lawyers' Careers in the New Millennium

When the AJD Project cohort began their legal careers, the profession was booming: the United States boasted more than 1 million lawyers (roughly 1 for every 264 citizens; Carson and Park 2012), and members of the bar held leadership positions in virtually every prominent sector of American society. A burgeoning legal press and even mainstream media outlets like the *New York Times* and the *Wall Street Journal* breathlessly reported six-figure starting salaries at large law firms, where skyrocketing profits made Wall Street titans of law firm partners. Like the "masters of the universe" depicted in Tom Wolfe's scathing yet valorizing 1987 novel *The Bonfire of the Vanities*, prosecutors and defense lawyers became stars via widespread coverage of celebrity trials, while personal injury lawyers plastered the highways with billboards promising larger-than-life settlements (and implying their own multimillion dollar incomes). And glowing profiles of public interest lawyers, like the Innocence Project staff, busy exonerating death row inmates, provided ample assurance that the spirits of Atticus Finch and Thurgood Marshall were alive and well. Law school applications hit an all-time high in the late 1990s, when AJD Project respondents joined a record cohort of 50,000 admitted students.

At the same time, a steady drumbeat of critics—including many prominent lawyers—was gaining resonance. Their criticisms were not necessarily new or internally consistent, though they underscored the enormous changes that had taken place in the latter decades of the twentieth century—changes that would only accelerate as the AJD Project cohort embarked on their careers.

These changes began almost immediately. In 2001, the tech bubble burst. The ensuing, if brief, recession hit the legal industry especially hard, and major law firms began laying off associates—even partners—the way General

Motors traditionally laid off assembly-line workers. By the second quarter of 2002, the US economy had swung again, now experiencing the biggest boom in history, with the growing number of large law firms undertaking an unprecedented hiring spree that opened the golden doors of these prestigious institutions to the graduates of regional and even local law schools who had never had such opportunities before. Then, in 2008, the economy crashed for the second time in less than a decade. The collapse of Lehman Brothers precipitated a global financial crisis that hit the legal services industry far harder than the bursting of the tech bubble had in 2001, precipitating a collapse of global capital, layoffs and law firm failures, declining incomes reported by solo and small-firm practitioners, the market entry of competitors from Legal Zoom to the Big Four accounting firms, a steep drop in applications to law school, and a sizable drop in the chances that law school graduates would obtain credentialed jobs. Apocalyptic headlines heralded "The Death of Big Law" and "The End of Lawyers" (Ribstein 2010; Susskind 2008).

This upheaval would continue throughout the first 10–12 years of AJD Project respondents' careers, reflecting broader social and political trends that were equally tumultuous. The AJD Project cohort began practicing law during the presidency of George W. Bush and in the shadow of 9/11, entered midcareer during the presidency of Barack Obama, and completed two decades as lawyers during the turmoil of the Trump years. Graduating from law school at the dawn of the Internet era, these Gen X lawyers joined a profession dominated by baby boomers but came of age in one significantly shaped by millennials and anticipating the coming of Gen Z. By 2019, when we last checked in via public record searches, we see a profession where law firm profits have hit record highs while legal professionals in government, public interest, and solo and small firms struggle to meet rising demand within margins tightened by the stagnation and decline of middle-class incomes and government budgets.

Scholars and commentators in the legal press seeking to explain this complex reality have generally defaulted to two sets of idealized heuristics. The first looks back to a golden age, nostalgic for a profession supposedly characterized by "lawyer-statesmen" whose conduct was driven by public purpose and professional pride rather than profit (Kronman 1993). The second looks forward, anxiously heralding the looming age of disruption, in which traditional legal institutions and practices will surely be transformed and degraded by the forces of globalization, technology, and deregulation (Susskind 2008). Neither captures either the complex realities of the profession's past or its likely future trajectories. Each is frequently deployed by self-interested actors who profit (directly or indirectly) from the comparisons and anxieties produced by the twin narratives. Both golden age and disruption rhetorics and responses have shaped the zeitgeist, importantly influencing many of the institutions, practices, and beliefs through which AJD Project lawyers navigated the first two decades of their careers. Understanding both the rhetoric and the reality of these competing depictions helps set the stage for the analysis throughout this volume.

The Golden Age and Its Pyrite Practices

The modern American legal profession traces back to the late nineteenth century. From the founding of the ABA in 1878 through the Roaring Twenties, a small, influential group of lawyers was shifting its focus from litigation to a new kind of work and a new organizational form—a sort of factory model for full-service legal practice frequently credited (although probably more than deserved) to the New York firm of Cravath Swaine and Moore (Galanter and Palay 1991; Swaine 1946).

The so-called Cravath System was distinguished from nineteenth-century legal practice (Swaine 1946) in four ways. First, the *work* of Cravath System firms emphasized providing a full range of services to corporate clients, as opposed to individuals, on transactional and commercial matters, as opposed to courtroom litigation. Second, the *lawyers* in these firms were hired directly from the country's newly emerging law schools, and they were expected to stay in an extended apprenticeship—including six to ten years of training under senior lawyers—to learn how to meet the needs of the hiring firm's corporate clients. Third, the Cravath System was an "up-or-out" scheme; after their probationary period, the best young lawyers were *promoted to partnership*, and the rest were asked to leave the firm (and, in effect, the entire sector of large law firms, as Cravath System firms hired virtually no lateral partners or associates). Fourth, Cravath System firms were *governed*, at least in theory, as true partnerships; all partners shared equally in the firm's profits and losses (through a "lockstep" compensation system) and in its decision-making.[1] For the next three decades, Cravath System firms sprang up in every major American city and more than a few smaller ones. Many saw them as representing the very pinnacle of the legal profession.

By promising a full suite of practices to handle all of a company's legal needs, the Cravath System was well positioned to take advantage of escalating demand. Its core internal elements aligned well with the client and labor markets emerging in the period (Mawdsley and Somaya 2015). From the Sherman Act (1890) to the New Deal, policy governing corporate conduct opened new areas of public and private law (Gordon 1984; Shamir 1995). The symbiosis between legislation and the legal field was not coincidental. Lawyers in government built the modern regulatory state with the promise of creating market stability through law, simultaneously creating a need for skilled business lawyers with ample personal connections to regulators to help companies steer through (and often circumvent) the legal and regulatory regimes.

The government and regulatory lawyers crafted modest regulations that helped mollify public criticism of the giant trusts but, ultimately, did not threaten corporate power. Often, they came to government from corporate law firms—and quickly returned when their time in government was over. From the perspective of Cravath System law firms, this was a virtuous circle. Government service and participation in law reform were considered signals of professional virtue, and they simultaneously enhanced firms' legitimacy and prestige while serving their clients' interests. Corporate lawyers and their clients had very stable relationships, corporate competition was limited, and clients simply needed to trust their lawyers and pay the bills. With that trust, corporations saw little need for internal legal resources (Gilson 1990).

Labor market dynamics contributed, too, as formal legal education began to replace apprenticeship as the dominant route for entry into the profession in the same period (Galanter and Palay 1991, 33). As law schools moved away from vocational training, they favored the "scientific" instruction of common law doctrines and rules designed to teach students how to think like a lawyer. The trend was reinforced by universities' aspirations toward national prestige and prominence and by the elite bar's push to increase its own prestige and power through the proliferation of law school accreditation standards set by the ABA and the American Association of Law Schools (Auerbach 1976). Fledgling lawyers graduated with precious little training in actual legal practice, which suited the hiring needs of Cravath System firms. Corporate law firms could easily sort and rank potential recruits through the ready mechanism of law school status and prestige, snapping up the most desirable graduates from schools such as Harvard, Columbia, and Yale Universities (Coquillette and Kimball 2015; Swaine 1946). Because they had a steady stream of corporate work, the Cravath System firms had the freedom to pay these young lawyers a respectable salary and maintain the internal training, promotion, and governance practices that ensured an abundance of talented applicants—and clients to absorb the cost (Wilkins and Gulati 1998). The result was what Galanter and Palay (1991) refer to as "the golden age of the Big law firm," an idealized image that cast a long shadow over the profession the AJD Project cohort would join almost four decades later.

Of course, this period was never really golden for most lawyers (Galanter 1996). As indicated above, one of the main projects of the newly formed ABA was to raise standards, wielding accreditation to shut down vocational law schools. As Auerbach demonstrates, these measures were thinly veiled efforts to stop "the pestiferous horde" of immigrants arriving from Southern and Eastern Europe, among them Jews and Catholics, from entering the profession. Similar professionalizing requirements included the imposition of increasingly rigorous bar exams (conducted in English) and the enforcement of a host of ethics rules prohibiting commercial practices like advertising, solicitation, and fee splitting, all of which were most likely to be used by immigrant lawyers (Auerbach 1976). When total exclusion proved impossible, professional elites did their best to confine these new entrants to the bottom rungs of the profession, where they would serve their own communities or toil in low-wage patronage jobs at the state and local level. They were certainly not welcome in the corridors of Cravath System law firms, which were interested in hiring only "men" who were "Nordic, ha[d] pleasing personalities and 'clean cut' appearances, graduates of the 'right' schools and ha[d] the 'right' social backgrounds and experience in the affairs of the world, and [were] endowed with tremendous stamina" (Smigel 1964, 37). Implicitly, these men were ideally supported by wives who stayed home taking care of children and the household chores.

Expressly discriminatory policies notwithstanding, the image of the large law firm held power far beyond the actual opportunities on offer. Throughout the golden age, the official narrative pushed by law schools and the bar held that law was a reliable and noble path to upward mobility. Even those lawyers who did not gain the vaunted positions as partners in Cravath System law firms but built their careers in solo and small-firm practice or in local government as prosecutors, defense lawyers, and judges could bask in the reflected glow of the "lawyer-statesmen" (Kronman 1993), moving from Cravath-style firms to key positions in business, government, and civil society. This paradoxical embrace flows, as Bourdieu and Wacquant (1992) argue, from the nature of the social field of the legal profession. Lawyers excluded from elite circles and relegated to positions within "machine-style" local politics (where their work was often at odds with the interests of corporate elites) were nevertheless incentivized to respect and internalize the values of the corporate bar on the reasonable expectation that they would, in turn, be respected and rewarded by their field's power brokers. Their adherence to norms that disadvantaged them personally reinforced the profession's tendency to reproduce its structure (Dinovitzer and Garth 2007, 2020).

Even the lawyers who rejected this golden age narrative still tended to define themselves in opposition to it. Thus, the rise of personal injury practice in the 1950s and 1960s created a David vs. Goliath scenario in which lawyers excluded from the corporate sector (often ethnoreligious or racial minorities) could potentially reap large financial rewards by representing accident victims against corporations and insurance companies. As local law school graduates gained control in state judiciaries, often after careers as prosecutors or defense lawyers, they were able to reshape the rules governing personal injury liability and damages to favor plaintiffs and their counsel. Then, once successful, the plaintiff's lawyers would mimic the corporate lawyers by seeking stature in bar associations and in philanthropic relationships with their law schools.

Continuity and Change in the Age of Disruption

By 2000, the legal profession the AJD Project cohort joined was far larger and more geographically concentrated, demographically diverse, structured by organizational incentives and internal career ladders, and overtly competitive and business focused than it had been in the 1960s. Despite these changes, so consequential for careers, the fundamental structure of the golden age bar remained. In this sense, hand-wringing about the age of disruption as a complete upending of the field's traditional institutions, career paths, and hierarchies was just as misleading as the valorization of the largely mythical golden age before it. The doomsday rhetoric would, however, prove to be another force shaping lawyers' careers.

SIZE AND CONCENTRATION

In 1960, there were approximately 250,000 lawyers in the United States. That population had doubled by 1985 and then doubled again as the new millennium dawned. The AJD Project cohort entered a far more crowded bar than the golden age lawyers before them had: with more than 200 law schools producing nearly 50,000 graduates a year. Although the global financial crisis sent law school enrollments plummeting (to a low of 37,056 in 2015)—with a few law schools shutting their doors (Tamanaha 2012)—the profession nevertheless continued to grow. By 2020, the American bar counted 1.3 million members.

The environment was increasingly competitive not only because of the rising ranks but also because of the rising cost of becoming a lawyer. The AJD Project lawyers began their careers carrying far more education debt than their predecessors had. In 1960, the median tuition and fees were $475 at private law schools and $204 at public law schools (Bader 2011). In 2000-adjusted dollars, that is roughly $2,700 and $1,100. But, by the actual year 2000, the average tuitions had ballooned to $21,790 (private) and $7,783 (public, though out-of-state students paid more than twice that price [Law School Transparency 2019]). The top schools, like Harvard and Yale, commanded still higher prices. Financial aid could not keep up, becoming primarily available (especially at elite schools) in the form of loans. Bearing in mind that many had taken out significant loans to fund their undergraduate degrees, it is easy to see how a substantial portion of the AJD Project cohort would report still paying off education debt throughout their first 12 years in practice.

Arguably, the impact of these two pressures was most acutely felt by lawyers in the individual hemisphere, where the demand for legal services (more precisely, the ability to pay for legal services) rose less steeply than the supply of available lawyers did. Lawyers in the corporate sector faced a different type of rising competition, the market's nationalization and globalization fueling a proliferation in the number and size of corporate law firms. As firms hired more lawyers and acquired smaller firms to extend their geographic reach, they courted bigger clients, profits rose, and they competed for the top graduates. At a certain point, however, that model would prove untenable.

Golden age law firms, no matter their ambition, tended to have just one office; the few exceptions rarely competed actively outside their home jurisdictions. That changed along with policy regimes: the legal problems facing corporations nationalized with the expansion of federal authority under the New Deal, through the rights revolution of the 1960s and 1970s, and via reforms following the corporate scandals of the 1980s and 1990s. The 1980s heralded a huge wave of corporate mergers and acquisitions that would last into the early years of the twenty-first century; now, even important local companies are often controlled by parent companies or investors in other states and countries. Rapid increases in the speed and accessibility of transportation and information technology mean that a lawyer in New York or Chicago can effectively service clients *anywhere*. As Henderson and Alderson (2016, 1252) document, large-firm consolidation has revealed stratification, aligning status to global, national, and, at the low end, regional markets. Global markets like New York and London are at the center of the corporate hemisphere, employing 80% of the lawyers in the 250 largest law firms, and generating 87.5% of these firms' profits in 2014. Key national markets are competitive, too, as law firms expand beyond their home jurisdictions to cities like Boston, Houston, Atlanta, and Denver in order to service existing clients with business in those cities or recruit new clients, thereby competing with local firms (themselves frequently angling to expand).

In fact, the most common way in which the national firms expand into new markets is through acquisition. By buying an already successful local law firm and/or luring lawyers away from successful local ones, these firms find a smooth path into the market, and, by building connections to local law schools and community organizations, they create the relationships and local knowledge needed to build a strong reputation. Put differently, amid nationalization, law remains a relationship business. Connections with local judges, politicians, businesses, and local community norms confer value.

Lawyers in the individual hemisphere are much more likely to have a local practice than are their corporate peers, though nationalization has shifted their work, too. A growing number of plaintiffs' class action and franchise law firms (e.g., Jacoby and Myers, Hyatt Legal Services) have sought to create a national presence (Kritzer 2002; Van Hoy 1995). The public interest bar followed the lead of national organizations like the National Association for the Advancement of Colored People's Legal Defense and Education Fund, moving toward directing public interest cases from a central office in a major market like New York or Washington, DC (Cummings 2004).

Another piece of the context for AJD Project lawyers' entry into the profession is the rollercoaster economy jolted by the dot-com bubble's burst in 2001. Firms from Silicon Valley to New York laid off associates and partners, though the recession was neither deep nor long. Much of the tech market cratered, with the rest of the economy remaining relatively unscathed. By the second quarter of 2002, the economy had recovered all its 2001 losses, and it was clear that the tech giants (the exponentially growing Google, Microsoft, and Apple) were far from busted. A new technological market—financial engineering, in the form of securitization (most prominently through mortgage-backed securities)—had arrived, and the legal market boomed.

Setting records with more than 7% growth every year for six years straight, the legal market moved in tandem with huge jumps in initial public offerings, domestic and global corporate mergers and acquisitions, and big-case litigation (Regan and Rohrer 2021). Strong demand produced an overall increase in law firm size and profitability as well as strong demand for new lawyers. By 2007, the country's 200 most profitable law firms collectively sought to hire 10,000 lawyers—close to 25% of that year's law school graduates (Wilkins et al. 2007).

But the corporate legal ecosystem eventually showed financial strain: meeting all their new legal needs by hiring high-cost law firms was expensive. To rein in legal fees, corporations began opting to establish or expand in-house legal departments; power within the legal field shifted, away from law firms and toward general counsels. In response, law firms ramped up the pressure on associates to bill hours and partners to generate clients. They redoubled efforts to recruit lateral, well-connected lawyers who had big books of business in high-value areas like capital markets and private equity. They shed partners and low-margin practice areas like employment law and trusts and estates (as with insurance defense in earlier years).

All these changes were accentuated by the global financial crisis. The economic turmoil in the wake of Lehman Brothers' collapse in the fall of 2008 initially devastated the corporate legal sector. The demand for legal services related to mergers and acquisitions and securitization work, which had driven six years of growth in the sector, dropped dramatically (Henderson 2014). Moreover, the withdrawal of this transactional work was not counterbalanced, as it had been in the 1991 and 2001 downturns, by any increase in the demand for litigation services. As a result, large law firms began laying off lawyers, starting with associates and support personnel, but quickly moving to partners, who were either deequitized or fired outright (Glater 2008). Indeed, entire law firms went out of business. Many other firms teetered on the brink of failure but were saved through mergers with—more accurately, in many cases, acquisitions by—stronger firms (Weiss 2009). As Albert Yoon (2014) documents, over 450 law firm mergers and acquisitions took place between 2008 and 2012, further bolstering the overall size, bureaucratic structure, and nationalization of the corporate hemisphere.

These changes, in turn, further strengthened the hand of in-house legal departments, which, armed with new technologies and sophisticated intermediaries, were able to unbundle services and parcel them out to the lowest-bidding law firms and/or the burgeoning alternative legal service providers (Wilkins and Esteban Ferrer 2018). This, in turn, added to the instability nagging at traditional law firm career paths; firms' economically rational responses meant emphasizing billable hours and short-term revenue generation, moves that disproportionately affect the careers of women and minority lawyers (Headworth et al. 2016).

But, as much as the global financial crisis has disrupted the corporate sector, its effects have, arguably, had an even greater effect on the individual hemisphere of law. Even before the financial crisis, solo and small-firm practitioners' incomes and opportunities had been depressed by wage stagnation and the expanding wealth gap. The precipitous drop in home values and the explosion in foreclosures only accentuated this gap as potential clients lost their jobs and saw their net worth wiped away by houses sinking "underwater" (their values dropping far below the remainder owed on mortgages). The associated loss of tax revenue hit governments hard, particularly at the state and local levels, forcing austerity measures that left little wiggle room for hiring lawyers (Burk 2019).

At the same time, the growth in legal technology posed a further threat to the incomes of solo and small-firm practitioners while creating a new bifurcation between those who were able to benefit from technological advances and those whose practices were threatened by them. This split dates back to 2001 when the celebrity attorney Robert Shapiro (who in 1995 was a member of the "Dream Team" representing O. J. Simpson) collaborated with a group of young engineers and entrepreneurs to form LegalZoom, the first company to harness technology to provide reasonably priced legal services to individuals and small businesses. Although bar officials in California and several other states waged a vigorous campaign to shut the company down, LegalZoom not only survived and expanded but also spawned a raft of competitors offering do-it-yourself legal tools and other forms of low- and fixed-cost legal services to individuals and small businesses. For entrepreneurial solos, cloud-based practice management platforms such as Clio and sophisticated research tools like Westlaw Next are great for leveraging up and running efficient, profitable businesses (Ambrogi 2020). Other solo and small-firm practitioners are rapidly losing potential clients to do-it-yourself legal websites that provide simple access and instructions and, thus, allowing individuals to do everything from creating a will to filing articles of incorporation (Kawamoto 2012).

Although these developments have certainly produced important changes in legal practice in both the corporate and the individual hemispheres, they have not resulted in the death of big law, let alone the end of lawyers. To the contrary, large law firms not only survived the global financial crisis but have also in some ways emerged stronger than ever. As we indicated, by the end of the second decade of the new millennium, law firm profits—at least at the top firms—were higher than ever (Jeffreys 2021; Thomas 2020), and a few years of seasoning at a big law firm is still considered an important credential for lawyers seeking to go into smaller, boutique law firms, in-house legal departments, government, and even most prestigious public interest positions. And, while lawyers in the individual hemisphere on average continue to lag their corporate counterparts in income and prestige, as our statistical findings and qualitative interviews document, lawyers from every sector of the bar continue to find and create pathways to successful and rewarding careers. The law itself remains an attractive career option: as this book goes to press, law school applications are on pace to hit the highest level in 20 years (Sloan 2021).

DIVERSITY

As we indicated above, elite corporate law firms have always had a symbiotic relationship with elite law schools. In many respects, this symbiosis has only strengthened in the years since the golden age as the exponential growth in the size and scope of corporate law firms drove these organizations to hire more and more elite law school graduates, and, during the peak of the boom years, a significant number of graduates from regional and even local law schools were able to break into corporate law more than before. Law schools therefore increasingly competed to attract top students willing to pay their ballooning tuitions. More than ever, they relied on their relationships with law firm partners, who could provide financial contributions, proximal prestige, and hiring practices that privilege their graduates. In return, the schools make it easy for their graduates to take positions at these firms, thereby reinforcing the widespread belief that the best way to ensure success is starting your legal career in a large law firm. Moreover, in addition to intensifying the connection between law firms and law schools, an important characteristic of the relationship between these two institutions has also been transformed in a way that would have been quite surprising to their golden age counterparts. Contrary to the explicit demand for homogeneity that characterized the mid-century relationship between law firms and law schools, by the time the AJD Project cohort entered law school, law firms were required to demonstrate a formal commitment to diversity, including at least a minimal number of women and people of color in their partnership ranks.

Demographic diversity is both disrupting and reinforcing the profession's traditional hierarchies. Take, for example, the entry of female lawyers. From just a handful at the end of the nineteenth century and less than 4% of the profession at midcentury, women constituted 27% of lawyers when the AJD Project cohort entered the profession in 2000. More importantly, they represented 40% of lawyers under 30 and 43% of law students. To be sure, high-profile, senior positions, including partner at a major law firm, were still predominantly held by men, but the rough match between the proportion of female law students and female law firm hires in every year since the mid-1980s adds credence to the durability of women's presence in the pipeline, securing further growth in the profession.

Yet structural inequalities have persisted despite progress in gender diversity, shaping women's careers once they enter the profession. Recall Constance, whose story illustrates the higher numbers of women who begin their careers in government, particularly at the state and local levels, rather than in private practice. Or consider the fact that many women who began their careers in law firms in the 1980s and 1990s have since exited, whether leaving the profession, leaving the corporate sector, or leaving the full-time workforce. Ongoing debates about this "'no-problem' problem" (Rhode 1991)—demonstrated by the patterned paths traversed by Alicia and

Paula—have highlighted the odd, persistent coincidence of women's growing presence in an ostensibly meritocratic profession and their continued under-representation in law firm partnerships and other prestigious positions.

The situation for ethnoreligious and racial minorities is even more complex. By 2000, the ethnoreligious cleavages that had defined the midcentury bar had all but disappeared (Heinz et al. 2005). The profession's consciousness of integration issues had moved toward African Americans and other racial minorities. Here, too, lawyers could point to historical progress: Prior to the mid-1960s, law schools remained virtually as racially segregated as they were in the 1860s. By the time the AJD Project cohort entered law school, minority students constituted 20.2% of all matriculants, with higher percentages at many elite schools such as Harvard and Yale as well as a number of urban law schools (Wilkins et al. 2000). In the early years, diversity efforts concentrated almost exclusively on African Americans. These efforts produced important gains. Thus, between 1965 and 1975, the number of African American students attending historically White law schools had quadrupled from 500 to 2,000 (Bell 1970; Leonard 1977), and, just a year later, 5,500 African American students were enrolled in ABA-accredited law schools (more than twice as many as the entire population of African American lawyers 16 years earlier, in 1960 [Abel 1989]). By 2000, the number of African American law students had almost doubled again: 9,272, or 7.4% of all law students (down slightly from a 1995 peak of 9,779, or 7.6%). By this time, however, the diversity agenda had expanded to include other traditionally excluded groups. As a result, the number of Latinx and Asian American law students also increased sharply (Li et al. 2020). Indeed, by the mid-1990s, Asian Americans had surpassed African Americans as the largest minority group in American law schools. Moreover, within each of the major minority groups, heterogeneity with respect to social class and parentage has greatly expanded since the early days of affirmative action; the sons and daughters of the first wave of African American lawyers to graduate from law school back in the 1960s and 1970s is entering the profession, as is a wave of first-generation immigrants from Asia, Latin America, and, in the late 1990s, Africa (Li et al. 2020; Wilkins et al. 2000; Wilkins and Fong 2017).

But the single most important difference between the minority students of the AJD Project cohort and those who first integrated law schools in the 1960s and 1970s is the same that defines the profession: gender. Since the mid-1980s, some two-thirds of African American law students have been women. As we will see, their career paths would be defined by many of the same obstacles faced by all women, plus special obstacles arising from the intersection of their race and gender (Crenshaw 1995; Wilkins and Fong 2017).

These gains in minority admissions were neither easy nor unchallenged. Beginning with *DeFunis v. Odegaard* in 1971, a series of court cases and ballot initiatives challenged affirmative action programs in public colleges and universities. These failed to eliminate affirmative action altogether, thanks to Supreme Court justice Lewis F. Powell Jr.'s endorsement of the Harvard Plan in *Regents of California v. Bakke* (1978). States, however, have continued to push back. In Texas, the state supreme court's decision in *Hopwood v. Texas* (1996) banned race-conscious admissions in the state's public law schools, and, in California, Proposition 209 imposed a similar ban via ballot initiative. Like debates in higher education and other spheres, the legal profession's internal fights over the legitimacy of affirmative action and the corresponding legitimacy of minority students (all of whom were affected by the presumption that they were admitted solely because of these programs) would be a prominent and persistent feature of the AJD Project cohort's experiences.

These efforts at diversity in law schools have spurred a corresponding set of initiatives to diversify the profession as a whole. Not surprisingly, these efforts began with the federal government when, in 1961, President John F. Kennedy signed an executive order authorizing federal agencies to use affirmative measures to recruit and retain African American lawyers. Two decades later, 31% of all African American lawyers were employed in federal or state government, more than any other single employment sector (Segal 1983).

Efforts to integrate the corporate hemisphere, however, have been decidedly less successful. As late as 1996, African American lawyers constituted less than 2% of the associates—and less than 1% of the partners—in the nation's top 250 law firms, with the number of Asian American and Latinx lawyers in these institutions lagging behind even these small numbers (Wilkins and Gulati 1996). In the last 25 years, the rhetoric around diversity in the corporate legal sector has ramped up significantly. Nearly every major law firm now has a formal diversity program, some employing a dedicated staff member to oversee the project. At the same time, general counsels have penned a series of letters and proclamations pledging to make a firm's diversity a significant factor in where their companies spend their legal dollars (Wilkins and Kim 2016). And the ABA and state and local bar organizations have launched dozens of diversity initiatives to address the underrepresentation of women and people of color in virtually every facet of the legal profession. Given all this attention, many law firm leaders and hiring partners now routinely assert that minorities become some of the corporate firms' most prized recruits, a stark reversal of the golden age calculus that treated everything other than White identity as a stigmatized, if not wholly counterfeit, form of social capital (Wilkins 2004b).

In 2004, Sara Lee's general counsel, Richard Palmore, one of the first African American lawyers to head a major corporate legal department, issued a "call to action" urging corporations to "make decisions regarding which law firms represent our companies based in significant part on the diversity performance of the firms" and to "end or limit" their relationships with firms that consistently failed to achieve diversity goals (quoted in Wilkins and Kim 2016, 37). Even so, progress on diversity has been achingly slow and incomplete. After rising slowly for more than a decade, the percentage of African American associates in the nation's largest law firms actually declined from 4.6% to 3.9% since 2009, with the percentage of African American partners continuing to hover around 2%. Indeed, in 2019, 7 of the 100 largest firms had *no* African American equity partners, with 20 others having only 1. Similarly, there have only been modest gains in the percentage of Asian American and Latinx partners, increasing from 2.7% to 3.3% for Asian Americans and from 2.3% to 2.6% for Latinx partners during this same period. Nor is this just a problem for the corporate sector. In the decade between 2000 and 2010, the percentage of racial minorities in the entire legal profession increased less than 1%, from 11.2% to 11.9%. And, lest one think that increasing these percentages is only a matter of time, the percentage of female partners in large law firms continues to hover around 20%—with the percentage of true equity partners typically thought to be significantly lower—notwithstanding the fact that women have constituted more than 40% of the entering associates in these institutions since the mid-1980s.

ORGANIZATIONAL STRUCTURE AND INTERNAL LABOR MARKETS

Finally, the legal profession's organizational structure and internal labor markets have also changed dramatically since the golden age, although in ways that have often reinforced the profession's underlying hierarchies. The interplay between change and replication is easiest to see in the corporate sector, where the number and size of large law firms has grown dramatically. Thus, in 1960, the country's largest law firm was New York's Shearman and Sterling, with 125 lawyers. Outside New York, few firms could claim 50 (Galanter and Palay 1991). In 2000, more than 250 law firms were larger than Shearman and Sterling was in 1960, the largest of them employing 1,000 or more lawyers (Henderson 2014); their offices spanned multiple cities and multiple countries.

Moreover, the Cravath System's four core elements had, by this time, each undergone significant change. First, the *work* of many US law firms had both broadened and specialized. Practices eschewed by golden age law firms were common to large corporate firms by century's end: litigation, criminal defense (particularly with respect to white-collar and corporate crime), and even plaint-iffs' work (as corporate clients became increasingly willing to file suit [Heinz et al. 2005]). On the other hand, the modern firms had abandoned the older, full-service model in favor of building expertise in specialized areas of law (evidenced, in part, by the careers of partners, often limited to narrow sub-sections of transactional practice or litigation [Henderson 2011]).

Growth in size and geographic scope has led many firms also to pivot away from the Cravath model's traditional *hiring* and *promotion* practices. At a certain point, there simply were not enough top graduates from elite law schools to go around; the most prestigious law firms began hiring lower-ranked students from the elite schools and, then, when they were all taken, graduates from less prestigious national, regional, and even local law schools. Virtually all US law firms now hire associates and even partners "laterally" from other law firms (and, to a lesser extent, government agencies and in-house legal departments), with several now sourcing most of their lawyers in this way (Henderson and Bierman 2009). The up-or-out promotion policy is disappearing, too, with firms innovating mesocategories of professionals such as "permanent associates" and "nonequity partners" (Henderson 2005; Wilkins and Gulati 1998).

The prototypical Cravath-style *governance* model has also changed signif-icantly. Although all US firms are still formally organized as partnerships (ad-mittedly, most have switched to limited liability partnerships or professional corporations), few retain the egalitarian decision-making structure and lock-step compensation system that formed the heart of the "partnership model" of large golden age firms. With the exception of a handful of top-performing New York law firms (including Cravath), US law firms are typically organized bureaucratically. Formal managers (including managers who are *not* lawyers) are conferred with decision-making authority, and compensation is deter-mined by an "eat what you kill" model in which partners are paid on the basis of their individual contributions to firm profits (Chambliss 2009; Chambliss and Wilkins 2002; Regan 2004; Wilkins 2007).

The organizational shift toward larger and more sophisticated in-house legal departments has figured into the pace of change. The companies that, in the 1970s, sought to purchase most routine legal services wholesale rather than retail led the way in developing the substantial in-house departments (Chayes and Chayes 1985) that would become the profession's fastest-growing sector in the 1990s (Daly 1997; Gilson 1990; Rosen 1989). As indicated earlier, the sophisticated general counsels in charge of these departments (among them plenty of former law firm partners) have used their growing power to destabilize their companies' long-standing relationships with primary law firms. This further accelerated the transformation of the traditional Cravath System's hiring, promotion, and compensation systems as law firms scrambled to recruit and retain star lawyers able to bring in business in a world where most general counsels took up a "hire lawyers not firms" mantra (Wilkins 2012). Soon, young lawyers found going in-house to be an attractive career option, especially young female lawyers, who regarded freedom from firms' billable hour requirements as a far better fit for balancing work and family obligations and/or, like Alicia (as we saw in the introduction), as a viable exit strategy should their promotion prospects wither in the firm setting.

The increase in the size and bureaucratic structure of law firms and in-house legal departments constitutes the most visible manifestation of the sprawling organizational structure of legal practice. But developments in other sectors reflect this trend as well. Although solo and small-firm practitioners continue to dominate the individual hemisphere of private practice, we now find plaintiff law firms of significant size and scope, many specializing in national class action litigation and large product liability cases. There are pronounced hierarchies *within* the plaintiffs' bar, too, where observers note a small number of elite plaintiffs' firms specializing in class actions and product liability litigation whose partners make incomes that rival or exceed those of top corporate lawyers and a much larger group of bread-and-butter plaintiff lawyers in small firms eking out a living on automobile accident and slip-and-fall cases (and referral fees for sending cases up the food chain) (Kritzer 2002).

The last half of the twentieth century was also marked by an explosion of public sector laws and regulations, amplifying the need for public lawyers to interpret, administer, and enforce this expanding legal infrastructure at every level of government (Clark 1992). In addition, public interest lawyers focused on two goals: keeping government bureaucracy growing and keeping the private sector, emboldened by deregulation and globalization, in check (Trubek et al. 2013). This still relatively small sector of legal practice is not without a hierarchy. This one is topped by institutionalized national and international public interest law firms and hybrid public-private firms. The elite ranks include the foundation-supported firms founded and expanded in the 1970s, which are more than capable of recruiting top law school graduates (Kornhauser and Revesz 1995). In fact, the public interest organizations often work with formal pro bono programs and departments at large law firms (Cummings 2004).

Finally, the growth of new entrants to the profession such as LegalZoom, Rocket Lawyer, and Avvo—used by many solo and small-firm practitioners to generate business in the individual hemisphere as well as by the corporate sector's managed legal service providers, outsourcing companies, and temporary staffing agencies (themselves corporations fueled by technology companies, venture capitalists, and hedge funds)—underscores the ongoing importance of organizational structures and hierarchies to the legal market (Ambrogi 2020; Wilkins and Esteban Ferrer 2018). In many cases, bar organizations have fought these upstarts vigorously as unauthorized practices of law. But, in 2007, the United Kingdom authorized alternative legal service providers and various other organizational forms of practice (via the Legal Services Act), arguing that they serve a public function in making legal services more available to ordinary individuals. US regulators face mounting pressure to follow suit by allowing similar innovations through legislation (Chambliss 2019; Flood 2011). These debates again indicate the dramatic shifts in the profession's formal norms—let alone its informal ones—since the golden age.

THE IDEAL AND THE ACTUAL OF

PROFESSIONAL NORMS

Well before the founding of the ABA in 1878, lawyers took great pains to portray themselves as members of a "noble profession," independent from both the market and the state. The bar remains at least rhetorically committed to this self-image, yet, by the time the AJD Project cohort entered practice, it was hard to square the rhetoric with reality. Everywhere these lawyers looked, there were glaring signs of the competitive marketplace of modern law: personal injury lawyers advertising on television, billboards lining the roadways into airports and clamoring for the attention of deep-pocketed corporate travelers, and firms from obscure to elite aggressively taking up lateral hiring and obsessing over profits per partner.

Working to quell the unease caused by this disjunction, bar organizations have, in recent decades, issued a slew of reports urging a return to professionalism (Nelson and Trubek 1992). Coming close to rebuking the standard golden age claim that Cravath System law firms were the very embodiment of professionalism, the New York State Bar Association issued a report declaring that midsize law firms (with 11–50 lawyers) had become the true guardians of the profession's core values, having "resisted the institutionalization of practice and the bureaucratic model" and demonstrated that "law is first a profession, and only secondarily a business." Even so, these firms were described as having only partially "mitigated the effects on the profession as a whole of the transformation of the large law firm," fingered as the "critical catalyst" in the profession's growing commercialism (New York State Bar Association 74–75). Importantly, however, this report was authored by the New York State Bar Association and not the more prestigious Association of the Bar of the

City of New York or the ABA. The large-firm lawyers the reports aim to influence largely ignore such efforts. Elite lawyers today are far less likely to be active in bar organizations—particularly general-purpose bar organizations open to all lawyers—than were their golden age predecessors, and the declining membership numbers are emblematic of the organized bar's declining control of lawyerly norms and practices. The ABA claimed half of all American lawyers as members in the late 1970s but just a quarter by century's end. In the same years, beginning with the Supreme Court decisions invalidating bar rules against lawyer advertising and continuing with the imposition of statutory, regulatory, and common law rules governing lawyer conduct, the law of lawyering has shifted to state control (Hazard et al. 2017). Clients are now the de facto arbiters of what, in a practical sense, constitutes professional norms of craft and competence, particularly in the corporate hemisphere, where general counsels are the ultimate judges determining how much professionalism they are willing to pay for (Gilson 1990).

Yet, as we noted in the introduction, the doomsday accounts focus not on a changing profession but on one risking extinction. Reports in the legal and popular press are filled with stories—mostly anecdotal—about the misery of big law in which elite firms' rampant commercialism renders associates' careers unstable and unrewarding. Associates and partners are portrayed as drowning in a sea of boring and ultimately meaningless work, cast aside the moment they fail to meet the firm's constantly escalating billable hour and revenue generation requirements. They are said to wither under the "hypercompetitive ideology" and its demands to provide 24-7 client-centered representation, complete loyalty and devotion to the firm, and maximal profit per partner regardless of meritocratic professional values or work/life balance (Wald 2010). Cynics portray the growth in law firm pro bono work as little more than a self-interested veneer of allegiance to noble professionalism, just one more sign that the traditional distinction between private interest and the public good has collapsed (Abel 2010; Adediran 2020; Cummings and Rhode 2010). With a touch of irony, others watching all this excoriation wink that the law has become the "only job with an industry devoted to helping people quit" (Abramson 2014).

LIVING IN THE CONTRADICTIONS

Collectively, these changes in size, demographics, institutionalization, and norms have produced a legal profession that differs significantly from both the idealized tropes of the golden age and the apocalyptic predictions of the age of disruption. Members of the AJD Project cohort have launched their careers in a legal marketplace of antinomies. Legal services constitute one of the world's largest professions, yet huge segments of the population have little or no access to them. The profession is increasingly diverse yet stubbornly stratified by race and gender (particularly at elite levels). Its dominant organizations are continually growing and expanding their scope while becoming more and more unstable. And it struggles with fears of commercialism and dissatisfaction while it continues to insist that law is a noble calling dedicated to craft and public service. The rest of this book documents how the AJD Project cohort has responded to work amid this host of competing pressures (and pressures to compete). Their strategies for finding career success illuminate both the continuing power and the permeability of the structures of the legal profession.

PART 2

The Structure of Lawyers' Careers

Change and Continuity in the Legal Field: From Walled-Off Hemispheres to More or Less Mixed Hierarchical Sequences

The AJD Project captures the trajectories of different law school graduates from different backgrounds, law schools, grades, gender, race, and ethnicity as they make their way through the first decades of their careers. The career paths experienced by lawyers in the AJD study are almost as varied as the number of lawyers in the study. Some held only one other position after their first job, while others worked in seven.

The sequencing of events is important. It highlights the fact that the initial position offers a potent form of capital that sets some but not all lawyers on a particular trajectory. For some lawyers, changing sectors becomes a way to leverage skills or expertise gained in a first job. For example, it may be that an early career in the federal government allows some lawyers to leverage specific expertise and trial experience into positions as equity partners in large law firms later in their careers, positions they might not have been able to attain had they remained in large law firms for their entire career. A career trajectory is not simply determined by one's starting position, however. It is the entirety of a career trajectory that needs to be considered: the precise ordering of job types, sectors, and absences from the labor force. It is in the ordering of positions that we can begin to understand which forms of capital are valued by particular settings and which individuals are able to mobilize that capital. And, when all these things are considered together and examined holistically, we can discern larger-scale patterns that offer insight into the structure of legal careers and into the relative value of experiences in particular work settings.

This chapter pursues an explicitly Bourdieusian approach to legal careers and the analysis of continuity and change in the legal profession. We reveal the new structure of lawyers' careers through sequence analysis, a technique that allows us to capture the ordering of career positions more fully. The analyses reveal some dominant trajectories that we can depict as Bourdieusian habitus of internalized career strategies differentially available to and even desired by different law school graduates. The sorting in the golden age took place on the assumption that only male White Anglo-Saxon Protestants from elite schools were capable of becoming the kind of corporate lawyers that clients would trust and retain. That assumption is gone. The much more open and meritocratic assignment into the most elite positions today, however, leads to considerable continuity with the earlier period not only in the hierarchy of positions but also in who specifically gets the rewards of that hierarchy. From this perspective, it is hard to see much disruption of traditional hierarchies in the current era.

Theoretical Perspective

In contrast to the discussion in chapter 2, which emphasized an internal perspective on changes in the profession, in this chapter we push the boundaries of social science research on the legal profession by stepping back from the recurring professional debates. We use the tools of field sociology to look at the issue of change and continuity from a more strictly sociological perspective. We refer to structure and agency, diversity, crisis, and competition, as does chapter 2, but here we mainly focus on how the structure evolves over time but also stays the same. In this analysis, therefore, we focus more on social class and social construction and on the arbitrariness of social constructs, on the one hand, and the relationship to hierarchies and power, on the other. Our agenda here is less about issues of concern to the profession and more about issues of change and continuity.

Looking sociologically at the legal field, the questions of whether there is fundamental disruption, whether there is enough autonomy, whether there is sufficient commitment to pro bono work, and whether there is a crisis of one thing or another must be placed in the context of the structure of the legal field, what it rewards and devalues, and how it is changing over time. There are enduring oppositions and debates that play a role in affirming the profession's status and that both shape and moderate change. The rules of the game for success in the field counsel affirming and enacting professionalism and autonomy as opposed to commercialism (at least symbolically), affirming the quality of the top law schools and their graduates, showing some commitment to pro bono work as evidence of the public service commitment, and protecting the professional monopoly. When the profession is most under attack, affirmations and criticisms around these issues heat up. Lawyers can gain attention and help make their careers by affirming these values. Few are embraced for arguing, for example, that commercialism should replace professionalism, that pro bono work is a waste of time, or that autonomy should succumb to client dominance. All this seems completely natural to the professional legal community, but we believe it is also important to explore how these debates and the changes that take place over time relate to the changing social context and the enduring structure of the legal field. The recurring debates themselves contribute to a story of continuity in professional ideology amid change.

Following Bourdieu, we see the legal field as a relatively autonomous space characterized by the rules of the game (contested and changing) and actors with different forms and values of capital seeking to use what they have to succeed in the game. The field changes over time in response to agents brokering resources that come from developments outside the field that provide opportunities and challenges to the existing rules of the game and the professional hierarchies that they sustain. The top of the hierarchy remains the corporate equity partners, and those who gain that stature tend to be White, male graduates of elite law schools with wives at home. This legal elite today is, it turns out, quite consistent with what the legal elite looked like in the so-called golden age of corporate law firms. We also show persistence in the lower hemisphere of the bar, in which graduates of less elite law schools continue to work in small firms, service individual needs, and work in state government. Yet much has changed.

In order to tell a story of continuity and change, we return to the classic period of the two hemispheres of Heinz and Laumann (1982) and describe the transformation to the modern era. The so-called lower hemisphere of the legal profession included graduates of urban and night law schools, typically children of immigrants who were often Catholic or Jewish. The legal profession was seen as a means of upward mobility for those in the lower hemisphere, who served individuals as solo and small-firm lawyers and also made up the infrastructure of urban government. The upper hemisphere was composed of graduates of elite law schools who were mainly White Anglo-Saxon Protestants and primarily served corporate clients. Those from the lower hemisphere did not cross over and hold positions in the upper hemisphere. There were relatively few women and members of minority groups in the profession, and those who were in the profession did not identify with corporate law.

The ecosystem fit together. The corporate law firm was at the top of the hierarchy. Law firms hired from leading law schools, mainly Harvard, Yale, and Columbia, and those who were hired participated with enthusiasm in the partnership tournament. Those who did not make partner were deemed failures. Clients were stable, and firms were associated with their prominent clients. Compensation was lockstep, and partner mobility was rare. Graduates of the elite schools who did not want to be corporate partners opted out at the beginning from what they called the *law factories*.

There was an increase in business competition beginning in the 1970s that brought real challenges to this ecosystem and hierarchy. Large firms and their clients had avoided litigation, which now became a weapon in corporate competition and in mergers and acquisitions, which were part of the new financialization of business associated with the rise of MBAs (Fourcade 2006) and an increase in deregulation. Law firms expanded greatly to follow (and try to hold on to) their clients and provide full service nationally and internationally. Partner profits grew, becoming part of the competition for status and, increasingly, for lawyers in the new market for laterals. As clients sought to lower their costs, long-standing law firm relationships and loyalties lost much of their significance. Partners were no longer secure in their positions, and those whose business generation declined were deequitized. Partnership took longer to attain, and, in order to maintain partner profits, a variety of nonequity positions became much more prominent: of counsel, nonequity partner, contract lawyer.

These changes meant that law firms promoted fewer associates to equity partner, instead retaining the ones who stayed at the firm in nonequity positions as employees. The calculus of the associate thus changed from one of a tournament toward partnership to perceiving the large law firm as a valuable starting position. The rise in prestige of in-house counsel also meant that those who left the large firm could go on to other prestigious positions. These shifts in the corporate sector had direct implications for the lower hemisphere of the bar: as law firms needed more associates, they began to recruit from lower-tier law schools. Yet the large law firms still promoted mainly their associates with more elite credentials to the equity partnerships.

The seismic changes traceable to an economy with greatly increased corporate competition were matched by changes inspired by political movements for social equality. Minorities, beginning with African Americans, struggled to gain places in the profession and are now expected to have equal opportunity to succeed in legal careers, including the highest ranks of corporate law. The societal changes associated with the civil rights movement meant that the *capital value of minority status* had gone up dramatically. Still, it has not translated to anything close to equality in the equity partnership ranks.

The women's movement also brought societal changes that have translated into capital values for corporate law firms. Since here, too, law firms are judged by their clients, their peers, and the legal press, women began to be recruited to join the corporate law firms in proportion to their representation in law school. It is a different story than that of racial and ethnic minorities, but it is very similar in outcome. And, while women are well represented among associates and non–equity track lawyers, their advancement into equity partnerships remains very limited despite the increase in the *capital value of gender diversity*.

One set of challenges also came from nonelite law school graduates, who had been traditionally relegated to positions in the lower hemisphere. Challenges to this division came from both internal and external events. For example, studies of Chicago lawyers show that Catholic schools worked hard to pry open corporate law firms, with the result that by the 1980s there was a critical mass in some of the corporate partnerships (Garth and Martin 1993). The dramatic expansion in the size of corporate law firms since the 1980s also resulted in the recruitment of the highest-achieving graduates from lower-ranked schools. This newfound openness came from a different imperative than the push for diversity did. It was driven primarily by the sheer need for more associates that came from the massive expansion of the large law firms. These graduates were highly committed to the partnership competition and eager to stay on because of the elite accomplishment this signaled (and few other options), and, given where they came from, they were also perhaps hungrier. Yet the odds of making equity partner were very small indeed. And, even though graduates of lower-ranked law schools tend to come from a less elite social class, we can say that there is a greater law firm commitment not to affirmative action for lower-ranked schools—or to those from a lower social class—but to a script of *meritocracy that includes graduates from nonelite schools*. It is not unusual to hear lawyers say that the degree makes no difference once they join the firm.

Associates, whether elite or nonelite, now leverage their initial experience in the large firm into a form of capital that allows them to build a career in these other settings. In this new model, a position in a law firm is treated paradigmatically as an apprenticeship that is recognized and valued in all practice settings—because the hierarchy of the legal field puts corporate law on top—as a great place to begin one's career. We have termed this "the new place of corporate law firms in the structuring of elite legal careers" (Dinovitzer and Garth 2020, 339). This transformation means that nearly all who can get corporate jobs take them, allowing the large law firm to maintain its legitimacy at the top of the hierarchy.

Sequence Analysis: The Pathways of Lawyers' Careers

A key feature of modern legal careers that is implicit in much of the discussion presented above is mobility. Lawyers' careers are now characterized by a much higher degree of mobility than they were in the golden age, when there was little movement from one practice setting to another or even from one firm to another. With the reconfiguration of the role of the large law firm in early careers, the rise in prestige of in-house counsel, and the broad expansion of positions in business, early careers are punctuated now by high rates of job changes. Within three years of graduating law school, about two-thirds of lawyers will have changed jobs at least once, and, while mobility slows in later careers, more than one-third of lawyers change jobs after year 7, and more than one-third change jobs after year 12 (see chap. 14). Despite the sheer scale of this mobility, it is not chaotic: careers in law tend to follow various well-worn paths, often depending on where the journey began, and, as was suggested above, the nature of the journey is also dependent on one's gender, race, and social class.

We rely on a statistical technique called *sequence analysis* to identify distinct patterns that are common among the careers of the lawyers in the AJD study. By identifying common threads and patterns among the unique careers, we are able to create clusters of typical pathways. Sequence analysis is a technique used by biologists to compare DNA sequences in order to find out the extent to which two DNA strands are homologous. The established degree of similarity then allows for conclusions about a common ancestor of two DNA strands. By applying this approach to career sequences, we look for patterns that bring together careers into more coherent groupings on the basis of prominent features.

The development of sequence analysis as a tool with which to understand careers comes from developments in life course research (Aisenbrey and Fasang 2010). Life course researchers are generally interested in micro-level events, such as important life events that they identify as *transitions* (such as marriage), as well as a more macro perspective that is interested in *trajectories*, especially across birth cohorts (Elder 1974). Sequence analysis, in contrast, seeks to identify patterns in trajectories. It allows us to observe and tell the story of the micro level of individual moves (such as a lateral move from a law firm into business) and to also zoom out and observe that there are commonalities across the ordering of these individual choices (which we see, e.g., in the mass movement of lawyers out of law firms and into business). Taken together, when aggregated across hundreds and thousands of lawyers, the individual choices that are observed in each sequence in fact reflect and reinforce broader patterns in the profession. This careful balance between the micro and the macro is important because, as Blair-Loy's (1999) sequence analysis of women in finance reveals, individuals themselves might describe their careers as the result of flukes or accidents, whereas the analysis reveals that there are in fact clear patterns and pathways.

Most importantly for our purposes, within the study of work and the life course, the theoretical underpinnings of sequence analysis consider the sequential development of work histories. This perspective is best captured by the concept of the career (Cornwell 2015). Careers are commonly thought of as being "built" through a series of job changes and promotions. For example, research finds that careers within specific settings have common trajectories (e.g., "climbing the corporate ladder"). A prime example is Stovel et al.'s (1996) analysis of careers at Lloyds Bank of London between 1890 and 1970, which identifies changes in career ladders and pathways from ascriptive status–based careers to achievement-based careers. The purpose of the analysis is not simply to identify types of careers but also to emphasize that each career trajectory is also usually accompanied by particular social scripts, much like the habitus we describe above. As Cornwell (2015, 28) elaborates: "People who find themselves on certain career trajectories develop different expectations about their current responsibilities and future prospects based on their understanding of other workers who are on similar tracks, which in turn directly shapes their performance." The analysis that we develop in this chapter clearly identifies a number of specific career trajectories, each with attendant social scripts.

The patterns that we find in these sequences preview many of the major themes that tie together the chapters in this book and empirically reflect our discussion of the era of change in the preceding part. The results we describe here show that sequence analysis is a powerful analytic tool that reveals the recurring trajectories across lawyers' careers and their implications for understanding opportunity and advancement in the legal profession, painting a picture of the broader structures that both create change and sustain inequality. Four patterns that we observed were particularly salient. (1) Careers continue to be divided and differentiated within and between the sectors of practice—namely, large firms, small firms, business, and the public sector—with very constrained mobility between sectors. For example, we observed mobility between large firms and business but not between large firms and state government, and we observed a continued divide between elite and nonelite career pathways. (2) First jobs tend to set career trajectories, especially among lawyers who start out in large firms, and continue to be the pathway to the most lucrative positions in the legal profession. (3) Race and gender continue to be salient, the sequence analysis showing that women and minorities are more likely than are Whites to have careers punctuated by episodes of unemployment and job changes. (4) Inequality determined by social origin, gender, race, and law school tier continues to be entrenched. Despite the opening up of the profession and the embrace of the script of meritocracy, those who succeed in the largest law firms continue to be White male elite law school graduates, while those who do not fit the mold either remain in nonequity positions or leave for other opportunities.

METHODS

The sequences we have constructed in this project are based on a chronology of the types of organizations (e.g., large law firm, federal government) in which respondents worked over the thirteen years of the study. We focus on organizational settings because where lawyers work allows us to understand not simply the kinds of work they do but also the prestige of the work they do, which of course indicates their status within the profession. In addition to organization, we also include whether respondents hold an equity partnership in a large and midsize firm, and we included spells of unemployment. We defined ten types of positions: equity partner in a large law firm (251 or more lawyers), nonequity partner in a large law firm (251 or more lawyers), equity partner in a midsize firm (51–250 lawyers), nonequity partner in a private law firm (51–250 lawyers), business (practicing and not practicing law), solo or small-firm lawyer (50 lawyers or fewer), federal government (not including federal court clerkships), state government, legal services/public interest, and unemployed. While these encompass the full range of organizations within which lawyers work, some distinct groups were too small to represent on their own—for example, law professors or public interest lawyers each have very unique career paths, but their categories are so small that the analysis would have become too cumbersome, and they are instead included in the category of legal services. As a result, our analysis will by definition miss some distinct career trajectories.

The empirical process through which we determine the commonalities between sequences is called *optimal matching*. This approach defines the distance between two sequences as the number of operations it takes to transform one sequence into the other (Cornwell 2015). These operations are *substitution* (changing one element into another), *insertion* (inserting an element), and *deletion* (deleting an element)—in our case, each element is a type of organization. The more operations it takes to make two sequences similar, the greater the distance between them. Once all the distances are calculated, we create groups of sequences that are most similar. It is important to note that creating groups or clusters of sequences is an exploratory and somewhat messy process. As our discussion below will highlight, each cluster is characterized by key features and career characteristics, but there will be some deviations from the most common sequences within a given cluster.

Of the 4,183 careers on which we have information, we are able to identify 12 typical careers into which we grouped all the sequences, groupings that we call *clusters*. We further aggregate these 12 clusters into four broader groupings based on the most common starting point of the sequences. These four groupings are a heuristic only and are used to simplify the presentation. The first grouping is of the large-firm starters, and it encompasses three different clusters. The first is a large cluster that identifies those whose careers primarily began and remained in the large firm. It is the second largest cluster in the analysis, comprising 19.4% of all sequences. The second is a cluster that emphasizes the relatively new and prestigious path from large firms to business (9.5%), and the third is a small grouping for those who transitioned from a large firm to a small firm (4.8%). Our next grouping includes four clusters that focus on small and midsize-firm starters. The largest—which is in fact the largest cluster overall, comprising 21% of all sequences—is of lawyers who began and ended their careers in small firms. The second identifies those primarily in small firms who experienced high rates of unemployment (5%), the third groups those in midsize firms who generally attained equity partnership (4.4%), and the fourth is for those who moved from midsize firms to small firms (4.2%). The third major grouping highlights careers in business. It includes one cluster (8.8%) of careers that mainly started and ended in business settings and a second of careers in business that are marked by a number of spells of unemployment (4.1%). The final grouping brings together various public sector paths: one focuses on state government (6.8%), another on legal services (6.2%), and the third on careers in the federal government (5.8%). Tables 3.1 and 3.2 describe the social characteristics and employment characteristics and practice settings of respondents in each cluster.

The analysis of the clusters offered below will highlight patterns in relation to some of the key forms of capital that we identify in this book as critical for understanding the trajectories of legal careers: most centrally race, gender, and ethnicity, law school attended, and starting at large law firms. Taken together, the findings fit well within a Bourdieusian understanding of social capital, showing that, while all careers are open to all, inequalities accumulate and that those who bring with them valued social capital are able to advance more easily. Taken together, the 12 clusters reflect and provide substance to the story of continuity and change that the introduction to this chapter and the remaining chapters of the book explore. They represent the prevailing pathways for lawyers' careers today. They show what kinds of education

TABLE 3.1 Respondent social and employment characteristics (%) and median income by career cluster

Social and employment characteristics, career satisfaction, and income	Career cluster													
	Big firms			Small/midsize firms				Business		Government/nongovernment public				
	Big firm	Big to business	Big to small	Small firm	Small unemployed	Midsize firm equity	Midsize to small	Business	Business unemployed	Federal government	State government	Legal services	Total %	Total N
Gender														
Woman	47.6	46.1	43.9	43.3	60.2	44.6	46.0	41.3	55.3	48.6	59.1	64.7	48.5	2,023
Man	52.4	53.9	56.1	56.7	39.8	55.4	54.0	58.7	44.7	51.4	40.9	35.3	51.5	2,150
Race/ethnicity														
African American	9.7	8.6	12.2	7.4	5.7	7.1	7.5	9.9	10.6	14.9	13.4	14.0	9.7	403
Latinx	10.2	9.8	10.7	9.5	12.4	6.0	9.2	9.6	7.6	9.1	10.9	10.5	9.8	406
Native American	0.9	1.0	1.0	1.7	2.9	2.2	1.7	0.8	2.4	1.2	2.5	1.6	1.5	62
Asian American	11.1	16.6	9.2	6.6	11.4	4.9	6.9	10.7	14.7	9.5	11.3	6.2	9.9	411
White	67.3	63.5	64.3	73.7	66.2	79.1	73.6	68.5	64.7	64.0	61.6	66.7	68.2	2,834
Other race/ethnicity	0.7	0.5	2.6	1.0	1.4	0.5	1.1	0.5	0.0	1.2	0.4	1.2	0.9	37
Law school ranking														
Top 10	23.5	23.7	13.3	1.3	1.5	9.3	4.1	8.8	9.6	17.1	2.9	10.2	11.5	465
Ranked 11–20	16.7	19.4	12.8	4.3	10.3	11.5	5.3	6.3	9.6	18.8	5.5	8.5	10.9	439
Ranked 21–50	22.1	25.7	26.5	15.7	27.0	25.3	22.4	19.6	18.6	21.7	19.7	22.8	21.3	859
Ranked 51–100	23.5	20.2	23.5	34.6	28.9	27.5	28.8	30.7	32.3	25.4	32.8	27.6	28.1	1,135

Tier 3	9.5	7.6	14.3	21.2	14.2	14.3	22.4	20.2	13.2	10.4	19.7	14.2	15.0	607
Tier 4	4.8	3.5	9.7	22.8	18.1	12.1	17.1	14.5	16.8	6.7	19.3	16.7	13.2	535
Children														
Men with children	68.9	70.6	68.5	69.3	65.5	67.6	77.4	66.7	71.1	71.2	73.5	65.9	69.4	2,148
Women with children	66.0	62.1	70.6	66.4	65.9	78.0	74.7	66.2	62.4	59.3	61.9	67.1	65.9	2,014
Unemployment														
Never unemployed	80.8	84.9	79.3	83.9	63.0	83.7	82.2	83.7	68.2	87.7	85.7	76.0	81.2	3,390
Has been unemployed	19.2	15.1	20.7	16.1	37.0	16.3	17.8	16.3	31.8	12.3	14.3	24.0	18.8	783
Partnership														
Equity	55.1	95.7	59.6	70.6	86.0	39.6	70.3	95.6	96.8	73.1	95.0	96.4	77.5	387
Nonequity	19.8	3.0	30.1	22.0	9.8	38.5	16.4	3.1	1.3	16.0	3.5	3.6	13.8	243
All other positions	25.1	1.3	10.3	7.4	4.1	22.0	13.3	1.3	1.9	10.9	1.5	0.0	8.7	2,171
Career Satisfaction														
Satisfied at wave 3	75.0	81.0	76.0	77.0	64.0	79.0	73.0	78.0	58.0	76.0	83.0	76.0	76.0	2,961
Earnings														
Median at wave 3	$171,500	$213,000	$122,463	$99,000	$72,500	$150,000	$115,000	$135,000	$100,000	$144,000	$87,500	$75,000	$120,000	2,488

TABLE 3.2A Respondent wave 1 practice setting by career cluster (%)

Wave 1 practice setting	Career cluster											
	Big firm	Big to business	Big to small	Small firm	Small unemployed	Mid firm equity	Mid to small	Business	Business unemployed	Federal government	State government	Legal services
Solo practice	1.0	0.3	3.4	14.4	8.7	0	4.3	0.7	0.8	1.6	0.5	3.5
Law firm 2–20	7.5	2.2	18.5	58.6	51.3	18.5	26.1	5.7	8.2	8.9	2.7	27.4
Law firm 21–100	12.4	9.9	7.5	3.6	8.7	65.6	50.0	11.8	5.7	7.3	5.4	4.5
Law firm 101–250	19.0	21.4	13.0	0.8	4.0	6.0	3.6	2.2	1.6	9.9	0.9	0
Law firm 251+	48.6	55.9	43.2	0.8	2.0	0.7	2.2	4.3	15.6	34.0	0.5	2.0
Law firm of unknown size	1.0	0.6	2.1	0	0	0	2.9	0.7	0	1.0	0	0
Federal government	3.6	2.9	4.8	2.6	2.0	2.6	1.4	6.8	5.7	30.9	4.5	4.0
State government	3.3	1.3	3.4	10.2	13.3	2.6	4.3	12.2	11.5	2.1	72.9	11.9
Legal services/public defense	0.7	0	2.1	3.0	2.7	2.0	1.4	1.8	2.5	0.5	8.6	15.4
Public interest	0.7	0	0	0.6	0	1.3	0.7	1.1	1.6	1.0	1.4	11.9
Nonprofit/education	0.7	0	0.7	0.9	2.7	0	0.7	2.2	4.9	1.6	2.3	15.4
Business, practicing	1.0	4.5	1.4	2.0	2.0	0	1.4	26.5	18.0	0	0	0.5
Business, not practicing	0.7	1.0	0	2.1	2.7	0.7	0.7	23.7	22.1	1.0	0	3.0
Other practice setting	0.2	0	0	0.5	0	0	0	0.4	1.6	0	0.5	0.5

TABLE 3.2B Respondent wave 2 practice setting by career cluster (%)

Wave 2 practice setting	Career cluster											
	Big firm	Big to business	Big to small	Small firm	Small unemployed	Mid firm equity	Mid to small	Business	Business unemployed	Federal government	State government	Legal services
Solo practice	0.1	0.6	12.0	27.1	18.3	0	22.8	0.7	2.5	1.5	0	6.5
Law firm 2–20	1.7	1.6	39.5	45.6	40.0	3.1	40.7	1.0	2.5	5.3	0.8	6.9
Law firm 21–100	6.6	0.9	8.4	6.1	6.3	77.8	17.2	1.6	3.3	4.9	4.0	1.9
Law firm 101–250	15.1	2.8	6.0	0.4	2.9	2.5	2.1	0.7	2.5	7.8	0.4	0.5
Law firm 251+	40.1	14.6	16.2	0.3	2.3	0	0.7	0.7	3.3	26.2	0	1.4
Law firm of unknown size	15.1	4.7	4.8	1.1	3.4	1.2	2.1	1.6	0.8	2.9	0.8	1.4
Federal government	8.9	2.5	3.6	2.4	3.4	4.9	0.7	3.3	5.0	36.4	3.6	1.4
State government	3.5	0.6	4.2	8.0	13.7	0	4.1	9.8	9.2	2.4	80.8	5.1
Legal services/public defense	0.8	0.6	1.2	0.4	0	0.6	0.7	0.7	1.7	0.5	4.4	20.8
Public interest	0.7	0.6	0	0.3	0.6	0.6	0	0.3	0	0	1.6	14.8
Nonprofit/education	5.8	2.8	1.8	0.5	0.6	6.2	0	2.6	7.5	8.7	2.4	33.8
Business, practicing	0.6	51.4	1.8	4.2	3.4	0	4.8	36.9	31.7	2.4	0	2.8
Business, not practicing	0.8	15.6	0.6	3.2	4.0	1.9	4.1	33.7	28.3	0.5	0.4	2.8
Other practice setting	0.1	0.6	0	0.5	1.1	1.2	0	6.5	1.7	0.5	0.8	0

TABLE 3.2c Respondent wave 3 practice setting by career cluster (%)

Wave 3 practice setting	Big firm	Big to business	Big to small	Small firm	Small unemployed	Mid firm equity	Mid to small	Business	Business unemployed	Federal government	State government	Legal services
Solo practice	0.9	1.0	21.2	26.4	29.0	0	20.3	0	2.6	2.9	0	5.6
Law firm 2–20	1.1	1.7	45.9	40.6	32.6		43.8	0	1.9	5.1	0	4.6
Law firm 21–100	9.5	1.3	5.5	7.2	6.2	77.2	7.8	0.9	2.6	4.6	5.5	0
Law firm 101–250	13.4	0	7.5	0.2	0.5	1.1	2.3	0	0.6	4.6	1.0	0
Law firm 251+	40.0	2.3	5.5	0	1.6	0	2.3	0	0.6	28.0	0	1.0
Law firm of unknown size	4.5	0	2.1	0	0.5	0	0	0	0.6	2.9	0	0.5
Federal government	10.2	2.0	2.1	3.6	2.6	8.7	0.8	2.7	4.5	33.1	10.9	2.0
State government	6.1	0.7	5.5	10.9	10.9	0	6.3	10.2	11.7	3.4	72.1	4.6
Legal services/ public defense	3.4	1.0	0.7	0	0	0	0	1.3	0.6	1.1	3.5	29.4
Public interest	0.9	0.3	0	0.2	0	2.2	0	0.9	1.9	0	2.0	9.1
Nonprofit/education	8.4	3.0	2.7	0.4	1.0	10.9	0	1.8	7.1	10.3	4.5	40.6
Business, practicing	0.9	65.4	0.7	4.3	7.3	0	8.6	34.1	24.7	2.9	0.5	0
Business, not practicing	0.2	15.6	0.7	3.4	5.2	0	6.3	34.1	27.9	0.6	0	1.0
Other practice setting	0.2	5.6	0	2.7	2.6	0	1.6	14.2	12.3	0.6	0	1.5

and career experiences open and close doors for particular kinds of career opportunities.

The sequence analysis thus provides a unique perspective on how career moves cluster together. In other chapters, we will analyze these transitions at the higher level of generality that is required for multivariate analyses of career processes. In the narrative chapters, we will analyze the evolution of individual careers on the basis of in-depth interviews that reveal how lawyers build their careers in the four distinct sectors of solo and small firms, large law firms, business, and the public sector. Thus, data collected with very different methods and analyzed with different techniques converge to present a portrait of a profession that is highly stratified yet dynamic at the level of practice organizations and individual career paths.

LARGE-FIRM STARTERS

One of the most significant transformations in the modern legal profession has been the growth of the large law firm. In 2008, at the peak of their recruitment, the large law firms collectively hired 10,000 entry-level associates in one year. This growth is directly reflected in the career sequences observed in the AJD study. Three of the clusters, which together account for one-third of the sample, describe the careers of individuals who primarily began in a large law firm. The first of these three is the largest (representing 19% of all the career sequences), and it is defined by careers that tended to remain within the large-firm setting. Indeed, we find that 40% of lawyers in this cluster are in a large firm of over 250 lawyers by wave 3 and that 70% have remained in a law firm of any size (with most in midsize to larger firms). The sequences for this cluster displayed in figure 3.1 show the prominence of beginning one's career in a large firm, along with many sequences with no other settings featured throughout their career. For those whose career led them away from law firms, 16% went to a government position (10% federal, 6% state), and 8% went to nonprofits or education. It is noteworthy that of the almost 100 AJD Project respondents who became law professors, about one-quarter are found in this cluster.

The prominence of law firms over the 13 years of the lawyers' careers in this cluster is in stark contrast to the overall pattern that we find in the AJD Project that describes lawyers leaving large private law firms (and, indeed, firms of all sizes) in significant numbers, and those career paths will be featured in other clusters. This first cluster tells us about the unique subset of lawyers who both began in and have remained in the large-firm setting. We find two distinct outcomes for those who remained in a large firm after

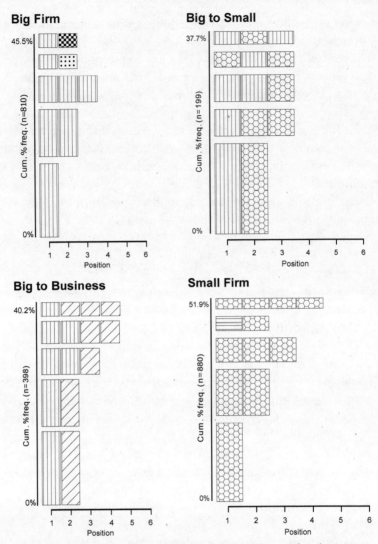

13 years: a small number (10%) who were promoted to equity partner in a large law firm and the remainder, who have remained in nonequity positions. This unequal distribution in advancement is related to other important characteristics: two-thirds of those who made equity partner are men, 87% are White, and the median earnings of equity partners are more than double those of nonequity partners ($386,000 vs. $167,000). This pattern very much reflects the new model of the large law firm in the twenty-first century, in which only

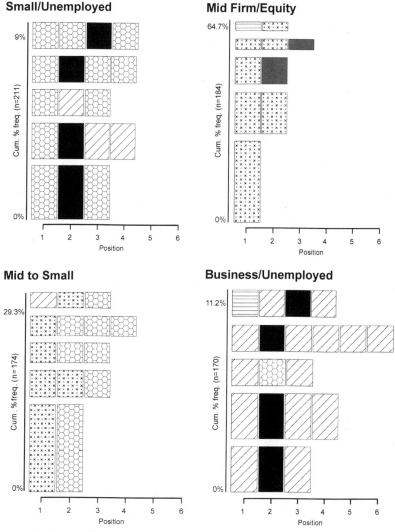

FIGURE 3.1. (*continued*)

a small number of lawyers receive equity partnerships while others are kept on in nonequity positions or go on to other practice settings.

Given the large-firm start, it is not surprising that this cluster has one of the highest proportions of elite graduates—40% attended top-10 or top-20 law schools. Yet a significant number graduated from schools outside the elite—46% from those ranked in the top 100 and another 14% from tier 3 and 4 schools. This is a notable differentiation from the closed world of the golden

Business

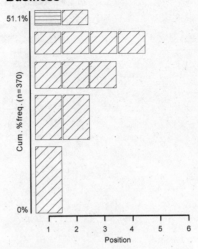

Federal Government

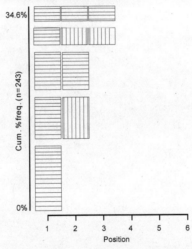

FIGURE 3.1. (*continued*)

age where only elite law school graduates were eligible for a position in a large firm. There is also evidence of the opening up of the large firm to women and racial/ethnic minorities and of the capital value of gender diversity and minority status that we discuss throughout this book. This cluster is almost half female (48%) and about one-third non-White, which is the sample average. Yet the data powerfully reveal that the acceptance of women and minorities within the large-firm setting is bounded: as we note above, despite the fact that they began in a large law firm, women and minorities in the large-firm

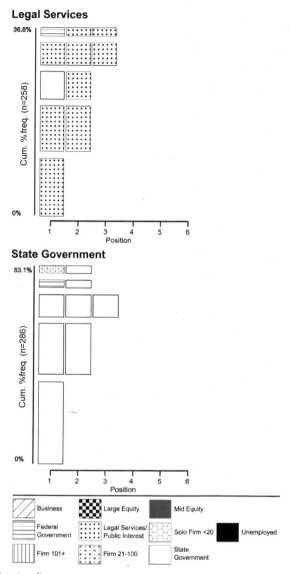

FIGURE 3.1. (*continued*)

cluster are less likely than are White men to be in equity partnerships by wave 3 (irrespective of the size of the firm). Thus, despite the increase in all forms of diversity in the large law firm, it appears to be limited mainly to entry- or second-level positions. Advancement in the large law firm remains the domain of privilege. As we will discuss in chapters 10 and 11, the patterns in the sequences revealed in this cluster exemplify law firms functioning as "inequality machines" that mainly push out minorities and women or shunt them off into nonequity positions.

The second large-firm cluster exemplifies another new feature of careers in large firms that we describe in chapter 8, namely, the synergy between large firms and business. This cluster brings together the careers of 398 individuals, the majority of whom began in a large firm and transitioned to a position in business (75% had a first position in a firm employing over 100 lawyers). A full 70% of lawyers in this cluster were in business by wave 3 of the survey. Three-quarters are practicing law, suggesting that these are indeed individuals who are working as inside counsel. The majority of sequences show positions in only two sectors—the large law firm and a business setting. Most went directly from a large firm into business. Some had more than one large-firm position before their exit to business, while others eventually held more than one position in business. A small number spent some time working in a midsize firm before transitioning to the business sector, and, interestingly, we also see a few (7%) who began their careers in the federal government (note that these positions do not include federal court clerkships) before moving into a large law firm and then into business. Median earnings in this cluster are the highest of all the clusters ($206,500). Taken together, these are elite careers, and it is not surprising that we again find an overrepresentation of elite law school graduates in this cluster—24% coming from top-10 law schools and another 19% from top-20 law schools.

The gender balance tips toward more men in this cluster (54% male), but it is slightly more diverse along racial lines, mostly owing to strong representation of both Asian American men and women (17% Asian American compared to 10% in the sample). While Asian Americans were overrepresented in large firms at wave 1, their overrepresentation in this cluster—which represents individuals who left the large firms even if it was to take up lucrative positions in business—is some evidence of their lack of fit for partnership. This lack of fit is reflected in measures of career satisfaction in this cluster, which were below average at wave 1 yet among the highest (81% reporting moderate to extreme satisfaction) by wave 3.

It is also worth noting that much of the public narrative about the path from law firms to business has been about work-family balance and the pressure to bill in the large-firm setting. There is some support in the data for this hypothesis: in waves 2 and 3, the hours worked by those in the large-firm cluster are generally higher than those in the large-firm to business cluster (though the difference is more pronounced in wave 2 than in wave 3), and the hours worked by those in large firms are generally higher than those in business. We also find that lawyers in business suggest that they experience less work family conflict than do the lawyers in large law firms. This certainly suggests that there are some pull factors to the business sector and that the business sector provides some very successful career options for lawyers. At the same time, there is much data to suggest that exits from law firms are the result of very strong push factors, and that we observe greater rates of attrition from firms among women and minorities is certainly suggestive that law firms continue to welcome and promote primarily White men.

The third cluster in this grouping of large-firm starters represents individuals who began in the large law firm and ultimately transitioned to a smaller firm or solo practice. The defining feature of this cluster is the near exclusivity of these two settings: a dominant sequence is simply one move, that from a large firm directly into small-firm/solo practice. Other sequences feature a few positions in a large firm before moving to a small firm, while others feature a first position in a large firm followed by a few positions in small firms, as respondents try to find the right fit. This is the smallest of the three large-firm clusters, which is not surprising given that the transitions we observe in it represent a change from the golden age, in which the client-type divide was rarely, if ever, crossed. We know that some of these smaller firms are so-called boutique firms that primarily serve businesses, but the salaries and pedigrees of most of the lawyers in this cluster suggest that they are generally not in boutiques. Lawyers in this cluster have the lowest earnings of all large-firm starters, but, at just above the sample median, those earnings are higher than those of most of the nonelite graduates who did not begin their careers in the large law firm.

In contrast to the elite pedigree found in the other two large-firm clusters, only 26% of the lawyers in this cluster graduated from a law school in the top 20. The lower proportion of elite graduates in this cluster despite the large-firm start suggests that, while large firms began hiring from a wider range of law schools, these hires were destined to be temporary workers who did not fit a long-term career in the prestigious large-firm setting. At the same time, it was a sufficient proportion to provide enough evidence for the new script of meritocracy within the large law firms. In short, the large-firm start provides differential payoffs that depend on law school credential along with gender and race. We also find more racial/ethnic diversity in this cluster: the proportion of African American women (and to a lesser extent men) is above average, along with Latinos and Asian American men. Again, these patterns bolster the story of continuity and change, with the large firm at the top of the hierarchy and much more open to changes at the entry level. It also shows the complicated nature of the capital value of gender diversity and minority status—and the script of meritocracy—with these traditional outsiders not fully embraced in the large firm.

SMALL- AND MIDSIZE-FIRM STARTERS

Despite the growth of the large law firm, careers in small and midsize firms continue to play an important role in lawyers' careers. About one-third of all sequences fall under the major grouping of small and midsize firms. There are four clusters in this group, two for small-firm starters and two for midsize-firm starters. The largest cluster of the four highlights careers in small firms (2–20 lawyers) and solo practice. Fully 21% of all career sequences are captured by this small-firm cluster, which is characterized by an almost singular presence in the lower hemisphere of legal practice. Most sequences are composed exclusively of positions in small firms and solo practice—not only are there are no instances of positions in large law firms, but there are also very few instances of positions in a midsize (21–100 lawyers) firm. Instead, as with the two hemispheres identified by Heinz and Laumann (1982), we see the continued homology between positions in small firms and state government along with a minor role for business, both practicing and not practicing law. One notable outlier is a small group of individuals who began their career in the federal government and then moved to a small firm.

Defying the out-migration from the private practice of law seen more generally in the sample, the majority (75%) of lawyers in this cluster remained in private law firms, with just over one-quarter working as sole practitioners by wave 3 of the study. For those working in law firms (and not solo practice), 42% obtained an equity partnership by wave 3, and all were in small to midsize firms of less than 100 lawyers. The relationship between the lower hemisphere of the bar and lower-tier law schools has persisted, with only 5% of the lawyers in this cluster having graduated from an elite law school (top 10 or top 20); median earnings are below the sample median. The demographic profile is striking: it is one of the Whitest clusters in the sample (73% White), with a significant underrepresentation of Asian American men and African American and Asian American women. It is also more male than female (43% women). Taken together, these patterns strongly echo the differentiation along the lines of law school tier, firm size, and client type that was documented close to 50 years earlier by Heinz and Laumann. Thus, despite significant transformations in the legal profession over the past half decade, we continue to find cleavages that have stubbornly persisted.

A second cluster also brings together careers in small firms, but this cluster is characterized by career volatility, including spells of unemployment and a greater number of positions over the course of the study. Sequence analysis provides a statistical measure of turbulence (Elzinga 2006), which is a measure of the number of job changes and the number of distinct types of positions in a sequence. We find that this cluster exhibits the highest level of turbulence compared to all other clusters. Fully 85% of the women and 80% of the men in this cluster have experienced at least one spell of unemployment. The cluster is predominantly female (60%), is one of the least elite clusters in the sample (6% graduated from a top-10 or -20 law school), and has the lowest median earnings ($73,000). The racial/ethnic profile is equally remarkable: despite the overrepresentation of White women, Latinas, and Asian American women, there is a dramatic underrepresentation of African American women (who constitute only 2.9% of this cluster, compared to 5.9% in the sample). Among the men, we find fewer White men and greater numbers of Latinos, Asian Americans, and Native Americans. The measures of career satisfaction suggest that this was not their intended trajectory. From an average level of satisfaction at wave 1 (78%), the lawyers in this cluster experience a 14% drop in satisfaction (down to 64%) by wave 3.

Examination of the sequences reveals positions in the lower hemisphere of the bar. The majority began in small firms and solo practice and ended in these settings as well, with a small handful attaining equity partnership in a small firm. For the small number who did change sectors, we observe moves primarily to state government and business. This cluster exemplifies not only the differentiation among the upper and lower hemispheres that has persisted in the modern legal profession but also the rhythm of careers that differentiates between men and women since women are more likely to experience spells of unemployment. However, it is important to note that women in this cluster are not more likely to have children than are women in other clusters; in fact, the proportion is identical. Thus, while some of the women in this cluster are unemployed in order to care for children, they are more likely than women in other clusters to be unemployed simply because they cannot find employment. In short, it is not the fact of having children but the spells of unemployment that differentiate the lawyers in this cluster from the men and women in other clusters.

There are two clusters that represent the careers of lawyers who began in midsize law firms (21–100). Together, they represent less than 10% of all the careers in the sample, suggesting that this not a common path (indeed, across the entire sample, only 12% of careers began in midsize firms). Careers in the first cluster, which we label the *midsize-firm equity cluster*, primarily started and ended in midsize law firms (21–100 lawyers). (Eighty-two percent began in a midsize firm, and 77% are working in midsize firms at wave 3.) The sequences are some of the shortest and simplest in the sample with very few job changes, and thus we observe the lowest turbulence score of all the clusters. There are a fair number of highly successful trajectories in this cluster: 38.5% of the lawyers made equity partner by wave 3, and 9% transitioned to positions in the federal government. Of the two midsize-firm clusters, this is the more elite (21% graduated from a top-10 or top-20 law school) and higher-earning cluster.

Careers in the second midsize-firm cluster tend to begin in midsize firms (21–100), though some lawyers first started in a different setting (with about 30% starting in small firms and state and federal government) before moving to a midsize firm. What defines the sequences in this cluster is that, in most cases, lawyers ultimately transition to a smaller firm. Seventy-two percent are found in solo practice or small firms (2–20 lawyers) by wave 3. In short, the careers of lawyers in this second cluster are punctuated by a greater number of job changes, featuring midsize and small firms. Only 16% are in an equity partnership in a small firm by wave 3. This is a less elite cluster (9% graduated from a top-10 or top-20 law school), and median earnings are in the lower end of the distribution. This cluster is also the Whitest in the sample, with only 26% non-White lawyers (compared to 32% across the sample). While there are fewer women than average in this cluster, it is because of the under-representation of African American and Asian American women.

BUSINESS LAWYERS

As we noted above, lawyers working in business have exemplified one of the most important shifts in the structure of legal careers over the past half century. As we demonstrated in the large-firm to business cluster described above, positions in business tend to come from lateral movement. Only 9% of careers began in business, but by wave 3 of the study 21% of AJD Project lawyers were working in business. The two clusters that we describe in this part are unique in that they identify lawyers whose careers began primarily in business settings.

The first and larger of the two clusters identifies lawyers who began their careers in business and remained in business settings over the course of the study. About half began in business, 14% began in midsize firms, and another 14% began in state or federal government. What further distinguishes these sequences is the dominance of business by wave 3 and the fact that none of these lawyers began in a large law firm. By wave 3, about one-third are practicing law as inside counsel (with most in Fortune 1000 organizations), and almost half are in business not practicing law. This cluster falls into a somewhat less elite category (15% graduated from a top-10 or top-20 law school), yet it is a fairly successful set of sequences, with earnings somewhat higher than those of the sample median. The cluster is more male than female (41% are women), and racial diversity is at about the sample mean for all groups.

The second and smaller business cluster is characterized by spells of unemployment and a higher rate of job changes. The level of turbulence in this cluster is equal to the turbulence in the small-firm/unemployed cluster, indicating a high level of turnover and instability. The plurality (40%) began their careers in business, with others starting in large firms (11%) and state and federal government (11.5% and 5.7%, respectively). This unevenness in starting position is also reflected in the fact that eliteness is a little higher than the previous business cluster (20% graduated from a top-10 or top-20 law school).

There are four features that unite these sequences: the high proportion that began in business, that the majority of lawyers are found in business settings by wave 3, that the vast majority (80%) of the men and women in this cluster experienced at least one spell of unemployment over the course of their careers, and that lawyers experienced a higher-than-average number of job changes. Earnings ($100,000) are below the sample median, and levels of career satisfaction are the lowest of all the clusters. It seems as if the trajectories on which they found themselves were not what they had hoped for, with this cluster showing a significant drop in satisfaction between wave 1 and wave 3 (from 69% to 58%). There is a strong overrepresentation of Asian American men (8.8% in the cluster vs. 4.5% in the sample) and African American women (8.8% in the cluster vs. 5.9% in the sample) in this cluster. Given the higher-than-average number of job changes and spells of unemployment, it is perhaps not surprising to find that women are overrepresented in this cluster (which is 55% female), with African American and White women driving this overrepresentation. Again, it is significant that a cluster defined by spells of unemployment overrepresents women and minorities.

GOVERNMENT, EDUCATION, AND NONGOVERNMENT PUBLIC SECTOR LAWYERS

Government continues to be an important setting in lawyers' careers, with 18% of respondents reporting working in government at wave 3. Yet government settings are specifically highlighted only by two clusters, which together account for 13% of all the career sequences. As a result, a number of career sequences that represent careers in government are captured by some of the clusters described above, most notably in the small-firm cluster, where almost 20% began their careers in government, and in the business/unemployed cluster, with 17% beginning in government. In both those clusters, state government served as a starting point in lawyers' careers, both building skills in small firms and serving as a stopgap for those trying to find their way in the profession (as in the business/unemployed cluster).

In contrast, the two government clusters we identify here represent sequences that feature positions in state or federal government, highlighting the fact that even careers in the public sector are highly differentiated. The state government cluster represents 8% of the sequences. It is the less elite of the two clusters, with only 8% of its lawyers having graduated from a top-10 or top-20 law school. The majority of careers in this cluster both started and ended in state government, though a small number moved to positions in the federal government. A very small number began in midsize firms (but none started in a small or large firm, with a notable absence of the large firm in these sequences) and legal services, both serving as potential starting points that lead to state government positions. It is clear that this is a feminized track, with women constituting 59% of the lawyers in this cluster, and median earnings are among the lowest, at $88,000. Despite lower pay, levels of career satisfaction in this cluster are consistently the highest or next to the highest, with 83%–85% of the lawyers reporting that they are moderately or extremely satisfied with their decision to become a lawyer. It is noteworthy that, despite the seemingly more family-friendly nature of careers in government, women in this cluster are less likely to have children than is the average woman in the sample (62% and 66%, respectively). This pattern does not hold for men, who are somewhat more likely to have children than is the average man in the sample. State government is also the most ethnically diverse cluster in the sample, and this diversity is solely attributable to women: African American women (10.2% of the cluster vs. 5.9% of the sample), followed by Latinas, Asian American women, and Native American women. This is a strong point of continuity with the post-1970s opening of the profession, in which women and minorities were concentrated in government positions (Heinz et al. 2005). While the explicit barriers and racism in the private sector (Spector 1972) may no longer be present, the similarities should give us pause.

The federal government cluster is decidedly more elite, with 17% of the lawyers in this cluster having graduated from a top-10 law school and another 17% from a top-20 school, which is the third highest concentration of elite graduates of all the clusters. The eliteness of a federal government starting position is reinforced by the high proportion of careers that began in the federal government and moved laterally to a large law firm (28%). In fact, 8% of all lawyers in this cluster were eventually promoted to equity partner in a large law firm, which is significant since only 10% of the large-firm cluster reported a promotion to equity partnership in a large law firm. The most common path to equity partnership is one position in the federal government followed by two nonequity positions in a large firm and, finally, the promotion to equity partner in a large firm. Another 7% of lawyers in this cluster were promoted to equity partnerships in law firms of other sizes by wave 3. For those who did not make equity partner, they either remained in the large law firm in a nonequity position or moved laterally to a smaller firm or to a position in business. About one-third of sequences remained in the federal government over the course of these lawyers' careers, in many cases remaining exclusively within this setting (which is a pathway more common for women than for men). It is equally notable that a full 7% of all sequences show positions as law professors by wave 3. These sequences demonstrate the high value of beginning a career in the federal government.

Median earnings are high in this cluster ($145,000), in part driven up by those working in a large firm. We also find high levels of career satisfaction that rival those for state government work, especially at waves 1 and 3. In line with the findings from the state government cluster, we also find that women in this cluster are less likely than is the average woman to have children, and, in fact, they have the lowest rate of parenthood in the sample (59% in the cluster vs. 66% in the sample). On the other hand, men in this cluster are more likely to have children than is the average man. We continue to find a greater-than-average level of diversity in this cluster, and, in this case, it is wholly attributable to the strong presence of African American women, who constitute 10.7% of this cluster. The number of African American women in both government clusters is a point of continuity with the early period (Wilkins 2012).

We also identify a third cluster for careers that are broadly in legal services, including education and nongovernment public sector positions. This cluster comprises about 300 individuals, primarily women (strikingly, it is two-thirds female), whose careers have been spent mainly outside the traditional practice of law. Only 57% are practicing law by wave 3, which is well below average. There is a diversity in the types of careers that are brought together in this cluster, especially in terms of starting points. About 20% began in small firms, 16% in legal services, 16% in nonprofits or education, another 12% in solo practice, and 9% in public interest. Despite this diversity, there are no sequences that began in large law firms. By wave 3, the sequences show that respondents found their fit: 41% are in nonprofits or education (with about half of these working as professors), another 30% are in legal services or public defender positions, and 9% are in public interest positions (the highest of any cluster).

Overall, 10% graduated from an elite law school, but those who pursued academic or public interest positions are more likely to have attended an elite institution. At the same time, the rate of unemployment is at about the sample average, as is the proportion who have children. Again, the pattern emerges that, even though it is a feminized cluster, we do not find higher rates of parenthood for women. African American women and Latinas are overrepresented in this cluster, while Asian American and White men are underrepresented. With the overrepresentation of women, we also find White women in a larger proportion in this cluster. That this cluster represents careers outside traditional legal practice and has one of the highest concentrations of women and African American women is good evidence that there are still strong patterns of marginalization in the modern legal profession.

Conclusion

The sequence analysis reveals a story of constrained social mobility that is fully revealed only once careers begin to mature. At the start of lawyers' careers, we witness in many of the sequences an opening up and reconfiguration of traditional hierarchies: women and minorities are welcomed into large law firms, as are graduates of some less elite law schools. This early mobility supports the efforts of the profession to welcome diversity and embrace the demographic change that it has faced.

Yet, as career trajectories unfold—with individuals and organizations making decisions about promotion (or the chance of promotion) and individuals getting married and forming families—we find the old hierarchies seeping back in and reestablishing much of the original structure. Individuals who do not fit the mold are shunted into less successful paths—those characterized by high rates of unemployment and job changes—or, when they do break into the more successful clusters such as in the large law firms, face a glass ceiling, remaining in nonequity positions while it is the White men who attain the status of equity partnership. We explore the mechanisms that underlie this glass ceiling in other chapters in this volume, highlighting implicit and explicit forms of discrimination and exclusion—the ways in which law firms work as anti-equality machines that structure opportunities differentially for women and minorities (constraining the choices men and women make when and in anticipation of when they become parents)—and the ways in which the lawyers are also able to make virtues of their necessities.

The sequence analysis highlights the very gendered form of the modern legal profession. Women are overrepresented in sequences that feature episodes of unemployment and are underrepresented in career paths that lead to equity partnerships or lucrative careers in business. We also find some patterns that seem to run against conventional wisdom. It is often argued that women do not succeed in law because they shoulder the disproportionate burden of parenthood. Yet, while the clusters that are imagined to be more family friendly are in fact very feminized (such as those in the public sector), the women in them are less likely to have children. While we need to investigate this further, it certainly suggests that the choices women make as they build their careers are more complex and constrained, especially as the field of law has been transformed by the growth of the large law firm. As law firms grew and required a larger labor force, they have provided part-time options and nonequity tracks. We find women overrepresented in these positions, and it may indeed be that these are the new family-friendly positions, offering the halo of the prestige and relatively high income of the large firm without offering their full rewards.

The reconfiguration of the field of law has also opened a limited number of new avenues for advancement. Most notable is that the path from large firms to business has provided a very successful trajectory for individuals who may not have met with success had they remained within the large-firm setting. The story of this set of sequences is that, having begun their careers in the setting that bestows prestige and facing perhaps limited opportunities for advancement, Asian American men and women are overrepresented among those who transitioned into business as inside counsel. As others have documented (Rosen 1989; Wilkins 2012), the position of inside counsel has been transformed into one of power and prestige, and it is thus significant to find that it has one of the largest concentrations of Asian American lawyers (and as a result is also among the least White) and that it is also one of the clusters with the highest levels of satisfaction and earnings in the study.

By identifying the common threads that tie together thousands of lawyers' career sequences, this analysis sheds light on the new structure of lawyers' careers. It highlights the importance of considering the full length of lawyers' careers because neither initial nor final position can tell the whole story. This analysis has highlighted the continuity in the structures of inequality that persist in the face of growing commitments to diversity and meritocracy, which help both to open up the profession and to ensure that there is very little change in the hierarchies that persist from at least the well-documented period of the 1960s and 1970s.

Bourdieusian field sociology posits that fields can be challenged and even transformed but that well-established fields tend to absorb change in ways that sustain the existing hierarchies of the field. This theoretical observation finds support in this chapter. It is remarkable that, in a period when partnership in a law firm became much less desirable, nevertheless almost all who can start in such a position do so, bringing in a critical mass of elite White men sufficient to sustain both the position of law firms in the hierarchy and the position of elite White men within the firms. Yet their assiduous efforts to hire women and minorities legitimated law firms' hiring as meritocratic. Indeed, law firms' leaders prominently complained that minorities and women left law firms for other opportunities and thus frustrated their efforts to promote them to partnership positions. The rise of corporate inside counsel might have led to hiring practices that opened up more to different law schools and to new graduates who could be trained by the inside counsel departments. But, instead, the ex-partners who "naturally" became in-house counsel "naturally" hired those they valued out of their own experience and prestige hierarchy. These and other challenges and reforms smoothly integrated with and sustained the long-standing hierarchical structure of the legal field.

Race, Class, and Gender in the Structuring of Lawyers' Early Careers

Using sequence analysis, chapter 3 demonstrated the variety of individual career paths and the distinct clusters of sequences that reflect the professional and social hierarchies of legal careers. This chapter examines the influence of race, class, and gender from law school through midcareer using multivariate analyses of career stages. The social characteristics of AJD Project respondents shape their entry point into the profession. Starting positions influence where respondents work at midcareer, when they were interviewed in wave 3. We supplemented this analysis with 2019 web data to investigate which respondents had become partners some 20 years after passing the bar. The results provide a compelling complement to the sequence analysis.

Class, gender, and race powerfully affect careers, from law school to first job through midcareer. These data illuminate how valued forms of social capital structure available opportunities. Social class, measured by parents' education, is strongly related to the field-specific status marker of law school credentials, with children of highly educated parents being more likely to have elite law degrees. The resulting education capital shapes first job options, and first job strongly shapes midcareer positions (e.g., as we saw in the sequence analysis, experience in a large law firm is a valued credential that opens up opportunities in other prestigious settings). People of color gain entry to higher-status law schools and begin their careers in large law firms at greater rates than do Whites, yet, like all women, they are far less likely to attain equity partnerships. Perhaps anticipating difficulties in law firms or perceiving lack of fit, women and people of color are more likely to gravitate to government and the nonprofit sector than are other lawyers. Before examining in-depth interview data in the next part, this chapter sketches the broad contours of career patterns traceable to respondents' social characteristics.

Entering the Profession: Race, Class, and Gender

The After the JD Project might, more appropriately, be titled the After Passing the Bar Project. Our sample, drawn from bar admittees in the 18 sampling areas described in chapter 1, navigated an extended pipeline of sequenced accomplishments: graduating college; applying to, getting into, matriculating in, and graduating from law school; and passing the bar. These stages are displayed by race/ethnicity in table 4.1, which combines current population and education statistics with the best available data on law school applicants, enrollment, and graduation and AJD Project data.

The general US population is 60% White, 18% Latinx, 12% African American, and 6% Asian American. The population of college graduates looks somewhat different: 63% White, 14% Latinx, 10% African American, and 8% Asian American. When it comes to law school, both African Americans and Asian Americans apply at slightly higher rates than their presence among college graduates would indicate but enroll at lower rates. Whites apply to law schools at lower rates than their college graduate representation would indicate, though their representation among law school graduates is similar to that among college graduates. Law school graduates are 64% White, 13% Latinx, 9% African American, and 6% Asian American. Thus, compared to their share of the college graduates, African Americans, Latinx, and Asian Americans are slightly underrepresented among law school graduates. Notably, African Americans and Asian Americans are also underrepresented among law school graduates compared to their share of applicants.

Within two years of law school graduation, 93% of Whites and 88% of Asian Americans pass the bar exam, compared to 84% of Latinx and 79% of African Americans. To estimate the race/ethnicity of bar admittees, we multiply the bar passage rates of each group by its percentage representation among law degrees awarded, then divide by the sum of the four groups for a total out of 100. Entering the bar, Whites are substantially and Asian Americans are slightly overrepresented, and Latinx and African Americans are underrepresented compared to their presence among college graduates.

Table 4.1 closes with Bureau of Labor Statistics[1] estimates of the racial/ethnic composition of the legal profession (across all ages) and the racial/ethnic composition of the AJD Project sample we are analyzing.[2] Given the broader and older age distribution of the BLS sample, it reports a lower presence of people of color than does the AJD Project sample, which is composed of year 2000 bar entrants and includes an oversampling of attorneys of color (at 70% White, 9% Latinx, 9% African American, 10% Asian American, and 2% Native American and others not shown).[3] We do not reweight responses for oversampling or nonresponse.

T A B L E 4.1 Racial/ethnic composition of pipeline to legal employment (%)

Race/ethnicity	General population[a]	High school graduates[b]	College graduates[c]	ABA applicants[d]	ABA matriculants[e]	JD recipients[f]	Bar passage rate[g]	Bar admittees[h]	Lawyers[i]	AJD wave 3 respondents[i]
African American	12.4	14.6	10.4	11.5	7.8	8.5	79	7.8	5.9	9.2
Latinx	18.4	20.2	14.2	10.2	13.1	13.2	84	12.9	5.8	9.5
Asian American	5.6	5.7	8.0	9.0	6.5	6.4	88	6.6	5.7	10.2
White	60.0	56.5	63.2	53.4	64.0	63.7	93	69.0	86.6	68.8

Note: For simplicity of presentation we only present the four largest racial/ethnic groups, who compose more than 96% of the general population. Column percentages do not add up to 100 because the data exclude other categories including American Indian, Alaska Native, Native Hawaiian, Other Pacific Islander, two or more races/ethnicities, some other race/ethnicity, or race/ethnicity unknown.

a U.S. Census, 2019 ACS 1-Year Estimates, https://data.census.gov/cedsci/table?q=United%20States&g=0100000US&tid=ACSDP1Y2019.DP05&hidePreview=true.

b National Center for Education Statistics (2019), public high school graduates 2012–13 by race/ethnicity, Digest of Education Statistics 2019, table 219.30, https://nces.ed.gov/programs/digest/d19/tables/dt19_219.30.asp.

c National Center for Education Statistics (2019), bachelor's degrees conferred by postsecondary institutions in 2017/2018 by race/ethnicity. Digest of Education Statistics 2019, table 332.20, https://nces.ed.gov/programs/digest/d19/tables/dt19_322.20.asp.

d Law School Admissions Council, 2019 ABA Applicants, https://report.lsac.org/View.aspx?Report=DiversityPopulationandPipeline.

e American Bar Association (2019), ABA Law School Data: JD Total First Year Class Enrollment Data, Aggregate, Fall 2019, https://www.americanbar.org/groups/legal_education/resources/statistics.

f Law School Admissions Council, JD Enrollment and Ethnicity 2019, JD Degrees Awarded, Standard 509 Disclosures, http://www.abarequireddisclosures.org/Disclosure 509.aspx.

g American Bar Association (2021). Bar Passage Study for Entering Law School Class of 1991, table 10, 32, https://www.americanbar.org/content/dam/aba/administrative/legal_education_and_admissions_to_the_bar/statistics/20210621-bpq-national-summary-data-race-ethnicity-gender.pdf.

h Calculated by multiplying degrees awarded (col. 6) by bar passage rate (col. 7) and dividing by the column total to get a value out of 100.

i Bureau of Labor Statistics (2019), table 11, Employed Persons by Detailed Occupation, Sex, Race, and Hispanic or Latino.

Matching the general perception that American lawyers come from relatively advantaged social backgrounds, the 1995 Chicago study found that 78% of all respondents had parents who were lawyers or worked in other professional, technical, or managerial occupations (80% for White attorneys and 54% for attorneys of color [Heinz et al. 2005, 66]). Similarly, three-quarters of AJD Project respondents have a parent who was a manager or a professional. This proportion is virtually identical across genders but varies substantially across race/ethnicity. Just 67% of African Americans and 60% of Latinx had managerial or professional parents, compared to 81% of Asian Americans and 78% of Whites.[4] African Americans and Latinx were also less likely than Asian Americans and Whites to have parents who graduated from college or attended some graduate school. Another dramatic difference is in parents' nativity: 93% of Asian Americans and 61% of Latinx have at least one foreign-born parent, compared to fewer than 30% of African Americans and just under 10% of Whites. Thus, each racial/ethnic group has distinctive class and nativity profiles.

Education Endowments: Privilege and Credentials

We do not endorse the ranking systems currently applied to postsecondary institutions, yet they are a social reality. As Espeland and Sauder (2007) have shown, rankings influence the behavior of both academic administrators and potential applicants, and, as Rivera (2016) writes, they serve as a palpable indicator of social hierarchy and, by themselves, tend to reproduce social hierarchy within professional fields. In other words, like race/ethnicity, higher education rankings are social constructions that nonetheless carry real-world consequences.

The status hierarchy of law school credentials has its roots in the status hierarchy of undergraduate institutions. We divided undergraduate institutions into three groups: national universities and liberal arts colleges ranked in the top 25 (i.e., the top 25 national universities[5] and the top 25 liberal arts colleges combined), national universities and liberal arts colleges ranked 26 through 100 (the top 26–100 universities and the top 26–100 liberal arts colleges), and other universities and colleges.[6] We divided law schools according to rankings reported by US News in 2003.[7]

Overall, 23% of AJD Project respondents attended top-25 national or liberal arts colleges.[8] The most likely to do so are Asian Americans (46%), followed by Latinx (35%), African Americans (29%), and Native American and other race/ethnicity respondents (19%). Proportionately, Whites are far less likely to have attended elite undergraduate institutions (18%). Still, owing to their representation within the sample, Whites occupy more than half the slots our sample held in top undergraduate schools.

The next two ranks of undergraduate institutions contribute roughly equal proportions to the sample overall. All racial/ethnic groups have a substantial number of graduates from institutions ranked from 26 to 100: 43% of White, 34% of Latinx, and 44% of Native American and other race/ethnicity respondents in the sample are alumni. While substantial proportions of African Americans and Asian Americans also attended undergraduate schools ranked from 26 to 100, the largest percentage of African Americans, 40%, graduated from undergraduate schools ranked below 100 (compared to just 20% of Asian American respondents).

Our sample presents a diverse set of undergraduate credentials. Asian Americans stand out as the most likely to have graduated from a top-25 undergraduate institution, though substantial proportions of African American, Latinx, and Native American lawyers did too. In every institutional category, Whites predominate numerically, at 56% of top-25 graduates and three-quarters of the tier 2 and tier 3 schools by rank.

We see very similar patterns in the cross-tabulation of race/ethnicity and law school rank, which is divided into five categories: those ranked in the top 10 by US News, followed by those ranked from 11 to 20, those ranked from 21 to 50, and those ranked from 51 to 100, then a combined category of those in tier 3 and tier 4. Overall, only 10% of the AJD Project sample graduated from top-10 law schools. Another 13% got their degrees from schools ranked from 11 to 20 and 22% from those ranked from 21 to 50. Larger percentages of the sample gained their degrees from lower-ranked law schools: 28% from schools ranked from 51 to 100 and 27% from law schools in tier 3 or tier 4. More than half of respondents graduated from law schools ranked below the top 50.

Asian Americans present the most elite education endowments: they are the most likely racial/ethnic group to have graduated from top-20 law schools (37%) and the least likely to hold tier 3 or tier 4 law degrees (18%). Some 15% of African Americans received top-10 degrees, and another 15% earned degrees from schools ranked from 11 to 20. Latinx earned top-10 law degrees at a rate of 14%, and another 18% graduated from schools ranked from 11 to 20. Yet more than 40% of respondents from each of these minority groups graduated from law schools ranked below 50. With the exception of Native American and other—19% of whom graduated from a top-20 law school—an appreciable number of minority respondents possess elite law school credentials, and a more substantial proportion graduated from lesser ranked law schools.

White attorneys present the least elite law degrees (after Native Americans and other), though they retain numerical dominance across each status category. For example, 9% of Whites in the sample graduated from top-10 law schools, but 61% of all top-10 law school graduates are White, and the 11% of White respondents who graduated from schools ranked from 11 to 20 represent 60% of that category of degree holders. Whites compose 70% of alumni from law schools ranked from 21 to 50, though 21% of White respondents earned law degrees from schools in this category. Substantial proportions of White respondents hold degrees from the least selective categories: 29% from law schools ranked from 51 to 100 and 30% from tier 3 or tier 4 law schools.

In contrast to the significant differences we see in education credentials by race/ethnicity at both the undergraduate and the law school level, we see no significant differences by gender. There is striking gender parity in all the status categories of undergraduate and law school degrees. We do, however, observe a strong association between social class (measured by parents' education and occupation) and education credentials. Lawyers whose parents had graduate or professional schooling were far likelier to attend top-25 undergraduate institutions (28%) than were those whose parents had a high school degree or less (18%), and children of managers (23%) and professionals (26%) were likelier than were children of blue-collar workers (13%) to graduate from top-25 undergraduate institutions. Class advantages are also pronounced with respect to law degrees: 29% of the children of parents with graduate or professional education earned top-20 degrees, compared to 12% of the children of parents with a high school education or less; and 23% of attorneys whose parents were managers and 25% of attorneys who parents were professionals graduated from top-20 law schools, compared to 13% of the children of blue-collar parents.

Table 4.2, reproduced from Dinovitzer and Garth (2007, 10), demonstrates the ordered relationship between law school selectivity and parents' occupational status and education. The occupational prestige scores are taken from an international standardized source (Ganzeboom and Treiman 1996), and parents' education is measured as the percentage of respondents with a parent who received graduate or professional education. There is a strong correspondence between law school selectivity and average prestige of parents' occupation. Children of parents with graduate education are far more likely to attend top-10 law schools, composing 68% of top-10 law school alumni in our sample. Graduates of the least selective category of law schools are half as likely to have a parent with advanced education; the majority of top-40 alumni have a parent with graduate education, compared to 42% or less of those graduating from lower-ranked law schools.

The profound class-based structure of law school credentials revealed in our sample is produced through a seemingly meritocratic tournament

TABLE 4.2 Law school ranking and measures of social stratification[a]

Law school ranking	Fathers' occupation prestige score (ISEI) (mean)[b]		Father with graduate education[c] (%)	Total N
Top 10	65.795	(16.525)	68***	174
Top 11–20	63.677	(17.228)	54***	253
Top 21–40	63.257	(17.506)	54***	310
Top 41–100	60.272	(18.230)	42	686
Tier 3	58.471	(17.617)	33***	383
Tier 4	57.231	(18.298)	34***	318

Note: Numbers in parentheses are standard errors.

[a] Table reproduced from Dinovitzer and Garth (2007, 10).

[b] Results from one-way Anova: $F = 13.099$, $p < 0.001$. Bonferroni post hoc tests reveal significant ($p < 0.05$ or better) contrasts between: top-10 graduates and those from schools ranked 41 and below; top-20 graduates and those from schools ranked 41 and below; top-40 graduates and those from tiers 3 and 4; top-100 graduates and those ranked in the top 10, top 20, and tier 4; tier 3 graduates and those from top-10–top-40 schools; and tier 4 graduates and all respondents except those from tier 3.

[c] Significance tests are for selected law school tier compared to all others.

* $p < .05$. ** $p < .01$. *** $p < .001$ (two-tailed).

among law school applicants. Status of undergraduate institution, undergraduate grades, and LSAT scores are powerful determinants of the selectivity of law school attended. Graduates of top-25 undergraduate schools have a 26% chance of having a degree from a top-10 law school, compared to a 7% chance for graduates of undergraduate institutions ranked from 26 to 100 and 4% for lower-ranked institutions.[9] Consequently, almost two-thirds (60%) of top-10 law school attendees in our sample attended a top-25 undergraduate institution.

Top-10 law school graduates also are more likely to have higher admissions credentials: higher undergraduate grade point averages and higher LSAT scores. LSAT scores differ significantly by law school rank in a unilinear trend. Using a normalized measure of LSAT to which a random value was added by the Law School Admissions Council to preserve individual anonymity, we see in table 4.3 that top-10 law school graduates had the highest proportion of LSAT scores in the top quartile (72%), followed by top-11 to top-20 law school graduates (51%), top-21 to top-50 graduates (29%), graduates of schools ranked from 51 to 100 (12%), and tier 3 and tier 4 graduates (5%).

To be sure, the role of LSAT scores in law school admissions has long been controversial. Women and minorities do not score as highly as other test-takers, and the scores prove only modestly correlated with first-year law school performance (Kidder 2001; Taylor 2019). Within our sample, we find

TABLE 4.3 LSAT score quartiles by gender, race/ethnicity, and law school ranking (%)

Gender, race/ethnicity, and law school ranking	LSAT score			
	Bottom quartile	Third quartile	Second quartile	Top quartile
Women	30.9	25.2	22.9	21.0
Men	20.0	24.8	26.8	28.4
χ^2	33.1***			
African American	56.0	26.4	12.0	5.7
Latinx	33.7	24.9	26.0	15.4
Native American/other	32.4	18.9	32.4	16.2
Asian American	25.7	18.3	29.1	26.9
White	19.6	26.0	25.8	28.7
χ^2	137.3***			
Top-10 law school	3.2	9.7	15.6	71.5
Ranked 11–20	3.9	15.2	29.6	51.3
Ranked 21–50	14.4	20.9	36.0	28.7
Ranked 51–100	26.0	35.7	26.4	12.0
Tiers 3 and 4	49.7	28.7	16.6	5.1
χ^2	637.5***			
Total (N)	445	444	445	444

Note: LSAT scores were transformed to ensure anonymity and then broken down into quartiles. For details, see the text.

a higher proportion of men who scored in the top quartile than women (28% compared to 21%, $p \le .001$) as well as significant differences by race/ethnicity ($p \le .001$). Among racial/ethnic groups, Whites have the highest proportion of top-quartile scores (29%), followed by Asian Americans (27%), Native Americans and others (16%), Latinx (15%), and African Americans (6%).

To assess the relative influence of social background, ascriptive characteristics, and undergraduate education credentials on law school credentials, we turn to multivariate analyses. We employed multinomial logistic regression to predict law school rank, entering gender, race/ethnicity, and parents' nativity and education in stages,[10] followed by selectivity of undergraduate institution, undergraduate grade point average, and LSAT score.[11] We imputed 50 data sets using multiple imputation by chained equations (White et al. 2011) and the multiple imputation then deletion approach (von Hippel 2007). In the first model, ascriptive characteristics and social background are both significant predictors of law school ranking. In the full model, race/ethnicity, parents' nativity and education, and all three types of pre–law school credentials are significant, though gender is not. Having one or more parents with a professional education is significant in predicting top-10 law schools and law schools ranked from 11 to 20 and from 21 to 50; having college-educated parents is significant in predicting top-10 and top-11 to top-20 law schools. There are significant positive effects for African Americans and Latinx across all law school ranks: African Americans have large positive coefficients for top-10, top-11 to top-20, and top-21 to top-50 law schools and a lower but still positive coefficient for schools ranked from 51 to 100. Latinx have relatively high coefficients for top-10 and top-11 to top-20 law schools, with lower but still positive coefficients for schools ranked from 21 to 50 and from 51 to 100. Asian Americans have significant positive coefficients for top-10 and top-11 to top-20 law schools, with the highest coefficient for schools ranked from 11 to 20.

The nested multivariate models reveal the salience of social background in predicting law school ranking. The strong class-based hierarchy of who attends more selective law schools is driven largely by pre–law school education endowments. Race and ethnicity have effects net of these endowments and of parents' education, perhaps reflecting law schools' diversity outreach (as we suggested in chap. 2, the positive effects for historically marginalized groups in gaining admission to top law schools and to corporate law firms partially chart efforts by these institutions to open opportunities for nontraditional groups and signify the complex social capital ascribed to gender and especially race in the contemporary period). It is possible to bring these patterns into sharper focus by examining the predicted probabilities for different groups while holding all other variables constant at their mean values.[12] Graduates of top-25 undergraduate universities and colleges have much higher odds of gaining admission to top-20 law schools than do their peer graduates from less selective undergraduate schools. The predicted probability of African Americans attending top-20 law schools is almost 25%, compared to lower probability for other groups, and that probability rises for all groups when we move to the less selective category of law schools ranked from 21 to 50, in which Latinx and Asian Americans close the gap substantially. African Americans and other groups of color are less likely to attend schools ranked 51 and lower, while the probability for Whites increases. It is this combination of class-based education endowments and racial/ethnic identity that shapes the selectivity of the law school degrees our respondents bring into practice. In turn, law school status has a powerful effect on structuring career paths.

First Practice Setting: Gender, Race, and Law School Status

Table 4.4 shows the practice settings in which respondents worked in their first jobs after joining their first bar (excluding judicial clerkships), broken down by gender and race/ethnicity. Before looking at the determinants of who works in which settings, it is important to consider the overall structure of lawyers' first jobs. Our practice setting variable includes seven categories.

TABLE 4.4 First practice setting by gender and race/ethnicity (%)

First practice setting	Overall	Gender		Race/ethnicity				
		Woman	Man	African American	Latinx	Native American/ other	Asian American	White
Solo practice/law firm 2–20	25.2	23.3	27.1	14.9	25.1	33.3	24.1	26.4
Law firm 21–250	19.8	19.1	20.5	14.4	15.3	12.5	15.5	21.8
Law firm 251+	20.4	19.8	20.9	23.6	23.0	16.7	24.1	19.3
Federal government	6.0	6.0	6.1	7.5	3.8	6.3	8.0	5.9
State government	9.6	10.1	9.2	15.5	12.0	10.4	8.0	8.8
Public interest and nonprofit/ education	7.8	10.9	4.6	12.6	8.7	8.3	6.4	7.2
Business	11.2	10.8	11.6	11.5	12.0	12.5	13.9	10.7
Total (N)	2,023	1,008	1,015	174	183	48	187	1,430
χ^2		30.2***		44.1**				

** $p \le .01$. *** $p \le .001$.

Three are private practice settings: solo and small law firms (up to 20 lawyers), midsize law firms (21–250 lawyers), and large law firms (251+ lawyers). Government positions are split into federal and state, and we combine jobs in public interest organizations, nonprofits, and education institutions into the sixth category. The seventh category, business, includes respondents who work for business organizations whether or not they are practicing law (for more on the latter, see chap. 5).

Private law firms dominated the AJD Project cohort's first jobs. One-quarter of respondents worked in solo and small law firms, 20% in large law firms, and 20% in midsize law firms. The next largest sector is business (11%), followed by state government (10%), public interest, nonprofit, and education organizations (8%), and federal government (6%).

Both gender and race/ethnicity are significantly related to first practice setting. Women are less likely than men to practice in solo and small firms and far likelier to work in the public interest/nonprofit sector. African Americans are much less likely to begin their careers in solo and small firms but are likelier than other lawyers to start in state government or public interest/nonprofits, and Latinx are less likely than other respondents to work in federal government. Other racial/ethnic groups do not notably depart from the overall distribution of practice settings.

Table 4.5 cross-classifies law school rank and first practice setting, indicating a strong link between elite law school credentials and entry-level jobs in

TABLE 4.5 First practice setting by law school ranking (%)

First practice setting	Law school ranking				
	Top 10	11–20	21–50	51–100	Tiers 3 and 4
Solo practice/law firm 2–20	4.4	15.1	20.9	30.4	34.5
Law firm 21–250	12.8	23.9	23.0	20.9	17.7
Law firm 251+	60.3	38.2	22.5	10.1	6.7
Federal government	4.4	3.9	7.2	7.0	6.0
State government	2.9	4.6	8.4	11.5	13.6
PI and nonprofit/education	10.3	7.3	7.9	8.3	6.2
Business	4.9	7.0	10.2	11.9	15.3
Total (N)	204	259	431	556	536
χ^2	384.1***				

*** $p \le .001$.

large law firms. More than half of top-10 graduates work at law firms with more than 250 lawyers, and another 13% work in midsize firms. The graduates of schools ranked from 11 to 20 have a similar profile, with two-thirds in midsize or large law firms. In contrast, the graduates of tier 3 and tier 4 law schools are far likelier to work as solo/small-firm attorneys or in state government or business. Note that, while the table displays hierarchical relationships between legal education and practice settings, there are no zero cells. That is, some graduates of top law schools do work in solo/small-firm practice or state government, and some graduates of tier 3 and tier 4 law schools begin their careers in large law firms.

Again, we are interested in the relative effects of these and other variables on practice setting. We employed multinomial logistic regression to predict respondents' first practice setting, entering the predictors in two stages: the first included the independent variables from the full model predicting law school ranking (including gender, race/ethnicity, parents' nativity and education, and pre–law school credentials), and the second added law school credentials (including law school rank, GPA, and law review service) and judicial clerkships.[13] We find that parents' education and elite undergraduate degrees increase the odds of initially working in a large law firm but that these effects drop below conventional levels of significance when we add law school credentials to the model. As in the model predicting law school ranking, the variables most proximate to first job had the most consistent effects. Even so, law school credentials did not completely displace the effects of undergraduate credentials on first job. For example, LSAT score has a significant positive effect on the odds of starting out in a large firm, public interest/nonprofit organization, or business compared to starting out in solo practice or a small firm. We found positive effects for elite law degrees, high grades, and law review service on working in large or midsize firms and that degrees from top-10 law schools increase the odds of starting out in public interest, nonprofit, and education settings.

In the final model, gender and race have effects net of education credentials. African Americans are more likely than are Whites to start out in any setting other than solo practice or small firms and have a particularly high likelihood of working in a first job in a large firm or in government. Women are more likely than are men to launch their careers in the public interest/nonprofit sector.

The starting practice setting patterns we find here largely mirror those of our law school analysis. More elite credentials lead to more prestigious early career practice settings. This pattern indicates an accumulation of capital whereby the social capital provided by an elite social background (what we might call *early social advantage*) is amplified and converted into education capital, which opens doors to more prestigious practice settings. This stepwise accrual process obscures the effects of social background, with the result that apparently merit-based legal credentials are the more visible and proximate determinants of lawyers' early careers.

Navigating Early Careers

THE SHIFTING STRUCTURE OF LAW JOBS FROM ENTRY TO MIDCAREER

To understand the evolution of lawyers' careers, it is important to consider the changing structure of jobs from entry to midcareer. Table 4.6 cross-classifies first practice setting by wave 3 practice setting. The first notable pattern is the changed distribution across practice settings. Midsize law firms dropped, over time, from employing 20% of AJD Project lawyers in their first jobs to employing only 13% by wave 3. Large law firms also declined, from 21% to 10%. That 11% of the first jobs but 20% of wave 3 settings were in business evinces a veritable exodus from midsize and large law firms into business. A second notable pattern is the importance of inertia—the tendency for lawyers to work in the same type of practice setting at wave 3 as they did at the beginning of their careers. The main diagonal of this table contains 44% of the sample; these lawyers stayed in the same type of practice setting for at least 12 years of their careers. The third notable feature is the distinct role of lawyers' "feeder" settings in structuring their "receiving" settings.

Half of lawyers found in business settings at wave 3 began their careers

TABLE 4.6 Wave 3 practice setting by first practice setting

Wave 3 practice setting	First practice setting							
	Solo/law firm 2–20	Law firm 21–250	Law firm 251+	Federal government	State government	Public interest and nonprofit/education	Business	Total
Solo practice/law firm 2–20								
n	259	76	47	21	30	22	36	491
Row %	52.8	15.5	9.6	4.3	6.1	4.5	7.3	100
Column %	55.0	20.7	12.2	19.3	16.5	15.6	18.3	26.5
Law firm 21–250								
n	56	126	31	4	8	3	6	234
Row %	23.9	53.9	13.3	1.7	3.4	1.3	2.6	100
Column %	11.9	34.3	8.0	3.7	4.4	2.1	3.1	12.6
Law firm 251+								
n	9	34	125	4	4	3	8	187
Row %	4.8	18.2	66.8	2.1	2.1	1.6	4.3	100
Column %	1.9	9.3	32.4	3.7	2.2	2.1	4.1	10.1
Federal government								
n	12	9	30	38	12	9	7	117
Row %	10.3	7.7	25.6	32.5	10.3	7.7	6.0	100
Column %	2.6	2.5	7.8	34.9	6.6	6.4	3.6	6.3

(continued)

TABLE 4.6 (continued)

Wave 3 practice setting	First practice setting							
	Solo/law firm 2–20	Law firm 21–250	Law firm 251+	Federal government	State government	Public interest and nonprofit/education	Business	Total
State government								
n	42	14	13	12	104	19	28	232
Row %	18.1	6.0	5.6	5.2	44.8	8.2	12.1	100
Column %	8.9	3.8	3.4	11.0	57.1	13.5	14.2	12.5
Public interest and nonprofit/education								
n	44	25	34	9	14	72	21	219
Row %	20.1	11.4	15.5	4.1	6.4	32.9	9.6	100
Column %	9.3	6.8	8.8	8.3	7.7	51.1	10.7	11.8
Business								
n	49	83	106	21	10	13	91	373
Row %	13.1	22.3	28.4	5.6	2.7	3.5	24.4	100
Column %	10.4	22.6	27.5	19.3	5.5	9.2	46.2	20.1
Total								
N	471	367	386	109	182	141	197	1,853
Row %	25.4	19.8	20.8	5.9	9.8	7.6	10.6	100
Column %	100	100	100	100	100	100	100	100
X^2	1,500***							

*** $p \leq .001$.

in midsize to large law firms (22% and 28%, respectively). These individuals far outnumber their business colleagues who began in business and, in the sequence analysis, would tend to belong to the large-firm to business cluster. As we saw in chapter 3 and will revisit in chapter 8, careers beginning in business tend to be less elite than those beginning in large firms and ending up in business settings. Respondents who begin in business graduate from lower-ranked law schools, earn less, and are less likely to practice law than are those who move into business from a large firm. Also, echoing the federal government cluster findings in chapter 3, we find that one-third of those in federal government in wave 3 began in a midsize to large law firm. One-quarter of those working in public interest, nonprofit, or education institutions in wave 3 started in these settings, while another 20% worked initially in solo practice and small firms. The path from private practice to public interest/nonprofit jobs is more common than a path that starts and stays in the nonprofit sector at midcareer. If we add these feeder cases to those in which lawyers began and ended in the same practice setting, we reach 65% of cases.

MIDCAREER PRACTICE SETTING: RACE, GENDER, AND CLASS

To this point, we have demonstrated the strong relationship between class, race/ethnicity, and law school credentials, between law school credentials and first job, and between first job and job at midcareer. By themselves, these three key connections would produce a classed, raced, and gendered job structure in the legal profession. Next, we investigate whether these race, class, and gender effects shape transitions from early to midcareer.

Cross-tabulations of wave 3 practice setting by gender and race/ethnicity show that, while women compose 48% of wave 3 respondents, they are slightly underrepresented in solo and small firms, midsize firms, large law firms, and business, overrepresented in federal and state government, and more decidedly overrepresented in public interest/nonprofit positions (64%).[14] These differences are statistically significant ($p \leq .001$) and match the feminized pattern we found for the legal services/public interest cluster in the sequence analysis. Differences by race/ethnicity also are statistically significant ($p \leq .05$). Whites (71% of wave 3 respondents) are underrepresented in the public sector positions of federal government, state government, and public interest/nonprofit/education institutions—the same settings in which African Americans and Latinx are overrepresented. Asian Americans are slightly overrepresented in federal government, business, public interest/nonprofit institutions, and large firms.

Next, we assess gender and race/ethnicity effects on wave 3 practice setting relative to other social background, education, and first practice setting variables in a multinomial logistic regression model.[15] Again, we entered the predictors in two stages. First, we entered all the variables that were significant in predicting first setting, including gender, race/ethnicity, undergraduate credentials, and law school credentials. This model shows that top-10 law degrees increase the odds of working in federal government, public interest/nonprofit institutions, and business and that degrees from law schools ranked in the top 20 increase the odds of working in a large firm of 251 or more. We also find that having edited a law review increases the odds of working in midsize to large firms and business.

In the second stage of this regression, we added first practice setting as a predictor. As in the models predicting law school ranking and first practice setting and reflecting the cross-tabulation results we discussed above, the strongest predictor of wave 3 setting is the most proximate variable: where lawyers began their careers. The highest coefficients in predicting each wave 3 practice setting correspond to the same practice setting at wave 1. The starkest example of this path dependence involves large law firms, with respondents who started in this setting being 4.2 times more likely to be working in large firms than in solo or small-firm practice at wave 3. Net of credentials and first settings, however, the effects remain significant for gender and race/ethnicity for African Americans, who are likelier than Whites to work in the federal government at midcareer, and both women and African Americans are likelier than are men and Whites to work in the public interest/nonprofit sector.

Native Americans

Native Americans make up a small portion of AJD Project respondents ($n = 70$; $n = 36$ responded to all three waves). Therefore, they are not always analyzed as a distinct category in this book. Here, we present a brief portrait of all Native American respondents in order better to understand this understudied group.

Notably, 41% of Native American respondents are from Oklahoma, which is one of our sampling areas. That is the highest concentration of any racial/ethnic group in one primary sampling unit. While there is near gender parity among Native American respondents, the proportion of women is slightly higher than the average for the sample overall (51% compared to 47%). The parents of Native American respondents have somewhat lower levels of education than do those of other groups, with 24% possessing a high school degree or less (compared to 19% for the sample overall) and only 40% being graduate educated (vs. 49% overall). Notwithstanding these education differences, however, Native American respondents' parents' occupy professional and managerial positions at rates within 1% of the sample mean.

Compared to respondents from other racial/ethnic groups, Native Americans possess substantially less prestigious education credentials. Only 13% graduated from top-25 undergraduate schools, compared to 22% of the overall sample, and nearly half (47%) attended undergraduate institutions outside the top 100 (vs. 38% overall). Similarly, a smaller share of Native Americans graduated from top-10 law schools than did any other racial/ethnic group (6.3% compared to 10.3% overall), and nearly half (46%) graduated from tier 3 and tier 4 schools (vs. 30% overall).

Given the social and education characteristics of Native Americans and the findings in this chapter, it is unsurprising that Native Americans are the least likely to start their careers in a private law firm and are more likely to start out in the public sector than are any other group except for African Americans. Moreover, a larger proportion of Native Americans begin in solo practice or a firm of 2–20 than any other racial/ethnic group, while the proportion that begins in larger firms is the smallest of any group. By wave 3, the concentration of Native Americans in solo practice and small firms is even more pronounced (40% vs. 27% overall), with only 12% remaining in midsize and large firms (vs. 23% of the sample). In 2019, Native Americans remained the most likely to be working in firms of 20 or fewer but were also more likely than any other group except for Whites to be an equity partner (although this category includes only four respondents).

Race and Gender in Law Firms: 20 Years In

As we discuss at greater length in chapters 10 and 14, we followed the career evolution of wave 3 respondents by conducting supplemental web searches in 2019. It was nearly 20 years since the AJD Project cohort began their careers and seven years since the wave 3 surveys. We successfully located 85% of respondents to all three waves in this way.

While the searches found the full range of organization positions our respondents held, we focus here on gender and race differences in achieving partnerships in private law firms. In 283 cases, respondents had clearly achieved equity partnership. In 155 additional cases, respondents' ownership status was unclear; taking a conservative counting approach, we deemed these "partner unspecified." In both, women were dramatically underrepresented. Half the web-based sample was female, but just 35% of the equity partnerships and

38% of the unspecified partnerships were held by women. Women, however, predominated in the non–partnership track positions in law firms: 54% of counsel and 59% of associate positions were held by women.

Whites dominated the partnership ranks. Some 71% of the web-based sample, they held 80% of equity partnerships and 70% of the unspecified partnerships identified in our searches. African Americans (8.7% of the web-based sample) accounted for 3.9% of equity partnerships and 7.7% of unspecified partnerships, Latinx (9.0% of the web-based sample) 7.8% of equity partnerships and 11% of unspecified partnerships, Native Americans (1.8% of the web-based sample) 1.4% of equity partnerships and no unspecified partnerships, and Asian Americans (9.2% of the web-based sample) 6.4% of equity partnerships and 10.3% of unspecified partnerships. In other words, 20 years into their careers, every group of attorneys of color is underrepresented in equity partnerships, though in some cases they match or exceed their representation in unspecified partnership positions.

In chapters 10 and 12, we will probe the mechanisms that produce these kinds of gender and race/ethnicity inequities in private law firms. But, for the moment, these differentials in achieving equity partnership after two decades of practice simply and forcefully underscore the persistence of gender and racial inequality across lawyers' careers.

The Structure of Careers at the Intersection of Race and Gender

Until this point, we have considered the influences of gender and race/ethnicity on the structure of lawyers' careers separately. Social characteristics operate intersectionally in the real world, producing unique experiences from the interaction of the sets of social characteristics with which we live. Thus, we reran our multivariate models, grouping together women of color, men of color, and White women, using White men as the reference group.[16] These analyses reveal that White men are particularly advantaged in the law career tournament and that the careers of women of color are uniquely structured. On the whole, people of color are likelier than are White men to attend high-ranking law schools, though men of color have better odds than do women of color. As a group, only women of color are significantly more likely than are White men to begin their careers in state government and to be working in public interest and nonprofit organizations in both their first jobs and by midcareer. That White men are the most likely to be working in the private firm sector by midcareer makes the findings of our 2019 web searches striking yet unsurprising: by 20 years into their careers, women of color are the least likely to be equity partners and White men the most likely (8% compared to

22%). Overall, these analyses show a dramatic exodus of women of color out of law firms and into public interest and nonprofit organizations. Coupled with high rates of retention in federal and state government positions, this patterned mobility underlies the concentration of women of color in the least prestigious and remunerative settings at midcareer.

Conclusion

This chapter has demonstrated how gender, race, and class structure the careers of American lawyers. Career outcomes are shaped by the accumulation of different kinds of social capital at each stage of the career process. The process begins when lawyers convert privileged social backgrounds into the college grades, elite undergraduate degrees, and LSAT scores that open the doors to elite law schools. Elite law degrees pave the way to more prestigious first jobs (most notably in large corporate law firms). The social capital of having worked in a large firm affords new opportunities, allowing these attorneys to move to corporations as inside counsel, to elite jobs in the federal government, and to smaller law firms. For a minority of attorneys—who tend to be White men with elite law degrees—starting in a large firm is the surest way to attain equity partnership in a large firm.

The predictive power of education credentials weakens as careers evolve, though education capital, gender, and race all continue to shape lawyers' career trajectories until at least midcareer. For example, men and Whites are overrepresented in private practice positions, women and racial/ethnic minority groups are overrepresented in the public sector, and graduates of lower-status undergraduate institutions and less selective law schools are overrepresented in solo practice, small law firms, and state government.[17] We find that men and Whites enjoy the highest rates of retention within their starting settings; in that this is related to White men's higher equity partnership rates in 2019, spending one's career in a single setting can be thought of as a career advantage.

By midcareer, African American, Asian American, and Native American respondents move from large law firms (sometimes into the business sector) at higher rates than do Whites and Latinx. This tendency may indicate that these groups are able to mobilize the professional capital they earned in their early careers to their advantage. An alternate, more pessimistic interpretation is that these groups leave large firms because they do not or cannot attain equity partnerships. After all, men and Whites are far more likely than women and all attorneys of color to have achieved equity partnership 20 years into their careers. Despite the salience of ascriptive characteristics and education credentials in shaping lawyers' careers, these effects disappear almost entirely when we add wave 1 practice setting to the multinomial logit model. Thus, our main findings include the observation that where AJD Project respondents begin their careers is the most powerful predictor of where they end up working at midcareer. This finding is consistent with the sequence analysis presented in chapter 3 as the largest clusters in private practice and federal and state government are sequences that remain within those clusters.

That each of the career points we have analyzed is predicted primarily by respondents' most recent social capital endowments suggests a high degree of path dependency in the capital accumulation—and, therefore, career advancement—process. The capital amassed at each stage of respondents' pre–law school careers is valuable but to differing degrees in differing career trajectories. The differences in these patterned trajectories typically become more salient over time. Consequently, the striking path dependency of lawyers' careers renders the imprint of class less legible, while gender and race continue to exert observable effects on later-stage career paths. These data come alive as we examine the narratives lawyers share about their own careers in chapters 6–9 as individuals with different types of social capital and facing different opportunities and obstacles make their careers.

Two Hemispheres Revisited:
Fields of Law, Practice Settings, and Client Types

The substantive fields in which individual lawyers practice are fundamental not only to the work lawyers do and the systems of expertise in which they are embedded but also to the career decisions they make. These fields of law (importantly, not to be confused with the field theory perspective, which regards the legal field as a unit of sociological analysis) have been implicated in the professional stratification documented by scholars as early as Hughes (1958) and continuing through Smigel (1964), Carlin (1962, 1966), Ladinsky (1963), and especially Heinz and Laumann (1982), who divided the legal profession into two hemispheres of practice: fields that served corporate clients and fields that served personal clients. At the close of *Chicago Lawyers*, Heinz and Laumann somberly assessed a "separate and unequal" legal profession:

> Different lawyers, with different social origins, who were trained at different law schools, serve different sorts of clients, practice in different office environments, are differentially likely to engage in litigation, litigate (when and if they litigate) in different forums, have somewhat different values, associate with different circles of acquaintance, and rest their claims to professionalism on different sorts of social power. . . . Only in the most formal of senses, then, do the two types of lawyers constitute one profession. (1982, 384)

The widely influential two hemispheres concept continues to be cited as a defining feature of the social structure of the American legal profession (Arewa et al. 2014; Dinovitzer and Hagan 2014; Remus 2017; Zaloznaya and Nielsen 2011). Yet, beyond a replication of the *Chicago Lawyers* study 20 years later (see *Urban Lawyers* [Heinz et al. 2005]), no research has empirically examined the continued utility of the two hemispheres thesis. In this chapter, we revisit Heinz and Laumann (1982) to examine whether the fundamental hierarchy of the legal profession, sorted by field of practice, has changed since the first Chicago study.

We pursue this question using data on the relative size and levels of specialization of fields of law, the segmentation of the bar by field, practice setting, and client type, the distribution of lawyers' efforts by client type, and the social characteristics of fields of law. We also consider the organizational features of practice settings, addressing the extent to which lawyers work in organizational hierarchies and how these may have changed the traditional organization of their work. While we focus primarily on wave 3 data for this analysis, we examine continuity and change in fields of practice and client type over respondents' early careers. For this reason, we need longitudinal data, so we restrict our sample of respondents for this analysis to only those who participated in all three waves of the AJD study ($N = 2,035$). Finally, given the focus on fields of practice, we further limit our analyses to lawyers who are practicing law at the time of their study responses ($N = 1,768$ at wave 1; $N = 1,571$ at wave 3). We conclude by analyzing lawyers who are not practicing law, a group that grows over the course of careers and makes up a substantial portion of lawyers by midcareer.

What Lawyers Do: The Relative Size of Fields of Practice

In all three waves of the AJD Project, we asked respondents who were practicing law to indicate how they allocated their time across 27 fields of law. In line with Heinz et al. (2005), we define field membership as spending 5% or more of one's time in a given field. The patterns, checked against data from waves 1 and 2, hold steady across waves with few exceptions, so, in table 5.1, we report only the wave 3 responses to this item, sorted by field and time allocation (5%–24%, 25%–49%, and 50% or more, responses adjusted to total no more than 100%).

The table reveals which fields take up the time of the largest number of practitioners as well as the distribution of small, middling, or large amounts of time spent working in each of the 27 fields. The largest field that emerges is civil and commercial litigation ($n = 494$), and there is a sizable gap between this field and the second largest, general corporate law ($n = 317$), as well as between the second and the third largest, employment law for management ($n = 226$). Many of the largest fields are associated with a business practice, though several fields identified with personal clients or government boast a substantial number of practitioners. The diversity in substantive expertise is shown in table 5.1.

TABLE 5.1 Time respondents spent in different fields of practice at wave 3 (%)

| Field of practice | | Time spent in field of practice (%) | | | | Type of field |
		5–24	25–49	50–100	Total	
Administrative law	n	34	14	71	119	Specialist
	%	28.6	11.8	59.7	100	
Antitrust	n	31	4	3	38	Generalist
	%	81.6	10.5	7.9	100	
Bankruptcy	n	58	11	29	98	Generalist
	%	59.2	11.2	29.6	100	
Civil/commercial litigation	n	180	100	214	494	Mixed
	%	36.4	20.2	43.3	100	
Civil rights/liberties	n	47	20	36	103	Mixed
	%	45.6	19.4	35.0	100	
Commercial law	n	99	35	52	186	Generalist
	%	53.2	18.8	28.0	100	
Criminal law (government)	n	23	10	82	115	Specialist
	%	20.0	8.7	71.3	100	
Criminal law (individuals)	n	38	36	76	150	Specialist
	%	25.3	24.0	50.7	100	
Employment (labor)	n	22	7	10	39	Generalist
	%	56.4	18.0	25.6	100	
Employment (management)	n	119	30	77	226	Generalist
	%	52.7	13.3	34.0	100	
Environmental law	n	27	15	28	70	Mixed
	%	38.6	21.4	40.0	100	
Family law	n	62	38	81	181	Mixed
	%	34.3	21.0	44.8	100	
General corporate	n	166	71	80	317	Generalist
	%	52.4	22.4	25.2	100	
General practice	n	124	14	12	150	Generalist
	%	82.7	9.3	8.0	100	
Health law	n	24	11	28	63	Mixed
	%	38.1	17.5	44.4	100	
Immigration law	n	20	3	30	53	Specialist
	%	37.7	5.7	56.6	100	
Insurance	n	54	10	38	102	Generalist
	%	52.9	9.8	37.3	100	
Intellectual property	n	62	29	108	199	Specialist
	%	31.2	14.6	54.3	100	
Municipal law	n	22	11	23	56	Mixed
	%	39.3	19.6	41.1	100	
Personal injury (defense)	n	35	18	52	105	Mixed
	%	33.3	17.1	49.5	100	

(continued)

TABLE 5.1 (continued)

Field of practice		Time spent in field of practice (%)				Type of field
		5–24	25–49	50–100	Total	
Personal injury (plaintiff)	n	46	11	33	90	Generalist
	%	51.1	12.2	36.7	100	
Probate	n	69	14	50	133	Generalist
	%	51.9	10.5	37.6	100	
Real estate (commercial)	n	93	22	48	163	Generalist
	%	57.1	13.5	29.5	100	
Real estate (personal)	n	71	16	24	111	Generalist
	%	64.0	14.4	21.6	100	
Securities	n	31	22	72	125	Specialist
	%	24.8	17.6	57.6	100	
Tax	n	41	10	34	85	Mixed
	%	48.2	11.8	40.0	100	
Workers compensation	n	25	7	32	32	Specialist
	%	39.1	10.9	50.0	100	

Specialization

In table 5.1, we see that fields of law vary in the degree to which they are populated by lawyers spending a lot of time, a middling amount of time, or a little time engaged in this work. To call out these differences, we created codes (see the right-hand column) indicating whether a field is a specialist field (in which more than half of lawyers who spend any time in the field spend 50% or more of their time), a generalist field (in which more than half of lawyers spend less than 25% of their time), or a mixed field (containing many lawyers who spend a small amount of time in the field and many lawyers who spend 50% or more of their time in the field). Relatively few fields are dominated by specialists: administrative law, criminal law for both government and individuals, immigration law, intellectual property law, securities law, and workers' compensation law. A dozen (nearly half the fields) are numerically dominated by generalists. These include small fields like antitrust law, bankruptcy law, employment law for unions, insurance law, and personal injury law for plaintiffs as well as the relatively larger fields of commercial law, employment law for management, general corporate law, general practice law, probate law, and both commercial law and personal real estate law. And nine fields are mixed. Civil litigation, for instance, contains 180 lawyers who spend 5%–24% of their time in civil litigation as well as 214 who spend more than 50% of their time in this specialization. Personal injury defense, family law, health law, and litigation barely missed the cutoff for specialist fields (almost half of lawyers devote more than 50% of their time to these fields) but are counted as mixed fields because the majority of lawyers who work in those fields spend less than half their time in that work.

Although the fields are variegated in terms of generalist, specialist, and occasional participation, there is a high level of specialization by field evident in our individual respondent-level data. We calculated the percentage of time lawyers spent in the field in which they spend the most time. The mean value was 78%, indicating that, on average, lawyers spend more than three-quarters of their time in their leading field. The median for this measure was 90%, indicating that more than half the sample spent 90% or more of their time working in their leading field; 38% of the sample reported spending 100% of their time in a single field. This is a significantly higher incidence than was found in the Chicago studies: in 1975, 23% of lawyers spent all their time in one field, compared to 33% in 1995 (Heinz et al. 2005, 37).

Next, we replicated the specialization index (SI) developed in the Chicago studies (Heinz et al. 2005, 37–38), again defining field membership as spending 5% or more of one's time in a field. The index ranges from 0 to 1, with 1 indicating complete specialization.[1] Heinz et al. (2005) reported a rise in the SI of the Chicago samples, from 0.488 in 1975 to 0.571 in 1995. Our wave 3 (2012) data yield a dramatically higher SI score: 0.776. The AJD Project sample is 36% more specialized than was the 1995 Chicago sample, which was 17% more specialized than was the 1975 Chicago sample.

In our data, the most specialized fields are both sides of criminal law, along with immigration law, workers' compensation law, intellectual property law, health law, administrative law, tax law, family law, and securities work. Interestingly, level of specialization is not associated with client sector; government, large business, and personal client fields are among the most specialized. In addition to our behavioral measure of lawyers' field-specific time use, we asked respondents in each wave to indicate whether they considered themselves specialists. In wave 1, 41% said that they were specialists, a figure that increased to 55% in wave 2 and 67% in wave 3. Thus, we find that individual fields and individual lawyers have become more specialized over time and that lawyers become more specialized as their careers progress. This pattern indicates that specialization may limit or direct career moves, in line with the way demand for certain kinds of legal work shapes the need to attract or maintain specialists. Additionally, looking to the chapter 3 sequence analysis, we can infer that individuals may well retain their legal specialty even when they change practice settings. For example, specialists in securities litigation or immigration may carry their specialty with them from the federal government to private law firms or corporate law departments.

Certainly, there are many differences across the two Chicago samples and the AJD Project sample (e.g., different time periods, local vs. national samples, and cross-sectional vs. cohort studies), yet the AJD Project data collected in 2012 seem to reflect a substantially more specialized system of legal fields than was documented in 1995 (see Heinz et al. 2005). Moreover, bivariate analyses of the geographic distribution of specialization suggest that the magnitude of the SI increase between 1995 and 2012 may be underestimated owing to the national reach of the AJD study. The average SI score for AJD Project respondents generally increases with city size at wave 3, usually in a step-graded manner with the population of the locale in which respondents are situated.[2] (Average SI in cities with populations under 100,000 is 0.64, compared to 0.80 in cities with populations over 5 million.) Thus, if we restricted our analyses to urban lawyers, more closely approximating the Chicago studies, we expect that the increase in SI scores would be even greater.

Copractice of Fields of Law

A signature finding of Heinz and Laumann (1982) was the profound segmentation of law practice by field, reflecting social divisions within the bar. Analyzing similar measures for our national cohort sample 40 years later, we see striking parallels. Using the 5% threshold for field membership, we computed the average conditional probability that a lawyer at wave 3 practiced in any given pair of fields. We then subjected the matrix of conditional probabilities to a cluster analysis, which groups related fields in clusters and shows which fields are separate from other fields. (For discussion of this technique, see Heinz et al. 2005, 29–37.) Figure 5.1 reveals a clustering of fields by client type and even higher levels of specialization (or lack of copractice) compared to either the 1975 or the 1995 Chicago surveys. Several fields are virtual isolates, as indicated by a lack of connections to other fields until we pass below the 0.1 conditional probability level (tax law, workers' compensation law, immigration law, and criminal law for government). Health law and personal injury defense are slightly less isolated and appear as part of a specialized cluster (0.011). And municipal law joins a pair of fields common to government lawyers, environmental law and administrative law, at the 0.011 level.

In general, the model lines up with the five stratified groups of fields identified in Heinz and Laumann (1982). At the top of the model, there are six

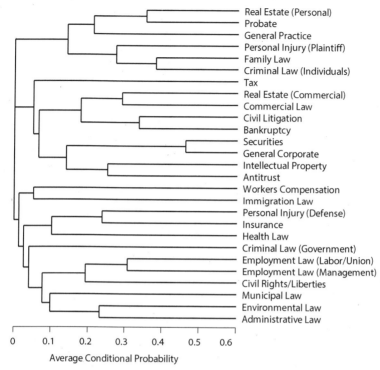

FIGURE 5.1. Hierarchical clustering of fields of copractice

personal client fields, with a set of large corporate fields following. Within this cluster, there is a strong affinity between securities and general corporate work—they join at 0.47 conditional probability. It also is interesting that intellectual property and antitrust connect at the 0.27 level, a pattern we can attribute to the connection between antitrust concerns, the practice of intellectual property law, and the settlement of intellectual property disputes (Hovenkamp et al. 2003; Leslie 2011; US Department of Justice and Federal Trade Commission 2017). After workers' compensation law and immigration law (two personal client field isolates), we see a cluster of business-oriented litigation and regulatory fields (personal injury defense, insurance law, and health law), then another isolate (criminal law for government) and a labor and civil rights cluster (including both sides of employment law). Finally, there is a government cluster made up of the near isolate municipal law plus environmental law and administrative law.

Just as Heinz and Laumann (1982) found, the personal client sphere is separate from the large corporate and general corporate spheres. None of these spheres connects with the government and labor spheres.

Allocation of Lawyers' Total Effort

THE SHIFT TO BUSINESS REPRESENTATION
IN LAWYERS' WORK

Heinz et al. (2005, 42) notably found a shift from personal clients to business clients in the allocation of lawyers' total effort between 1975 and 1995. In the former, there was a 53%/40% split of effort between corporate and personal client sectors (7% went to government or general practice); in the latter, Heinz et al. cite a 64%/29% total legal effort split (again, with 7% to other or unassigned fields). Our replication of the time allocation analysis is reported alongside the Chicago results in table 5.2, with adjustments to compensate for the modifications in field lists presented to AJD Project respondents.

We see in table 5.2 a strong similarity between the 2012 AJD Project results and the 1995 study results reported in Heinz et al. (2005), with a roughly two-to-one predominance of business over personal clients in time allocation. The percentage of lawyers' total effort spent on the corporate client sector is 67% and on the personal client/small business sector 30% (the remaining 3% is general practice, other fields, and unassigned). However, because we also find that business clients are concentrated in large cities, this predominance might be greater if we restricted analysis to urban lawyers as in the Chicago studies.

Comparing the size of fields across surveys reveals some significant changes in practice areas. For example, we see the decline of antitrust, litigation, and personal injury work for plaintiffs, the rise of intellectual property and criminal prosecution, and the emergence of health law, immigration law, insurance law, and workers' compensation law as distinct fields. As we noted in chapter 2, these shifts may reflect changes in the political economy of lawyering; in this period, the government made it harder to bring plaintiffs' antitrust cases and personal injury cases while boosting criminal prosecutions via the War on Drugs and passing new and complex regulations concerning intellectual property, health care, and immigration. Taken together, however, the split of effort between business and personal client sectors remains quite similar to that found in the 1995 survey of Chicago lawyers.

DIRECT MEASURES OF TOTAL EFFORT ON CLIENT TYPES

To this point, our replication of the analysis of effort allocation and client-defined clusters in Heinz et al. (2005) has helped us uncover how it held up over time and in a national context. But the AJD Project also allows us to

TABLE 5.2 Estimated distribution of lawyer effort, 1975–2012

Field of practice	1975 (Chicago lawyers)		1995 (urban lawyers)		2012 (AJD wave 3)	
	Practitioners (n)	% of lawyer effort	Practitioners (n)	% of lawyer effort	Practitioners (n)	% of lawyer effort
Corporate client sector	**543**	**53**	**562**	**64**	**1,224**	**67**
Large corporate fields						
Antitrust (defense)[a]	47	2	20	1	38	0
Commercial litigation[b]	91	4	215	14	314	6
Insurance[c]	—	—	—	—	102	3
Real estate (commercial)	74	4	105	6	163	4
Corporate tax[b]	51	3	57	4	44	1
Employment (management)	39	2	71	5	226	6
Securities	53	2	56	3	125	5
Cluster total	256	18	404	32	751	25
Regulatory fields						
Employment (union/labor)	18	1	31	2	39	1
Intellectual property	45	4	44	3	199	8
Administrative law	52	3	20	1	119	5
Environmental[d]	23	<1[e]	56	3	70	2
Health law[c]	—	—	—	—	63	2
Cluster total	123	9	137	9	422	18
General corporate fields						
Antitrust (plaintiff)[a]	24	1	9	—	—	—
Bankruptcy[c]	60	3	49	2	98	2
Commercial	102	3	63	3	186	4
General corporate	262	11	142	6	317	7
Personal injury (defense)	73	4	80	7	105	4
Cluster total	396	22	282	18	557	17
Political fields						
Criminal law (government)	20	2	25	3	115	6
Municipal	30	1	25	2	56	2
Cluster total	46	3	48	5	168	8

(continued)

TABLE 5.2 (continued)

Field of practice	1975 (Chicago lawyers)		1995 (urban lawyers)		2012 (AJD wave 3)	
	Practitioners (n)	% of lawyer effort	Practitioners (n)	% of lawyer effort	Practitioners (n)	% of lawyer effort
Personal/small business client sector	**424**	**40**	**330**	**29**	**743.3**	**30**
Personal business fields						
Civil litigation[b]	90	3	123	5	180	2
Real estate (personal)	152	6	84	3	110	2
Personal tax[b]	57	2	52	2	41	1
Probate	195	8	79	3	133	3
Cluster total	296	19	230	13	385	8
Personal plight fields						
Civil rights	41	2	45	2	103	3
Criminal law (individuals)	91	5	41	3	149	6
Family law[f]	237	9	114	6	180	6
Personal injury (plaintiff)	120	6	87	6	90	3
Immigration[c]	–	–	–	–	53	2
Workers compensation[c]	–	–	–	–	64	2
Cluster total	296	21	208	16	477	22
Other fields and unassigned time	**162**	**7**	**170**	**7**	**150**	**3**
General practice[g]	–	–	–	–	150	2
Other fields and unassigned time	162	7	170	7	128	1
Total practitioners	**699**	**100**	**675**	**100**	**1,571**	**100**

Source: Data for 1975 are from Heinz and Laumann (1982); data for 1995 are from Heinz et al. 2005.

[a] Antitrust was not disaggregated into plaintiff and defense categories in 2012; this category was designated as defense for comparison with 1975 and 1995.

[b] Respondents in the litigation category were divided into commercial and civil, and respondents in the tax category were divided into corporate and personal on the basis of the ratio of these categories in 1995 for comparison with the Chicago studies.

[c] Insurance, health law, immigration, and workers compensation were not included as categories in 1975 or 1995.

[d] Plaintiff and defense categories of environmental law have been combined for 1975 and 1995 for comparison with 2012.

[e] Bankruptcy was not included in 1975 or 1995, so we have substituted data for banking for comparison with 2012.

[f] Family law and divorce have been combined for 1975 and 1995 for comparison with 2012.

[g] General practice was included only in 2012, so we compare this category to "Other fields and unassigned time" for 1975 and 1995.

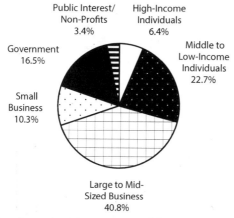

Public Interest/
Non-Profits
3.4%

High-Income
Individuals
6.4%

Government
16.5%

Middle to
Low-Income
Individuals
22.7%

Small
Business
10.3%

Large to Mid-
Sized Business
40.8%

FIGURE 5.2. Allocation of respondents' time spent serving different types of clients at wave 3

examine this issue more directly, calculating the percentage of total work-ing hours lawyers spent on the six client types discussed above.[3] Figure 5.2 presents these wave 3 results as a pie chart, where allocation patterns shift slightly from our time-in-fields analysis. In wave 3, the biggest client group is large business, which receives 40% of lawyers' total hours. Yet, even if we add small business to large business, only 50% of lawyers' total time is spent on business clients—much less than the 67% we calculated for the corporate client sector in the time-in-fields analysis. The second largest client group is middle- to low-income individuals (23%), followed by government (17%) and then relatively small proportions for high-income individuals (6%) and public interest, nonprofit, and education institutions (3%).

The results from these two different approaches to determining the al-location of lawyers' time by client type are broadly consistent. Both show the predominance of large business as clients of the legal profession. And because they are calculated in quite different ways—one at the field level and one at the level of individual responses—it is not surprising that the specific pro-portions differ. Yet the differences suggest taking caution when interpreting time-in-fields analyses. When we shift to an individual-level analysis, large business is less dominant over other client types; most strikingly, the portion of time spent on government clients rises with this methodology.[4]

The distribution of lawyers' effort indicates inequality in the provision of legal services, while the distribution of earnings reveals dramatic inequality in professional rewards (an inequality that grows over time). Figure 5.3 sets the stage for this analysis by displaying the share of total earnings by the four quar-tiles of AJD Project respondents at waves 1 and 3. At wave 1, the top quartile outearns the bottom quartile 3.3:1 and claims 42.1% of the overall earnings

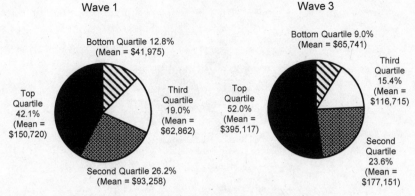

.FIGURE 5.3. Mean earnings and share of earnings by quartile at waves 1 and 3

reported by the sample. By wave 3, the top quartile earns 52% of the total earnings and 5.8 times as much as reported by practitioners in the bottom quartile. Earnings are remarkably unequal and polarize over the course of lawyers' careers. Our wave 3 results show that the share of overall earnings belonging to the top quartile roughly matches the percentage in the 1975 Chicago study (54%) but is lower than the 61% the 1995 Chicago study found. However, the increasing divergence between the earnings of the top and the bottom quartiles over the first twelve or so years of AJD Project respondents' careers suggests that this difference might be attributable to the early career stage of the AJD Project sample and that the legal profession as a whole has experienced the same dramatic growth in inequality as has been seen in American society more generally (see Chetty et al. 2014; Chetty et al. 2017; Piketty and Saez 2003).

We will dig into the individual determinants of lawyers' earnings in chapter 12, but here we consider earnings inequality by practice setting, the context in which markets, client types, and organizations intersect. As expected, the gaps are sizable. Solo practitioners and those working in state government and public interest and nonprofit organizations report the lowest earnings.[5] Federal government lawyers do better than those in other public sector settings. At the top end of the earnings spectrum are lawyers working in the largest law firms and as in-house counsel to business organizations. The effect of practice setting on earnings has grown substantially since the Chicago studies, with practice setting accounting for 36% of the variance in the AJD Project cohort's earnings at wave 3 (compared to 19% in Heinz et al. [2005] and 8% in Heinz and Laumann [1982]).

Figure 5.4 juxtaposes the distribution of practitioners among practice settings and the share of the overall earnings attributed to each setting. Lawyers in business and large law firms (about one-third of the practitioners) earn nearly half (48%) the total income of all practicing lawyers. Lawyers in midsize firms command a share of total earnings roughly commensurate to their share of the total number of practitioners. And state government, public interest/nonprofit/education institution, solo practice, and small-firm lawyers have lower average earnings. These data confirm the vast differences in economic resources accrued in different segments of the legal profession—a level of inequality that likely holds consequences for the vitality of various legal sectors.

FIELDS, CLIENTS, AND MARKETS

In table 5.3, we examine two central features of fields—the clients they serve and the markets in which they are situated—by analyzing the prevalence of selected client types and practice locales with the highest and lowest populations among selected fields in the AJD Project sample. Here we define membership in a field as spending 25% or more time in that work, and we select 14 fields representing the major sectors of practice (government, corporate client, and personal client). We treat civil litigation as a boundary field between the corporate and the personal client sector, and we include a column reporting the prestige score of each field from Heinz et al. (2005).

The first three columns of table 5.3 document the client profile of the 14 fields, listing the percentage in each field who spend 50% or more of their time on a particular type of client. The data confirm our selection of fields as their sectors' representatives. The three government fields contain a preponderance of lawyers spending most of their time on government clients, the

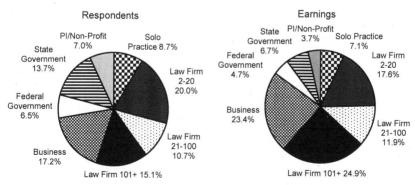

FIGURE 5.4. Percentage of respondents and percentage of earnings by wave 3 practice setting
NOTE: N = 2,961.

TABLE 5.3 Field prestige scores in 1995 and client type and city size for respondents in selected fields of practice at wave 3 (%)

Field of practice	Client type			Employer city size		Respondents in field (n)	1995 prestige score for field of practice
	Large business	Government	Mid and low-income individuals	Population up to 1 million	Population above 5 million		
Government sector							
Administrative law	36	44.7	9.4	15.3	28.2	85	34
Criminal law (government)	2.2	71.7	1.1	32.6	26.1	92	35
Municipal law	2.9	67.7	17.7	29.4	23.5	34	38
Corporate client sector							
Employment law (management)	52.3	23.4	3.7	12.2	29.9	107	38
General corporate	62.3	2.0	2.0	15.2	39.7	151	66
Intellectual property	73.0	3.7	2.2	7.3	32.9	137	71
Securities	61.7	12.8	4.3	2.1	46.8	94	85
Personal injury (defense)	70.0	11.4	10	8.6	32.9	70	17
Litigation sector							
Civil and commercial litigation	51.0	11.5	15.3	17.2	33.1	314	67/28
Personal client sector							
Criminal law (individuals)	0.9	0	94.6	28.6	29.5	112	17
Family law	1.7	11.0	78.8	40.7	22.0	118	4/8
Immigration	18.2	9.1	48.5	9.1	45.5	33	7
Personal injury (plaintiff)	9.1	0	86.4	29.6	27.3	44	14
Probate	0	1.6	57.8	20.3	26.6	64	28
Total	38.8	16.6	23.7	16.6	33.0	1,571	

Note: Respondents are allocated to client types if they spend at least 50% of their time serving that type of client.

business fields contain a preponderance of lawyers spending most of their time on business clients, litigators split their time between business and other types of clients, and lawyers in personal client fields spend most of their time on middle- to low-income client work. The next two columns show the representation of lawyers practicing in the smallest locales and the largest cities among the selected fields; these data indicate a clear relationship between fields and markets. Lawyers working in the corporate client sector are concentrated in large urban markets, and lawyers working in the personal client sector and the government sector are more numerous in the least populous locales. For example, 47% of securities lawyers are located in the largest cities (only 2% work in cities with populations under 1 million), while 41% of family law specialists practice in cities with populations under 1 million (and 22% in cities with populations over 5 million). The government and personal client sectors are present in both small and large cities, but large corporate fields are functionally limited to big cities.

THE GEOGRAPHY OF OPPORTUNITY

That the AJD Project sample is national in scope allows us to address differences across locales and markets, as well as lawyers' geographic mobility and the status dimensions of geographic locations. In chapter 1, we explained how the survey design aimed to capture the complex interplay between the global, national, and local factors shaping legal careers. Our cluster analysis of the 18 legal markets from which respondents were sampled generated three geographic groupings of legal markets along those lines. The "global" cluster comprises New York City, Washington, DC, and San Francisco/the Bay Area. The "national" cluster, which has global connections, includes the legal markets in Chicago, Los Angeles, Houston, St. Louis, Atlanta, Boston, New Jersey (outside Newark), and Minneapolis. The third, the "regional" cluster, includes the rest of the seven AJD Project sampling units: Connecticut, Florida (outside Miami), Indiana, Oklahoma, Oregon, Tennessee, and Utah (Dawe and Nelson 2021b). There are important differences in lawyers' careers across these clusters. For instance, location influences the amount of international work that lawyers do, the kinds of clients they represent, their most common practice settings, their earnings levels, and earnings inequality. When lawyers choose their geographic location, they are selecting from different market contexts that offer different kinds of economic and professional opportunity.

Unsurprisingly, our analysis finds significant differences in the education and social capital of lawyers working in each cluster. Global markets clearly dominate when it comes to recruiting graduates from top-10 law schools. Overall, 11% of the AJD Project sample graduated from top-10 law schools, but 32% of the respondents sampled from New York City, one-quarter of the San Francisco/Bay Area respondents, and almost one-fifth (19%) of the DC respondents did. In contrast, the regional markets dominate in recruiting graduates from tier 3 and tier 4 law schools. Overall 30% of the AJD Project sample graduated from tier 3 and tier 4 law schools, but over half of respondents sampled from Tennessee, 49% of respondents from Oklahoma, and 48% of respondents from Connecticut did.

Relatedly, in a separate analysis, we considered the number and characteristics of lawyers who began their legal careers in a state different from the one in which they attended law school and those who changed jurisdictions between their first jobs and their wave 3 responses (Dawe and Nelson 2021a). These data show that three-quarters (76%) of respondents began their legal careers in the state in which they went to law school. Notably, they dominate in some national and regional locales: Houston (97%), Minneapolis and Oklahoma (91%), Indiana (88%), Tennessee (86%), and Oregon (85%). The remaining lawyers, the law school movers, tended to be from more privileged social backgrounds and/or elite law schools: 72% of the top-10 graduates in the AJD Project sample began their careers by moving away from the state in which they earned their degree, compared to 20% of the graduates from law schools ranked 11 or below (Dawe and Nelson 2021a, 6). Reaffirming this connection, we find that those practice settings that contain larger percentages of top-10 graduates have larger percentages of law school movers: nearly 50% of lawyers who began their careers in federal government and nearly 40% of those who began in large law firms were movers. Roughly equal proportions of men and women move between law school and their first jobs, but there is a statistically significant relationship between race and law school movement ($p \leq .05$): 33% of Asian Americans but just 13% of Native Americans moved for their first positions. African American and Latinx respondents are somewhat more likely than average (24%) to be law school movers (28% and 26%, respectively), and Whites are somewhat less likely than average (23%).

Once AJD Project respondents were settled in their first jobs, they rarely move geographically. At wave 3, 74% of respondents remained in the state in which they began working 12 years prior (Dawe and Nelson 2021a, 17). While law school movers are nearly twice as likely as stayers to move to different states in their early careers (38% compared to 20%), moving is still relatively rare: nearly two-thirds (62%) of law school movers were settled in their first-job states at wave 3. To the extent that there *is* significant geographic movement, it is toward larger cities. At wave 1, only 19% of AJD Project respondents lived in a megacity (i.e., one with a population at or above 1 million), compared to 41% at wave 3. Midsize cities (with populations ranging from 500,000 to 999,999) lost their share over time, dropping from 19% to 7%. Once again, there is a well-ordered relationship between law school status and mobility; top-10 graduates are the most likely to have moved by wave 3, and mobility drops in tandem with law school ranking. As with law school movers, those lawyers who are geographically mobile during their early careers are those who begin in the most high-status practice settings, including large law firms and the federal government. Early career movement does not vary at a statistically significant level by gender or by race.

Moving is not equally valuable for all lawyers or all practice settings. On average, law school movers earn significantly more than stayers at wave 1 ($95,003 compared to $78,840 [$p \leq .001$]), yet the earnings differences between law school movers and stayers and early career movers and stayers are not statistically significant at wave 3. Early career stayers are twice as likely as early career movers to make equity partner by wave 3 (18% compared to 9%), and, as might be expected, they tend to practice in smaller communities and smaller law firms. For their part, both law school and early career movers are much more likely than are law school and early career stayers to have become inside counsel by wave 3 (19% compared to 13% for the former and 19% compared to 12% for the latter). This pattern corresponds to the data on movement out of large law firms and the requirement to move locations in order to take inside counsel positions, as documented in chapters 3 and 4.

Among men, movers outearn stayers by 8% at wave 3 ($201,091 compared to $186,636), while, among women, movers earn 11% *less* than do stayers ($149,549 compared to $133,036). Although these differences are not statistically significant, this pattern suggests that women enjoy fewer rewards for their mobility, perhaps because they are more likely than men are to move because they are trailing spouses than because they are pursuing their own career opportunities.

SOCIAL CHARACTERISTICS OF FIELDS OF PRACTICE

Heinz and Laumann (1982) found a distinct overrepresentation of ethnoreligious groups in certain fields of law: Jewish lawyers in divorce, Irish Catholics in civil litigation, and White Anglo-Saxon Protestants in securities. By the time of Heinz et al. (2005), these patterns had changed substantially, and ethnoreligious distinctions were far less salient. Heinz et al. hypothesized that, owing to the entry of growing numbers of women and people of color practicing law, gender and race would become more important axes of inequality by field of work.

In table 5.4, we explore a set of salient social characteristics by the same selected fields of practice as were discussed above. Beginning with religious affiliation, we find that Catholic and Greek/Russian Orthodox lawyers make up 29% of practicing lawyers in the AJD Project sample. This group is no longer overrepresented in the litigation field and now underrepresented in personal injury defense, where Protestants (32% of the sample) are overrepresented. Protestants, meanwhile, are no longer overrepresented in securities work. Our measure of divorce law is not precisely comparable to the field as specified in the Chicago studies, though we find Jewish lawyers (6% of the sample)[6] underrepresented within our broader category, family law. Other notable patterns by religious group include a concentration of Catholic/Greek/Russian Orthodox lawyers in municipal law and employment law for management but their vast underrepresentation in immigration law. Jewish lawyers are overrepresented in administrative law and underrepresented in personal injury law (on both the plaintiff and the defense sides). Overall, however, ethnoreligious identity is not a clear determinant of field of legal practice.

Women (47% of the practicing lawyers in the sample) are over- and underrepresented in several of the selected fields. If we use an absolute 10% divergence as a guideline for a meaningful difference, women are overrepresented in administrative law, employment law for management, family law, and immigration law, and they are underrepresented in intellectual property law, securities law, and personal injury for plaintiffs.

Because these fields span the corporate and personal client sectors, client type cannot explain these gendered patterns. Status, however, seems to be key. Intellectual property had the second-highest prestige score (see table 5.3); it may favor lawyers with a scientific background, which, given the lesser presence of women in STEM (science, technology, engineering, and mathematics) fields, may also help explain the dominance of men in that area of law. Securities law is also a traditionally high-status field. While the AJD Project did not collect prestige scores, we note that securities has by far the highest proportion of top-20 law school graduates, a frequently used measure of law firm status (Uzzi and Lancaster 2004). In our data, just 34% of securities law specialists are women.

We find family law and immigration law at the opposite end of the status spectrum, these fields having received the lowest prestige ratings of the 14 fields surveyed in Heinz et al. (2005). Perhaps not coincidentally (see Abbott

TABLE 5.4 Social characteristics of respondents in selected fields of practice at wave 3 (%)

Field of practice	Religion			Gender	Race/ethnicity				Parent education		Parent occupation		Law school ranking	
	Catholic/ Orthodox	Protestant	Jewish	Woman	African American	Latinx	Asian American	White	High school or less	Graduate/ professional school	Blue collar	Professional	Top 20	Tiers 3 and 4
Government sector														
Administrative law	21.4	32.1	10.7	57.7	8.2	4.7	8.2	76.5	15.5	58.3	4.0	48.0	28.2	20.0
Criminal law (government)	27.0	28.6	4.8	39.1	6.5	13.0	10.9	69.6	17.4	51.1	6.0	46.3	16.3	27.2
Municipal law	37.5	25.0	8.3	50.0	2.9	8.8	8.8	73.5	15.6	31.3	0	35.7	20.6	17.7
Corporate client sector														
Employment law (management)	38.3	28.3	5.0	64.5	11.2	7.5	10.3	67.3	14.2	51.9	5.5	48.4	29.9	20.6
General corporate	32.4	36.1	6.5	45.0	4.6	11.9	9.9	70.9	14.9	52.7	7.4	38.0	32.5	16.6
Intellectual property	23.6	34.8	3.4	30.7	7.4	6.6	14.0	69.9	20.6	51.5	7.0	44.7	32.9	23.4
Securities	35.9	31.3	4.7	34.0	8.5	11.7	10.6	68.1	13.0	55.4	7.4	43.2	45.7	11.7
Personal injury (defense)	17.3	44.2	1.9	47.1	7.1	7.1	7.1	74.3	22.9	37.1	6.6	36.1	10.1	46.4
Litigation sector														
Civil and commercial litigation	26.9	32.8	7.5	39.8	8.0	9.9	8.6	70.4	14.2	54.0	4.0	45.6	25.1	26.1
Personal client sector														
Criminal law (individuals)	29.1	32.6	7.0	48.2	11.6	12.5	5.4	69.6	15.3	48.7	4.1	38.8	13.1	35.5
Family law	25.9	38.8	3.5	61.9	9.2	7.6	4.2	73.1	15.3	47.5	12.4	41.9	7.9	41.2
Immigration	9.5	38.1	4.8	66.7	3.0	21.2	33.3	39.4	18.2	45.5	11.5	46.2	18.8	43.8
Personal injury (plaintiff)	30.6	38.9	2.8	22.7	4.5	4.5	4.5	84.1	18.2	52.3	2.4	41.5	9.5	38.1
Probate	20.5	34.1	4.6	56.3	3.1	3.1	9.4	82.8	17.5	55.6	10.4	41.7	17.7	32.3
Total	**29.1**	**32.1**	**6.1**	**47.1**	**8.5**	**9.3**	**9.5**	**70.5**	**17.2**	**50.3**	**6.1**	**43.4**	**23.7**	**26.6**

1988; Sandefur 2001), both fields centrally involve family relationships. Not only is this kind of emotion-laden work not "professionally pure" in Abbott's usage, but stereotypes about women's relative ability to deal with such issues may also contribute to their overrepresentation in these fields. Personal injury law (on the plaintiffs' side) was ranked as slightly more prestigious than family law and immigration law, though this is the sort of adversarial field in which gender stereotypes may amplify discrimination against women (Pierce 1995), leading to their underrepresentation. Interestingly, however, gender bias does not appear to operate across all litigation fields; women are not underrepresented in civil and commercial litigation or personal injury defense.

All things considered, we posit that, as Menkel-Meadow (1986) has argued using cross-cultural data, gendered field sorting hinges on prestige, contributing to the higher likelihood that women will practice in less prestigious fields of law. Additionally, it appears to reflect and reinforce gender stereotyping regarding aptitudes and certain kinds of lawyers' work.

Race and ethnicity have only a small number of specific effects on fields of practice. Latinx and Asian American lawyers are overrepresented in immigration law (by a factor of more than 2 for Latinx and more than 3 for Asian Americans), possibly reflecting foreign language skills or clientele concentrated by race and ethnicity. Whites are dramatically underrepresented among immigration lawyers but somewhat overrepresented in the personal injury plaintiffs' field and in probate. Here, we suspect a sort of racial legacy is at work: the plaintiffs' personal injury bar in Chicago and other large cities has, in the past, been dominated by Irish Catholics (Heinz and Laumann 1982; Parikh and Garth 2005) and White attorneys in probate, in accordance with the well-established fact that Whites' family wealth far outstrips African Americans' and Latinx's (Barsky et al. 2002; Conley 1999; Krivo and Kaufman 2004), may be continuing a historical legacy of dominance among advisers to wealthy White families. We find no other major differences in field representation by race and ethnicity.

Our measures of social class include parents' education and parents' occupation. In table 5.4, we include measures of the lowest- and highest-status group on each variable. With regard to measures of social class, we see only weak associations with field and no strong affinity between more privileged parents' background and client sector.

The selectivity of lawyers' alma maters proves a more proximate measure of professional prestige and shows a stronger connection to the divided client sectors of legal practice. Here, we use two measures of law school prestige to consider legal field sorting: graduating from a top-20 law school (as did 24%

of the practicing lawyers in the sample) and graduating from a tier 3 or tier 4 law school (27%). Again using a 10% difference from the sample mean as an indicator of a meaningful disparity, we find that just one of the five business fields, securities, has an overrepresentation of more elite law school graduates. It is also the only field in which lower-tier law school graduates are underrepresented. Top-20 graduates are underrepresented in family law and personal injury law (both plaintiff and defense). In fact, 46% of personal injury defense lawyers and 38% of personal injury plaintiffs' lawyers graduated from the lowest-status law schools and 10% from top-20 schools. Thus, both personal injury fields appear to occupy a lower-status position in the profession, continuing the low prestige ratings they received in the 1995 Chicago survey.

Personal client fields attract a preponderance of less selective law school graduates. None of these five fields has more than 20% top-20 graduates. The proportion of tier 3 and tier 4 law school graduates exceeds the sample mean for all five personal client fields and for family law, immigration law, and personal injury for plaintiffs by more than 10%.

Today, fields of practice are marked by gender, race, and law school status. The status stratification of fields remains, as in 1975 Chicago, but the differentiating characteristics have shifted away from ethnoreligious background and social class and toward gender, law school status, and race.

Practice Settings as Organizational Hierarchies

The 1975 Chicago study ascribed little importance to the characteristics of the organizations in which lawyers worked (Heinz and Laumann 1982), but, by the time of the 1995 replication study, transformations in these organizations were recognized as major drivers of professional change, including the rise and economic dominance of large law firms and the growing stature of inside counsel to business (Heinz et al. 2005, 98–139). As in much of the professions and organizations literature, the authors sought to determine whether organizational change fundamentally altered the professional autonomy of lawyers, including their power to run their organizations, choose the clients they represented, and control strategies of representation (see Brock et al. 1999; Derber 1983; Falconbridge and Muzio 2008; Hanlon 1999; Hinings 2006; Johnson 1972; and Van Hoy 1995). Heinz and Laumann (1982) posited that one of the paradoxes of the two hemispheres was that lawyers in the corporate hemisphere enjoyed more prestige but less professional autonomy. Personal client attorneys were better able to pick and choose clients and tended to deal with less sophisticated or legally knowledgeable clients, allowing them wider control over legal strategy. Heinz et al. (2005, 114–20) largely supported this earlier contention. While rejecting a deprofessionaliza- tion hypothesis (more on this shortly), it highlighted significant differences across practice settings that affirmed personal client attorneys' greater profes- sional autonomy.

The AJD Project provides a rare opportunity to revisit this issue using some of the same measures employed in the Chicago studies. We begin by examining the characteristics of the organizations in which lawyers work. A basic distinction is that between organizations controlled by profession- als (*heteronomous* organizations) and those controlled by nonprofessionals (Freidson 1986; Scott 1965). Lawyers working in heteronomous organiza- tions may still have control over their work but be constrained by the author- ity structure of the organization (Nelson and Nielsen 2000). Solo practices and private law firms are the clearest examples of heteronomous practice set- tings, and, as we saw in chapter 4, most of the AJD Project lawyers work in these types of organizations across all waves. But there is a steady decline in employment in professional organizations across stage of career: 73% of practicing lawyers worked in these settings at wave 1, 64% at wave 2, and 59% at wave 3.[7] The slope reflects the exodus of lawyers from law firms to business over the course of their careers. Businesses, which attract a growing percentage of lawyers to positions as inside counsel or roles that do not in- volve practicing law, represent the clearest category of organizations not run by lawyers (in a professional capacity). Given our focus on practicing lawyers, we limit the analysis here to inside counsel; we get to those lawyers working in business settings but not practicing law later in the chapter. At wave 1, 4% of practicing lawyers worked in business, increasing to 12% at wave 2, and 16% at wave 3. Public interest, nonprofit, and education organizations, which employ 6%–7% of the sample at all three waves, are more likely to be run by lawyers and provide relatively high professional autonomy, and the 18% of lawyers who work in federal or state government at wave 3 are likely to work in units in which there is considerable autonomy from nonlawyer officials or that are controlled by lawyers (such as the judiciary). The 2% of lawyers who work in nonprofits or education institutions are expected to have a level of professional autonomy dependent on the circumstances of their position and organization. Law professors, for example, may be employed by a university but enjoy considerable freedom in a professional role. Overall, we find that most American lawyers today work in organizations run by lawyers, though women less so than men (at 54% vs. 63%, respectively, at wave 3).

We examined three measures of organization size by practice setting at wave 3: total employees, number of lawyers in the organization, and number of lawyers in the respondent's office.[8] Nearly one-third of the sample are solos or work in firms with 20 or fewer lawyers. Another 7% work in public interest, nonprofit, or education organizations with a median size of fewer than 100 employees. The remainder, 61%, work in large organizations with median employee counts ranging from 100 to 6,300. Still, their own practice groups are much smaller. The median number of lawyers in organizations is 27, and the median number of lawyers in their office is 11. Consider, for example, law firms with more than 100 lawyers. Their median number of lawyers is 500, but, owing to branching, the median number of lawyers in each office is 110—still large, though far more modest than the firm as a whole. Differences between overall organization size and office size are even more pronounced in government and business, where the median number of lawyers in the office ranges from 7 to 20. These much smaller office sizes would facilitate the kind of personal interactions between lawyers we might expect in a traditional organization of lawyers' work, including those characteristic of the golden age.

Yet most midcareer lawyers work in chains of supervision. We asked respondents at wave 3 whether they supervised anyone, whether they were supervised, and whether, in turn, their supervisor was supervised. The responses included 76% who supervised others, 66% who were supervised by someone else, and 60% whose own supervisor was supervised by someone else.[9] Solos are an outlier at the low end, with virtually none reporting that they worked under supervision, while 100% of lawyers in federal government and 92% in state government were supervised. An additional 86% of lawyers in public interest, nonprofit, and education organizations and 94% in inside counsel to business roles had supervisors. Women occupy more subordinate roles in supervisory hierarchies. They supervise others at a lower rate than do men (71% vs. 80%), are supervised at a higher rate than are men (72% vs. 60%), and are less likely to have the power to reward those under their supervision (54% vs. 61%). All differences in supervisory status by practice setting are statistically significant, as are all differences in supervisory status by gender except for whether supervisors are supervised.

What are the implications of supervised hierarchies for whether lawyers control their work processes? At waves 2 and 3, we asked, "How frequently are you required to design important aspects of your own work and to put your ideas into practice?" Additionally, as part of our battery of satisfaction questions, we measured lawyers' satisfaction with their degree of control over how they work and how much they work. Here, we discuss the wave 3 results, but the patterns are similar across waves. Overwhelmingly, lawyers told us they design and execute important aspects of their work. The mean rating is 5.9 on a 7-point scale.[10] Still, this varies by practice setting. Solo practitioners post the highest ratings, at 6.4, followed by small-firm lawyers at 6.0. State government attorneys score the lowest (5.3), and lawyers in other settings score within a narrow range, from 5.7 to 5.9. Women, across settings, average 5.7 compared to men's 6.0. The measure of satisfaction with control over how you do your work elicited high ratings, too, with an overall mean of 5.9. Again, solos responded with the highest levels of satisfaction, at 6.4, followed closely by attorneys from small firms at 6.1, attorneys working in nonprofits and education at 6.0, and lawyers working in public interest and nonprofits at 5.9. Lawyers in midsize firms employing from 21 to 100 lawyers posted the lowest levels of satisfaction with the work process, with an average rating of 5.6. In contrast to a 2015 Harvard Law School career study (Wilkins et al. 2015), we do not find a significant gender difference on this measure at wave 3.

Control over the *amount* of work is a different story. Here, the overall satisfaction rating is 5.1. Solos again lead the sample in satisfaction with a mean of 6.1, while the least satisfied are lawyers working in large law firms with more than 100 attorneys (4.7). Lawyers in all settings except solo practice and small firms report levels of satisfaction below the overall mean. While women are less satisfied than are men on this dimension at wave 1 (4.3 compared to 4.5), the gender difference has disappeared by wave 3.

When we analyzed these three items by position within the organization, we found that hierarchy clearly shapes control over work. Notably, contract attorneys rate their satisfaction with control over the design and execution of their work at a particularly low level (4.1 compared to 5.9 for the sample overall).[11] Their satisfaction with control over the work process measures 4.8, compared to 5.9 for the sample overall. Contract attorneys represent just a small number of practicing lawyers in our sample, a mere 23 (1.5% of our sample). Thus, the growth of alternative service providers like Axiom has not yet directly transformed lawyers' careers, even if such innovations are already reshaping the contours of the legal services market. In general, lawyers in positions of ownership (solos and equity partners) or authority (business owners, judges, law professors) record higher ratings on control over their work. Satisfaction with control over the amount of work falls along lines of organizational authority and varies by practice context. Business owners, judges, and solos are among the most satisfied on this dimension. Law professors also assign above-average satisfaction ratings. Those least satisfied with their control over how much work they do are nonequity partners, public defenders, contract attorneys, associates, those with the title *supervising attorney*, and of counsel.

These data clearly indicate that most midcareer lawyers control how they do their work, which contradicts arguments that lawyers have become deskilled or deprofessionalized since the golden age. Far more problematic, however, is their apparently scant control over how much they have to work. Satisfaction levels on this dimension vary by the number of hours lawyers work in different practice contexts: the least satisfied are lawyers in the largest law firms, which are notorious for the high number of working hours they demand of their attorneys. And women differ from their male colleagues in their perceived level of control over the design and execution of their work, though their satisfaction ratings remain relatively high.

NONPRACTICING LAWYERS

Lawyers who are not practicing law in their jobs represent a nontrivial—and growing—segment of the bar. The Chicago studies found that, in 1975, 7% of lawyers worked in positions that were not defined by a knowledge of law, and this figure had increased to 9% by 1995 (Heinz et al. 2005, 157). AJD Project respondents were asked to self-report whether they were practicing law in their current jobs, and 25% reported working in a nonpracticing position in at least one wave of the study. In wave 1, nearly 1 in 10 AJD Project lawyers was not practicing law (9%). This grew to 15% at wave 2 and 18% at wave 3,[12] suggesting that lawyers are more likely to work in nonpracticing positions as their careers progress.[13]

We find a smaller share of nonpracticing lawyers who have never practiced law than was found in Heinz et al. (2005), reflecting AJD Project respondents' greater movement into and out of nonpracticing positions across survey waves. Heinz et al. found that 40% of nonpracticing lawyers in their sample had never practiced law, while only 27% of nonpracticing AJD Project lawyers at wave 3 were not practicing law at any wave. It is significant that the movement we find between practicing and nonpracticing positions is bidirectional. Nonpracticing lawyers have not simply left the profession. For example, one-third of the nonpracticing lawyers at wave 1 were practicing law by wave 2, and 25% of nonpracticing lawyers at wave 1 or 2 were practicing law at wave 3.

Like Heinz et al. (2005), we find that nonpracticing lawyers lack a distinctive social profile.[14] Women are somewhat less likely than are men to be practicing law (80% compared to 83%), though the difference is not statistically significant. Asian American respondents are the most likely to be practicing law (85%), followed by Latinx (83%), Whites (82%), and African Americans (78%). Asian Americans are concentrated in business settings, which we might expect to reduce their rate of law practice, but the overwhelming majority of Asian Americans working in business organizations at wave 3 were, in fact, practicing law (76%). However intriguing these differences may be, they are not statistically significant. Parents' education and parents' occupation do not vary by practicing law, and top-10 graduates are only marginally more likely than tier 3 and tier 4 graduates to be practicing law (83% compared to 81%) at the 12-year point of their careers.

Age is the only social characteristic by which practicing and nonpracticing lawyers differ at a statistically significant level. On average, nonpracticing lawyers are 1.5 years older than practicing lawyers ($p \leq .001$). Nonpracticing lawyers' greater mean age is related, in part, to their greater likelihood of having earned additional postgraduate degrees (31% compared to 19% for practicing lawyers). The mean age for lawyers with additional degrees is three years older than for lawyers with law degrees only, reflecting in part time spent working toward degrees before attending law school and in part a divergence in pre–law school work experience.

The social characteristics of practicing and nonpracticing lawyers are similar, though their jobs, organizational contexts, and workplace experiences turn out to be remarkably different. The most common practice setting for nonpracticing lawyers is business organizations, yet more than half worked in nonbusiness settings at wave 3.[15] Public interest and nonprofit organizations are nearly as common a setting for nonpracticing lawyers as are business organizations (35% compared to 40%). Another 20% work in state and federal government and the remaining 4.3% in law firms. Thus, fewer than 5% of nonpracticing lawyers work in organizations run by lawyers, compared to nearly 60% of practicing lawyers. Nonpracticing lawyers earn significantly less than do practicing lawyers at wave 3 (reporting a mean income of $110,000 vs. $156,000) and work significantly fewer hours per week (43 vs. 48).[16] They are more likely to have additional jobs (26% vs. 15%), indicating that they are nearly twice as likely as practicing lawyers to supplement their earnings from their primary job with income from extra paid work.

Nonpracticing lawyers enjoy less workplace authority than do practicing lawyers. They are significantly less likely to supervise others (58% compared to 76%) and are significantly more likely to be supervised (74% compared to 66%) and to have a supervisor who is supervised (77% compared to 61%). Nonpracticing lawyers, who are concentrated in business settings in which discretionary rewards and incentives are commonplace, are more likely to have the authority to reward supervisees. When it comes to satisfaction ratings, we find no difference in the amount of control practicing and nonpracticing lawyers report over their work, how they do it, or how much of it they do. Significant differences emerge on five dimensions of job satisfaction. Non-practicing lawyers are less satisfied than are practicing lawyers with the intellectual challenge of their work and their amount of work-related travel, which may be traceable to their relative concentration in business organizations. They are significantly more satisfied than their peers, however, with workplace diversity, the value of their work to society, and work/life balance.

Conclusion

Although the AJD Project surveys were conducted from 2003 through 2012 and were based on a national sample of one cohort of lawyers, we see in this chapter remarkable continuity in the organization of lawyers' work from the Chicago studies conducted in the mid-1970s and the mid-1990s. Using the same methodology employed by Heinz and Laumann (1982), we confirm their finding that lawyers' work for business clients (claiming some two-thirds of their total effort) far outstrips their work for personal clients. We also find higher levels of specialization and profound levels of segmentation by field of practice, with distinct clusters of fields indicating a lack of copractice.

In the 1995 Chicago replication study (see Heinz et al. 2005), ethnoreligious segregation by field of law was weakening; today, it has largely eroded. Instead, the AJD Project surveys highlight gendered fault lines and, in very specific cases, field segregation by race and ethnicity. Women are over- and underrepresented in several fields of practice, evincing patterns of field sorting that seem to reflect gender stereotypes and broader social subjugation, in that they are channeled into areas of family law and other, less prestigious fields of practice. Race figures most prominently in the selection of lawyers into immigration law, where Latinx and Asian American lawyers are overrepresented.

Taken together, our comprehensive data on fields of practice, practice settings, and client types testify to the continued vitality of the two-hemispheres conception of the legal profession. Some of the axes of social differentiation across fields have shifted, from religion and ethnicity to gender and race, but the underlying structure of inequality among American lawyers remains the distinction between lawyers who represent business and lawyers who represent persons or who work in the public sector. Our data reveal that within this fundamental structure there is dramatically growing inequality in earnings across spheres of practice as lawyers working in corporate law firms command significantly higher earnings while lawyers in other practice settings see only modest wage growth. In this highly segmented and highly stratified professional system, as Heinz and Laumann (1982, 384) remarked, lawyers are members of one profession "only in the most formal of senses."

PART 3

The Narratives of Lawyers' Careers

Fast Tracks and Long Hauls

In part 1, we introduced our analysis of the strategies and serendipities inherent in making legal careers by reviewing foundational theoretical frameworks and scholarship, particularly Heinz and Laumann (1982) and Heinz et al. (2005). In part 2, we examined the AJD Project data to identify patterns and pathways shaping careers in the American legal profession today, noting continuities and changes in lawyers' social characteristics, clients, specialties, and practice settings and their mobility across the persistent hemispheres of legal practice that Heinz and Laumann (1982) identified four decades ago.

Part 3 breathes life into these quantitative patterns and trends by zooming in on lawyers' practice settings and career moves within and across them. Each chapter begins with statistical data about a focal setting (private law firms, solo practice, business settings, and the public sector, including government, public interest organizations, and nonprofits), then draws on extensive qualitative interview data to show how individuals navigate their own careers. Many AJD Project respondents were interviewed multiple times. With these rich data and the ubiquity of LinkedIn and other online sources, we can follow their strategic and sometimes shifting approaches to their careers as they mature in the law and update their career trajectories through the present.

For the most part, our interviews were open-ended invitations for individuals to narrate their careers. We wanted to know about their family backgrounds, the reasons they went to law school, how they obtained their jobs, whether and why they changed jobs, what kind of work they did (mundane and exceptional alike), and where they hoped and expected to go in the future.

From a more theoretical perspective, we were interested in tracing how the lawyers are able to deploy various kinds of capital—including degrees, social networks, job experience, entrepreneurial initiatives, supportive spouses handling childcare and household duties, and cultural capital that fits in particular settings—and take advantage of serendipitous opportunities to move into particular positions. Each narrative contributes to a collective biography of what is valued and disvalued in making lawyers' careers and how those with particular kinds of capital may naturally follow well-established patterns that amount to a Bourdieusian habitus. It is not just a matter of how individuals and groups deploy their assets; it is also a matter of how those assets (and potential liabilities, like unemployment and law degrees from low-ranked schools) are valued in particular practice settings at moments in lawyers' careers. Individual agency is seeking to gain recognition for forms of capital that may not generally be recognized within the current hierarchical structure of opportunity in the legal profession.

The interviews illustrate that almost all positions in law are nominally open to all who pass the bar, no matter where they attended law school, but they also show how access to certain career paths is distributed both systematically and unevenly. The distribution reflects traditional and slowly changing hierarchies enshrined in the field's meritocratic veneer. It rewards those who have the family resources, education opportunities, and personal drive and talent to reach the elite law schools, individuals who from birth have been prepared for the next test and entrance into the next select school. Relatively few individuals, however talented and driven, can overcome a lack of family resources and early education opportunity to gain places at the top law schools.

As an example, we have shown in earlier chapters that elite law school graduates are more likely than others in the AJD Project cohort to start their careers in large corporate law firms, regardless of their intentions about becoming partners. Their habitus is a natural fit for the existing culture of this practice setting. Over time, some who profess no partnership interest will change their minds, usually those whose cultural capital is shared by the organization's partners. Others—even those who intended to become partners—will leave. This group is disproportionately composed of women and minorities who, luckily, find their early career corporate law firm experience rewarded in other practice settings and have now created their own well-worn career path. Leaving large law firms for jobs as in-house counsel reflects the capital value of a corporate background. It also offers a way to flourish without the unique pressures surrounding billable hours and client recruitment.

The interviews reveal that success in these law firms is organized around the billable hour, so we investigated how various individuals are seen as good investments by mentors and sponsors who fast-track them to partnership.

Again, we heard a recurring story: White men with elite law school credentials and wives at home have the easiest path because they are deemed most
able to work long hours and generate or preserve the business or wealthy
individual clients essential to firm prosperity. That tendency, too, pushes
women and minorities out of the large-firm setting. One knowledgeable minority woman told us she had beaten "thousand to one odds" to become a
partner. There is a substantial literature on the work/life tensions that female
lawyers face (Brockman 2001; Epstein et al. 1999; Rhode 2011; Sommerlad
and Sanderson 1998; Wallace 2008). The interviews provide rich examples of
how those odds are stacked in opening and closing various career paths for
lawyers.

The interviews also evidence the "great divide" between the career paths
of those who start out in large law firms and those who do not (see chap. 3).
The former will find that this early experience pays dividends throughout
their careers and in all their future practice settings. This divide overlaps with
other differentiations, including demographics and class background. In every job setting, therefore, we can see a division between today's version of the
two hemispheres of Heinz and Laumann—roughly between those who serve
corporations and those who serve individuals—discussed in earlier chapters.
Surprisingly, we even see this divide in chapter 7, where we contrast the solos
who started with few advantages compared to those who came out of large
corporate law firms with prestige and a stable of well-positioned contacts.
Chapter 8 examines careers in business and illustrates the strongest embodiment of the divide, where the established path connects large corporate law
firms to in-house counsel positions in major corporations.

Today, all positions are open to all lawyers. But merit remains very specifically defined to fit the hierarchies of the legal field. These meritocratic standards continue to enshrine the advantages of elite schooling and privileged
social class backgrounds, however. Others are excluded not on the basis of
identity, as they once were, but because they are now framed as falling inef-
fably short of the standards.

Although different positions reflect differential values of particular assets,
the overall pattern favors those lawyers with the traditionally valued mix of
symbolic capital (grades and elite degrees), cultural capital (e.g., comfort in
country clubs and on golf courses), and social capital (here, the networks that
come with elite schooling and positions in elite settings). Put in stark terms,
the narratives that follow are consistent with a version of meritocracy that is
also not inconsistent with the characterization of the American legal profession as raced, gendered, stratified on the basis of social class, and, in general,
snobby.

There are both struggles and remarkable success stories in each setting, however. The interviews show that the legal profession allows upward mobility (if not equal opportunity). We see many individuals who do not find a fit in corporate law firms or whose credentials denied them access to elite careers but who are thriving in their careers and pleased not to be working in large law firms. Many brilliantly invent new kinds of practices and practice settings. Most believe that law school was a good choice, despite also noting that careers in law require more work than they anticipated when they made that selection.

Chapter 6 begins in law firms, where billable hours and various forms of capital organize the anointment of partner material. Chapter 7 examines solo practice, the setting of ordinary practice and long-standing scholarly depreciation, arguing for a reinterpretation on the basis of its own internal divisions. In chapter 8, we look at those pursuing business careers, mainly as in-house counsel. And, in chapter 9, we look at public interest law and careers in government, elucidating the divisions and the relative uniqueness of the elite idealist at the heart of the scholarly literature.

6

Moving Up and Moving On: Careers in Law Firms

As the previous chapters have shown, the corporate hemisphere of the American legal profession and its ideal-typical career has been oriented toward making partner in a private law firm. In the up-or-out hierarchy of the Cravath System, those associates who failed to make partner had few alternate career paths. Some filled respectable but distinctly less esteemed positions as inside counsel to their firms' corporate clients, and a select few, mostly relatives of leading partners, became permanent associates. Despite decades of change, this aspect of the profession proved durable. In 1991, Galanter and Palay documented the persistence of the promotion-to-partnership system, identifying it as the defining feature of the modern law firm, and, in 2008, Galanter and Henderson again confirmed a structure organized around a core of equity partners supported by larger numbers of associates and non–partnership track attorneys. Associates—and now nonequity partners—continued grabbing for the brass ring of partnership, as did the women and people of color newly admitted to what Galanter and Henderson call this "elastic tournament," though they remained at a distinct disadvantage.

By 2000, when the AJD Project cohort entered practice, the labor market was no longer limited to the graduates of elite law schools. Law firms' rapacious demand could be satisfied only by extending recruitment to a larger range of law schools and lawyers. Further, few of the AJD Project cohort in general expected that they would stay with the same firm for their entire career, let alone win—or even compete for—equity partnership. Lawyers' careers had gained a visible level of mobility. Sequence analysis reveals, as we explored in chapter 3, what have become well-worn paths out of large firms into a variety of now respectable and even prestigious positions. By wave 3, roughly half of those who started their careers in large and midsize firms had left. Meanwhile, the upper echelons of partnership remained for the most part bastions of White, elite-educated men (especially those with wives at home).

The vast literature on careers in large law firms reflects the upward bias of scholarship on the legal profession, teasing out patterns of inequality by gender and race in the distributions of partnership and attrition (see Kay et al. 2016; Gorman 2006; Gorman and Kay 2020; and Wilkins and Gulati 1996), in the inheritance of firm clients and in rainmaking (Briscoe and von Nordenflycht 2014), in the career guidance and relative influence of mentors (Kay and Wallace 2009) and patrons (Lazega 2000), and in the quality of assignments (Kay and Gorman 2012), recognition of origination credits (Sterling and Reichman 2016), and embrace of family-friendly work policies (Kay 1997). The continued concentration of elite White men in partnership roles has been explained by the firms themselves, however, as evidence not of inequality but of one of three natural processes: meritocratic measures of who is best able to attract clients, family responsibilities nudging women toward jobs off the partner track, and external opportunities that draw excellent women and minority attorneys out of large firms (often for government positions). Our qualitative interviews, by contrast, show throughout this chapter that layered processes smooth the path to partnership for White men with elite credentials while women and minorities must defy the odds to do the same. Quantitative employment history data presented in chapter 10 support this argument.

Large law firms are highly bureaucratized, with overlapping systems that regularize their hiring. This means that their ranks—especially incoming cohorts—are typically marked by a measure of gender parity and a beyond-symbolic inclusion of ethnic and racial minority lawyers, even if their partnership level stays much more homogeneous. Things are different in the less bureaucratic midsize and small firms, which are more flexible in their hiring in terms of grades and law schools. But that flexibility is also a double-edged sword: these firms are characterized by increased subjectivity and ad hoc decision-making. Less than transparent firm policies amplify the need for individuals to establish good relations with the higher-ups, who, in these smaller settings, have even greater influence over lawyers' careers. In this setting, the reception toward and advancement of women and minorities depends greatly on the power dynamics and attitudes of particular individuals.

A common feature of private law firms is that partners generally are selected to fit into the world of the billable hour tied to the firm's clientele. This feature is especially bureaucratized at the large firms, but it figures in the organization of firms of all sizes, with the major exception of those operating on contingent fees. Associates have billable targets to reach, exceeding targets may lead to bonuses, and how an associate is doing is related generally to hours worked. Firm productivity and profitability come from hours billed. Partners then are chosen because, for example, they have a book of business that will lead to many hours of work throughout the firm and, thus, law firm profits. They might also or instead be seen as the kind of person who will generate business and perhaps also be someone to whom clients will naturally be handed down. Law firms of all sizes feature enduring racial/ethnic inequality (see chap. 10) in terms of access to equity partnership, and part of the mechanism is the long-embedded idea of what a business generator looks and acts like. While White men from top law schools with supportive wives at home may begin in large firms with the presumption that they are partnership material, minorities and women must affirmatively prove that they are. Certain related rules are central to the partnership game: for example, one must demonstrate excellence in accumulating billable hours as an associate, a commitment not every associate can make, including many women in traditional relationships. Our quantitative data show that more hours worked at wave 2 and wave 3 correlated with being partner in both waves. One must be perceived to fit within that community of partners, themselves seen to embody business generation for the firm's clientele. And potential partners must develop mentors and sponsors who facilitate billable hours and who themselves are rainmakers attesting to and committed to helping the chosen future rainmakers.

The interview data and analysis presented in this chapter enrich the existing literature on careers in large law firms by taking up the standpoint of the lawyers navigating these settings and making judgments about whether to stay, where to go, and what kind of career to pursue. The first portion of the chapter is divided into two sections (large law firms and midsize and small firms). Then we attend to salient dimensions that shape lawyers' careers: gendered choices and challenges, spouses, and the impact of sexism on career development. Individuals may move through private law firm settings, yet we have placed their narratives within large-firm and midsize-firm sections by virtue of their career trajectories' centers of gravity. We will take up solo and small-firm attorneys' narratives in the next chapter.

Large Law Firms

To consider contemporary legal careers in large law firms, we organized our findings in line with the persistent orientation of attorneys within them: partnership. We contrast the careers of those in the AJD Project cohort who were

fast-tracked, the women and minorities who defied long odds, and the attorneys who coveted partnership status but did not achieve it even though
they continued to practice in the large-firm setting. As the brass ring in an
ostensibly meritocratic profession, making partner is often regarded as a sort
of apotheosis. But that elevation hinges on perceptions of fit—the existing partners' as well as the aspirant's—as encoded in the *je ne sais quoi* quality of having
the right stuff to attract a given firm's desired clientele.

MAKING PARTNER ON THE FAST TRACK AND
FROM THE OUTSIDE LANE

You may recall James, a sort of ideal-type fast-tracker, from chapter 1. Though
he did not initially set out to join a large law firm, let alone make partner, it
seemed that he had all but stumbled into equity partnership in a major Washington, DC, firm by the time of his wave 2 interview. Tellingly, he and his
wife met as young attorneys working side by side, yet she transitioned into
practicing law in a government setting even before they had children and
had left the workforce to care for their children by wave 3. Still, she hoped
to return, assuming she could secure another position that would prioritize
her husband's demanding schedule as an equity partner in his law firm (especially during trials).

Though James once planned to join the Justice Department's Honors Program after a federal clerkship, a friend's suggestion brought him to the firm,
where he figured he would stay a few years. But, he noted: "Nothing has driven
me away. I mean . . . I wouldn't have told you coming in that this is something
I was looking for, but I've been happy." He easily found mentors and sponsors
who helped him tap into information and networks and "talked . . . about other
things I should be trying to do or what they've heard that's out there in the firm
that I should try or people to work with or avoid working with." Unlike others,
he felt that his firm cared more about building relationships than about generating business, telling us: "While I'm sure no one would look down their nose
at you if you were out there trying to gather business, it's not something that is
stressed." So he seemed relatively unstressed himself.

We asked, in our wave 2 interview, what it took to become a partner. James
cited having a "broad range of skills" and "fit [with] the culture," conceding
that both qualities were "easy to say and . . . harder to identify." From his new
partnership perspective, with the power to anoint up-and-comers, he concluded: "I mean, you're looking for . . . the next generation of people we think
are stars." Not every White man with elite credentials has this experience (or
a spouse willing and able to step out of the workforce to take on the bulk of

parenting), but the example shows how natural, in retrospect, the fast track can appear, especially for those on it. The fit within the traditional law firm hierarchy produces a recognizable, polished, and impressive law firm partner.

The fast track looked slightly different for Raymond. A White engineering professor, Raymond had a successful career before he decided to go to law school. He attended a high-ranked law school, then followed friends' advice and moved to Silicon Valley to practice. There as a tax lawyer his engineering expertise allowed him to become "heavily involved in discussing with taxpayer engineers the underlying facts and the products and the intellectual property." Thus: "I got a chance to really dig into the client's businesses, which clients love." After several years in his first large-firm job, the partners he worked with left, taking "98% of [his] billings" but extending an invitation for him to join them. He did. He stayed. He made nonequity and then equity partner. And, in 2011, 12 years into his career, he moved to *another* large firm.

A father of two with a wife at home, Raymond gave a different explanation when we asked what it took to make partner: "So I had good hours, good client contacts. You have to be, you have to have a certain—I don't want to say *je ne sais quoi*, but it's a partner potential. You have to be seen as somebody who's likely to be able to bring business into a law firm. Is this somebody you . . . [and] other partners . . . would put in front of clients or potential clients?" The third firm in which he worked had provided a larger and slightly better platform, and it reunited him with local partners with whom he had worked in his first firm: "They kept telling me how great . . . [the third firm] was." From his perspective, moving was acceptable because of those relationships: "The unknown, the largest unknown is probably not what you're doing but who you're doing it with or who you're doing it for." Though he worked in more firms than James, Raymond tells another straightforward career story— the fast track that turned welcoming relationships in a first job into invitations to a second, where he made partner, eventually following his relationships into a third firm.

Rufus, another White man with elite law school credentials, expected he'd achieve partnership at his first law firm, but his plans were derailed by the Great Recession. "I guess the vote would have happened at the end of 2009, and . . . I would have made partner at the beginning of 2010," he recalled. Like an eternally disappointed baseball fan, he was told to "wait until next year," only to be offered a counsel position rather than the partnership he anticipated. So he looked for a lateral move, finding a position at another large firm—not "in the same sort of league as the first" but "still a fine firm"—where he already knew and had worked with some of the attorneys. Since they had been headhunted, he said, he "reached out to them" and was able to secure a position "with a guarantee" that he would make equity partner. After achieving that goal, he moved to a top-tier firm, maintaining his status as an equity partner. He was "actually very, very happy" in his second job, but he was lured away by his relationships with individuals working in the third firm. He too has two children and a wife at home. The highway to equity partnership for Rufus was perhaps detoured by the recession, but his network of colleagues and mentors kept him on the fast track.

In the AJD Project cohort of qualitative interviewees, just two women became equity partners in large corporate law firms. Rather than accessing the fast track, they defied the odds by achieving partnership from the outside lane. Juliette, an Asian American woman, was a hard worker with elite credentials. She served as law review editor at her regionally leading, top-50 law school, completed a prestigious clerkship, and began working as an associate in a large law firm. A litigator with considerable trial experience, she was active in diversity efforts and public service, both in her firm and in the profession more broadly. She made partner in the same firm where she began her career.

Juliette recognized frankly that her rise to equity partnership was a statistically rare achievement. She was the only member of her entering class still at the firm and one of just a few partners of color there. And she made partner while working part-time (80%). Though diversity consultants told her all this added up to a "zero" chance of partnership, she found ways to deal with the challenges she faced owing to her gender, race, age, and part-time status: "I feel like I have to work harder than other people to be seen as legitimate. There's a part-time stigma that I've gotten over. I mean, after 11 years. . . . There's a female Asian lawyer stigma, and an age stigma. I don't look like a lawyer, so I have to demonstrate that. . . . [I have to do] advance prep. When I'm going into a meeting, I'm not going to go into a meeting without a speaking role designated in advance. . . . I'm never going to get caught in the situation where I'm at a meeting and I'm not speaking substantively about something." Even as an equity partner, she continued to make deliberate career choices in order to prove her mettle to anyone who might question her qualifications.

When we asked how she defied the odds, Juliette pointed to several things, including her ability to get business without inheriting clients from more senior lawyers in the firm: "Inheritance is just. . . . I *wish* that would happen, but it doesn't really happen. To me, at least, you have to hustle, and work your networks, and be responsive. . . . It's a lot of matter origination." That is, it involves bringing in clients and getting credit for the work done for them even if she did not do the work herself. Juliette also spoke about the importance of not only her sponsors within the firm but also her father, a prominent White lawyer in the same city, in enhancing her credibility, helping to generate local business, and providing crucial guidance: "I mean, that's a huge leg up and a privilege . . . to have somebody like your dad to go to. Because I'm very involved in diversity efforts in the firm, and how our chief diversity officer tries to frame [good mentoring is], 'If your best friend's child came to work at your law firm, what would you say to them to help them?'" Juliette's father was able to provide this direct advice, whether big picture (like investing time in building business), detail oriented ("you need to do your time sheet every day"), or socially useful for climbing the professional ladder ("never cry in front of a partner," something she "needed to hear"). Among her other "legs up," Juliette counted the fact that she, too, had a stay-at-home spouse to help take care of their children and household responsibilities.

It was still a challenge to gain partnership status. On her third, ultimately successful try, Juliette swore it was the last time she was "going to put up." Among the stumbling blocks, she identified the slow post–financial crisis economy, sponsors who were good but not current on the right tactics for advancing in the firm, and the firm's growth and geographic expansion, which changed the standards for making partner over time. When the firm finally recognized her talents, her business generation, and the importance of the diversity she brought to the table, the national leadership embraced her, too. Juliette is now a member of her national firm's governing body.

The second female equity partner in the AJD Project cohort was Constance, the legal ethics specialist whose story appears in chapter 1. Constance's journey to partnership is remarkable. She is a Latina graduate of a tier 3 law school who made partner in a major corporate law firm, and her initial career track was pretty common among talented, hardworking graduates of her law school, though it looked nothing like the start one would choose if gunning for partnership. The key event was serendipitous: working on a case involving legal professional ethics. Her collaboration with an ethics expert from a private firm precipitated a new trajectory into an emerging legal niche and a partnership in the small firm, which in turn led to her partnership in a large firm when hers was acquired. Constance never had to go up for partnership as an associate seeking the approval of partners making their decisions on implicit opinions about who has the right stuff.

SIDETRACKED: FAILING TO MAKE
PARTNER IN A LARGE FIRM

When Pamela, an Asian American woman, graduated from her top-15 law school, she was in high demand—by her count, she had "21 callbacks" for jobs before she passed the bar. She chose to begin her career in the new office of a large, elite law firm, where she had no specific long-term goal beyond "just take it day by day." At her wave 1 interview, she was relatively happy as a litigator working in a branch office of a national firm: "So you get the exposure to the big clients, but you still get a nice family sort of feel." Most of her court experience came through pro bono prosecutions, she reported, which seemed to be consistent with the partnership track. "It . . . takes initiative and . . . a certain amount of ballsiness to go out and spend that much time on pro bono. I think a lot of people may be afraid to not be doing the income-generating work, but I've heard nothing but good things and praise," she said proudly (and notably in terms that fit with the masculine litigation culture of her firm, as we shall see).

By her wave 2 interview, Pamela was a nonequity partner at the same firm, and she was beginning to sense her path toward equity partnership would be far more frustrating than her experience finding her first job. Asked about her place in the organization, she said: "Obviously, I know how to run cases now. . . . I'm fine in court. I do plenty of pro bono cases . . . but to do the type of case that [the firm wants equity partners to bring in] I need to step to the next level and be handling my clients and making the key strategic calls myself." She recalled that she had "tried to bring in about six clients over the last two years." Unfortunately, "the matters were too small" for her firm to take on. An edge crept in as she shared her feeling that all this would be different if she were a White man: "It's not an overt discrimination. In no way do I feel that because I'm Asian I've been discriminated against. . . . [But] there is a bit of a paternalistic attitude toward women. You can either be relegated to the role of being sort of a submissive, little worker bee or, if you're more assertive— and I'm definitely more on the assertive side—I feel that sometimes I scare the guys a bit." While male colleagues were "dropping the F-bomb here and there," Pamela sensed it "scares them a little" if she does the same, even when "it's appropriate." So, too, did her assertive response when a witness was "not doing what I want them to do" or when "I'm expressing extreme displeasure and I say so in a meeting." And she felt shut out of relationships in the firm:

> Male lawyers would say: "I couldn't have my wife do the same things that you do. . . . There's only one person who can wear the pants in the family, and that's got to be me. . . . I couldn't handle it if my wife was doing that." Or even small social things like a partner will say to another partner, "Hey," you know, "We should get together. Why don't you have your wife call my wife?"

Given her descriptions, it was no wonder Pamela sighed: "So you feel like you can't win."

Nor was it a surprise that, at wave 3, Pamela had left the firm. The reason for her departure stood out, in fact, only because she was *asked* to leave the firm. She had joined a case late, after another lawyer failed to get along with the client. "There were several . . . equity partners on the case," she recalled, "and they gave me terrible work. They had me do the document review and document productions." It was the kind of work that, "in the past, on other cases," she'd done because "[she]'d been told [she] had to be a team player." But: "That came back to bite me in my reviews when they said, 'You didn't do enough substantive work.'" Thus, Pamela insisted on being "able to handle a witness or . . . work up some substantive legal part of the case." Reluctantly, the legal team "threw her a bone" and gave her ownership over a part of the case that, through her work, "became a third of the case . . . [and] eventually won us the case." Her integral role in the win did not get the recognition she felt she merited: "And, right after that, they said thank you very much and 'we anticipate that we won't need your services.'" The recession hit, and she received a nice severance package alongside the intimation that she was an insufficiently skilled lawyer.

Pamela looked for other positions, though becoming pregnant "kind of forced [her] hand" and the situation "turned into a mixed blessing," such that she told us: "I've had three and a half years off with my daughter." Without her income, she and her husband had to give up the condo they had just purchased, though his career as a practicing physician supported the family and allowed Pamela to continue volunteering via pro bono prosecution in two separate cities. The volunteer work paid off. She was ultimately able to parlay it into an offer of permanent employment. Since our last interview, she has moved into a prosecutor position in a major city.

Regarding her experience in the firm, Pamela described:

> There's so much backstabbing and maneuvering and hitching your wagon to the right star. . . . You're supposed to be on the same team. . . . But this was more like being on the reality show *Survivor*, where you just have to watch for people stabbing your back and your real enemy is not the opposition but the people on [your] own team.

In the *Survivor*-style, macho man's world of litigation, Pamela never found a comfortable or valued space. The talent and diversity she brought to the job had been highly valued at the outset, and she made it to nonequity partnership, but she was never really in consideration for equity partnership. Where the men on the fast track described being promoted, repeatedly, on the basis of their "business potential," Pamela floundered even though she sought to bring in potential clients. Gender certainly played a role. According to our quantitative data, however, so did being Asian American. Despite being well-represented "success stories" at wave 2, Asian American lawyers are far more likely to leave firms than are White lawyers.

This brings us to Todd, an Asian American man with elite credentials. He received an undergraduate science degree from a prestigious university, graduated from a top-20 law school, and joined one of the country's largest, most lucrative law firms. Interested in intellectual property, he was recruited by a rainmaking partner (reputedly one of the country's top 10 intellectual property lawyers) and made nonequity partner himself within his first five years. Though he was on track to make equity partner by 2010, Todd told us, he had not been promoted by the time of his wave 3 interview, in 2015. With palpable frustration, he explained that his recruiting partner, the source of most of his work, had retired. Worse yet, rather than handing clients off to Todd, "he passed them on to people . . . who were five or six years more senior" than Todd.

After twelve years, Todd moaned that he was stuck "in a service role." He lamented that he had relied on his mentor and believed that, "if you did good work, over time . . . you would have your own clients" and get ushered into equity partnership. When we asked where he would like to be in another five years, he said he wished to have that book of business—a steady and repeat stream of clients—and partnership: "I just don't like the uncertainty or the lack of clarity. Worrying, like, oh, what if, you know, that partner doesn't want to give you work anymore?" Todd never mentioned bias at this megafirm, even though, unlike the three White men we profiled on the fast track, he was never adopted or mentored on the path toward equity partnership. Though he had elite credentials, he did not have a professional network that might have helped him sustain clients after his recruiter's retirement or find a new position where he had a better chance of getting ahead. Considering this, we find it notable that Todd's prepartnership departure from a megafirm fits with a statistical pattern observed in our data and many other studies: Asian American lawyers have the highest attrition rates from law firms.

According to his LinkedIn profile, Todd left the firm after 15 years. He never made equity partner. He went on to work as a consultant, as counsel in another law firm, and as inside counsel (now senior university counsel) in a large university health care system.

An Arab American lawyer in an elite law firm, Amir, like Pamela, is representative of both the welcome extended to new attorneys who bring diversity into large law firms and the subsequent discomfort that attends minority status in this professional setting. A first-generation American, Amir graduated from a top-15 law school and started his career in an elite corporate firm in Chicago. In our first interview, when we asked about relationships with his fellow associates, he already saw himself as separate from his peer cohort at the firm: "I don't hang out with them as much, I'm married, have a baby. I'm a religious guy, so I don't play poker, and I don't drink. But we do get together sometimes." We circled back to these relationships when discussing whether his ties to the Middle East might conceivably help build his client base—an idea he dismissed, noting only that "clients sometimes get a kick out of" his Middle Eastern roots and that it could become fodder for jokes when he worked closely with a Jewish associate: "The client might say, 'Come on guys, you're working on this agreement; why don't you figure out the Palestinian struggle?'"

The uncomfortable humor took on a new edge for Amir after 9/11. Still very early in his career he felt a shift in how he was perceived. His ethnic background became more salient, and others seemed to think he could or should speak for all Arab Americans: "You have a senior associate or partner who comes to you and says, 'Why are they doing these suicide bombings?' And they want to understand. In a way, I *can* explain it in a little bit better way than they're getting in the media. But do you want to even start talking about the plight of Palestinians when somebody's very emotional?" In this interview, Amir was still relatively enthusiastic about the law firm, his chances of making partner, and the options that would open to him later in his career, "sticking it out . . . and being involved in the Chicago community": "I would love to maybe someday be asked into the Chicago Council of Foreign Affairs or Chicago Economic Club or any of these other . . . general institutions of the city that make Chicago so great."

All that had evaporated by our wave 2 interview with Amir. He had left the firm, he explained, having endured the practice-group leadership of a lawyer who was "very obnoxious . . . hardheaded": "And the more I was working in the group, the more I had to interact with him, the less buffer I had with either senior associates or junior partners, and that experience was like a hazing." Further, the demanding schedule of the large law firm kept him so busy he could not see a way to build a practice that tightened his connections with the city's Arab American community: "My sense of separation from community work and activism was growing because I simply had no time." He reported that, at first, he had switched to a midsize firm. When he still felt out of place, his confidence took a hit. He suffered from clinical depression and left this firm, too, in order to become involved in politics. Now he was starting his own small law firm focused on health care and his ethnic community:

A huge chunk of Muslim Americans are in the healthcare sphere. Either they're physicians or they're entrepreneurs within the healthcare field. Many of them are also very entrepreneurial. . . . They want to start something new, etc., and they don't want to pay $600 [per hour]. Growing up in [that community], you have an appreciation. . . . I can build off my own natural clients. Yes, they're not heads of banks. They're running individual [practices and groups], but it's enough to make a living, so that's what I'm doing.

Where Amir once saw little chance that his Arab connections would be an asset in terms of his legal career, he had, by the third interview, learned the value of his contacts within the specifically Arab American medical community. His wife was a physician, with her own connections and the ability to support their household with three children as Amir grew his firm. His new clientele and expertise gave him new capital in the legal field, making him attractive in a new way as potential partnership material. By 2017, it seemed that he had acquired the right stuff: he was an equity partner in a prominent regional firm, focusing on corporate law and the health care industry. He changed firms again in 2018, bringing his specialized practice profile to another regional law firm.

Recall the story of Lynden, the African American lawyer we met in chapter 1. Although he tried hard to succeed, he never found his way to real consideration as a large-firm partner. Nonetheless, his stint in a large law firm may well have facilitated his move to a responsible position in a federal regulatory agency and, after that, to private industry as inside counsel.

Our final example of a large-firm starter who got sidetracked in the partnership tournament is Wendy. An Asian American lawyer from a middle-class background, Wendy graduated from a select private college and a top-30 law school and began her career in one of DC's top regulatory law firms. At wave 1, she told us it had taken her a while to feel comfortable in the position but that she "turned a corner" in her second year: "By then I'd worked with enough people to know . . . the partners, and I'd go back to them for projects when I didn't have work. . . . That's kind of where I developed a relationship with the partners in the communications group." In that first stretch at the firm, she also got married, had a child, and moved to working part-time. Her husband, a lawyer for the federal government, had been home on parental leave with their baby for four and a half months at the time of the interview, leaving room for Wendy to "come back and at least try for partnership" after her maternity leave. She was, she explained, planning to attend "a fifth-year training coming up": "And that tells you, 'OK, this is what you need to start doing . . . if you're going to be on partnership track.'"

Wendy was returning from her second maternity leave at the time of the second interview, and she thought she had lost momentum in the partnership tournament: "It has been eight years; most firms have an eight-year track. . . . I've been held back a year . . . well, they say 'due to the [partner-heavy] structure of my department' . . . but also because . . . I've taken leave and I've been reduced schedule. . . . So I'm . . . on a slower track generally." Her reduced schedule was roughly 85% time, with roughly 1,600 billable hours as an annual target, and she generally liked the work even though her closest contacts at the firm had moved on ("I don't really know anyone anymore," she said, adding that she did not have time to make new work friends): "Overall . . . I think I'm in a place where I like the work that I'm doing, I like the people I work for, and it works for my family. So it's hard to disrupt that." She would be happy to go back to 100% time, though she figured the expectation would then shift to "120%." Thus she said plainly: "I try to get my work done and get out of here when I can." At her last employee review, she had been told that she was "on track" to make "of counsel," not partnership.

Indeed, Wendy was "of counsel" at the same firm at wave 3. Basically content, she billed 1,900 hours per year at a minimum, though she would need to start generating new business if she hoped to get promoted further. As "of counsel," she worked directly with long-term clients of the firm (for which she "certainly wouldn't get origination" credit) rather than bringing in new business. Effectively, she landed in a well-paid position at a large, elite law firm, one akin to a government agency position, in which her experience and credentials are valued, but her career shifted to one with relatively low expectations. She was outside the reward structure available to equity partners. A statement from her wave 2 interview seemed to hold: "I try to do a good job here, but you know I'm not going to take more time away from my family to try to aim for [partnership]. . . . I've . . . come to that realization a few years ago, and I'm fine with [it]."

These accounts are representative of our sample of large-firm partnership experiences, though patterned data is not without its outliers. We are sure that, in the contemporary American legal profession's large law firms, there are White male attorneys with elite credentials and wives at home who try and fail to make partner and that there are minority women with nonelite credentials who sail through to equity partnership. But the patterns we see demonstrate that credentials, gender, ethnicity, race, and class are all implicated in the particular meaning of the partnership track in this practice setting. The AJD Project individuals who missed the so-called brass ring were all open to equity partnership, yet their attempts to achieve it looked very different from the fast-tracked, White men's career paths as well as the paths of those with different backgrounds and identities who managed to defy the odds and make partner. The saving grace may be that the sting of not making partner was mitigated, for all these lawyers, by their ability to go on to secure, still-lucrative positions, even making successful legal practice setting transitions facilitated by their years of experience in the large firms.

Midsize and Small Law Firms

The issues we have seen are not unique to large law firms. Fit, in fact, can be magnified as a determining factor in career opportunities in smaller, less bureaucratized practice settings where the leading partners typically set the tone and evaluations and promotions are far more subjective and less transparent. Alicia, whom we met in chapter 1, for example, did everything to become a partner in a midsize firm in a major legal market. She even took over, on short notice, the entire portfolios of a partner and another lawyer who suddenly left the firm. But her partnership vote fell short, and she heard that a partner had commented that she was "not pretty enough" (suggesting that women needed to have a certain look to generate business as a partner). Despite other partners' predictions, the promotion was not approved the following year either. Alicia ultimately moved to an in-house position.

As with the previous sections, our narratives on midsize and small firms "follow the money," looking to the perception that a given lawyer has the potential to generate significant clientele or income for his or her firm—that he or she has the right stuff to deserve equity partnership. Here, however, we key in on the ways in which the business generation imperative is interpreted by attorneys working to find a niche and advance within their firm. Perception remains important, while these accounts also demonstrate the politics and implicit biases involved in assigning or claiming credit for business generation.

NAVIGATING SUCCESS IN A MIDSIZE FIRM

Max's career narrative lays bare some of the constraints and opportunities of working in a midsize law firm. His parents were middle-class, and he graduated from a local undergraduate college. He went to law school—one ranked around 50—aspiring to become a sports lawyer. Indeed, he interned over the summer for a professional sports team and hoped he could go work for it after graduating from law school. Unable to realize that ambition, he became an associate in a midsize firm that had a sports law group. But the group was too small to provide him with an opportunity to do sports law. Instead, he shifted to litigation and specifically to a niche products liability practice. Thus, in

2005, at our wave 1 interview, he was married to a practicing nurse, owned a home, and had paid off his student loans (he had accomplished that in his first six months at the firm). He was very active in his church, doing work he considered pro bono (though it did not come with formal credit at his firm).

Max was doing well, though he admitted he still wished he had gotten a position with the professional sports team with which he had interned and continued to approach the sports franchise about employment opportunities. Denied the opportunity he was passionate about, he settled for a comfortable career path within his firm. He thought his firm paid a bit below the going rate, a reasonable trade-off, perhaps, for the fact that, in five years, he had worked only about four weekends. Plus, he had a mentor to guide him on the partner track (said to be about seven years, though the exact timing was "rather vague"): "I think my partner takes pretty good care of me, making sure that I am meeting my billable quota and at the same time giving me the opportunity . . . to do the depositions, to do court hearings, to do the experts." His mentor recommended activities to bolster Max's partner profile, such as "becoming involved with the Defense Research Institute . . . making contacts." This partner was also "big on firm citizenship": "So for your nonbillable work you're going to their softball games, you're going to all the summer associate events, making the firm your family type of mentality."

Max stated the problem candidly: "I just don't know if I'm necessarily groomed to be what he'd like me to be." It seemed to him that the partners "only socialize with their own partners," who become "their core group of friends": "[They] hold functions on the weekend. Some of them are mandatory attendance." He continued: "It really becomes a lifestyle, which, as I look at it, maybe I don't want that to become my lifestyle long term." Max's mentor was pushing him toward partnership in ways he knew were not available to everyone in his cohort: "Those who don't really have an anchor in the firm, some place or another, a person they can trust, they uniformly have trouble." When this partner left the firm in a lateral move, he invited Max to come, too, and his sponsorship continued in the new setting, despite Max's doubts about his career path.

At wave 2, Max was "senior counsel" in the new firm. He had two children, and his wife now stayed home to care for them. They had purchased a larger house, using the first as a source of rental income. Max had not had a case go to trial, and the recession had affected his firm, but he was active with motions, discovery, and settlement conferences and had not yet taken a salary cut. He had no trouble working the requisite hours while also taking four weeks of vacation a year, keeping up with his church activities, and rarely working weekends. The more business he did for this one partner, the more business he got. We asked how he felt about his job, and he ticked off the benefits: it met his financial needs, provided a fairly good work/life balance, and was anchored in a mentorship relationship with "the same guy for about eight years." He still hesitated when it came to discussing his future, telling us: "I don't know if I can do this long term, let alone . . . *want* to do this long term." He then backed away, acknowledging: "Even if I were to switch jobs, even if I were to look, obviously, in the law community, I don't think it gets much better because you become a low man on the totem pole, . . . and then you lose the benefits that are acquired from a long-term relationship." Musing about alternative jobs, he mentioned teaching law, joining an international justice mission, or joining a nonprofit providing legal services to low-income individuals, but he did not want to move geographically. At wave 3, he was still working for the same law firm. By this time a father of four, he had been promoted to equity partner.

At his firm, Max explained, the financial calculus involved distinguishing between origination credits and billing credits. He became partner through billing credit, for which "there is no magic number, no magic formula, . . . [but] an expectation that you can keep yourself sufficiently employed as well as keeping at least one other person sufficiently employed here at the firm." His main billings had stemmed from one client, for whom Max and his mentor became the national discovery counsel in 2009. That led to his 2010 promotion to income partner and his 2012 promotion to equity partner. He expressed gratitude because the client relationship provided "a steady source of business, a steady source of revenue to have next to your name." On the other hand, it was repetitive, and he felt "pigeonholed."

"The equity partnership, you've got different levels," Max reported, "and so in order to hold your position there you've got to still keep those numbers pretty much the same next to your name. . . . As a result then you become very narrowly tailored into that area." He called himself a "cog in the wheel," telling us he remained at the firm because "you do what you need to do in order to make the money to get through life and so you don't always get your first choice." He added: "But, at the same time, if I have to practice law, this is a great place to do it." What he meant was that he was still able to be active with his church and local organizations. In fact, when he finally left the firm in 2017, it was to become a full-time pastor for a community church. As of this writing, his bar license is inactive.

Max was a well-regarded lawyer who made partner yet never found a place in the profession that fit his dreams and ambitions. He was successful in a way that seems specially to fit a midsize firm, moving ahead almost as seamlessly as some of the fast-tracked large-firm starters while remaining ever-so-slightly uncomfortable in the partners' closed social world. The salary helped his family thrive, and the job left leeway for community involvement, the pull of which would eventually help him, after 16 years, make good on his desire better to align his values with his work.

Samir was a first-generation South Asian American with a Catholic mother and a Methodist father who immigrated for their own education opportunities. A standout tennis player, he attended a leading Roman Catholic undergraduate college, did a one-year fellowship abroad, and returned to the city where he grew up to attend a major state law school. When he earned his JD and accepted his first position at a small law firm, he was carrying $100,000 in education debt (most of it would be paid off by the time we met). Six months later, he was recruited by a larger defense litigation firm whose lawyers he had impressed in court. At the time, the firm had several offices and around 70 lawyers, but, when we had our first interview, it had expanded to 200 attorneys (50 of them in Samir's office alone). Samir was 13 years into his career, billing roughly 2,000 hours (as required), and had made nonequity partner.

What, we asked Samir, would it take for him to move into equity partnership? He did not know: "Even when I've asked, nobody's been able to explain it. It just kind of happens." It could not, he felt, be based on business generation and billing alone: "I've actually brought in more receivables than some people who have been recently made equity partners, so there's other factors. It probably has a lot to do with political clout. It also has to do with who's in with the in-group." Despite feeling that he had good mentors as well as good billing, he had not yet gotten the partnership nod.

Samir focused his strategy on building networking capacity. He remained an avid tennis player and worked with nonprofit tennis groups, he was heavily involved with his undergraduate institution and got client referrals via his fellow alums, and he was active in his church. His was one of the clearest accounts in our data of a skilled networker's modus operandi:

> And sometimes the line between personal and professional blurs, whether it's tennis or, you know. . . . I've talked business with people at church, etc., but I've gone to those things that I like. Like the work that I do for the basilica, which is my church, I do about 100–150 hours of pro bono activity work for them a year, and so that's my pro bono client. Nobody bats an eye at it because it *is* the biggest parish in the state.

Then there was Samir's active participation in bar associations and informal mentoring. He figured he was involved in five or six different breakfast and lunch groups, finding that his attendance inevitably resulted in building new business and connections. "My worlds cross," he commented. "I'm a hybrid. . . . I always look at my contact sheet and what I have on Outlook . . . I think, 7,500 contacts."

As his firm's hiring partner, Samir advocated strongly for diversity: "I hold no bones about it that I'm predominately looking for diverse attorneys. It's tough to say that, but it's exactly what we need to do." The firm had a "mixed" record on diversity, he noted: "For coming up through the ranks as a diverse attorney, I'm probably . . . I'm the rarity." In his office, only two of the partners were people of color, and none were among the senior associates in the pipeline.

Samir's comfort, 13 years into his career, was evident. He was engaged to be married and said that, in five years' time, he expected either to be at the firm as an equity partner or to be working as an associate general counsel. It appeared he knew that his knack for business generation and his active embrace of the firm's diversity efforts would, at some point, result in an invitation to equity partnership, and it did. According to our follow-up web searches, he is now comanaging partner of the firm and chairs its diversity and inclusion committee. He is an adjunct professor at his alma mater. He is a husband and a father. His promotion delayed for "political" reasons, he is now a "partner with power."

We interviewed Skylar, a White women, only once, at wave 3. Her story is one of remarkable personal agency, of strategizing and researching and striving to carve out a successful career in a legal setting designed by and for White men. Skylar did not know any lawyers, nor did she particularly feel called to the profession; she told us she went to law school because her schoolteacher parents pushed it and she did not want to "end up" working at a factory near her rural hometown. So, after earning an undergraduate degree at a state college, then teaching English abroad for a year, she was offered a scholarship to a top-50 law school in the Mideast.

Skylar hated law school. She enrolled in a number of clinics, hoping to discover her passion for a practice area. After spending time in criminal prosecution, plaintiffs' personal injury practice, and environmental law, still nothing inspired her. After ending her engagement, she decided to approach the question of her legal future systematically, cold-calling a purposely selected sample of local lawyers and asking them to talk about how they felt about their jobs. Only intellectual property lawyers, she reported, were consistently happy in their practices. To follow their lead, she figured, would require a degree in biology, so she temporarily returned to her home state, living with her parents as she dug in. Three semesters and a summer term later, she was ready.

The legwork paid off, and a small patent boutique invited Skylar to join as its seventeenth attorney in January 2001. She quickly passed the patent bar and became a substantial originator of business. Though a partner was dismissive toward what he thought would be a small niche of a local company's intellectual property business, which he therefore did not take up personally, Skylar picked it up and ran. She built up that relationship, and it became a key to her success. She was voted into partnership in 2007.

"I've worked really hard, and I've fought creatively and pushed myself and also have had some stunningly [good] luck, stunningly amazing opportunities," Skylar recalled. But she also talked about enduring constant sexism. "The guys" would say, for example, that "women can't be good patent lawyers" because they did not grow up working on cars. She noticed that, in the office, her male colleagues were addressed as "Mister" and that she was called "Skylar," so "everyone would assume that [she] was there to get the coffee." Having grown up in the rural West, she explained, she "kind of expect[ed] this shit." The workplace environment "was just like playing with boys back home": "When you hung out with the boys [as a girl], you couldn't whine about anything, you had to keep up no matter what, you know?" When she called out the sexism, "they just put [her] in the tomboy category or something," she said with bemusement, pointing out that even media articles about her in those years always mentioned that she was tough, raced motorcycles, and had been on the judo team in college. Perhaps demonstrating a much deeper toughness, Skylar had at this point become a mother to two children, one of whom had a medical condition that required special treatment, and Skylar fought to change the state's policies regarding medical coverage so that her son could get it. (She continues to work pro bono on similar cases.)

Skylar left her first firm after 11 years. She thought that the partners were too conservative, unwilling to take risks, and that the firm was poorly managed. From several options, she chose to take her substantial book of business to one of the city's larger firms. She did not start as an equity partner, though she had a chance to build up a patent practice department from scratch. Again, she did her homework, reaching out to her already "decent network" to learn what people in the tech industry, including her husband, looked for in a patent attorney. The responses were unanimous: they "weren't getting help figuring out how to write a patent strategy that would be supportive of their business goals." Proactive Skylar and those working with her ably filled that niche, but she did not thrive at the firm: "I wasn't in charge of anything officially; I didn't have any rank." There were also "cultural problems." "Not only were [colleagues] unwilling to back me up, but . . . there were no consequences attached to blowing me off," she remembered. When the firm cut down its support for her business generation efforts, she hired a headhunter.

In 2014, Skylar moved to a large firm with multiple offices and a strong intellectual property practice. When we interviewed her in 2016, she had just made equity partner and was leading the firm's tech industry group. All but two of her clients came with her in the move, and she said she had been able to put together a terrific team and handle a range of matters for her clients (from licensing, patent prosecution, and immigration issues to trade secrets). The new job was not without its downsides: though there were female partners, there were fewer female associates in the partnership pipeline than she would have liked to see, and it seemed that the firm had a tough time hiring minorities. Her male colleagues seemed more often to hand off their clients to lawyers more like themselves than to her. But leadership was responsive, and she was relatively content.

"I love being a lawyer, I love my career," Skylar said, and she and her husband had gradually figured out a balance that allowed them to juggle full-time careers and family, an evolving process. The sharing of household chores had "been really good," but "it hasn't gotten good by osmosis." In other words, it was another area in which she had approached a problem, gathered data, and figured out the best path forward. An involved parent and a busy lawyer, she reported that she always dropped the kids off in the morning and picked them up at 5:00 P.M., even though she sometimes had to work evenings. Clients had her cell phone number: "Nobody doubts my commitment. So I get a lot more latitude than a lot of people do. I leave to go to school events, and this week [my daughter] just finished kindergarten, and then her like marathon of freaking camps, and so I just wanted to have a week off [to be with her]."

Mitchell's career was very local. The son of a minister, Mitchell graduated from a liberal arts college in 1985, got an Ivy League MA in international affairs, taught political science at his undergraduate alma mater for two years, and began a PhD at a state university, all before dropping out to pursue his interest in the applied politics of land use by attending a local private law school on a full scholarship. "I loved law school," he enthused. And he was proud that he had no law school debt: "I tell [prospective law students] . . . they should really think about where they want to practice. If they want to practice [in this city], then I don't think it really matters whether they go to [a public university law school] or to private law schools." The latter, he said from experience, might not have high rankings, but they still come with "great networks" and they're all "respected in the community."

After earning his JD summa cum laude, Mitchell got a one-year clerkship with the state supreme court, then joined the state attorney general's office. He briefly pursued a city council bid, then was hired back by the attorney general's office when he lost the election. At that point, he "was assigned to transportation, which was perfect . . . because that's where the land use happens at a state level": "It's for the Department of Transportation, and so that's really when I started doing eminent domain work, which is the bread and butter of what I do now." Five years in the attorney general's office paved the way for a move to a large law firm in 2007, and he was promoted directly to equity partner in 2010.

In Mitchell's experience, the firm did not require an aspiring partner to develop a specific book of business: "You really just have to demonstrate that you can. . . . And then, of course, you have to demonstrate that you can do the work, and bill the hours, and that you've got the competence to become a shareholder." But Mitchell remained unsure about the specifics of what constitutes the right stuff for promotion: "And then I think, really . . . I can't really point to anything specifically, but I think, also, there's a factor that what you're doing fits with the economic model for the firm, because there are some people who don't get shareholder, not because they haven't met all the requirements, but the firm doesn't see them fitting into . . ." And, with that, he trailed off. In terms of his own promotion, he returned to the significant support (and business) of a senior partner who was "very important in helping [him] navigate firm politics and . . . a big supporter . . . when it came to [his] election to shareholder status."

When asked whether he would get clients when this mentor retired, Mitchell again seemed unsure: "The thing is . . . in one sense maybe I will, because if there is a firm client who has an eminent domain issue or a property tax issue, the call is to [him]. . . . But when you do this work, you don't have . . . a lot of repeat business. . . . So I'm not going to inherit a book from [him]." He was "expected to bill" 1,700–1,850 hours a year, yet he totaled more like 2,200 and felt pressure to work at least one day each weekend: "I think probably this is true. One of my partners said, 'You can work as a lawyer five days a week, but if you want to practice, it's six days a week.'" Taking a vacation was acceptable, he thought, though more than a week was probably unworkable: "I like what I do, but I feel like I do need to get away, too. I'm now at the point where I'm, sort of, cultivating and maintaining clients and so forth. I really feel compelled to get out the phone and see if I've got emails and respond to emails, and even if you're just doing it a little bit while you're on vacation, still, it's a constant reminder."

Married to a computer programmer (who had primarily been a stay-at-home mother to their son, an adult by the time of our interview), Mitchell was active in the bar association and served as chair of the eminent domain section of his county bar. He no longer aspired to run for public office, though he remained interested and involved in politics. Responding to our prompt about where he saw himself in five years, he speculated that he would stay put while his son was in college but then consider moving. He might, he said, "start [his] own shop." In our follow-up searches, after the AJD study's interviews closed, we found a news article in which Mitchell was named chair of the board of a progressive nonprofit organization working on local and state government issues and also the news that he had joined a small firm in his city as a partner in 2016.

Katrina, another midsize-firm starter, never made partner even though she, too, worked hard, made carefully researched decisions, and "loved the work." Her parents were middle-class and well educated, and, with her grandfather's support, she was able to earn her undergraduate degree and JD without any debt. Because there were no lawyers in her family and she had no immediate network, she chose to work as a paralegal for a plaintiffs' firm before attending law school. She gained considerable responsibility, working there even during law school and as an associate once she graduated. When her boyfriend got a job abroad, she went with him and worked remotely but realized that she was not interested in returning to the firm as an associate: "It was a wonderful, wonderful experience. I worked myself to the bone. I mean, they were demanding and exacting, and we had really interesting cases and high damage catastrophic personal injury type cases and a lot of consolidated actions and class actions, so it was complex litigation, and it was very involved," she remembered. Going abroad had not, however, offered the break she needed, and she left the firm after seven years' service.

Next, Katrina was hired as a litigation associate in another midsize firm in the same legal market. Starting in 2003, she worked in a group specializing in the representation of public bodies. But, because public clients preferred to work with the most senior attorneys, she gained only limited trial experience (and never as the first chair in a significant case). The billing for this practice was also inherently conservative—in industry terms, it was a low-profit practice group—so, when its managing partner left to join the judiciary, the firm cut the practice. Katrina and another associate were let go in 2012. She was married and, unbeknownst to her in that moment, pregnant.

Katrina reflected on her experience as a nine-year associate as if trying to figure out why, rather than becoming a partner, she had been so disposable:

> I used to mentor associates there, and I was always a better advocate for them than I was for myself, but I didn't do myself a service there because I never said, "I want partner, how do I get there? Help me get there, make it happen for me." . . . On the other hand, I don't think that there was a good system that

said, "We want you to get there," you know? . . . [No one] advocated for me in that respect. . . . It actually is a travesty because my boss—I mean, I love her to this day, and I keep in touch with her— . . . if anyone was going to do it, it was going to be her. . . . If I look at myself objectively, I did everything right, and I was a huge asset to them, except in the billing department.

She noted that she constantly marked down her billing time, which in retrospect was a mistake because she reduced her recorded billing time. Her frustration was evident: "I kept the clients, and I kept them happy, very much so, and always kept them coming back for more and actually asking for me to work on specific things." Still, she never managed to get serious attention as a potential partner.

Realizing she was not cut out to be a stay-at-home parent, Katrina returned to practice in an offshoot of her second firm, helmed by people she "respected," that she "held in high esteem," the ones that "mentored [her] at the second firm." Then, after five years as of counsel at that small firm, she changed legal practice settings, moving into the state judicial system.

Gendered Choices and Challenges

We have already seen that gender has a pervasive impact on legal careers, one built into the structure of the legal profession. When women leave law firms, the firm narrative is typically that they left for "lifestyle" reasons. In fact, the "choices" made by women are structured by law firm stereotypes and stereotyped expectations, such as the assumption that men are natural rainmakers and women are not. Patriarchy indeed is pervasive in lawyers' careers. The following sections focus on the impact of patriarchy in the lives of female lawyers in the midsize and small-firm contexts.

CHILDREN AND TRADITIONAL GENDER ROLES

"Somebody's gotta pay attention," Audrey said, as she spoke about how being a parent affected her career choices and trajectory. Fresh from an elite law school, she began her career at a prestigious law firm in a major city on the West Coast and thrived on the long hours in her litigation practice. Pointing out that "big firms get a bad rap for not being . . . supportive environments," she said that she found the opposite: "I worked on a lot of . . . very complex pieces of litigation. . . . I thought it was a great place to work. I worked with really good mentors, who were really kind, and I got a lot of great standup [speaking roles in litigation practice] and good experience. But I worked all the time. I mean, *all* the time." Then:

> I got pregnant with our first child, and . . . I just felt like I couldn't go on there. . . . I was pregnant, and I had these trials lined up in front of me, and I knew that I could ask for help, but . . . the people that I had seen go off track . . . I . . . didn't see them thriving there. . . . So I quit suddenly. . . . I gave them two months' notice, and I finished my work. . . . I didn't take my maternity leave; I left all the benefits behind me.

After a year out of the labor market, Audrey considered going into government or legal aid work, but she and her husband instead decided to move to a regional market in the Midwest, near their hometowns. There, with her elite firm experience, she could essentially pick where she wanted to work. She "had really specific criteria": "I wanted to be at a place that I thought promoted women, had more flexibility, had a lower billable hour target. . . . I mean, I interviewed with a bunch of firms, but I was really only seriously considering a couple." She became very successful as head of litigation, helped reshape firm practices regarding maternity leave, and made partner. She also crafted a work schedule that worked for her family. Her husband, whose job was less flexible but more predictable, drove their three kids to and from school and made dinners, while she worked nine to five (plus extra hours in the evenings, after putting the children to bed). And still: "Every day I'm on the verge of quitting my job, to be honest. . . . It seems like it should get easier as your kids get older, but it gets harder, and we've . . . hit that moment in my life. . . . I've got kids in a lot of activities and just kids who [are] . . . developing into people, and they've got stuff going on, and somebody's gotta pay attention. And we've sort of been struggling with what to do about that." Indeed, in our follow-up searches, Audrey had made a major change: She relinquished her partnership status, became of counsel to the firm, and took on the position of public interest counsel. Effectively, she redefined her professional role (in which she was thriving) and gave up a hard-earned achievement to participate more in her children's lives.

Marcia was a graduate of a midwestern state law school and worked in litigation for a midsize firm in a major market. She was married to a graduate of the same school (he worked in an elite firm) and knew when she was hired that they planned to have children. Thus, she was "vocal" about creating family-friendly reduced-hour policies and joined a committee with one of the partners: "We basically drafted an . . . arrangement that, ultimately, I was not happy with, but it was better than nothing." New parents would be able to reduce their billable hour targets by 20% for two years after welcoming a child.

In 2006, Marcia had a son. She planned to take three months off but needed extra time after experiencing postpartum complications. When she returned to the office, she requested a 60% schedule so that she might stay home two days a week, but the firm held firm to its 80% rule for those on the partner track: "I was the first person ever to use the policy, the policy that I knew was going to do this to me, and they said, 'You go 60%, then you stall in partnership.'" Reluctantly, she agreed. At the time of her next review, she had been working without a secretary, and her "files were a mess." She was doing the work, she said, and the clients loved her, but the partners "lit out" at her in her review. One of the partners criticizing her was a woman who had earlier said to her: "Either you're a mother, or you're a lawyer. What's your priority?" A new parent, Marcia had already billed 250 hours over her requirement for the period, and she was working five days a week. The firm would not put a lock on her office door, yet she was pumping milk at work. It was miserable. When the reviewers told her, "You need to spend more time on your filing," Marcia decided she had had enough.

"What is it to be a partner in a firm and be miserable and hate your life and have your kids prefer the nanny?" Marcia noted. She approached a supportive partner, who had spoken against her negative review, to see whether she could do contract work for him: "I wrote up the proposal; he pitched it. [The firm's partners] were very, very unhappy. . . . They really had hoped that I would come back onboard and go toward partnership." It seemed that Marcia had the qualities her firm valued in a litigator but that its leadership was unwilling to support her effort to achieve partnership part-time, on her terms. Leaving felt like it was a death knell for her career—and Marcia called it the "best move [she] ever made." Traditional gender roles and a hidebound law firm turned a promising potential partner into a dead-end contract lawyer.

Tara too stepped out of her profession owing to gendered roles within her family. She had grown up in the West with successful, professional parents and was so taken with moot court in high school that she knew she intended to go to law school. After her undergraduate time at a state university, she took some time to see where she might like to live. She waited tables, she sold ads for a journal, and eventually she married a man from her hometown. The couple returned home so that she could attend a local law school, with her marketing professional husband and her mother helping her pay tuition. Happily, she had just $30,000 in loans to pay off after earning her JD, and she secured a job with the leading midsize firm where she summered. Having begun law school "thinking [she] would do public service or something," she excelled in corporate law and began her career in the private sphere. Her path would be winding.

For a year and a half, Tara was a full-time associate, and then she went to 80% time. Once her first child was born, she reevaluated and realized she had lost interest in a partnership: "You know, when I looked at other women who were partners . . . the ones that did have kids just seemed like their lives were so chaotic." She had another child, and her work goal became just getting sufficient billable hours. Estate planning work—"substantively . . . not my first choice"—was at least flexible, so she gradually increased her workload as a contract lawyer, leaving the associate track. That path closed when the economy declined and the firm sent the limited estate work to a staff associate instead. Tara moved to another midsize firm, staying three years before she became frustrated with one of the partners. Looking back, she commented: "At that point, I was really questioning whether I wanted to practice law [or parent full-time]. So, I did that for a year, and decided I do not want to be a stay-at-home mom. I just felt bored. I didn't feel intellectually challenged." She considered her options and returned to work as a contract lawyer, then jumped at an opportunity at a small law firm.

Tara noted: "I was contemplating getting a divorce, so I thought, 'Well, I need to start worrying about money.'" Hired as a 50% time associate, she was offered more money: "And it's gone from 50% to 80%, with the idea that I will be going to full time." Her divorce was moving forward, and her career was looking up. The small firm turned out to be a much better fit. Once she got past what she called "a huge culture shock" ("I honestly really questioned my choice"), she realized that she had found large-firm work "kind of oppressive." By contrast, she told us: "I enjoy it much more working at a smaller firm . . . not so much pressure on billable hours." Though "there was zero training" and "no policies and procedures," she found the atmosphere "autonomous" but "collegial" and said: "I'm probably in the best spot of my career in a long time ever just because I feel like I'm back on track . . . and viable." A partnership was back on the table as Tara talked about where she saw herself in five years: "This is really the first firm where I thought, Oh, being a partner actually looks appealing."

Tara's career was shaped by gendered choices and family roles. She even picked her specialty in trusts and estates on that basis. At one point, she practically halted her career. As circumstances changed—her children aged, and she got a divorce—so did her viable career options. When last we checked, she was the sole female partner, presumably nonequity, and one of three women working at her 20-person firm.

SPOUSES

We met Piper, a staff attorney at the DC circuit court's legal division, at her wave 1 interview, where she ran down her background information. She was a solidly middle-class, midwestern kid who went from an elite undergraduate college to an elite law school (her father had trained as a lawyer but did not practice). Her mother used a recent inheritance to cover Piper's education debt. Though she started her career at the white-shoe New York firm where she summered, Piper lasted only six months in corporate law because it did not involve close reading of statutes, regulations, and cases, which was "why [she] went to law school." Deciding to shift to environmental law, which her firm did not handle, she moved to an elite national firm's DC office. "It was a pretty good experience actually. . . . They gave me a lot of responsibility, the hours were pretty good for what it was, and so I was pretty happy for about five years." But the firm did not clearly communicate to her that they saw her becoming a partner. And she could plainly see how a female partner with nonelite credentials was treated: "almost like she was a glorified administrator of the practice group." Although it was a close decision, she moved to an appellate court staff position at the DC circuit, which appealed to her given her interest in appellate cases.

At wave 2, Piper was a newlywed and had elected to move to a regional southern city because that is where her husband, laid off in the Great Recession, secured an in-house position. At wave 3, the family had two children, and Piper was working in a law firm with about 140 lawyers. She landed there almost by chance when the upstairs neighbor in the new city made the connection. He was the firm's former head and brought her in for an interview: "This law firm does a lot of energy work in oil and gas, and I had done a lot of regulatory and environmental work. . . . It's been a really good fit." The firm also agreed to Piper's request for a part-time position. On its end, Piper acknowledged, the firm found her attractive because of the schools she had attended and the prestigious firm in which she had worked in DC. The firm's partners tended to mention the latter whenever she was introduced to clients.

Assessing her position, Piper said: "In some ways, I think this is the most intellectually stimulating job I've had." She added: "It's just hardcore regulatory, which I've always liked, like reading the regulations, going back to the regulatory history." It was very "academic." Plus, while she noted hints that some partners were sexist, the firm was relatively progressive and meritocratic. She did not "necessarily want to make partner," which would involve focusing more on "business development" and possibly losing her relatively flexible schedule. At a billables expectation of 1,300 hours, she rarely worked past 4:45 P.M. on weekdays and was able to take six months off after the birth of her second child. Her husband, she noted, "keeps the trains running on time at home" while working 8:30 A.M. to about 7:00 P.M. daily, but they no longer had a nanny (both spouses wanted to do more childcare), and it would be hard for her to take on more hours in the evenings and on weekends. On the whole, Piper had a pretty successful gendered career: though she was the trailing spouse in her move to the South, she found a midsize firm that valued her prior elite law firm experience, provided the kind of academic work she preferred, and kept her hours manageable.

Allyson was another trailing spouse in our AJD Project cohort who eventually found a successful path in the legal profession, though she had nearly gotten a divorce in the process. She grew up in the Northwest with successful professional parents, then attended a leading undergraduate university, worked at a domestic violence–related nonprofit for a year, and graduated from a top-30 law school in the East. Between her undergraduate years and law school, she married a PhD student, and, when he got a job offer in the Northwest, she sought out the firms from their chosen city. Given her record, she secured offers from every firm with which she interviewed. After completing her law degree as a visiting student, she took a job with a nationally recognized large law firm with an office in the city where her husband worked. She spent two years at the firm, billing just under 2,000 hours a year. But the stress of the job and "family and personal issues" led her to quit rather than "destroy my marriage."

After a brief pause, Allyson worked her networks and got hired at an 80-attorney firm. She appreciated the informal mentors and lighter work demands at her new firm, but she also noted that the firm was far less transparent than her previous firm had been about work expectations and her prospects for making partner. She was encouraged to "start thinking about how you're going to differentiate yourself . . . basically how to make your own practice." At the wave 2 interview, she expressed her uncertainty: "I don't think I'm *not* on the partnership track, but at the same time nothing formal has been said." There was only one female equity partner. After a conference of the whole firm, the female attorneys met and discussed how the networking to obtain clients they were encouraged to do was in fact "a man's game."

Outside work, Allyson was incredibly athletic (though she gave up running marathons when it contributed to her need for personal leave), active with her church, and trying to have children. Her husband did more than his share of the chores (together they had little difficulty managing household duties), and the couple had almost no debt. As for a five-year plan, she said at wave 2: "I don't have anything in particular in mind right now for that. I wouldn't be surprised if I'm not at the firm. And not, not because of anything negative about the firm. Just I think hopefully by then I'll have some kids and I'll be, I'll find a place that I think really fits with that lifestyle. . . . And it may be the firm, but it could just as easily be somewhere else."

At wave 3, in 2016, Allyson had changed firms while on leave to adopt a child in Asia. She was unhappy at her previous firm, citing "poor management" and the fact that she was primed before maternity leave for making nonequity partner. And, though, as she said, "Gender issues don't get under my skin much," there were signals that the firm's culture remained sexist. She recalled that once, while she was helping a female litigator with extensive document analysis, other attorneys ("mostly guys") popped their heads in throughout the day, asking questions like, "Are you girls in here doing your nails together?" So, when a lawyer from a rival firm invited her to come over to that office, she was primed for poaching: "No one was expecting me . . . but in the next four hours . . . [he] walked me around. . . . I did the interviews there on the spot."

Remembering that she was "very up front" that she didn't have her own "book of business," Allyson learned that the firm had a very large new client and that one of the partners needed significant help to serve that client's needs: "And what the firm said was, 'We need you now, and we want your years of experience and your ability to run transactions, and we don't need you to have your own book.'" Better yet, this midsize firm with multiple regional offices was much better managed than her last firm was.

Allyson did well immediately but bore a "gender penalty." She made nonequity partner and then equity partner, but she and other women obtained the equity partnerships a year later than expected while at least one man got his well before the usual time line. "I don't know what the heck was going on. I don't think *they* knew what was going on," she noted. Then the partner she was working with went on sabbatical. He did not return, and she and a male partner "divvied up his book." She was expected to shift seamlessly to working under this male partner, which confused the big client. For years, this major client would ask why she was not the liaison since she was "the one that we work with day in and day out." They asked Allyson whether they could hire her directly, but she responded: "No, it doesn't work that way. Just leave it alone." And then there was the "night and day thing" with her compensation. The firm told her that they would give her some "origination" credit for the existing clients, but "the numbers that they were publishing never reflected it." She did not push the issue because she was friends with the lawyer who got the credit and her pay was still "way over the line compared to everyone else," yet she was taking notice.

At this point, Allyson had three children and felt torn between home and clients. She felt guilty leaving the office, rushing to be home at 6:00 P.M., even though "everybody else was gone" before she was anyway: "And this is the lifestyle that people are already leading. I just hadn't picked up on that."

Her outside activities were time-consuming, and, between coaching a track team, founding a networking group, serving on nonprofit boards, and her parish involvement, time was tight. When her husband was not traveling for work, he prepared all the meals: "He's incredible. He and I manage it all," she said proudly. Still, sometimes she found she would say to her husband: "'This week, don't forget. Monday, Tuesday, I've got this, this, and I won't be home until. . . .' And then occasionally it's, 'But I'm going to be in Korea then.'" Nonetheless, at this wave 3 interview, she said: "We manage it."

Allyson is a driven high achiever who made career choices that supported her ambitions as well as her family's needs.

SEXISM

When we talk about gendered choices, it is easy to forget that they arise from sexism and patriarchy. Once it is baked into structures and practices and norms, misogynistic constraint can look more like personal choice or lack of fit. Still, there are stories in which the blatant sexist discrimination cannot be avoided. Penelope told one such dramatic story—and told us how she put the pieces back together when gender discrimination destroyed her career.

Penelope's parents never graduated from college. Her father was a blue-collar worker, though her mother had worked her way up into management. Raising their daughter in the suburban East, they saw her blossom during a fifth-grade project on the judicial system and immediately encouraged her to consider the law as a profession. She said she never considered anything else. After attending a small liberal arts college, she spent a year working for a prominent domestic relations lawyer, then attended a local law school.

Penelope finished her first position, a year-long stint as a staff attorney in state government, during an economic downturn. She felt fortunate to find a position in "a construction law firm that was a spin-off of a large firm," and, though it offered little practical experience, she worked on a team of three or four lawyers in the small operation for four years. From there, she moved to a slightly larger firm that focused on insurance defense, gaining experience in depositions and motion practice. Next, she took a friend's advice about the poor chances for partnership at her small firm and moved into a construction law position in one of the city's larger firms (more than 150 lawyers). Another nine years later she was a nonequity partner.

The story of why she left was, as Penelope put it, "sort of a blood-curdling": "I left because of rampant misogyny and gender biases. . . . It was so bad that, when I left, they had hired the region's best employment lawyer because they thought I was coming after them. . . . They just assumed that I would. So it was really awful." In the end, she decided not to sue, saying: "Part of me would love to, but my friends are equity partners there. It's their business, too."

Construction law, Penelope noted, was generally "hostile for women," and she worked as "the last woman of four" in a group with seven or eight men run by a senior male partner: "Well, it wasn't really bad until the last three years, so then. . . . As long as I was sort of in my place as an associate bowing down and looking up, everything was fine." It seemed like a good sign when, in 2011, she made nonequity partner and the firm asked her "to develop and run a women's initiative to help" because it was losing women: "And to their credit, they were very interested. They gave me free rein wherever I needed to [go]." But it was about the same time that the recession finally hit her practice group: "The big issue is that my oldest boss did not like the women's initiative [and] . . . stopped giving me work. . . . I didn't quite have a client base big enough to support myself." For three years, she simply worked harder, trying to make up for the shortfall. She was unhappy but tried to think about her career: "I don't want to walk away from this if I could inherit the origination credit for the clients I have actually now developed and taken on myself. . . . Because they will tell you that origination credit doesn't matter, but it absolutely does matter. It drives me crazy that they say it doesn't matter because it always comes up in every review. . . . So, I was trying my best to hold on and see if I would get his architect client." Then the troublesome male partner finally announced he was retiring and began taking a male lawyer around to meet his clients. Penelope was bothered. The other lawyer "had been practicing for one year longer": But: "I had more trials than him, I had gotten more clients than him, I had done more firm service than he had, I had done more marketing, more community service than he had." At the end of the day, this colleague made equity partner, became leader of the practice group, and inherited a "$3 or $4 million book of business from the big guy, including my clients who only ever called me."

Penelope went to the firm leadership, pointing out that the women's initiative was designed to stop these sorts of practices. "[You] wanted me to run the women's initiative," she told them. "One of the problems that is well-documented is that business is given from one White guy to the next White guy, and I'm asking for your help. I'm not asking to receive *your* origination credit with clients I don't know. Only . . . having origination credit for my specialty that I've been working with for years." The response, in her recollection, was: "We're not going to get involved. You need to handle this yourself." She tried to have that conversation with the male lawyer, who "at this point has been made leader so he's in some sense a boss." She recalled, wryly: "[He] did not receive my request well."

In 2014, as the "big boss's" retirement drew near, Penelope noted: "I was reviewing some documents and it was clear that our client was not telling us the full truth. So I emailed the big boss . . . 'Hey, something is up. We need to talk this week.'" She tried for two days to contact him while she was out sick with a cold. On the third day, she had training through the women's initiative, so she emailed again: "I have to go to this implicit bias training. Why don't we touch base tomorrow? If you want to look at what I'm talking about, the documents are on my chair, and then we can catch up tomorrow."

Penelope returned from the training and found an email from the boss saying: "Hey, I haven't been feeling well. I sent you an improvident email. Let's talk tomorrow." He had forwarded that email to the next highest-ranking person in the group, stating: "You have no idea how this pisses me off. I have been looking for her for days. I'm out for five minutes, and I get a 'you're not there.'" Penelope continued: "So, he's lying. But that wasn't enough. . . . His follow-up email, was, 'But she has time for implicit bias training' . . . sprinkled with a lot of F-bombs and other things." The next day, he sought to "apologize," instead heaping insult on injury. Penelope remembered that he began: "You know, we need to forgive each other for the things we do wrong. I'm not going to say that you're *bitchy*, but you can be prickly." She continued:

> I started shaking at my desk and feeling really nauseated and just decided it was time to go. But, when I left, rather than having the standard exit interview with the chief operating officer, I called for a meeting of more than half the board, and I sat down with exhibits and a time line, and I went through every single thing. Because the firm was losing women. And the women would leave, and the firm would say, "Well, they just want to spend more time with their family." Because the women don't hold them accountable. They don't *tell* them why they are leaving. . . . And if they don't tell them why they're leaving . . . it lets them off the hook. . . . I had seen—as part of the women's initiative, we had run studies of salaries—I knew where all the skeletons were hidden, the women were paid far less than the men were. And you know, they can chalk it up to, well, "he brings in more clients" and "he, you know, he's more profitable," but they don't look at the system behind it.

After her exit interview, the firm "found [her boss] in violation of the HR policy." When Penelope heard that, when she left the room, the retiring partner had gotten up and told the group he planned to leave her some of his business but had instead "lost faith and confidence" in her, she said: "I really came unhinged. . . . I tried cases in those three years, I brought clients in, I mentored people, I served on the hiring committee, I ran the women's initiative. . . . I did the marketing events. . . ." Galled, she went to firm leadership, and they "talked it through." But: "He was retiring, so there was not much they could do to punish him." At least "they did take his bonus and unanimously donated it to a women's organization."

Penelope became inside counsel for the architecture firm she had worked closely with while at the firm, but, once it became clear to her that she "couldn't spend 40 hours a week staring at a wall and hoping for something," she decided to open her own practice. The clients that had been given to the less deserving man were now all her clients with the new firm. She stopped litigating, choosing work that was "very much catered toward [her] sanity and [her] health," and "working with only the people [she] want[ed] to work with": "In the first seven months, I made my retirement, bonus, and covered my self-employment tax. And I'm charging my clients half of what I would have charged them [at the firm]." She has built her firm on the idea of doing things in innovative ways: "So, there's only so much flexibility within the system, but things like flat fee and donating a portion of proceeds to 501c3 of the client's choosing [made a difference]." She centers her practice on the architects (less "old boys") and meets her clients in their offices.

Looking back, she said: "One of the best parts of my career frankly was working on the women's initiative and being able to dive into issues truly relating to practice that are not just about being a lawyer." She mentioned, however, that, as years went by, she did not bring up her own story when advising other attorneys: "I have mentored plenty of younger women lawyers, and it's hard because I wouldn't share with them the things that were happening. . . . They were going to face their own battles, and I didn't want them viewing the world through my lens. If they came to me and said, 'I'm being mistreated,' then I would step in and do something." Penelope's husband works in the tech industry. They had no children: "Personal choice. I've never been a big kid fan, and my husband wasn't either, so we just decided we would just keep adopting rescue dogs and that was good for us, and we were going to live our life. . . . That's what always made me laugh. It's like, I'm the closest thing to a man that these people [in the law firm] have, you know?"

Penelope survived and was transformed by experiencing and working to end sexist discrimination, and she managed to regroup with her own solo practice. Her story demonstrates that even a firm trying to be enlightened is unlikely to address big issues when it comes to the behavior of a rainmaking partner and that even a woman taking a leadership role against it might suppress her own story about professional sexism. In the end, she described herself as "recovering," yet she had soured on the premise that the legal profession was, in general, a good career for women.

Conclusion

Large law firms tell a story of looking to find the next generation of legal stars and selecting them for equity partners. Yet, generation after generation, that group continues to look very White, very male, and very elite. If you ask the partners, women and minorities—now valuable entry-level attorneys seen as bringing talent and diversity to firms (not to mention fulfilling their bureaucratized commitments)—could be great colleagues but tend to leave the partner track for lifestyle reasons or because other positions are more attractive. That characterization is not wholly untrue, but it is the result after the fact of how individuals experienced law firms. Well-credentialed White men were much more easily embraced by partners with power, were steered into the proper silos, and were assumed to have a business-friendly personality that is part of the right stuff for equity partnership. Those who did not get the benefits of that welcome and embrace ultimately looked elsewhere for work, including options that did not depend on perceptions of an ability to generate business or have a business-friendly personality. In the midsize and small law firms, perception also favors White men, and the crucial processes of handing down clients and distributing origination credits bear this out.

We also see minorities and women whose quantifiable rainmaking skills cannot be denied. In many cases throughout this chapter, however, gendered expectations disrupted potentially promising trajectories. Female attorneys spoke about orienting themselves to spouses, children, and business as they worked to make their careers, following spouses to new cities, accepting gendered practices, committing to partnership or a more balanced lifestyle, schooling spouses on sharing chores, embracing contract work, and, of course, divorcing partners and firms.

7

Rethinking the Solo Practitioner

The literature on the legal profession has subordinated solo practitioners since Jerome Carlin's (1962) classic study portrayed them as a precarious and ethically challenged group of low-status lawyers who could not make it into corporate law firms. Deemed irrelevant to the careers of elite law school graduates considering public interest or corporate profit, solo practice has been largely ignored by scholars, leaving Carlin's image unchallenged. The AJD Project data allow us to reexamine this practice setting. We begin with an overview of the scholarly literature, which assumes that elite corporate law and public interest careers are the most rewarding and prestigious. Solos are seen as the others. Almost by definition they do not do enough pro bono, serve the public interest, or have the expertise to serve lucrative clients or major causes. We then present four main findings from the AJD Project.

First, *solo practitioner* is not a fixed category of individuals at the bottom of the profession but an evolving status, part of the process of making careers where one or even a few individuals become business owners rather than employees. Solo practice may be a way station to employment in other settings, the beginning of a law firm, or an end point. Thus, the idea of solo practice as a fixed category is misleading. Second, solo practice is more entrepreneurial than other practice settings, but being entrepreneurial is not just a personal characteristic. Solos make careers through what they can access: family connections, language skills, ethnic affinities, friends from school, a niche that they find or stumble into. Some solo careers are created by friends or colleagues who push an individual into a practice. Third, and relatedly, this solo category contains today's version of the two hemispheres hierarchy, which rewards those with the presumed merit of elite law degrees and with early career corporate law experience. The diaspora of attorneys who begin in corporate law firms affects who goes into solo practice and what that practice brings in terms of clients and rewards. Solos who start as associates in large law firms have advantages that are unavailable to those who start in small firms or other settings. Fourth, despite this pervasive inequality, individuals who develop solo practices demonstrate the possibility of upward mobility through entry into the American legal profession.

These practices also contribute to the legitimacy of the legal profession, to positive (and some negative) images of lawyers, and to lawyer adaptation over time to new practice areas and settings. Those whom we define as the *lower* category of solos are the ones who serve racial, ethnic, or linguistic minorities or build a practice out of a sense of mission, while those in the *upper* category rely on a ready-made network of corporate lawyers and clients. Both groups are characterized by some innovation.

The Picture from Existing Scholarship

The academic literature on solo practitioners is thin. Carlin's (1962) classic study portrayed solos in Chicago as unhappy, leading precarious lives, hustling for business, and prone to ethical lapses. Presaging Heinz and Laumann's (1982) two hemisphere thesis, Carlin described the bar in stark class terms. The lower class of solos, he suggested, was in effect created by the rise of corporate law firms staffed by graduates of a very few schools and closed to the ethnic and religious groups dominant in the city. He concluded dismally that "most individual practitioners in the metropolitan bar are men of fairly high ambition who haven't made it" (90). Solos (and to some extent small firms) largely did residual work, including "the undesirable cases, the dirty work, those areas of practice . . . that are felt by the large firms to be professionally damaging . . . [including] local tax, municipal, personal injury, divorce, and criminal matters" (8).

Carlin highlights the difficulty of building a practice and the way in which many lawyers are limited to their neighborhood and its residents, often a particular ethnoreligious group: "Over half the respondents acknowledged that at least 50 per cent of their clients were drawn from either their own or some other ethno-religious group, and almost a third reported that 50 per cent or more of their clients were drawn from their own ethno-religious group" (1994, 56). It was difficult to move out. Carlin notes that there are personal injury lawyers, divorce lawyers, and criminal defense and collection lawyers who substantially outearn others. They succeed financially—owing to regular sources of clients like bondsmen, police, and "chasers"—but resent the exclusiveness of the corporate bar and its domination of the bar associations.

Carlin also describes a group of solos resembling small-scale corporate lawyers, typically serving one business client or source of relatively large real estate transactions: "The upper-level real estate and business-corporate lawyers . . . have not only the advantage of a more permanent business clientele and a greater sense of accomplishment in their work, but they have also been able to carve out a fairly secure niche for themselves in the practice of law" (1994, 80).

Jack Ladinsky (1963) also focused on solo practitioners, echoing Carlin in highlighting the gulf between corporate lawyers and solos: "Poorly trained lawyers are likely to be in individual practice. They lack the skills provided by high quality education and specialized work experience to handle the more complex legal problems of modern society. Low quality education is one reason why solo lawyers are rarely invited to join big firms. By default most solo men end up doing the 'dirty work' of the bar: personal injury, divorce, criminal work, collections, title searching, etc." Night law school pedigrees are seen as a source of weakness, as is family pedigree: "The requisite of any profession is availability of clients. The average solo lawyer has no contacts with big business. Neighborhood, ethnic group, family, and perhaps organizational contacts are the relations from which he can build a clientele. Firm men, on the other hand, come more often from high occupational family backgrounds, and are more likely to establish and cultivate relationships which yield business and corporate clienteles" (1963, 53).

Two decades later. Heinz and Laumann (1982) divided Chicago lawyers into two hemispheres, one serving organizations, mainly corporations, and the other serving individuals with "personal plights." Solos go into the "lower hemisphere," with almost nothing in common with corporate lawyers, including law schools attended and ethnoreligious identity (White Anglo-Saxon Protestants vs. others).

Carroll Seron (1996) conducted another rich study of solo and small-firm lawyers, this time in New York City and surrounding areas, including some very rich suburbs. Advertising had been liberalized since the earlier studies, and Seron found that most solos had adopted this strategy. Yet the role of social networks and contacts remained of paramount importance in building successful practices. His study illuminates the common need to invest time in building client relationships—typically after work—and how traditional gender roles limit this investment by women.

Seron also found the sense of financial insecurity and some of the stratification noted by Carlin. In the affluent suburbs where IBM is headquartered, solo and small-firm lawyers thrived serving businesses that served IBM. She also found opportunities in Manhattan in the interstices of the corporate law firms handling condominium sales. More generally, she found that entry into solo and small firms came from government and other solo and small firms and sometimes even from Wall Street firms. Our data reveal a similar phenomenon.

Jerry Van Hoy (1997; 2001) studied the emergence and social organization of franchise law firms in the personal client sector, documenting the challenges this new organizational form faces in the legal marketplace and its continuities with the organization of traditional small law firms.

A Quantitative Portrait

The basic portrait painted by the aggregate statistics is consistent with the pejorative scholarly image. At wave 1, in particular, it appears that most solos are in fact individuals who lack other options. The proportion of tier 3 and tier 4 graduates working in solo practice is more than double that of graduates of higher-ranking law schools (7% compared to 3%, respectively). While the racial and ethnic composition of solo practices largely follows that of the sample, women are somewhat underrepresented, making up 36% of solos compared to their much higher presence in public interest/nonprofit/education organizations, legal services, and state government (at 80%, 68%, 66%, and 53%, respectively). These gender relationships moderate by wave 3, at which point women make up 49% of solos. Earnings are much lower in solo practice than in corporate law firms; wave 1 median earnings are $50,000 for solos vs. $135,000 in firms of 251 or more lawyers. And, while no more likely than others to graduate with law school debt in the 75th percentile, solos are more likely to have high debt at wave 3 (40% for solos vs. 20% in other settings).

There is continuity in career paths involving solo practice, with a number working as solos in all three waves. Nearly one-quarter of wave 3 solos were solos at wave 1, and almost half were at wave 2. The sequence analysis shows that those who move into and out of solo practice most often link to small firms, state government, or business not practicing law (chap. 3). Solos are more likely than other lawyers to have multiple jobs and frequently work part-time (particularly women). Two-thirds of wave 3 solos expect to stay in that setting for more than five years.

The statistics are therefore consistent with a sense of solo practice as part of the lower hemisphere resulting from fewer options for lower-tier law school graduates. Solos report higher depression scores than do lawyers in other settings—suggesting high stress—but are generally satisfied, particularly with their work/life balance and the altruistic and social elements of their positions. The statistics mask the relatively small segment of solo practice that belongs in the upper hemisphere. At wave 3, solos earned a mean of $90,097 and median of $70,000, and the bottom quartile earned a median of less than $45,000. Eight percent of solos earned $200,000 or more, which is the threshold for the 75th percentile of earners across all settings. Although the proportion of top-quartile earners among solos is lower than in business or larger firms, it is higher than in any public sector settings. Thus, there are clearly large income earners and many who make relatively little. There are relatively few graduates of top-10 law schools in solo practice, but there are some.

The statistics also mask the fluidity that we see in the qualitative interviews. Solo practice is part of a process that includes start-up positions in small firms. We exclude established small firms that are more bureaucratized with firm clients that the associates typically work on. This is, admittedly, not a fine line, but we can see that people start solo and add partners or even team up with a friend. These represent the world of solos in terms of what we see in the qualitative interviews.

The Lower Hemisphere of Solo Practice

The first set of interviews updates and revises the classic scholarly understanding. We see the precariousness and some of the ethical challenges of solo practice and the connection of many solo practices to racial, ethnic, or linguistic minorities often linked to urban geography. Yet the narratives also challenge the notion of solos as failures fighting over the residual and dirty work that corporate law firms do not want. Instead, they feature stories of upward mobility and entrepreneurialism and of solos' central role in creating the demand for and supply of legal services to particular clients. We also note the mission-driven nature of some of these careers, reinforcing Luz Herrera's (2007) theme about the public interest in solo practice.

UPWARD MOBILITY AND PRECARITY

Born in suburban Florida, Sean graduated from a state university where he majored in religious studies. While he initially aspired to become a rabbi like his father, he decided to go to law school late in the year. The Florida schools he contacted recommended that he delay applying until the following year, so his parents suggested he apply to an independent law school in California, where they had relocated. He matriculated in January and graduated with the top of his class, passing both the California and the Florida bar exams on the first attempt. When he applied to law firms in Florida, none had ever heard of his law school.

Getting desperate, Sean applied for a job at an amusement park. His friends advised him to contact Neil, a solo practitioner with two small offices (one being at home). Against his father's advice, he took a job with Neil for a "paltry" salary. The firm practiced "threshold law," meaning that, if it came across the threshold, they practiced it.

Sean reported that Neil ran a "smoke and mirrors" practice but that he learned a lot at the firm, "not only about the practice of law, but about the business of law practice." He, also knew from the beginning that he needed to market and network, telling us: "I came to town, and I called every person I knew. My father had a good base of people here, fortunately."

Sean left Neil's firm two years later, moving to a small firm as a generalist. He considered leaving law altogether but did not see any other options. He continued marketing and building networks that would eventually help build a stable practice. He worked with the Optimist Club, for example. Most members could not even afford his low hourly fee, but some did bring him business. He also formed a social networking group with "a financial consultant, . . . a banker from a local bank, an accountant, a mortgage broker, a real estate agent, and a copy leasing guy" that helped generate a half dozen leads in three months. He was also very involved in the local Jewish community and attended bar association luncheons, describing himself as a "people person."

At the time of our second interview twelve years later, Sean had experienced a number of career and personal changes. He had gone in-house for a salary of $120,000 (up from $66,000) but left three years later when he discovered that the company was being investigated by a grand jury. He started his own practice, working as a solo for three years before expanding to a larger office. He hired a lawyer who ended up cheating the firm out of money and another who further drained the firm and then had to file for personal bankruptcy because he could not finance the firm's debt. He also went through a divorce during this period.

Throughout this period of hardship, Sean continued networking. He met an individual through his work with the local chamber of commerce who invited him to join his small firm, where profits were strictly "eat what you kill." He succeeded at this new firm, generating most of his work from referrals. He ran for public office and got to know the general counsel for one of the political parties in the state, who gave him some regional work. He remarried, and, like his first wife, his second was a stay-at-home mom. He stayed at this law firm until 2018, nominally as a partner. He returned to the second firm where he had worked, probably because of the insufficient credit he received for the business he was generating.

One key to Sean's success, despite the precariousness of his practice, was his determination to build business through networking: "Most of my clients I am very friendly with on some level. So is it marketing when I go out and have a beer with one of the loan officers? Ostensibly, yes, but we could just be out having a drink. And, so, it really is a very blurred line because, for us, it's all about the opportunities. . . . For the average attorney, relationships are the lifeblood." He was also open to new practices, like election law. Thus, despite the bumps along the way, he was able to transform his lower-tier credentials, local connections, and entrepreneurial drive into a satisfactory practice.

Sophia, whom we interviewed in 2003 and 2015, is also from Florida. Her mother, a Cuban immigrant, was a nurse's assistant, and her stepfather was a tradesman. While she received undergraduate scholarships, she did not receive assistance for law school. She graduated with substantial education debt ($120,000) and indicated that she had experienced financial stress.

Sophia had married her husband while in college, and he got a job first, which constrained her employment choices. Further limiting her options, she had chosen to go into construction law. She joined a small firm but quickly became uncomfortable with the way the staff was treated and felt that the firm atmosphere was discriminatory. She and her husband wanted to start a family soon, so she was also concerned about work hours, but she felt that she could not even present a proposal for a flex schedule. She left after a year to join an eight-lawyer firm that exclusively represented a large insurance company. During her interview, she discussed the firm's position on flex schedules. Her husband was a firefighter who worked 24 hours on and then 48 hours off. The partner who interviewed her implied that they would allow a flex schedule, but, when she wrote out a formal proposal, the boss never even considered it. She stayed there for two years.

Sophia was hired by a firm specializing in construction litigation. The managing partner agreed to let her try out a flex schedule and offered to raise her salary by $5,000 in six months if it worked out. He kept his word. She really liked the firm and was hopeful that she would be promoted to nonequity partner in six or seven years.

When we reinterviewed Sophia in 2015, she had divorced and remarried, and she had a child from each marriage plus two stepchildren. She had left the last firm when, after working on an important case with the managing partner, she was not promoted and the managing partner did not even discuss the possibility of a partnership with her. Sophia and her husband—who had been her moot court partner in law school—decided to start a practice with a third lawyer who promised to bring them 45 real estate closings immediately. They opened an office in anticipation of the work, but the proposed partner gave the closings to another lawyer. Sophia and her husband had to restructure the entire business. She still practiced construction law with her husband, working also by contract with her prior firm; but it was not her focus.

Sophia's divorce had been contentious, ending up in appeals court before a custody issue was settled. That experience led her to become disillusioned with the law and in particular the litigation system. She no longer spent time marketing to build her clientele. She worked only on cases that came as referrals from the earlier managing partner, himself now in solo practice. She told us that her family was "in a transition." Her husband had just "finished his second full year . . . of seminary because he's received his calling to teach, so he's been going to . . . [school] part-time."

Sophia said that, if she had the resources, she would not practice law. It appears that she and her husband were unable to transform their practice into an adequate revenue-generating business. They lacked strong local connections and a practice with a network to support it. According to LinkedIn, in 2019 they still had their practice, but it appears her main focus was elsewhere. Her profile also listed a high-ranking position in a local church and ongoing contract work for a national dietary supplement company.

There is little left of Sophia's passion for construction litigation. Gender roles, law firm conservatism, and probably some prejudice stymied her in law firms, with the result that, ironically, she ended up doing individual work for the one lawyer who treated her nicely even though he, too, disappointed her when it came to a partnership. This story is of an individual coming from disadvantage and becoming a lawyer, with some successes, but ultimately it is a reminder of the precarity that still characterizes many of those who take a chance and start their own firm.

Annette grew up on Chicago's South Side and was the first person in her father's family to attend college, graduating from a state school before enrolling in a local law school. Her family was actively involved in local politics, and she knew she wanted to go to law school. She made the trial team while an undergraduate and clerked at both the state's attorney's office and the public defender's office. She also interned in a large law firm and "decided that really wasn't for [her]." She joined the state's attorney's office on graduation and stayed there for six years.

Annette and her husband met working at the state's attorney's office, and they started a real estate law practice because the state's attorney's office "allows lawyers to do any work that does not bring [them] into court to supplement [their] income." Her mother was a real estate broker, and the practice allowed Annette to repay student loans. She decided: "Well I've been doing it for a while; let's see where it takes us." She also liked that the work was based on flat fees instead of billable hours.

Annette started the firm from referrals from her mother's network, and, when she had enough business, her husband joined her. She described the importance of marketing to clients: "I was always good at marketing, so I tend to think that the best way to market yourself to real estate agents . . . is to market the way they do." One of her innovations was to post her and her husband's pictures the way realtors do, for example, at bus stops. She has led seminars for new agents run by the biggest real estate brokerage in the city.

Annette and her husband have been able to buy a three-story home in the city and use the downstairs as their office, allowing her to spend time with their toddler and put him to bed before returning to the office to finish up her day.

Annette provided further evidence of innovation and entrepreneurialism: "Somebody approached me about short sales, and so I did one, and I think this is going to be big business, so I started teaching classes for the agents, and we became well known as . . . the king and queen of short sales." Her firm's 2019 website reveals that they have an elegant downtown office and that short sales continue to be important to their practice.

Identity

In addition to precarity and upward mobility, the next interviews that we describe also demonstrate the strategy of building a successful and rewarding solo practice on the basis of racial or ethnic identity.

We interviewed Alejandro in 2003, 2009, and 2014. He and his family emigrated in 1979 from Mexico City, where his father had risen from sweeping floors to a managerial position. Starting over in California, both parents built successful small businesses that allowed them to give him a middle-class upbringing. On graduation from a lower-tier law school, Alejandro had relatively few career options. When we interviewed him in 2003, he already was in his fourth job. He described the ethical challenges of practicing immigration law and his efforts to find a position where he could thrive and maintain professional standards. He had been working for about a year at a small, professionally run immigration firm, which he loved because the lead partner gave him "a lot of leeway" and let him "handle his cases from the get-go."

Alejandro described the professional network of immigration attorneys that he had made through the American Immigration Lawyers Association and several bar associations. He had a "full Rolodex" and a "ton of cases." He got clients from "word of mouth": "People know me, people see me. I volunteer all the time. I've done volunteer work for [a television channel], getting call-in phone calls; at the schools here. . . . I'll go out and give free advice. . . . We went out to the parks here . . . and gave advice, brought in business." Although he was thriving, he said that he was not anticipating a partnership and that he felt he was generating much more business than his salary was rewarding him for. He planned to start repaying his student debt the following year.

Alejandro's wife was also an attorney. She worked as a government lawyer. For family reasons, Alejandro worked only weekdays 9:00 to 6:00. He and his wife had a nanny for their two kids: "She gets there about 8:30 and leaves when I get home. She cooks, cleans, washes, does everything, takes care of both the boys." He noted that, whether he stayed at his current firm or left, "regardless we're going to open up our own practice": "I plan by the age of 50 to retire, and I think it can be done. . . . I never imagined in my wildest dreams that immigration could lead to that, but now I know it can. What the community needs is someone who cares, someone who is willing to do a good job, and I think that I can do both and make a living at it."

By 2009, Alejandro had left the firm and opened up his own office, earlier than he had planned. His previous firm was having difficulties, and, despite his revenue generation, he had a partially negative review that seemed to him inaccurate. He reported that he was told, "You know, you're a nine to five guy": "And I said, 'Yeah, and I told you that from day 1 when I walked into this office.' I said, 'Well, here's my two weeks' notice.'" His wife stayed in her government position.

Although Alejandro specialized in immigration, after three years in solo practice he was devoting one-third of his time to criminal law. He had generated clients by serving on the board of the Hispanic Bar Association, the YMCA, and the local school board. Television was also important: "I've developed a very good relationship with the Spanish channel here, and so, . . . when it's . . . [a] criminal issue . . . immigration issue more than anything, I'm the one that gets the [airtime]." He also worked for the Mexican consulate for some time, which enhanced his standing in the Hispanic community. He continued to thrive: "Business is great. . . . Business is growing well and steady, and it's word of mouth." He had just realized his goal of buying a Porsche and had two paralegals working for him.

When asked how his practice stays afloat, Alejandro responded: "The way I do it is . . . one of my paralegals and I have a goal. I need to generate $1,000 a day that has to come through that door paid and that'll cover my expenses and then some. . . . I've never had a cash flow problem. I've never been in the red. I started off with a $5,000 loan from my mother, and I paid her off the very first month." He invests time in networking: "You know, and that's one thing I have developed is a golf game because I've been invited through different organizations to do stuff like that." Yet he maintains a flexible work schedule, coaching his kids' football and baseball teams and working "about 35 hours a week" while earning about four times what he did at the previous firm.

By 2014, there were then nine people on Alejandro's payroll, including his brother, his mother (as a notary public), an attorney doing court appearances as contract work, and his father doing marketing. He noted proudly: "I've built an office where . . . I think not only am I happy, but the people that work for me are very happy." He indicated on a map of the United States all the places where he had practiced. He clearly had developed a national practice. He described his personalized approach:

> I go above and beyond what people expect. On my business card, to this day, my cell phone is there. My direct email is there. If people need to speak to me, they speak to me. I might have eight other people working for me, but I'm always accessible. I don't get upset when they call me at 2:00 in the morning on a Saturday night. That's the part of the business that I'm in.

His wife was now a district attorney, and they had four children: "She loves what she does. Wears on her a little bit, but she loves what she does."

Ninety percent of Alejandro's clients are Spanish speaking. He noted the trepidation in the Hispanic community about "getting swindled": "I always . . . explain to them, Look, I'm not going to get rich off of you. . . . But I am a businessman." Referring to a mutual relationship of trust, he stated he did not send bills: "Of over a thousand clients, twenty-three of them are late." He built a practice serving mainly Mexican Americans around the idea of integrity and availability in what was too often a shady area of practice. As of 2020, he had another lawyer working in his office.

We interviewed Jacob in 2003, 2009, and 2013. He attended a state school and a law school ranked below 100. He is of Armenian descent and is well integrated into the local Armenian American community. His mother works for his cousin's small law firm, and his father "is a blue-collar worker, still working at 67," but they managed to send him to private school.

Jacob started working at his cousin's firm at 16, holding a variety of positions: "law clerk, bookkeeper, receptionist, legal research, library maintenance." The firm, which also employed his godfather, did a variety of plaintiffs' work. His job was "predetermined" before he started law school. He was guaranteed a job but regretted using the awaiting position as an excuse for not focusing on grades.

Jacob worked very hard in this first position and had the highest caseload in the firm, including his own cases of relatively low economic value. He had done two trials but knew that a partnership was not in his future: "The big ego of a trial lawyer, this is his firm, you want your own, do your own." He enjoyed being a lawyer: "The job allows you to come to the rescue, kind of the knight in shining armor or the unsung hero so to speak." But he was also stressed and afraid to take a vacation because of his caseload. At that time, he was afraid even to think of going solo given the responsibilities that entailed. He expected to stay at the firm for the foreseeable future.

By 2009, Jacob had had two more positions and was divorced. He left his cousin's firm in 2004 for an opportunity to become general counsel for a small business in another county. He was helping the client resolve a major dispute with his partner, and the client offered to triple his salary to relocate and work on the dispute. But he was there only five months. He started a solo legal practice, and, although the specific client relationship ended, the client "introduced [him] to persons here who became referral sources as well . . . [particularly] physicians who are in the . . . community who've now been a big referral source . . . because [he] still do[es] primarily plaintiffs' personal injury." The physicians liked the relationship because "they don't get paid much [from health insurance], . . . so they would rather get paid on a lien basis—in other words, from an outcome of a third-party case": "After I would get the referral, of course, I'd expect to pay them, or we would get a lien going."

Jacob was pleased with how this had worked out: "[Physicians have] still been my bread and butter. . . . And then their family members refer others, and it's just become a chain. . . . So it's growing and growing. I have no advertising budget—zero." He also suggested that he preferred contingency fees. One limitation of his practice is his avoidance of larger cases requiring several experts, "which requires a big bankroll": "As a solo practitioner, I don't have the resources to do that. . . . I just do auto accidents, which is a lot simpler."

Jacob became active in the local chapter of the Armenian National Committee and had some friends whom he "knew growing up who now happen to also live [in his new locale]." He had 27 cases and did not have a secretary or a paralegal. He typically worked 30 hours a week and reported high satisfaction: "There is no downside. I'm very blessed." He still owed $50,000 in education debt, but he now owned a home and rented a small suite. He said that his standard of living had increased significantly, but he also noted: "If you're chasing the Louis Vuitton, the expensive cars [you might be disappointed]— I drive a Jeep. Can I drive a nice expensive car? Yes, but I'm happy with a Jeep. . . . So I keep my lifestyle where it is."

When we interviewed Jacob in 2013, he was in partnership with a friend who practices criminal defense. He was in a lower-rent but nice office area and had repaid his education debt. He was engaged and had a two-year old daughter: "I do it nine to five or come in at seven if I have a busy day. But I'm home in time to greet the girls. . . . I'll prepare dinner for them, spend time with them. And, if I have to come back, my office is only . . . four minutes away. . . . So I do still have that wonderful flexibility."

Jacob's practice reportedly had grown, largely thanks to referrals from former clients or physicians, and could now handle larger cases with expensive experts. His Armenian community activities continued, as did the relationship with the Consumer Lawyers' Association that he began with his cousin's firm. Jacob denied that his practice particularly served Armenian American clients but noted why this clientele was attracted to his practice:

> A lot of them will target me because of my ability to speak the language. . . . And my abilities and my reputation, I guess, too. But I don't advertise. . . . I don't target them. But they will call me. . . . And persons in the community that know me. And that's why I would get an Armenian client. . . . But it's not a high percentage. I would say maybe 20 percent.

He hoped to be able to afford an administrative staff so that he did not have to do everything by himself.

Jacob seems to have found his niche with referrals from doctors treating patients in automobile accidents. Like most plaintiffs' lawyers, he was not atop the personal injury food chain, and he had done only one trial since leaving his cousin's firm, but he was proud to be a plaintiffs' attorney. He had clearly gone through some financial precarity earlier in his career, and he still had no support staff, but he had found a practice that sustained him and his family. His upward mobility was facilitated mostly by his links to the Armenian community. He did not reach out to the community as much as stay largely within it.

We interviewed Stewart in 2014. Although, he had spent most of his career in state government, we focus here on the law firm that he and a friend started in the midwestern city in which he grew up. His African American identity and his wife's Vietnamese identity were central to his practice. He was the firm's rainmaker.

Stewart's parents were physicians, and, explaining why he went to law school, he said: "I've always enjoyed the law, and it was always in my mind that I was going to look at becoming a judge or run for office. . . . I just love politics." He attended a historically Black college before returning home for law school. His father's role as a physician was part of his political ambition: "What threw me toward law school was the idea . . . that my father is . . . an OB/GYN in town and he's delivered . . . many of the individuals, especially African Americans, that live there." He went to a top-20 state law school and hated it: "Really terrible. . . . It was bad among the Black students and much worse between the Black students and the White students. . . . I did not make good grades in law school. I was magna cum laude and Phi Beta Kappa coming out of [college], and my grades were terrible in law school." He clerked for a large law firm during law school, but, when the partners saw his grades, they declined to hire him.

On graduation, Stewart spent two years working for the state house of representatives and spent another couple of years working with environmental camping programs before taking and passing the bar. Furthering his interests and his politics, he and a friend opened a practice in his African American neighborhood: "He's a White guy, but it worked out great. And so then I started practicing. . . . I got married. I needed to make some more money, and I needed to get serious about law, I needed to get serious about politics, and the way to get serious about politics is to open up a law office, so that was what I did." The firm did transactional work and litigation.

It was difficult for Stewart: "You constantly had a feeling of incompetence starting in a firm where you were kind of on our own and you know we had other lawyers who were friends that would help us and talk us through different things, . . . but it was really just a baptism by fire." The clients were locals through his network: "I know a lot of people . . . from politics and this and that, and so I really made the rain for the firm just from the people that I knew and us being right on this good corner right in the African American neighborhood." There was one problem, however: "[Clients] didn't always pay."

Another source of clients materialized when, after seeing her picture on his desk, an existing client realized Stewart's wife was of Vietnamese descent: "The next day I had 17 Vietnamese clients. . . . So my clients were African American, there were White clients too, and there were Vietnamese."

Stewart felt that the firm was pretty successful while it lasted: "We ended up taking on a law clerk and two other partners in the practice. So we built the practice, and it did well, and we ended up I was really proud of some of the law that I did while I was in practice, . . . [including] helping small businesses and nonprofits, which never paid a lot, but I really enjoyed it." But not all aspects of the practice were enjoyable: "It was really the criminal law that paid the bills. That's the one where they wrote the checks and some family law too, but the family law is just miserable."

Success did not come without costs. Stewart noted: "I was unhappy as a private attorney, and it was very stressful. . . . I wasn't spending a lot of time with my family. My family was growing, and I was working you know six days a week, sometimes six and a half days, and so I was doing things that I didn't like." He also felt very uncomfortable with aspects of criminal practice, like defending a child abuser:

> So we're humming along. We have four attorneys and a paralegal and a secretary and an intern. Things are going well. . . . Over the course of just about three months the law practice really dissolved. One of my partners was activated [into military service]. . . . Another partner got hired [by a major employer], and another did not like practicing in the Black community.

Then a political acquaintance called him about an opening in the Department of Corrections. He applied and was hired in 2005, and LinkedIn shows he remained there in 2020.

While at the firm, Stewart entered politics, with some success: "I [ran] for office, but I got redistricted out." He said that he ran "a good race" and that there still might be politics in his future. His state government job actually pays better and is more financially stable than his private practice was. He enjoys the government position and now has time to spend with his growing family and his wife, who also works in government.

The firm was in many ways successful, built on Stewart's political ambitions and local connections. It was always precarious, but it built a payroll, handled some notable cases, and appeared to be sustainable. It also provided a platform for Stewart's political ambitions. A variety of circumstances conspired to end the firm, but it appears that Stewart's own reluctance to embrace the role of adversary lawyer and hired gun for criminal defense was part of the decision to shutter.

Kareem majored in biology at a California state university before attending a top-100 law school in California. He went straight to law school because he wanted to get married and "no Indian parent's going to let you get married to his daughter if you're not a professional." Kareem's father is an engineer and his mother is a medical technician, and they moved to the United States from India when Kareem was very young.

During law school, a student mentor advised Kareem that, as a biology major, he "should do intellectual property because that's a really good field to get into, it pays a lot": "And I was like, well OK, so I just did it." He did not have opportunities in corporate law firms coming out of law school. His first job was clerking for a solo practitioner, also East Indian and Muslim, whom he contacted because of that affinity. The solo originally needed someone to handle trademark, copyright, and licensing issues, but that business did not pan out, so Kareem stayed only eight months.

At a seminar, Kareem met a senior partner from an intellectual property firm that wound up hiring him to work exclusively on patent cases. He worked with one main partner, who also would frequently advise him and take him to lunch. This partner taught him conventions like sending cards to people he met and sending Christmas cards: "That's the way to build clients." He stayed at the firm until 2004. He started looking for another position owing to the lack of a steady stream of patent cases and because he wanted to make more money.

Kareem graduated from law school with $65,000 in debt, which he had already repaid when we interviewed him in 2003. Part of his motivation was the Muslim prohibition against paying interest. He was married and had a 15-month-old son, and his wife was pregnant. She worked at an Internet startup, and they had a babysitter for day care. Kareem "loved" his career at that point in time.

When we interviewed Kareem in 2009, he had moved several times, first to a boutique patent firm and then to a prestigious corporate law firm, a position he craved:

> I've always wanted to work for a big firm . . . because you go into a room and you're like, "Hey what firm did you used to work for?" Everybody's announcing, and you'd be like, "This firm." Then you have to kind of give some background information. I just got tired of doing that, and I really wanted to work for somewhere where people immediately recognize you. So once I got into [the new firm] I just felt like it was like the Holy Grail.

He left in 2008 when, owing to the recession, the firm lost its biggest client, but the luster of that firm stayed with him.

Kareem began contemplating starting his own practice. He was connected to the Indo-Pakistani and Muslim entrepreneurial communities in the Bay Area and decided to build on these identities. He partnered with the lawyer he originally clerked for, "a general practitioner, but his emphasis is bankruptcy work": "So he's booming [in the down economy]." His partner was well-known and respected in the Muslim community and had been contemplating retirement. The practice was essentially built on the partner's ties to the Bay Area Muslin community, and Kareem introduced new technology, including billing software.

Kareem also began teaching intellectual property law at night at a local law school to build his name. Most of his clients were Indian or Pakistani. At first it was difficult to attract enough patent work, so he was forced to become more of a generalist, work long hours, and endure the stress of an uncertain cash flow.

When we interviewed Kareem in 2014, the firm had expanded. He indicated that the stress period ended in 2009, explaining the transition as follows:

> I was doing my [intellectual property] and corporate work and nonprofit work, and then at some point I figured out because [his partner's] been doing this for such a long time he's done everything basically, which is a huge resource in addition to his specialty. So for any Indian or Muslim entrepreneur who wanted to set up a company . . . I relearned how to set up companies, set up LLCs. But then my clients started having more and more needs, like, "Hey I want to do a merger," "I want to . . . acquire this," "I want to do a first round of finance," whatever. So I got introduced to this other attorney who was 20 years out of Harvard with an MBA who just did corporate work who needed work. . . . So I developed a relationship with him. I developed a relationship with this other patent attorney in New York, and then we kind of grew.

According to Kareem, the other two were lawyers in big firms who did not take to networking: "So they get pushed out, I guess. But their work is first-class." He contracts out his clients' work, which is done by Harvard-trained lawyers for $300 per hour rather than the $700 per hour large firms charge.

At the time of the interview, Kareem and his wife were expecting their fourth child. After being unemployed, his wife was working again in the technology sector. Explaining his improved quality of life and his network of contract lawyers, he described a long vacation where he could be in touch with clients every day through the Internet and then delegate any legal issue that needed to be resolved. His niche continued to be South Asian Muslims, particularly in Silicon Valley.

As of 2019, it appeared that Kareem was phasing out his partnership with the very senior lawyer, who likely retired, and has taken on another lawyer as of counsel who has an established practice in the New York City area. The new office is in a more opulent part of Silicon Valley, and the firm's website notes a generalist practice with a focus on technology.

The strategies for building a practice through identity all succeeded to some extent, yet there are also limits. For example, there is typically a need to expand a practice toward the general, partly because the clientele may become limited to a particular community, and partly because it is hard for someone like Kareem to combine an identity-based practice with a limited specialty, especially one like a patent law practice that is also strong in many large law firms and boutiques. Alejandro's and Stewart's expansion into criminal law reflects this pressure to move toward general practice. Part of the pressure on Jacob is that he has not been able to become more of a generalist.

One feature of these identity-based practices that the literature does not address is that they are almost inevitably to some extent mission driven. They serve underrepresented populations either in their field of practice or through community engagement. Kareem, for example, helped mosques that were pushed to report on their members' activities. We now focus on interviews highlighting this aspect of solo practice.

MISSION- OR VALUE-DRIVEN LAWYERS

Toby, our second example of a successful immigration lawyer, grew up in the West with parents who were educators. He graduated from a small liberal arts school and returned home to substitute teach in an urban school district, which he described as "very eye-opening." He joined a religious-based volunteer corps that focused on immigration issues, especially those linked to Central America. The position helped perfect his Spanish, but he is not of Hispanic descent. He married and decided to pursue his interest in immigration law, attending an urban law school ranked below 100, and even taking an internship with an immigration court. He also worked as a part-time paralegal in an immigration boutique and from there "just kind of stepped into the role of an associate."

After seven years, the managing partner told Toby she was hiring a family member and could no longer afford him. Toby had been considering going solo and treated this as a "blessing in disguise." The transition was amicable, and his clients elected to follow him. He built a successful practice, with most clients coming "from word of mouth." His clients came from a range of home regions, including Africa and Central America. His income rose every year, including during the economic downturn. He also did considerable marketing with Lawyer.com, which includes client feedback, and direct advertising in community newspapers.

After going solo for five years, Toby partnered with another immigration lawyer whom he had met through bar committees and who had different linguistic skills. Together, they had a bump in business with the liberalization of gay marriage and the Supreme Court decision on the Defense of Marriage Act: "We are like in the thick of it with our gay and lesbian clients who . . . have foreign spouses." Because he took an early position on immigration equality, he was also one of the few lawyers on a closed referral list.

The practice and partnership were flourishing. Toby never had cash flow problems, and the business continued to grow. He kept to a 40-hour week, sharing care of his three children with his wife, who works three-fourths time. He and his partner use a contract lawyer as needed but do not plan on bringing more lawyers into the partnership. He is active in his church and has repaid his loans.

Toby reflected on his beginning in solo practice in a windowless office, comparing it to his downtown office: "Downtown seemed very kind of untouchable or unreachable or unattainable . . . very kind of hoity-toity and out of reach." Remarkably, his career follows almost a straight line from his religious-oriented community service to his successful practice. The marketing has been low-key, and even the LGBTQ business came only because of his early support of LGBTQ immigration rights. This is a classic kind of a mission-driven and successful solo practice that has grown into a small firm.

We interviewed Dorah in 2005 and 2009. Web sources indicate that she remains a solo practitioner representing indigent clients as a court-appointed attorney in child welfare and probate law. Hailing from a middle-class entrepreneurial family in the South, she attended law school in her midthirties. Her family paid 20% of her expenses. After receiving her undergraduate degree, she taught for several years at the high school level in her state, followed by some work in fundraising. She then entered a convent, traveling overseas in "peace and justice work." She felt she needed to "retool," perhaps for nonprofit work, and left the convent after ten years for a law school ranked below 50. Her legal career reflects the values that she showed in her work for the convent.

Dorah entered law school with a specific interest in human rights and reframed that interest into criminal defense for the indigent, participating in public interest clinics. She had no interest in corporate law. She received a judicial clerkship specializing in the family calendar, including cases of neglect. She stayed for two years: "[The experience] helped direct me in the practice that I have now."

Following the suggestion of a lawyer who appeared in the court where she was clerking, Dorah joined a suite of offices and began working with a senior solo who had overflow work that helped her develop a practice. While their formal arrangement ended after a year, she continued in the suite and built a successful practice on the basis of court referrals, which she attributed to the quality of her work and her reputation among judges and staff in the court where she had clerked. She also benefited from her inside knowledge of how to submit bills to the courts who referred cases.

Dorah identified as lesbian and discussed how both she and her partner had to take care of her partner's father, who had dementia. She is not interested in earning a large income and considers her income adequate. She is motivated by intellectual challenge and a desire to help people: "I really feel like I'm in the place where I have wanted to be, . . . a place where I can help people with the set of skills that are needed. . . . It satisfies . . . my desire to help people, and it's also intellectually challenging." She has considered adding a partner and applying for a public defender position but has opted to remain solo.

Despite her low pay, Dorah was repaying her $75,000 debt on a ten-year plan and noted her frugality: "Well you know . . . I live pretty modestly. . . . I know how to live on less than $10,000 a year."

Dorah started almost classically in an office suite, building her career by representing poor people, by building a reputation that expanded opportunities, and by having the business sense to generate income. We consider this a mission- or value-driven career, a kind of solo, for-profit (but limited profit), public interest career.

We interviewed Blair in 2009 in a major midwestern city. She had taken her time as a relatively unmotivated undergraduate student in a regional state school and was an Americorps volunteer for two years, working with battered women and at-risk young people. Following the advice of the administrator, who took her aside one day and said, "Kid, you gotta go to law school," she enrolled in a top-50 midwestern state law school at the age of 30. She "loved law school" and did well.

At that point, Blair assumed she would "do something like advocacy for battered women or public defender work or some lefty lobby." She did some public interest internships during law school but wondered whether she should "follow the herd" into corporate law. One summer in the family practice department of a relatively large firm changed her mind. Her first position was a clerkship in juvenile court. She applied not out of interest but because there was an opening, and it felt like a random move. She left after a while "because it [was] making [her] cry every day."

Blair's next position came from a law school friend who offered her "a sweet gig" as the monitor of a large class-action settlement unrelated to juvenile justice or family law. She stayed for three years as a staff attorney, honing her writing skills, and "[learning] a lot about what neutrals should not do."

Blair then started a generalist practice with a law school classmate coming from a small firm. The firm was open for just over a year: "Our relationship, our friendship deteriorated. . . . Our business relationship fell apart very quickly. . . . I got to the point where I did not want to answer the phone because I just knew there was somebody on the other end of the phone who was going to ask a question I couldn't answer." Both lawyers were miserable and terminated the firm.

Blair applied for many positions but interviewed poorly in part because of her lack of self-confidence. She was doing temporary and one-off jobs when "a good friend [through the monitor's office] who'd been doing family law . . . said you should become a guardian ad litem," a position that required a 40-hour supreme court training session and not a law degree. She thought this could be "an anchor": "something that . . . I can feel decent about while I try to figure out the rest of my life." Another friend pulled her into a legal aid position, but that office turned out to be "in absolute disarray."

Blair knew she had to find something else: "I was still pursuing this guardian thing. I'd finished the training in the . . . interim." She demonstrated entrepreneurialism by calling different county directors to see whether they had volunteer opportunities: "Most of them didn't, but I got a call back from [one] who asked me to come down for an interview." She thought the interview was for a volunteer position: "But I walked out with a contract for full-time independent contractor. . . . So I did the guardian ad litem work, and . . . within ten minutes I'm like, 'Aha.'" Evidently, the county was looking to upgrade the quality of that office owing to the many trained but unqualified people seeking to provide those services. At the time, she "wasn't thinking of it as a career thing": "I was just sort of thinking like I gotta feel good about myself." The job paid poorly, but she loved it.

Her legal training and writing skills quickly made Blair a favorite of the family court judges. She took mediation training and began getting referrals for mediations she could do on the side. When a change in law eliminated full-time guardian ad litem positions, she told her friends, and "the doors [blew] off" in the demand for her services.

Blair's practice was a variation of pure mediation: "I didn't do a ton of mediation, but I did a lot of parenting consulting." Blair "joined a consultation group that happened to [include the] few people who get all the [parental consulting] business": "And, through those folks, I met more folks. . . . And so I'm in . . . four consultation groups right now. And, through that, I met all the bigheads." She now does training: "For the first time in my life, I have mentors and people who grease the skids for me. . . . It's this incredibly warm and welcoming and incredibly generous community. And it's primarily mental health providers, but there are a few attorneys. . . . There are a number of folks who have training in both." She estimated that 96% are women.

Blair works from home and says she puts in fewer hours compared to practicing in a firm. She is an adjunct professor and is active in civic activities, especially those connected to her practice. Her social activities revolve around her professional group. She did not express concern about her debt but noted that the $60,000 she borrowed will be repaid two years after her mortgage is: "I'll be paying my student loans into my 60s." Her female partner is an artist.

Blair is a talented attorney who did not know what she wanted to do, even though her friends directed her toward positions that might fit her interests. Lacking an entrepreneurial spirit and confidence, she failed disastrously when she teamed up with a friend. But her small niche as a guardian ad litem blossomed into a thriving solo mediation practice focused on child custody issues. Her friends recognized what comported with her values and skills, and she found a community of like-minded friends. She is prosperous and enjoys her lifestyle.

INVENTION

Blair's interview reveals another feature of solo practice that is ignored in the literature: invention. Blair was not particularly entrepreneurial, but her legal writing skills and the guardian ad litem position helped her develop a legalized role as an adviser to divorced parents. She in effect invented and helped advance the legalization of a position that today we would call *JD advantage*, but this term ignores the process of moving it toward more law.

Annette's real estate work exemplifies a recognition of opportunities to bring legal analyses and lawyers into such issues as short sales and to expand their role in title insurance. Alejandro moving into "crimmigration" helped invent a field of immigration practice addressing the growing connection of criminal law to immigrant status. Toby recognizing the importance of changes in LGBTQ law to immigration law was both inventive and value driven.

The Upper Hemisphere of Solo Practice

We now turn to a group of solo lawyers who have more in common with corporate lawyers than with the solos discussed so far. This group represents a small but apparently growing segment of solo practice, one facilitated by technology, including virtual work, and the market value today of the networks—strong and weak ties—and symbolic capital that comes from experience in a prominent law firm. Unlike those identified by Carlin (1962) and Seron (2007) as close to the upper hemisphere, this group started in corporate law firms. They are both connected to corporate law firms and separated from them by their perceived lack of fit in those spaces. Their stories are of both corporate law firms and solo practices that most had never contemplated.

Monica graduated from a local Chicago law school and was hired by the large firm at which she had summered, largely practicing class action defense. Her previous work as a paralegal led her to litigation, and her grades secured her the position. She aspired to advancement within the firm and got a senior partner to mentor her and provide informal information about how the firm worked. He also provided work and was an effective teacher but lacked political pull. She was relatively satisfied with her position and speculated that, if she left, it would be to do something totally different, perhaps solo practice.

By the second interview (2008), Monica had gone solo. She left the firm after being reviewed for partner in 2007. The economy was slowing, and the firm made no promotions. Her coworkers told her that, if anyone had been promoted, it would have been her. But she was skeptical. She noted: "One particular partner I work with, every year it seemed like he would say, 'Well, she did great at XYZ, but we're not sure if she can do this.'" And the task would be something she had already done for someone else. She continued: "So the next year I would do that for him, and he'd go, 'She's great. She did this, this, and this, but I'm not sure if she can do this,' and I . . . felt he was someone . . . had he really pounded the table for me, I [would have been promoted]." After the sudden death of her mother and serious injury to her father in a automobile accident, she reevaluated her position in the firm.

The final straw came when Monica was assigned to represent an Alaska-based company. She had to be constantly available to the client (adjusting for the time differential). She finally went to the partner in charge and asked to be removed from this assignment. It took five weeks for the partner to respond to her. It was now obvious to her that the firm always comes first and there was no room for personal life.

Resignation did not sever Monica's ties. After going solo, she did the same work for the same clients: "[They] wanted me to continue working with them, so I actually share the cases with my old firm." One of the cases she continued was a huge class action that she had worked on since joining the firm. Her ability to service the class actions was rewarded as a solo, even though it did not lead to a partnership.

Monica reported that she had so much work as a solo that she expected to earn more than she had at the firm. She caught up with friends, and the down economy of 2009 actually helped her. The litigation continued unabated, and the firm could retain her at a cost savings for clients.

By her third interview in 2013, Monica had celebrated the five-year anniversary of her solo practice. She still had some of the work from 2009 plus small class actions and other litigation. At least 80% of her practice was class action defense. She had done some networking initially but no longer had to spend a lot of time on business development. Technology facilitated her management of these cases, and some of the tedious work was now handled by e-discovery firms with contract lawyers. She recognized that her previous affiliation brought her credibility as a solo.

In her first interview, Monica had expressed interest in writing fiction, and she published her first novel as an e-book in 2010. The book did well enough that she was bringing it out in paper and audio formats. When some big cases resolved in 2012, she decided to focus up to half her time writing a second book. She was also working as an adjunct legal writing professor at her alma mater. She was still single and owned a home.

Each year Monica earned as much or more than she made at the law firm (although, of course, less than if she had stayed).

Our web search finds that Monica had moved to a seven-person law firm as of counsel in 2018, doing precisely the work she was doing before. She has now written nine books, all in print.

Bradley graduated from a local Los Angeles law school after studying engineering at one of the service academies. He grew up in the Northwest, where his parents owned a restaurant. At the time of the first interview, he was working at the large Los Angeles–based law firm at which he had summered in law school. He was attracted in part to the firm's patent law practice and was assigned to cover technology, including everything from golf clubs to Internet-based inventions. He had assisted with a few patent litigation cases but primarily did patent prosecution.

Bradley thought that he was "getting good training" and liked the work, especially solving the "puzzle" of new technology. He had decided to concentrate the first two years on "learning the work." He lived with his girlfriend and still had law school debt.

When we reinterviewed him in 2009, Bradley had left the large law firm and opened a solo practice. He was renting shared space in an office building near his home and had access to resources on his floor: including conference rooms, a receptionist, and office supplies. He explained the timing of his move to solo practice as follows:

> As I was starting to bring in clients, I just saw that there was an opportunity to develop my own client base. And the partnership track was . . . still four or five years out, and so I figured if I'm having success bringing in clients maybe . . . there was an opportunity to do it on my own. I had one potential client that was coming online, so I made the decision, OK, let's time this so at least I had one month . . . of work . . . seeing if any other clients would come with. So it was . . . a bit of a gamble, but it worked out.

The partners were very accommodating when Bradley left the firm, and some of his clients came with him. His solo practice focused mostly on patent prosecution, and his target clients were midsize companies without in-house intellectual property lawyers.

Bradley noted that most of his business came from referrals from past clients and contacts. He had clients referred from his academy friends, and some of his friends are now clients. He got married in 2004. His wife is an artist and had her own studio. They owned their home.

The economic downturn did not affect Bradley's practice materially, except that some clients were slow to pay. To his advantage, "people [were] shopping around a little bit more." When we asked about the disadvantages of solo practice, Bradley reported that some clients have substantial patent portfolios and that he may be unable to handle all their work. He likes working for startup companies. He does not do the corporate formation work but handles the intellectual property portfolio and refers the corporate work to others, who in turn refer patent work to him. Unlike in the large firm, he can receive equity from start-ups.

When we interviewed Bradley in 2013, he had moved to a new office building in downtown Los Angeles. He and his wife now had three children. She still pursued her art but no longer worked outside the home. They had recently bought a house in a nice area near downtown. He now employed two associates and had some part-time interns. His practice was about 70% patent law and 30% trademark law.

Moving downtown enabled Bradley to join lawyers' networking groups, one of which had "become pretty reliable for referrals [for] patent matters." He is also active in the Los Angeles Bar Association's intellectual property group and gets referrals from his academy friends.

Bradley makes time for his family and tries not to work on the weekends. He and his wife are involved in their church. He had a small amount of debt remaining from law school. His website shows offices in Seattle and Los Angeles.

Nicholas graduated from a state university in the Northwest and a top West Coast law school and comes from a family of solos. He proudly told us: "My father was a solo, my grandfather was a solo, and my great-grandfather as well. It's a long line of mavericks. I like the label of solo just because it fits in with the family tradition."

Nicholas expressed dislike for most of his law school classmates, but relationships with two law school friends have made his career. After summering in an elite Wall Street firm, one of his close friends steered him toward an entrepreneurial Silicon Valley firm, where he was hired doing corporate work focusing especially on start-ups. He loved the firm: "All the partners are very young. . . . There are opportunities here to get rich very quickly from their equity programs." But the recession forced the firm to merge with a large, traditionally organized law firm. "It just wasn't fun anymore." So Nicholas left without a plan. He got a real estate license and dealt in subprime loans and did odd jobs with friends who had left law firms. He had good relationships with several clients from the law firm and was able to continue that representation with the firm's permission. He reviewed contracts, compiled board minutes, attended board meetings, and performed other related tasks for clients he knew.

Nicholas had the opportunity to form a firm with friends but preferred to work as a solo: "It just suits me better." He did find his situation a bit precarious, but he had connections from his firm who were now general counsel who gave him some work, which he did about three days a week. For about half his clients he took equity and reduced his direct fees. He worked an eight-to-five schedule and then exercised for a couple of hours and ran marathons.

When we interviewed him in 2018, Nicholas noted: "I'm happy where I am . . . having a full stable of clients and making more money than I'd ever made before. . . . And, professionally, I've gained a lot more skill sets, and there's a lot more opportunities." All his business came through word of mouth, particularly from a Silicon Valley investment bank one of his classmate friends was connected to. The bank would assign a trusted lawyer to take private companies in their portfolio public and "have a babysitter basically." For example: "I started working with an energy company as an outside attorney. . . . [The company] grew a lot from 2006 until 2011, [when] we sold [it]." The investment bank relationship has led to several other private company clients. For example, he became involved in a venture started by an executive from a company he had worked with and served as general counsel and vice president in 2018. Although he is a full-time employee, the arrangement allows him to work on noncompeting outside engagements. His career has been characterized by relationships of varying formality while working essentially as a solo.

Nicholas also joined a virtual law firm with one of his two closest law school friends: "So it's kind of a hobby on the side. I have my own paralegal, . . . and I can charge more for her now because we're in a law firm, and I can charge more for myself now because I'm in a law firm, so it's a win-win." Indeed, he attributed all his success to this pair of friends with similar backgrounds, "country boys" like him: "So those are . . . really the only two I'm in contact with, but, luckily, they are both very smart and very successful at what they did and know a lot of people, and, yeah, they're the rainmakers, really. I just live off their coattails. . . . But for them I'd probably be homeless living under an overpass." Nicholas has invested in several start-ups, converting hourly fees to income-generating property, allowing him also to own a cabin in the Sierras.

We interviewed Bryce in 2006 and in 2018. The son of a mathematics professor from New York City, he attended a prestigious liberal arts college and one of the city's top law schools, earning a JD and an LLM in taxation. He graduated without debt, thanks to an inheritance from an aunt. He summered and took an associate position at an elite white-shoe firm, where he stayed for five years.

Bryce developed an interest in corporate and banking law partly through volunteering for a credit union before law school. Limited engagement with the technical aspects of his work motivated his departure from the firm: "So I was a math major. . . . I enjoy doing that kind of stuff, and I found that very constraining at a law firm. . . . I was really effectively running deals. . . . But . . . there were whole worlds that I was just not involved in . . . regulatory aspects, the negotiation aspects, the accounting aspects. And I kind of said, you know what, these are all really interesting things."

Bryce's mentor at the firm was a tax partner: "[A firm colleague] said you've got to get in and work with [the partner]; he's the top of the field you know. . . . And so I angled very specifically to work with him, . . . and he really showed me the ropes in this subspecialty. . . . Even within the law firm he would say . . . this is what's going on, these are the people that matter if you want to stay and become a partner." He felt somewhat guilty leaving his sponsor but was souring on the brass ring of partnership, wondering: "How . . . shiny a ring is this actually?"

Aspiring to run transactions and not just do the legal work, Bryce joined the product development team of an investment bank postrecession: "I had the opportunity, and it was a lot more money." He noted some improvement in his lifestyle, working fewer hours and rarely on weekends: "My hours are more reasonable now that I've left the firm, but . . . it really is a strain." His salary was lower than it was at the firm, but most of his compensation came from a year-end bonus. To his surprise, he was also doing legal work about one-third of the time.

Bryce was married to a corporate lawyer and had one child. He noted that he and his wife were in a "classic conundrum": "You know sort of traditional gender roles are very much playing out . . . like . . . I would not feel OK being a house husband. I also make a lot more money than she does." They had a nanny, and his wife was "looking at other positions that might be a more reasonable trade-off": "She's not interested in making partner anymore . . . [perhaps] in-house or nonprofit or even the United Nations." By the next interview, they had divorced.

By 2018, Bryce had "bounced around" banks for a while. During the financial crisis of 2008–9, he "lost [the] fire in the belly": "So [when] the axe fell one day I knew it was going to." He had not considered going solo "because it just wasn't in our field of experienc[e]." Then a couple of people he knew—litigators and a few corporate lawyers—went solo, and in 2012 he followed suit.

Bryce was told: "[If] you have enough money to weather the first two years, which I did, you'll look up in three years and never look back. And so now I'm there. It's been five years." He reported:

> This feels like an amazing fit. Doing well financially, I hired two accountants because they're cheaper than lawyers, and . . . I don't need other tax lawyers yet, but that may well come as I slowly grow. So it's thriving; it's doing great. I have control over my hours. But, more than that, I'm engaged again. . . . And now I've found that, again, I really love doing this. I don't spend as many hours total because I have. . . . Well, I was married, and then I was divorced, and now I'm married again, so I have two kids, one from a prior marriage, one from my current marriage. So I don't pull the crazy hours.

Bryce now has the flexibility to spend time with his son. At the law firm: "Flexibility was really completely absent . . . certainly from law firm practice. . . . And the view on the ground in the trenches was anything the firm told you about being flexible was a complete and total lie, and, if you fell for that, you were too stupid to be at the firm." Bryce describes his marketing skills as an "ineffable gift." Still the "plurality" of his practice comes from referrals from corporate law firms. His elite law firm experience was the foundation of his practice. As of 2020, his firm included an associate, two accountants, an office manager/paralegal, and a marketing professional.

Interviewed in 2004, 2009, and 2018, Ricardo is the son of a Cuban refugee who grew up in a "working-class family" with few resources. A first-generation college graduate, he went on to graduate from a highly ranked law school. He spent his first summer at an elite New York law firm through a program targeting minorities and his second at another elite firm.

Ricardo never found comfort in a large law firm, moving from New York to San Francisco and back seeking a better fit. Discouraged, he described "a very inhospitable environment." He felt out of place while associates golfed with partners, discussing yachting off the coast of France and NCAA basketball. His engagement waned, and the New York firm eventually let him go, but his credentials provided opportunities.

Ricardo moved to Chicago with his wife. Also a lawyer, she had decided to stay home with their children. After brief, unfulfilling stints with Chicago firms, Ricardo relocated to southern California, joining a prestigious Los

Angeles–based firm to do mergers, acquisitions, and general corporate work. Despite receiving assurances that he would be promoted to partner, he did not believe it. Also: "Frankly I was growing tired of the late nights and billable hours." He was lured away to become general counsel at a small energy company. The position turned out to be too good to be true: "I was inundated with up-the-ladder reports of violations of law and breaches of fiduciary duty by other members of the management team. It turns out the company was in dire straits."

Six months later, Ricardo and his wife decided to move again, but the economy was softer, and it took almost a year to find work. He eventually took a position at a large law firm in Texas: "Half of my wife's family is here . . . lots of free babysitting as well." However, the new firm was partner heavy, so "the junior partners do the job that senior associates typically do." Consequently: "The quality of my work here is not nearly as good as it was elsewhere." Ricardo did not discuss partnership: "They're happy with my work, but, at a time when the pie is shrinking, it's not a really prudent time to be discussing promotion." He had "a much better personal life": "I get to see my children for dinner every night; I come in at a leisurely 9:30 in the morning, bill my eight hours, and go home. . . . This is definitely the easiest job I've had ever." But he also had "fewer opportunities to run deals . . . and lower pay."

Ricardo and his wife had three children, and she had just taken an in-house position with a large company. Their combined education debt had decreased from $300,000 to $70,000. He concluded: "I'm trying to resist my natural urge to move on."

By 2018, Ricardo had declined a partnership and left the Texas firm after four years, remaining in the same city. After he and his wife attempted to start a venture-backed technology company, they started their own law firm out of their home:

> We . . . saw some opportunities present themselves to us, and we had folks who I know through my network reach out to me and ask me if we'd be in a position to assist them with various legal matters. And given that we were drawing no compensation for several years . . . we started to take on small engagements here and there. . . . I was also doing some contract work as of counsel for [his prior firm]. And the work that we were originating through our law firm just grew, and grew, and grew, and it reached a point where we were able to focus exclusively on the firm, and it's been quite successful.

The contacts came from "the large firms" at which he had worked, mainly the Texas-based firm, where he had done deals himself: "So I had direct contact with lots of decision-makers. And what we do at our firm is we provide the same, virtually identical service to what I provided at the larger firms, only our rates are . . . roughly half what they were. . . . And so it's not a difficult pitch for us to win business from clients, given the ever-increasing billable hour rates at the large firms." Another lawyer from his previous firm had also joined them to do commercial real estate. The firm's revenues grew quickly, rising from $200,000 a year to $1.5 million in the current year.

The firm's marketing was low-key: "We invest in just being helpful. . . . [It's] an interesting market . . . a big city that feels like a little town. I feel like a lot of the business folks know each other personally." Ricardo had helped the chief executive officer (CEO) of a public company he had represented at the firm on his exit from his company. He did not charge him. In turn, the former CEO introduced him to a billionaire headquartered in the city who then became a major client and also a source of referrals from other business elites.

Ricardo and his wife did not exploit their identity as a "woman-owned, minority-owned law firm," turning down an invitation-only conference by a major company for minority-owned law firms: "We just don't need it. And I'm really trying to build a brand that's associated with high-quality legal work, and I . . . don't want to come to be known as an affirmative action law firm."

Ricardo highlighted two features of the firm's business strategy. First:

> We've been very careful with our brand, and so all of our attorneys are graduates of top-tier law schools and alumni of top-tier law firms. . . . And that helps a great deal. I've had clients in meetings . . . brag about my background. Because otherwise I'm just some random guy with a name they've never heard of. And, given that it's Texas, I'm possibly discounted because I have a Hispanic surname, so they like to do that.

Second:

> I think I am pretty entrepreneurial. I'm not risk averse; neither is my wife. . . . My dad is a car salesman. . . . Every negotiation is a sale. You're selling something, right? . . . I may not go out there and do much networking, but I still do need to pitch. Yeah, I get recommendations from the billionaire and my other clients, but I still need to pitch and close the deal. Yeah, I would say that it's more than just resting on my laurels and having a good reputation.

Working solo was far more satisfying than was working at the firm:

> For the first time I've been enjoying what I do. I really never enjoyed being at a large firm. There are so many things about it I didn't like. I haven't had a boss in years. I accept or reject clients at my discretion. I have a personal relationship with all of my clients. . . . I make better money than I would at a large firm. . . . Oh and my teenagers all want to be lawyers and come work.

The firm's website today shows three lawyers, highlighting the savings and flexible billing of a "virtual law firm," while also suggesting the importance of its network of boutique firms.

The last example illustrates an alternative method of cofounding an entrepreneurial practice. Emilio, a Mexican American lawyer whose father drove a truck, learned to use his identity as a solo. A first-generation college graduate, he attended an elite law school and began at an elite law firm. With support from scholarships, he incurred only moderate debt, which he had repaid.

Emilio did not enjoy law school but described the firm in mixed terms:

> It's great people, really smart people, committed people, but I was there . . . for almost three years, and I did three depositions, and two of them were expert depositions, and the rest of the time was just writing demurrers or doing those document reviews, that kind of stuff, which is what younger lawyers do anyway. But, again, you have to remember where I started from, the first person from my family to graduate from college, the first person from my family to be a lawyer. . . . It was a shock going into [the elite law school], and then it was an even bigger shock ending up at [the law firm]. And I had good mentors, but the people who were my mentors, one left a little less than a year after I started there, and then the other mentor that I had left about 18 months after I started. . . . So that . . . left me in a little bit of a lurch.

He considered partnership at first: "But you kind of see the writing on the wall. . . . After a couple of years, especially when the people . . . I was working with left, you have to find somebody to be a mentor."

After three years, Emilio moved to a small litigation-focused firm that a partner from his firm told him about. He stayed for ten years, becoming a partner, before partnering with a friend from his first firm and taking several key clients from the second. They have received additional work from referrals: "Everyone hustles to get some work. . . . Pretty much everyone here [networks], and we have to do it to grow." The firm hired three associates and anticipated needing more to manage overwork. Emilio learned a lot about the business of law from books and consulted with friends about the logistics of starting a practice. His wife has a high-ranking position at a nonprofit working 14-hour days: "I don't feel the pressure to be home as much as I would otherwise." He usually worked until 7:30 P.M. and occasional weekends. He and his wife had no children at the time.

Emilio's firm emphasizes its diversity and has been very successful. Its website trumpets the elite law firm credentials of its lawyers, now seven plus the two founding partners. Describing his attraction to law practice, Emilio said: "There's an element to being a lawyer that's. . . . I think it's a lot of fun . . .

a lot of arguing, a lot of fighting. There's somebody on the other side who gets paid to point out my mistakes, and I get paid to try to find their mistakes. I think that's a lot of fun." Reviewing his career to date, he noted: "When I started, I thought I would be at a large firm for a long time. That changed rather quickly, and, when it did, I never really envisioned having my own firm. That was never part of my plan. I'm very risk averse. . . . I think . . . if [his friend] hadn't shown up . . . I probably would still be at [the firm] being second-fiddle partner."

Rethinking the Solo Practitioner

These accounts of solo practice as a process, not an end state, contrast with the scholarly literature on solos as a group of failures with marginal careers. The lower hemisphere features considerable innovation and entrepreneurialism, and the upper hemisphere is a significant and distinctive segment of solo practice. The differences between the two reveal the accumulated advantage of those with access to leading schools and brand-name corporate law firms vs. those from lower-ranked schools and practices serving individuals rather than businesses. Nevertheless, those without upper-hemisphere advantages enjoy rewarding careers often involving public service.

Lower-hemisphere solos often encountered economic uncertainty developing a viable practice without a ready-made network forged in corporate law practice. Their strategies are localized, often connected to family, where they grew up, or racial/ethnic or linguistic networks. Relatedly, they often saw their practices as mission driven—providing ethical and affordable service to underserved communities. This feature of solo practice is virtually ignored in scholarly literature and is largely missing in the upper hemisphere.

There are similarities in solo careers across hemispheres. Like the ethical challenges described by Carlin (1962, 1966), we found jobs that "were too good to be true" in both hemispheres. Both were marked by innovation, developing new types of legal services, clients, and organizational forms—like virtual offices. Both hemispheres sought work/life balance. Corporate client solos almost always judged their lifestyles against the demands and inflexibility of corporate law firms.

Both personal-client and corporate-client solos showcased entrepreneurialism, pursuing connections to potential clients, and persuading them to bring them work. Solos in both sectors made deliberate decisions about staffing, office arrangements, and marketing, referencing terms like *hustling* and *making a sale*. Yet, as Seron (2007) observed, most marketing involves promotion through referrals and word of mouth rather than advertising.

Moving Inside: Practicing Law
in Business Organizations

In this chapter we examine the career narratives of lawyers in business, both those who practice law inside business—inside counsel—and those who are not practicing law. As we discussed in chapter 2, there has been a sea change in the professional status of lawyers going in-house to business since Smigel (1964) described them as failures in the chase for partnership in Wall Street law firms. This characterization of inside counsel persisted through the 1970s (see Slovak 1979, 1981; and Heinz and Laumann 1982) but has been swept away with the ascent of corporate counsel to positions that allow them to dictate the terms of relationships between corporations and business (Heineman 2016; Nelson 1988) and the emergence of inside counsel positions as highly desirable compared to associate and partner positions in law firms.

Yet the entry to positions in business typically comes through positions in law firms, after practicing lawyers have developed specialized expertise in fields serving corporate clients and, often, mobilized social networks to make the move to business. Once in business, attorneys pursue strategies for advancing within the organization or for advancing to more senior positions in other businesses. Our capital assets approach illuminates how attorneys develop the kinds of social capital that allow them to gain entry to business positions and then move up within the world of business and law. This change was not inevitable. The ascendency of corporate counsel could have led to competition with corporate law firms for the most desirable law school graduates; it could also have led to a different kind of recruiting, for example, targeting those who were not on elite tracks but would be well trained and competent. But, within the American legal field, changes such as the rise of corporate counsel are generally absorbed in ways that protect traditional hierarchies. Business initially drew on corporate partners to become in-house leaders, not trusting their own lawyers, deemed as failures in gaining partnership status. Not surprisingly, as they gained power, general counsels looked to the large law firms with graduates from high-status law schools to build their departments. As corporate law firm partnerships became both harder to get and less desirable, one reason to start in such law firms *became* the high value placed on that experience, seen no longer as a failure but instead as a valued legal credential, one that was especially well suited to get into prestigious in-house positions. This is a track strong enough to stand out in the sequence analyses of chapter 3.

For over a century, the *habitus* (Bourdieu's term for the internalized "strategies" that actors follow to make careers given the structure of the legal field) of graduates of the high-prestige law schools has militated in favor of a default position in a corporate law firm after graduation (and/or clerkships). This habitus still exists, but it now incorporates an expectation that most will not be among the chosen few with sponsors for partnership, that many also will not feel welcome or comfortable or willing to live with the demands in terms of time and commitment of the corporate law firms. Now some lawyers naturally look at in-house as a very nice option. Thus, we argue, there is a discrete group of lawyers, including many women and minorities, who enter the inside counsel positions with welcomes through the front door and see people just like themselves thriving on the inside.

Attorneys with less elite credentials and no corporate law firm experience enter business law through various side doors, sometimes by working in an industry before getting a law degree or by building a resume based on corporate experience rather than law school credentials. As with the solo practitioners who succeed through serendipity or passion, these careers are much more varied than the big law to big corporate counsel track. They are rarely in the top corporations unless they gain access by working their way up, often aided by a personal relationship or a merger that moves them into a larger company.

One difference between the law firms and corporate counsel is that the business setting opens up possibilities to move one's career more toward business without necessarily changing companies or even positions. Here, too, there is a range of evolving options. As we will see in the next chapter, law school graduates in state government positions often try to move from positions that are deemed to be not law to positions where the law is recognized and valued, which usually means a higher status for law school graduates. In the for-profit side, this hierarchy is embedded in the career distinction between *JD-required* positions and *JD advantage* positions (terms that the National Association for Law Placement [NALP] uses in its placement reports), with the former more prestigious and even more valuable in reporting law school placement statistics. Positions such as those in human resources, intellectual property, compliance, or legal and business affairs may be combinations of law and business, and historically they have carried less prestige than those identified specifically with law. Today, they can be steps up or down depending on the setting and the rewards. When intellectual property became legalized and central to business, for example, its position changed in the hierarchy.

At the elite level, in particular, lawyers may go into investment banking or business consulting as a perceived step up, and in these positions the role of law can vary enormously. The professional and financial service firms compete for legal talent at the highest level, especially at the entry level for JDs/MBAs, but also later in careers.

Prior to the increase in the prestige of inside counsel, the conventional wisdom rationalized the high status of partners in the law firms by deprecating corporate counsel as too beholden to their employers and unable to assert any autonomy since they could be fired if they did not do what they were told. There is a somewhat more recent literature about deskilling, routinization, and perceived loss of professional autonomy, the supposed conditions of employed lawyers in business or in public bureaucracies (Derber 1982; Spangler 1986). There is now a counterliterature—one based on the new roles of corporate counsel—suggesting that general counsel represent the new site for lawyer-statespersons (Heineman 2016), partly because corporate law firms must now compete so assiduously for corporate business that they may compromise their integrity. There are many examples. The fact that the same people with more or less the same backgrounds are found in the corporate counsel and in the corporate law firms makes it likely that they will employ their legal skills in the same way in relation to business. There are temptations and also some incentives to take potentially unethical matters up the ladder.

Debates about losing or gaining autonomy are staples among lawyers, including in the books used for legal profession classes. That emphasis helps, from a sociological perspective, build the image of the profession as more than simply hired guns. Those who fight for the principle of autonomy are rewarded for the benefit they bring the profession generally. They help promote the image of lawyer-statespersons at the top of the profession. The argument of autonomy also may help keep at bay the idea that lawyers should be more accountable for their choices of clients (except, e.g., when they are public defenders). The assumption of autonomy makes the representation of corrupt clients seem less worrisome perhaps.

The big difference between business settings and law firms is the billable hour's continued domination within the corporate law firms, despite decades of predictions of its demise. Success in that setting is all about the billable hour. The billable hour itself has structural impacts. For example, one aspect of the law firm experience is a dedication to availability that, many interviewees suggest, precludes any personal life. The willingness to drop everything for work is built into many associates' lives since they are not infrequently given assignments on Friday afternoon that are due Monday morning. This is so firmly built into the relationship that a general counsel who spoke in Bryant Garth's legal profession class said that, if he were unable to finish something Friday afternoon, he would send it to a law firm only too happy to have the additional hours billed. And a gunner associate would be reluctant to say, Please give this to someone else. The narratives of moving from law firms to corporations often involve the desire to leave the demands of the billable hour. And, again consistent with the way in which the developments all relate to each other and existing hierarchies, the rise of in-house counsel and the ability to demand more work from corporate law firms reinforces the billable hour in law firms.

We organize this analysis around the distinction between the two basic types of sequences that we saw in chapter 3—the elite track, which we identified with the front door, and the less elite track, which does not connect to high-ranked law schools and prestigious corporate law firms. With respect to each group, we also explore the way in which business and law interact in some careers. Some lawyers are chasing the rewards that come to some business careers; others find that, when they moved from business careers into law school and law careers, their most valued capital was their business expertise and networks.

Statistical Profile of Lawyers Working in Business

Chapter 4 documented the exodus from large and midsize law firms to positions in business. Chapter 5 demonstrated the dominance of business-oriented fields of law by lawyers working in business compared to their counterparts in large law firms. But the sequence analysis presented in chapter 3 is the most helpful in terms of understanding the careers of lawyers in business. In chapter 3 we found that there are three career sequences characterized by positions in business. All three of these sequences feature business as an end point, but only two of these clusters tend to begin in this setting as well. The first sequence that primarily begins and ends in business contains 8.8% of respondents, about half of whom were practicing law at wave 3. The second business starter sequence is the smallest of all the clusters (4.1%) and is characterized by more frequent job changes and spells of unemployment. Forty percent of this group began their careers in business, with the remainder coming from a variety of other settings, and the majority were working in business at wave 3. Women and racial minorities are overrepresented in this cluster, and 80% have been unemployed at least once in their career. The third and largest business sequence ("big to business") is composed of the 9.5% of sample respondents who began their careers in large law firms before moving to business in-house counsel positions.

The three business sequences map onto the career trajectories we contrast in this chapter, with big to business approximating the elite track from large firms to in-house counsel positions and the sequences that begin in business or small firms representing the side door. Respondents in the big to business cluster are relatively elite, with 24% graduating from top-10 law schools and 43% graduating from schools ranked in the top 20, and, at wave 3, this cluster had the highest median earnings in the entire sample ($206,500). In contrast, only 9% of respondents in both business starter clusters graduated from top-10 law schools. At wave 3, respondents in the larger of the two clusters earned roughly the same amount as the sample overall, while the smaller cluster earned a median of $100,000, less than half the median earnings of the big to business cluster. Thus, there appears to be a status distinction generally within the business sector between attorneys who are inside counsel and those who are in nonpracticing positions. To be sure, there are elite JD-MBA programs whose graduates start in investment banks, private equity firms, or hedge funds, but the numbers are dwarfed by those for whom business is a generally less prestigious alternative. For example, an appreciable number of lawyers start their careers after working full-time in business, then attend night law school and usually seek to use their business experience to find a position where the law degree is valued, whether in itself or in some business-law mix.

Corporate counsel have become leading spokespersons for diversity in the legal profession (Headworth et al. 2016). Without the long organizational history of favoring White men with wives at home, legal departments in business have been more open. It is not surprising that we find people of color and especially Asian Americans well represented in inside counsel positions. As we saw in chapter 6 and will see again in chapters 10 and 12, law firms of all sizes are dependent on personal relations and billable hours and often make structurally biased judgments of who fits in and deserves the perception of a presumptive rainmaker. These perceptions tend to drive out women and minorities before they achieve equity partnership positions. Corporate counsel is appealing to many of those individuals, including some who just did not want to be a partner. African Americans, who make up 9% of the sample overall at midcareer, are slightly overrepresented in inside counsel positions

(10%). In contrast, they make up 8% of lawyers in law firms of 251 or more at midcareer. Asian Americans, who make up an additional 10% of the sample at midcareer, make up 14% of inside counsel positions, a figure slightly higher than their presence in large law firms, where they make up 12% of attorneys. Whites remain the predominant group in inside counsel positions at 65%, but this figure is somewhat lower than that reflecting their presence in the sample at midcareer (68%). Whites make up a higher percentage of those in business who are not practicing law (74%).

Women are well represented in inside counsel positions. They hold 48% of inside counsel positions, compared to their presence at 49% in the sample overall. But they are much less likely to work in business if not practicing, holding only 39% of those positions.

Becoming Inside Counsel

THE ELITE PATH TO INSIDE COUNSEL

The front door to corporate jobs is opened by elite education credentials and first jobs in large law firms. Trevor, a gay African American man who graduated from an elite undergraduate institution and a top-20 law school, began his career in one of the leading law firms in a national market city. Although he stayed at the law firm for five and a half years, he said he never had the goal or the expectation of making partner. The law firm was instrumental for his long-term goal of practicing entertainment law, and he began looking for inside counsel positions in his second year at the firm. To position himself for this move, he did extensive networking in the entertainment field, drawing on law school alumni contacts. He was hired by a major entertainment conglomerate and has remained with that company through to the present. He now is vice president for business and legal affairs for one of the divisions of the company. He knew coming out of law school that the easy track into entertainment law was to start in a corporate law firm that did entertainment law, build networks, skills, and credibility and wait for an opportunity.

Claire is an Asian American woman who also graduated from an elite undergraduate institution and a top-20 law school and practiced in a leading employment law firm for five years. With her eyes set on an inside counsel position to provide a better work/life balance, and knowing that she needed to acquire the skills necessary to move in-house, she took a position in a law firm that emphasized counseling over litigation. This move was facilitated in part by her social networks, particularly among the Asian American community. Former coworkers who had left her first firm for another notified her that they were looking for people, and she was hired without an interview. Her next career move was also aided by her connections. Two years later, a friend from law school who was working as head in-house counsel for a large corporation contacted her to let her know the company was hiring and to see whether she was interested in the job. She pursued the opportunity and landed a position as in-house counsel.

Claire notes that her primary motivation for moving in-house was to pursue a more manageable work schedule, and she reflected on how a law firm partnership seemed impossible for women with children: "When I was in a law firm, I couldn't envision myself being partner because I looked at every woman there, and either the husband didn't work, or they had a nanny and they never saw their kids. There were not two working parents making it work in a happy way." Claire and her husband worked as inside counsel in companies in close proximity to each other and could readily drop their children off at school on the way to work. LinkedIn shows that Claire was later promoted to director and assistant general counsel and has subsequently moved into the same role at another large company in the same locale. One key feature of her personality was that, while she saw no way to manage in a large law firm, she was extremely ambitious and told us, for example, that she would move if she did not get the promotions she sought.

Paula, whom we discussed in chapter 1, was looking toward partnership in a large law firm. Her elite law school credentials and experience and her status as a Latina at a time when firms were looking to burnish their images as committed to diversity made her a plausible candidate for promotion. Yet she came to realize that there was really no place for her to gain the mentors and sponsors needed to make partner, especially if she was not willing to abandon hopes for raising a family. She shifted toward a focus on lifestyle, justifying a move to inside counsel and, indeed, a general slowing of her ambitions so that she could give more attention to her family. Her ethnicity and ability to speak Spanish facilitated a move to a family-friendly position in a media firm that did not make the intense work demands of a corporate law firm.

Although Spencer, a White man, attended a law school ranked from 51 to 100, he had graduated from an elite undergraduate institution that one of the partners involved in hiring had attended and, thus, landed an associate position at a major Wall Street law firm. When we interviewed him six years into his career, he had established himself as an expert in mergers and acquisitions but wanted to move away from the intense work demands of Wall Street. He hoped to do similar work but inside a corporate law department. He spoke about the job searches he already was conducting, looking for the right kind of opportunity in the right geographic location. LinkedIn reports that he indeed had moved to an inside counsel position in a large financial corporation where he had become associate general counsel for mergers and acquisitions. We have no sense of whether he had any aspirations to become a partner. Perhaps, like Trevor and Claire, he saw the corporate law firm as a first step leading to a good opportunity as corporate counsel.

Darby, a White woman, graduated from a top-10 law school. Her father had practiced in big law before starting his own firm, and she followed in his footsteps in her early career. She started out working in a large global law firm, where she stayed for two years. When we interviewed her at wave 1, she had moved to another global firm and expressed that she was already intending to move again. After working in the second firm for one year, she took a position in federal government in a high-status regulatory agency. She stayed with this agency for eight years and had planned to remain longer. But, as she reported: "I had a friend who worked here [a tech company], and he knew they were looking for somebody. And so, while I was on [maternity] leave, he sent me the job posting and said, 'Are you interested?' So I talked to them, and it just kind of happened." She was hired by the tech company to continue on the business side of the same field of regulatory law she had practiced in government. Although she had intended to return to her government job after her maternity leave, her move was inspired by a desire for greater compensation and a regular schedule. Her husband also worked as inside counsel in a major corporation in the region. Darby expressed dissatisfaction with her corporate employer and spoke of her desire to move to a different company. LinkedIn reports that she has left the business world to become an administrator in an elite law school. Her career is evidence not just of the front door but of combining elite credentials with major connections and an upper-class family, including a very successful lawyer father. It is a career of one opportunity after another.

THE SIDE DOOR TO BUSINESS POSITIONS

In contrast to the elite paths to in-house positions, the side door to corporate counsel is opened not by elite credentials but by accumulated expertise, carving out a niche, or personal relationships. The corporations that nonelites work for are most often, but not always, different from the major companies that characterize the business sites of those individuals just described. Some opted for business opportunities on graduating from law school. Some already were working in business when they went to law school, sometimes at night, and then continued in a business career. Some had to overcome the lack of high-status credentials by demonstrating their skills in law practice and working their way into positions of greater responsibility. And, as with the more elite law school graduates, a career in law and business can become a dead end. Or one can start in a small company, and it can become a major one through mergers and acquisitions.

Patrick, a White man, attended a well-regarded public university as an undergraduate and a tier 3 law school, both within commuting distance of his home in the Northeast. We interviewed him six years into his career. Even in law school he knew he did not want to pursue private practice: "Going through law school I realized I wanted to be in more of a consulting type of position. I definitely did not want to be in litigation. I did not find what I heard about law firms very appealing. So this [i.e., business] is what I was more interested in, and an opportunity arose, so I took it." He "wanted to go in-house counsel." He had an opportunity in a local broker-dealer company with several hundred traders and a staff of 15 or 20. He found this position through a "friend who was already in that firm" and "running their compliance department": "That's where the opening up came." He took the job on graduation and stayed there three years. He worked both in compliance and in management, given that "it was a mom-and-pop type of firm. . . . The father was the CEO, the daughter ran the human resources department. . . . It was like walking on eggshells a lot of times."

Through Monster.com, Patrick landed a job as chief compliance officer and general counsel for a larger—55 employees when he started—but still relatively small investment firm that supports advisers for high–net worth investors. Right from the start he saw that advancement in this kind of business required him to move toward the business side: "There's no place up on the legal ladder, but I'm moving more into their operations ladder." In interviewing for the job, he noted: "I made it clear to the boss that, look, I like doing legal, and I like doing compliance, but I really want to run, I really want to help run this firm. I want to do operations; I want to move towards that area." Building on his experience in his first position, early on he took on a lot of operational responsibility. Since then he has hired lawyers to perform compliance and legal work. He stated that his position was now 25% legal and that he has become the chief operating officer of the company.

Patrick said the most satisfying aspect of his job was the "autonomy and room to grow": "I pretty much have freedom to act at my own will. There's really no one overseeing me directly." He puts in a lot of work hours—nine to seven on weekdays, sometimes on the weekend, an hour at home at night. He graduated law school with $130,000 in debt and is paying it down on a thirty-year schedule. He made $200,000 a year at the time he was interviewed. LinkedIn in 2019 reported that he still was chief operating officer of the same investment firm, which has grown substantially. While definitely not on track to move up the ladder of corporate counsel positions, he took advantage of the smaller companies he worked in to build a substantial and relatively highly compensated role in combining some law with managing the business.

Calvin, a White man, is an example of someone who worked for a business firm before and during law school and eventually returned to the same business firm after a few years in practice elsewhere. He came from what he described as "humble origins," raised by a divorced mother with four children who worked as a secretary. After majoring in finance at a large public university, he went to work in the trust department of a large bank. He attended the night program of a law school ranked from 51 to 100 and took a job at a midsize insurance defense law firm after graduating. It was at this point that we interviewed him the first time. When we asked where he thought we would find him in five years, he said that he hoped to be doing similar work but as an in-house attorney so that he would have more manageable hours. When we interviewed him five years later, he had returned to the bank where he had worked before and during law school. He had "gotten a tip" that the bank was creating a new position that involved a combination of banking and legal skills.

Calvin's new position was in a different part of the bank from his previous work there. Calvin was now in the investment side of the bank, preparing legal agreements for institutional investors. He did not report to the law department, although he had a "dotted line" to it. He remarked on how he played a different role in the organization than did the lawyers in the law department: "You've got to have money coming in the door to keep the business running. So my approach might be a little bit different from someone in the legal department proper because I'm a little more practical about it. I plot policy. I interpret policy and work with folks who make business decisions as well as the legal department to figure out where we can bend and where we can't."

Calvin talked about how his work/life balance is far superior to what it was when he worked in the law firm. He makes more money, works 8:00 A.M. to 4:30 P.M., with four weeks of vacation, paternity leave, and investment holidays. His stress is "a fraction of what it was." Asked where we would find him in five years, he said "definitely" at the same bank, which he said was "a great company." According to LinkedIn in 2019, his prediction was correct. He is now a senior corporate attorney and senior vice president. His major asset as a lawyer was that he had worked in and knew the bank that rehired him after law school. For both Calvin and Patrick, there was no particular trajectory established for them if they wanted to move up outside the companies in which they landed, but Calvin's position seems to have been tailor-made for him.

Sebastian, a White male, was working in an energy company as an engineer after graduating with a BS in chemical engineering when he went to law school at night in a school ranked from 51 to 100. On graduation, he became an associate at a large law firm in a major city and practiced environmental law. After two years, he was recruited back to industry by his former boss, almost immediately being made director of corporate health and safety, with some 15 staff reporting to him, including three attorneys. He was not planning to stay at the firm in any event:

> I would see the partners who were in their forties and fifties, and they were still—even though they were partners in the firm—they were still killing themselves developing their business and all that kind of stuff, and I guess I was just uncomfortable with having to develop and maintain my own business. . . . I knew I wasn't going to want to work at the firm when my wife and I were going to have a baby.

The lifestyle was important: "It's kind of my own schedule here. I come and go how I want. . . . At the firm I was probably billing like I said probably 50–55 hours a week, but I was working 75–80 hours a week of unbilled total. So, yeah, my hours have gone down considerably." His favorite part of his new job was that he can be proactive in the company. When he worked at the law firm, a call would come in about a worker who had been killed, and he was "always trying to save somebody's skin": "Now I feel like I'm in a position where I can actually do something about it before it happens, build up the system to better handle safety and environmental impacts as opposed to just putting out fires."

Sebastian clearly stated his ambition to move up the corporate ladder in the environmental field to become a general counsel: "In the environmental world it's the head of environmental and counsel." He was already at a Fortune 500 company, and he felt that he had received the training he needed to make the move up and that it was just a matter of "what's the right opportunity and when." Asked where he would be in five years, he said a general counsel in his current company or another company. LinkedIn in 2019 showed that he had stayed with his current employer for six years before moving to another energy company to become vice president for global environment and safety and environmental counsel. Through his technical background and legal experience, he had found a fast track to a high-ranking corporate counsel position.

Samantha, a White woman, also had trained and worked as an engineer for several years, managing hazardous waste issues for a local government and then a private company. Given that she already was doing analysis and compliance, she decided to pursue a law degree in her hometown at a law school ranked from 51 to 100. She then drew on her engineering background and worked as an associate in an environmental practice, following an expert/mentor whom she had known for twelve years. He brought her to the firm, and then she followed him when he quickly moved from one large law firm to another. At her first interview with us, three years after graduating, she indicated that she wanted to continue to work in environmental law but not at the intense pace of private practice. She also thought that her mentor did not have the same clout in the second firm as he had had in the first. In our second interview with her, she told us how she had been contacted by a headhunter about an in-house position doing construction law. Her hours were more predictable but still long: 8:00 A.M. to 7:00 P.M., five days a week. She noted a downside: "You have fewer people that can make demands of you [when you are in a law firm]." She did not project happiness in her position. She suggested that she would stay: "If I, honestly, if I made a change, it wouldn't be to go to another legal position. It would be to get away from it." LinkedIn in 2019 revealed that she was still at the same company in a senior counsel position. She had not been able to realize her aspirations of moving out of the legal department.

Peggy, Brooks, and Angela all eventually succeeded in business but faced barriers at some point owing to their lack of elite credentials. Peggy, a White woman, had a relatively high-status education background. She graduated from a leading public research university as an undergraduate, received a master's degree in a scientific field from a top-20 research university, and self-consciously pursued an intellectual property specialty at a law school ranked from 51 to 100. She then practiced as an associate in a small intellectual property law firm for some seven years and was recruited by a headhunter into an intellectual property position at a large tech company. She worked as a senior counsel in that company for almost three years, but, when that company was acquired by another tech company, she was not retained. Paraphrasing her words, the new company did not want her, and she did not want the new company. Although her comment was opaque, we inferred that the new employer was looking for attorneys from more prestigious law schools with large-firm experience.

Peggy experienced a few months of unemployment and then practiced as a contract attorney with another large tech company. She was recruited by her former supervisor at the previously acquired company, who had since moved to another large tech company. When her former supervisor received a position to fill, she reached out to Peggy, and she began there 11 years into her career. At that tech company, Peggy progressed through a series of more responsible positions, adding expertise in the legal aspects of new technologies in the industry. She suggested that, barring a ruinous firing or some other misstep, after an attorney lands a position as inside counsel it is much easier to find another job as inside counsel. Thus, while the graduating law school classes after 2008 faced a very difficult hiring environment, those already in inside counsel positions can mobilize their networks among other inside counsel to find a new position. Peggy also suggested that her hours were not necessarily better than they would have been in a law firm, although it should be noted that her experience was limited to a small firm:

> Yeah, well there's this myth that. . . . Well, I think it's a myth. That you take the pay cut for the hours cut, and I just. . . . I mean I think that may be still true in certain cases, but I just don't think it applies across the board anymore. As far as I can tell, it hasn't for several years now. Certainly, when I first went in-house in 2007, we were working crazy hours there. Maybe that was just the [tech company] thing.

In 2020, LinkedIn showed that Peggy stayed at that tech company for seven years before moving first to a position as chief technology officer and associate general counsel at a small tech company and then to a position as vice president of products and operations at a large financial services corporation. Thus, despite a short period of unemployment, her career in business appears to have flourished.

Brooks is a White man who also had very strong, if not elite, academic credentials when he graduated from law school. After attending a top-25 public university as an undergraduate with a social science major, he attended a law school ranked from 51 to 100 while working as a paralegal for a prestigious Wall Street law firm. After five more years at the firm, Brooks learned over drinks that there was no way he could progress from paralegal to lawyer at the firm. The lawyers told him:

BROOKS: "Go somewhere else. If you want us to make phone calls, let us know. We'll happily try to get you further in your career. It's just your pedigree doesn't match up with what we like to have."
INTERVIEWER: Do they actually say that?
BROOKS: By that point I had done some trials with partners and had some very frank late-night conversations after a couple of drinks. They were up-front with me about it. I respected that. I still do. I still use them. . . .

Eight years' experience, if it's a good eight years of experience, who cares that you got a B– in [civil procedure] your first year of law school? ... But they do.

Brooks then left his position as a paralegal to take a position as a lawyer in the litigation department of a tech company. His first business employer was then acquired after he spent four years there; then that company was acquired five years later by a larger, international tech firm. Over the course of these three transitions, he gradually assumed more responsibility over litigation matters. He described the gradual accretion of larger and larger cases in his first company job. Each transition to a new, larger company led to increased responsibility. But each transition entailed developing relationships with a new management team and coming to understand how different cases fit into the company's overall operations. Asked where he would be in five years, he said he did not know because it depended on company management. The 2020 LinkedIn page for Brooks shows that he has remained at the last acquiring company for more than five years and has risen to the position of associate general counsel for litigation.

In some respects the story of Angela is similar to that of Brooks at the start of his career. A Latina, Angela began her career in law working as a paralegal for a large national law firm for seven years. At the end of that period, she attended a tier 3 law school in the same national market city. On graduating from law school, she had, she explained, difficulty landing a job in a law firm:

ANGELA: When I started looking for jobs and going out and interviewing, it didn't matter to them that I had worked at a law firm as a paralegal for seven years. So two things. One is it held me back that I had never worked at a law firm as a lawyer, and the other thing was that I had actually stayed somewhere for seven years.
INTERVIEWER: That was bad?
ANGELA: That was bad. Apparently, in this new day to stay somewhere too long, your view of the world is too small.

While still in law school, Angela took a position as a law clerk in a video game company and continued there after graduating from law school. Although she suggested that gaming companies are volatile and that many do not survive or are taken over by other firms, she stayed at that company for 10 years, rising from law clerk, to associate legal counsel, to director of business and legal affairs, to vice president for business and legal affairs. Her 2019

LinkedIn profile shows that, after having left that first business employer, she has held eight different positions in the computer game industry over 10 years, some as a consultant and contract attorney, some as general counsel. One of these contracts evolved into a position as senior counsel for a major company in the entertainment industry, where she has worked for the past four years. This appears to be a very solid destination after working for another firm as a contract employee in the same community.

While the preceding cases are of lawyers who stay in the business sector, some of our cases reflect the opposite trajectory. Sergio, a gay Latino, worked in a major bank in a large urban center conducting trust and international transactions. He attended night law school and night business school, eventually completing a JD and an MBA. (The law school is ranked in tier 3; the MBA program is unranked.) He was interested in pursuing nonlaw jobs in banking when the father of a friend hired him to run his small company's operations and assist in marketing a new trust vehicle. When the demand for these trust products ended, Sergio took a year off to travel internationally, then returned to hang out his own shingle doing immigration and trust law. LinkedIn in 2020 shows that he is still with a very small law firm specializing in immigration law. His career matches in some respects that of Jacob (chap. 7), who began in a small firm operated by family members, exited with a kind of in-house position, and then went solo.

Emily's career has largely turned away from law, a legal detour if not dead end. Emily is a White woman who was working as a registered nurse when she decided to go to law school. Her mother worked as a legal secretary for a judge, which sparked Emily's interest in law. She enrolled in a public law school in the midwestern city in which she lived but was not drawn to opportunities for associates in law firms. On graduating, given the soft law market at the time, she took a position as a claims manager in a large health insurance company. She found the work frustrating as she felt that she was always the bearer to her manager of the bad news that the company would have to pay a claim. After 18 months, she joined a medical malpractice group within a law firm of 100 or more attorneys. She reported that it was a "terrible" experience, one marked by a lack of respect and support for associates, including even from a female partner who was particularly tough on female associates. She told us that, while the firm had very set goals for billables, it did not train associates how to work efficiently to reach their goals. She would work evenings and weekends, but it was still tough to reach the billable goals, and the firm required associates to do a lot of "face time." After an unexpected and "horrible" negative review, she concluded that the firm was not treating its associates as professionals. Disillusioned by her brief career as a lawyer, she left the law firm after one year and returned to nursing. She earned a master's degree in nursing, had a baby, and took a part-time job working for the state government reviewing medical complaints against health care providers. She informed us that her law license is no longer active. Our web search shows that she has since earned a postmaster's certificate in nursing and is now working in research. She evidently took two runs at finding a legal career that drew on her nursing background, saw no other good opportunities, and went on to a different career as a researcher (where her law degree might at times be valuable).

A Note on Work/Life Balance

As noted in chapter 3, many of the in-depth interviews with lawyers in business indicate that a regular work life—not subject to the demands of law firms' billable hours requirements or just the workplace norms of law firms—was a major attraction of moving to business. While this was mentioned more often by women than by men, both women and men discussed how their work lives were now more manageable. When we look at our survey results, it looks like inside counsel report average hours per week that are only somewhat below the most intense practice setting of law firms over 251 lawyers. Large-firm respondents at wave 3 report a mean of 52 hours per week compared to 49.5 by inside counsel in business (Dinovitzer et al. 2014, table 4.1). A quarter of large-firm respondents work 60 hours per week or more, compared to 16% of inside counsel. Inside counsel work appreciably more on average than do government and public interest/nonprofit lawyers. They work more than solo and small-firm practitioners, are virtually tied with midsize-firm lawyers, and are slightly bested by lawyers in law firms of 101–250 attorneys. What we rarely see in the inside counsel interviews are statements such as this one by Bryce, quoted in chapter 7: "Anything the firm told you about being flexible was a total lie." What you do hear is that there are many in-house counsel who work hard. Trevor, for example, noted that he and his colleagues in the entertainment company are "overworked" and that he would like to hire more people. Also, they are always on call: "We're all connected all the time. . . . We're always checking and responding to questions and stuff over the weekends." But the strong perception among the interviews is that, if the respondents moved from a large law firm to a corporate counsel office, they would improve their lifestyle. The dominance of the billable hour in the corporate law firms cannot be denied.

Conclusion

The narratives of attorneys working in business demonstrate the different kinds of social capital that operate in the business world to produce different and variable career outcomes. The interviews reflect the structure we identified in the sequence analysis presented in chapter 3: there is a fundamental status divide between big law firm to business careers and careers that start in businesses or small firms. The first group follows an elite path from selective law schools, to large law firms, to positions as inside counsel. This path valorizes the traditional status hierarchy of law schools and law firms as preeminent in providing sophisticated legal representation to large business, even as it is configured as a negation of the billable hour system of corporate law firms. The second group enters business through various side doors, the door depending on different kinds of social capital, often linked to the specific technologies or knowledge requirements of the business itself, which often are not dependent on professional status as such. The STEM graduates have some advantages in this process. The existence of these two sets of paths has not been well recognized in the literature on the legal profession, the upward bias in scholarship and in media coverage emphasizing only the former. Yet both are part of the world that connects law to business, and both reflect and reproduce the stratification system of American law.

One of the reasons we see so much variation in the nonelite careers is because there simply *is* more variation. In contrast to the elites, who have a well-worn path by now, for nonelites moving into business is many different things, and they get there in many different ways. Moreover, the capital that they need to draw on is also more diverse, as opposed to the elites, whose main sources of capital are their law school credentials and their law firm experience (plus their race and gender). As seen in the sequence analyses, the trajectories of nonelites are generally much more of a mixed bag. Instead of very identifiable paths through corporate law firms, clerkships, public interest fellowships, or competitive federal government positions, nonelite careers in all these settings come from such diverse forms of capital as friendship networks, a particular expertise such as engineering, linguistic and ethnic or racial ties, and especially creatively building on wherever they happened to find an entry into professional practice.

Finally, the career narratives of lawyers in business—both the elite and nonelite versions—suggest that the theoretical focus on lawyers' autonomy, as with respect to lawyers in private practice, does not reflect the lived experience of lawyers serving business. For these attorneys, the move to business or the building of careers within business does not seem to present the moral dilemma posited in traditional professionalism literature. The topic never came up in the interviews. Rather, in different ways, using different mixes of social capital, going in-house is a way to gain the rewards that go to those advancing the interests of business but without the dependence on the billable hour and all that goes with it.

Commitment, Careerism, and Stratification: Careers in Government, Nonprofits, and Public Interest Organizations

The literature on government, nonprofit, and public interest organizations—a sector conceived as such in the late 1960s and celebrated for assisting the underrepresented or unrepresented—focuses on the relatively few law school graduates who enter it. Law professors especially seek to encourage the idealists who reject corporate law firms in the name of the public interest. We will therefore begin our discussion with narratives from those holding public interest and nonprofit positions. We next turn to federal government positions and then state government positions. All are usually subsumed under the category of public service positions, but, not surprisingly, there are more factors at stake in most of these positions than the pure commitment to public service. As these narratives reveal, lawyers must find ways to support themselves, navigate their personal lives, and build careers whatever their ideals.

As with the other sectors we have analyzed through career narratives, we see the operation of a status hierarchy within this sector. Public sector positions are very different from each other in terms of where lawyers are recruited from, how they are compensated, and their status within the legal profession, and they relate to the broader hierarchy of the profession in different ways. Some of them are gateways to relatively prestigious positions in large law firms, corporate law departments, or law school teaching; some lead to established practices in the personal client hemisphere. Others are ends in themselves, the lawyers holding them planning to spend the rest of their careers in them.

Because public service careers offer relatively low pay compared to corporate law or business careers, elite law schools encourage them through loan forgiveness programs targeting those law school graduates who take them. A substantial scholarly and journalistic literature has grown up that portrays these careers as desirable, "service-oriented" or "social change" alternatives to "greed-oriented" careers in corporate law firms. In schools where corporate law jobs are available to a substantial proportion of students, there is even a self-conscious public interest track that is relatively successful in channeling some students into public service careers (Bliss 2018). The perceived battle surrounding this choice is well chronicled in a literature seeking to find ways to encourage students to reject corporate law in favor of public service. *Broken Contract*, by Richard Kahlenberg (1999), exemplifies this perspective in the popular press. It is organized around the author's struggle at Harvard Law School to avoid the path of least resistance, that into corporate law. He ultimately resists and chooses a federal government position.

There is also a strong literature on how and why law students tend to shift their focus away from public service as they move through law school (e.g., Albiston et al. 2021; Bliss 2018). The conclusion of a recent article is indicative of the prevailing scholarly focus: "Our findings underscore law schools' vital role in producing legal professionals committed to social justice. It is essential that law schools invest in the institutional programs necessary to nurturing and training the next generation of public interest lawyers so they may meet the challenge of the current crises and help chart a path to a stronger democracy" (Albiston et al. 2021, 286). The research seeks to find ways to inspire law school graduates to embrace and persist in public interest careers. The focus is almost entirely on the importance of ideological commitment.

There is not much literature on those government positions generally included in the public service category, but there is some discussion of actors in the criminal legal system. Criminal prosecutors and public defenders are open to graduates of all law schools, with state and local positions occupied mostly by graduates of local law schools and federal positions mostly held by graduates of high-ranked law schools. The focus of the literature is on the role these actors play in a failing justice system. Scholars and journalists show how overworked they are, the most common example being the public defender. One recent article, for example, notes that a lack of resources, a high caseload, low pay, and the relatively high stakes of their work leave public defenders unable to serve their clients properly, thus creating great personal stress (see Baćak et al. 2020).

The literature on public interest law highlights the importance of nurturing an ideological commitment that will turn law school graduates toward public interest law and result in their staying committed. Similarly, it is argued that a career as a public defender would be more attractive if more resources were committed to the justice system. Both approaches could be true, but neither recognizes that there are many factors that lead law school graduates to seek public interest or public service careers. As elsewhere, race, gender, ethnicity, law school status, and performance in law school matter. And, as we saw in chapter 3, there are well-worn tracks that differentiate the lower-status and less well-paying careers of those in state government and the more elite careers in federal government.

Our qualitative interviews also suggest patterns for graduates of the highest-status law schools and those lower in the law school hierarchy. The most obvious patterns that make up a public interest habitus are among the more elite graduates. One path includes mostly women in top law schools who embrace a public interest track, gain prestigious fellowships such as a Skadden or an Equal Justice, and then begin careers at relatively high-profile public interest organizations. These careers are the closest to the ideologically committed law school graduates posited by those who argue for more public interest lawyers. The lawyers choosing them reject corporate law careers. Even here, however, the decision to work in the public interest sector may relate to many factors, not just ideology. A second path typically starts in a large law firm or a clerkship and leads into a federal position—such as an assistant US attorney general—that frequently later translates to a partnership in a corporate law firm defending white-collar prosecutions. This career track is also idealistically embraced in the interviews, but the difficulty monetizing it—something everyone knows about—makes actually doing so more complex. And a third path starts in a law firm and leads to other federal government positions that may or may not lead back to corporate law.

The positions in state government and in the less prestigious parts of the public interest/nonprofit sector suggest a lower-prestige habitus, individuals who start at and stay in state government or move from positions such as solo practice into state government. These are individuals who have adapted to a more realistic set of job options—those that afford job security, good benefits, and a modest income. Indeed, many of those going into prosecutor and defender positions are from schools at which at best only a small minority of the graduates had access to large law firms. Those obtaining such government positions hardly need the encouragement of, for example, loan forgiveness and other incentives designed to lure graduates away from corporate law. They are pleased to get hired at the state or the local level. Women and in particular women of color are also more likely to pursue these paths, citing the fact that they do not fit in private practice. Anticipating or already experiencing bias because of their gender, their race, or the school they attended, they choose a government job. We also see examples in state government of the mission-driven law school graduates celebrated in the literature, those whose commitment to public service began before law school and persisted into their professional careers. There is idealism, and there is also making a virtue of necessity.

After providing a statistical profile of public sector respondents, we organize this analysis according to the three major subtypes of public sector jobs: public interest and nonprofit, federal government, and state and local government.

Statistical Background

As we saw in chapter 4, almost one-third of our respondents work in the public and nonprofit sector. The largest group comprises attorneys who work for state and local governments, who make up 12% of the sample, followed by attorneys employed by nonprofits and education institutions (7%) and the federal government (6%), those who work in legal services or public defenders' offices (3%), and those who work in public interest organizations (1%). In contrast to the private law firm jobs we examined in previous chapters, for the most part public sector and nonprofit jobs are not located in organizations with up-or-out hierarchies that depend on client generation and profits.[1] Thus, we see not the structural draining of careers out of public sector jobs that we saw with private practice but modest growth in the percentage of the sample in the public sector, from 25% at wave 1 to 31% at wave 3.

Public sector jobs vary in terms of how lawyers enter them and their propensity to stay in them. The career sequences outlined in chapter 3 show that state government attorneys are the most likely to have graduated from a lower-ranked school and begun and stayed in state government across waves 1 and 3: 58%. For those who did not start in state government, the most frequent feeder position for wave 3 was solo and small-firm practice, which led to 20% of wave 3 state government positions. Forty-four percent of federal government attorneys at wave 3 started in the federal government at wave 1. The main feeder for those who did not start in the federal government was law firms employing more than 250 attorneys, which was a path for 25% of federal government attorneys at wave 3.

Public interest/nonprofit jobholders come from more diverse origins. Only 24% of attorneys in public interest/nonprofit jobs at wave 3 started there in wave 1, and there is no dominant feeder among wave 1 positions. There is considerable evidence that those who go into the well-known and established public interest organizations have elite law school credentials and often elite fellowships and federal clerkships. It is also clear that law schools hire only from the top schools and the top firms and public interest organizations, especially but not only for tenure-track positions (George and Yoon 2014).

As we saw in chapter 4 (table 4.4), women are slightly overrepresented in government positions and substantially overrepresented in the nonprofit sector. People of color are somewhat overrepresented in federal and state government jobs and more significantly overrepresented in public interest/nonprofit jobs.

Public Interest Organizations, Nonprofits, and Education Institutions

ELITE TRACKS

Amanda, who attended an elite undergraduate university and a top-10 law school, traced her passion for social justice to her upbringing in a "liberal Jewish East Coast family." While during the years of the booming tech economy she was surrounded by law students who were heading off to corporate law firms, she interned at an employment-focused civil rights organization and won a fellowship to continue working there after graduation. After spending a few years there, she became deputy director of a law school center focusing on work/life balance. It was here that she decided she would like to teach. She moved to a visiting faculty position at the same law school, then to a tenure track teaching position at a different law school—one ranked from 51 to 100—where she is now a full professor teaching courses in employment law and work and family. The transition from elite public interest to teaching, often in clinical positions, is a frequent path into the legal academy. Amanda acknowledged that she came from privilege: "I mean I grew up solidly upper middle class, and pretty much everything I've done has been privileged by that fact, including being a public interest lawyer."

In a similar vein, Leslie is a White woman who attended a prestigious liberal arts college, traveled the world working for nonprofits that cared for homeless children, and then attended an elite law school to pursue her interests. Although she "hated law school" because the teachers were largely old White men and her fellow students were primarily interested in making money, she began working on housing law issues at a nonprofit the summer after her first year. She later interned at another housing nonprofit, where she went to work after graduating, supported by a prestigious Skadden fellowship. After relocating to be with her husband, she applied through a nonprofit hiring website to a nonprofit law clinic that included housing law as part of its portfolio. She has remained with the organization and is now director of the housing section. Leslie is a clear example of a lawyer on the elite track who knew that she intended to be a public interest lawyer. She has not strayed from that trajectory during the 20 years of her career. Her husband is a lawyer in private practice, which helps ease any financial burden.

Lilly entered a joint program at a top-20 law school, obtaining a JD and an

MA in social work. She is a White woman whose father is a lawyer and whose mother is a social worker. Her choice of a combined program largely dictated her public interest career path. She never applied or even considered applying for a position in private law practice. She considered job offers only from public interest or government employers and chose a public interest job because it "fit with [her] schooling" and allowed her to concentrate on disability rights. After getting married, she moved to Australia for three years. During this time, she did some contract work on disability rights for her previous employer. When we interviewed her at wave 3, she was back working with an organization advocating for disability rights. At that time, she told us that she now had two children and took the position in part because it gave her flexibility for family responsibilities. When we checked Facebook, we found that she had since worked as a consultant for three years and was currently the executive director of a disability organization in the midwestern city where we found her in wave 1. She has been with this organization for four years.

Alexandra is a White woman who began her career with a fellowship at a prestigious public interest law firm in a large midwestern city after graduating from one of the top law schools in the same city. She never intended to practice in a firm and knew she wanted to do public interest law: "I was interested in doing direct service, [which] was one of the reasons that I picked the fellowship and also the supervision I was going to get."

Alexandra said further:

> I went to law school to do this work so it's not like I learned in law school about public interest law. I had worked for some nonprofit agencies, and at 25 I was getting sick of sitting at a board meeting where I felt like there was an answer that I could clearly answer but they turned to the lawyers to say, "Well, what do the lawyers think about this?" So I thought, "Maybe I should become a lawyer so that, when I speak, people will listen to me."

She told us that she did a summer clerkship at a large firm in the same midwestern city during her second summer, but the reason was to earn money to pay for her bar year. In her wave 1 public interest job she had major responsibilities:

> I do a lot of policy. I do—policy isn't exactly right—I meet with the [city] housing authority and negotiate their lease terms, their procedures, things like that, and as the [city] housing authority is tearing down all its buildings, they're rebuilding these mixed-income developments, so a large piece of what I do is sit at the table for these—each new mixed-income development has a working group to decide on what the tenant selection plan should look like, what the . . . everything . . . what the site should look like, what the lease should look like. So I represent the tenant organization for local advisory council presidents

who get to sit at the working group. I serve as their counsel, and my supervisor also serves as counsel on different work—in all different developments.

Alexandra was engaged to be married when we talked to her at wave 1. At that time, she said that she did not think that she would be a "lifer" in public interest and that she would lose her loan forgiveness when she got married. However, at that point she hoped she could extend her fellowship for another one or two years. Our web searches indicate that, after getting married, she and her husband moved to a city in the East. Her bar membership is inactive, suggesting she is no longer practicing law. It appears that she and her husband are active in their temple and that she is active as a volunteer in a prominent international nonprofit organization.

Less elite but with a similar story is Serena, a White woman who took the public interest track in the law school of a high-ranking public university. During the summers, she worked at a legal aid clinic in a major city, her objective being to get a legal aid job on graduation. Her law school mentor encouraged her to start her career at a plaintiffs' union law firm after graduation. After a short time, she relocated to a regional law market where she worked for a nonprofit that supported loan forgiveness for recent law school graduates representing disadvantaged clients. Our 2019 web searches found that she was the executive director of the organization, which now is housed in the state bar association.

Arthur is the only man on this elite public interest track that we interviewed. He is White and attended a prestigious liberal arts college and then a top-10 law school, where he intended to combine law with a PhD in sociology. He was devoted to public interest from the time he was a student at law school. After law school, he had a clerkship with a federal court of appeals judge, and that was followed by a Skadden fellowship. Putting aside plans for a PhD, after law school he worked for two years in a shelter. He then went into private practice in a large firm for two years but then returned to work with the homeless. For the last five years, he has been the initiative director of a nonprofit whose total focus is on developing solutions to homelessness. Arthur not only exemplifies dedication to public interest law; he has also been able to structure his life to be able to live on a very modest income. His wife (whom he met as an undergraduate) is a consultant on community organizing and projects to help the homeless.

THE NONELITE WORLD OF PUBLIC INTEREST LAW

We present two examples of nonelite public interest paths that, like nonelite paths in other sectors, seem more serendipitous and less planned than more conventional high-status trajectories. Christopher, a White man, has spent his career, from the summer after his first year of law school to the present, working in the same conservative legal advocacy nonprofit. He attended a top-50 undergraduate university and a tier 3 law school. He got his job because he was the swimming coach of the child of the president of the nonprofit. He asked the president about the organization, which led to an interview for a summer job, which in turn led to work throughout law school and a full-time job on graduation. Christopher was enthused about the intellectual challenge and policy impact of the work he was doing. He recognized that his salary ($100,000) was much higher than those most public interest attorneys commanded. Although he mentioned that his dream job—a federal job vetting candidates for judgeships—might draw him away, he was very satisfied with his current position. Our 2019 web search found him at the same organization in a high-level legal position. He likely did not have the credentials typically required for his ideal position, but he was well paid, and his position aligned with his own values.

Bartholomew—a White man who graduated from a law school ranked in the range from 51 to 100—is a case of an attorney who was not initially committed to a public interest path but has spent his entire career in public interest work and shows no sign that he intends to move. He was interested in international law in law school and had obtained a master's in international relations. But, by his telling, his tier 3 law school did not provide many opportunities for jobs in international law, and he made some strategic errors in his job search by not accepting offers that might have led to international work. Having followed his wife, who worked in the arts, to a national law market city, he was exploring jobs in immigration law when he began volunteering at a nonprofit that represented low-income families in family law cases. The nonprofit offered him a job, which he accepted to help pay the bills. He has been there ever since. Our interview suggested that he was not especially happy or unhappy in his position. He contemplated seeking other positions but did not act on those thoughts. His wife was in development and thus probably made a salary that was greater than his, and he seemed more or less content with the life his public interest position provided.

Federal Government Careers

It is apparent from our interviews that law jobs in the federal government are generally prestigious, are relatively well paid, offer interesting work, often are held for a considerable time, but also—in many cases—allow for exit to attractive private sector jobs. The classic pattern, illustrated by our first interview, is the assistant US attorney position.

Our three interviews with Adam, a White man who graduated from a top-10 law school, exemplify how social background, elite credentials, and professional ambition can lead to a successful career as an assistant US attorney. Adam grew up in affluent circumstances and reported that his decision to go to law school was informed by talking to professional friends of his parents. He obtained a federal district court clerkship after having lunch with a judge whom his parents knew. While the judge had clerks lined up for the coming year, he offered Adam a clerkship for the following year. The large law firm that had offered him a job agreed to let him work for a year at the firm before doing the clerkship and offered to keep him on after he finished his clerkship. He instead opted for an assistant US attorney position. The US attorney who hired him was nationally famous. Adam was working in a specialized unit in the office, and he spoke enthusiastically in the wave 2 interview about the nature of his work: "It really is a great job, and I think it's one of the most unique jobs a person can have as a lawyer in terms of the experience, the level of responsibility, really just in terms of everything." By the time of the wave 3 interview, he had been promoted to a supervisory position, and our 2019 web search indicated that he had been promoted to chief of his section. He then left his position to become a partner in a large global law firm, a position he still holds today, specializing in white-collar crime. He had told us at his wave 3 interview that his wife, who was a lawyer in corporate practice, encouraged him to make such a move since she intended to leave private practice once they started a family and that he was planning to do so. Checking her law firm, we found that Adam's wife is still at the large law firm where she began her career. Her bio at the firm emphasizes her pro bono work and the fact that she chaired the firm's domestic violence pro bono program. We do not know whether she has changed her hours or her work patterns.

Alexander—also a White man who graduated from an elite undergraduate university and a top-10 law school—represents another example of an attorney with high-status credentials who gained prestigious positions in the federal government. We can infer that Alexander came from an upper-class background. A "generous grandmother" paid for his law school education so that he incurred no debt. After graduating from law school, he clerked for a federal appeals court judge. He worked for a few years in a large law firm in the regional city that was his hometown. He regarded his law firm job with disdain: "Any case was only as important as . . . the dollars and cents spent on pursuing it or settling it, . . . [and] there's very little practice in court [and a] very substantial aversion to trial." He was contacted about a high-level policy position in the Department of Justice in Washington, DC, by a friend from an elite law school who knew him through a conservative political organization. He jumped at the opportunity in the hopes that it would lead to a position in the assistant US attorney's office in his hometown.

Alexander's wave 2 interview took place in DC. When we asked how he felt about his work and what he liked the most about his job, he responded:

> I would say being able to work with people whom I respect enormously on issues that I care about a great deal. That applies to a bunch of different things. It applies to immigration reform, and it applies to Supreme Court appointments, but very talented people all working together toward a common objective—usually a highly complicated process; and the outcome is really important.

By wave 3, Alexander had gotten his wish and had moved to an assistant US attorney position in his hometown. He still loved his work, even more so than the policy work he had done in DC. When asked about future plans, he indicated that he wanted to stay in his current position, hopefully gaining more and more complicated cases and, possibly, supervisory responsibility. The 2019 web search indicated that he remained an assistant US attorney and had been considered for high appointive office.

Carrie, a White woman, had some of the same characteristics as Adam and Alexander at the start of her career—an undergraduate degree from a top-25 university, a law degree from a top-30 law school, a federal district court clerkship, and an entry-level position with a large law firm. When we asked why she decided to leave a large law firm job for the federal government, she replied: "In the back of my mind I did not want to go to a firm, and it felt almost like it would be a dead-end job. I would end up for the majority of my career doing what other people wanted me to do and not being a leader. But another part of it is that I just loved public service. And every time I thought about this job [in the US attorney's office] I would just smile." She described how throughout her life she had done a lot of volunteer work, how the religious university she attended had promoted service activities, and how she had spent two years in a public service program working with disadvantaged children.

She did not miss the egocentrism and rivalry that she saw in law firm practice or the demands to work weekends for no apparent reason: "I don't miss having to be at the whim of all of the partners. I mean there almost every Friday night I would be upset, angry, because I had just received a project that was due Monday morning. I mean I got the Friday four o'clock project more often than I didn't." She perceived that her law firm peers were largely unhappy. They liked the money, they liked the opportunity for experience, but they seldom got an opportunity to see the big picture when it came to what they were working on.

In contrast, even early in her federal government career Carrie was responsible for and largely in control of her cases. When we asked what she most liked about her current work, she replied: "I guess maybe it has meaning. Maybe that's what I'm most satisfied with." All assistant US attorneys are required to commit to four years in their jobs. While she thought that her job would be an easy stepping stone to private practice if she wanted that, she indicated that she had no plans for a quick transition: "I think right now it's strange because I've always known what I was going to try to do the next step. And I think right now I want to do well here." Indeed, we learned from our interview at wave 3 and from our web search that Carrie stayed with the US attorney's office for more than 10 years, conducted numerous trials, and rose to become senior counsel. According to web sources, she recently left the federal government to join a midsize law firm that specializes in her area of expertise. The firm website touts her experience as a litigator for the federal government. She returned to private law in a far stronger position than the one she was in when she left it for the assistant US attorney position.

While assistant US attorney positions represent a particularly elite track within the federal government, there are several other attractive paths in federal employment. For Lynden, the African American man we described in chapters 1 and 6, the move into federal government was as a refuge from private practice. Lynden never gained responsibility for clients or major cases, and, as practice groups in the law firm began to splinter, he was terminated. He was never in the right silo. After an extensive job search, he was hired by the federal agency where he was working when we interviewed him at wave 3. According to LinkedIn, he stayed there for eight years, gaining two significant promotions. Like Adam, Alexander, and Carrie, Lynden was struck by how quickly he became responsible for writing his own briefs and appearing in hearings. In private practice, he would "grind out a brief," but the "whole thing [would] be rewritten for no reason." But in the US attorney's office he gets to do his own writing: "I get to speak in front of this judge."

While Lynden expressed satisfaction with his job, when we talked about future plans, he was candid in saying that he hoped to be in the private sector to make more money because his son would eventually be attending college. He was not in the same strong market position as the assistant US attorneys or the just slightly less prestigious Department of Justice lawyers. According to LinkedIn, however, he succeeded in making the transition, moving to an inside counsel position in the Midwest in a large corporation in the industry that he had dealt with in his previous agency. We do not know whether he sought positions in law firms or was soured by his previous experience.

Two federal government interviewees, Mindy and Barbara, graduated from tier 4 law schools but landed jobs in the federal government through the prestigious Department of Justice Honors Program. Mindy is White and was the first in her family to obtain an advanced degree. Her mother is a small business owner who did not really understand what Mindy does but was very proud of her. In our wave 1 interview, Mindy indicated that she did not see herself going into private practice. She was hired into federal immigration work and had her choice of several locations in which to work. Her initial thinking was that she would work in immigration until she could move into an assistant US attorney position, but immigration law provided considerable opportunities for professional growth: "The opportunities I see in my new position [in immigration] I think I want to explore before I make that jump [to being an assistant US attorney]. . . . I have a feeling there's some great things that are going to be opening up, some really good opportunities where you're given an opportunity that nobody else has ever been given before." She spoke of how exciting immigration law was: "It's always changing . . . and always in the public eye. . . . It keeps you on your toes. You're required to read to keep yourself updated. . . . It's been a professional growth for me because not only have I learned an area of law, but, with us doing a lot of asylum refugee cases, I've learned a lot about the world."

The trajectory of opportunity within Mindy's agency and her legal specialty continued throughout waves 2 and 3 of our study. Mindy was promoted to supervisory positions with broad regional responsibility and had foreign tours of service. When we asked whether she thought about leaving her government job, she spoke of how good she felt her job was.

According to LinkedIn, Mindy stayed in her government job for 17 years before moving to a large law firm that specialized in corporate immigration law. She now holds the title of partner. The firm has offices in nine cities in the United States. It exemplifies the relatively recent growth of relatively prestigious and lucrative practices in immigration law for corporations seeking to recruit from and place employees in many parts of the globe.

Barbara, an Asian American woman also from a tier 4 law school, has spent her entire career representing the federal government in immigration cases, first under the Immigration and Naturalization Service, and then under the successor agency, the Department of Homeland Security. She observed that those who entered government employment through the Honors Program were different than the large number of lateral entries that have begun to populate the agency in recent years:

People who came in through the Attorney General Honors Program like I did almost all of them have always wanted to be in public service. You find more . . . are maybe idealists who can better deal with limited resources. . . . With people who lateral in, most of them have come from either . . . being solo practitioners or having worked for large law firms. They came because they want a better quality of life usually. . . . You find they're realists and pragmatists and less because they believe in the mission or believe in service.

When we asked whether she has considered moving to private practice, Barbara gave us a categorical no, saying that she went to law school to do public service. She had applied for other positions within government but would not leave for private practice. Web sources indicate that she is now working as a judge in immigration court for the US Department of Justice. She is one example of a lawyer who persisted in a public career as a way to stay true to her ideals. She also was rewarded through advancement.

Carl, a White man who graduated from a top-30 law school, provides a contrasting story. He had served in the marine corps for three and a half years. Prior to going to law school, he got an MA in international relations and had worked for the Central Intelligence Agency (CIA) for two years. When we interviewed him during wave 1, he was working for the Securities and Exchange Commission (SEC) in DC. At wave 2, when we interviewed him again, he had moved to the Department of Treasury in financial crimes enforcement. A friend of his at the SEC recommended that he apply for a position at Treasury. He was hired there and has been there ever since, serving in a policy position. Carl said that he likes his position at Treasury much more than he did his position at the SEC. His disappointment, however, was that he thought he might have the opportunity to do security and intelligence work. Technically, his current position does not require that he be an attorney. He told us that he never expected to be thrilled to be a lawyer. From his discussion, we got the impression that he may have wished he had stayed at the CIA. This career in government has not led to the professional fulfillment he had hoped for. He is married with two children. When we interviewed him, his oldest child was in college, and his youngest child was a junior in high school.

Finally, we have an example of someone working in the federal government after working in legal services. Olivia is an African American woman who graduated from a state university and studied law at a top-50 public law school in the South. Her mother was a loan officer, and her father, who had passed away, had been a mechanic. Her first position was at an urban legal services organization in the state where she studied. She did general civil work, including housing, bankruptcy, and divorce. She knew that, after law school, she wanted to be able to live in the city in which she was currently located, and she was looking for a position that would allow her to have balance in her life. She moved to a position in the office of general counsel of the Social Security Administration (SSA), where she handled disability cases and defended the rulings of administrative law judges. She referred to the work as "transcript litigation." She writes the brief, and then the US attorney argues the case. She considers herself a specialist since she concentrates on appellate work. This position is very different than the one she held at legal services. Most of the lawyers in the office are women. She missed the client contact of legal services but noted that the pay was much better now. She liked being a government lawyer since it allowed her to "have a life." She was single with no children at the time of the interview, and she owned a home. From Internet sources, it appears that she has moved to another major city in the South, still with the general counsel of the SSA. She evidently is married since she now uses a different last name.

State and Local Government

FAST-TRACK STATE GOVERNMENT POSITIONS

While working in state government would not be considered analogous in terms of prestige to working in the US attorney's office, there are state positions whose cachet is comparable to that of federal fast-track positions. We had one lawyer in particular with this profile. Fred is a White man who graduated from a top-10 law school. Prior to law school, he had attended a criminal justice program in which he learned of the district attorney's office in one of the global legal markets. From that experience, he knew exactly the position he was aiming for. After his first year of law school, he worked in the US attorney's office. After his second year, he clerked at a large well-known law firm. When he graduated from law school, he had a federal clerkship with a US district court judge. However, there was a six-month delay before he could start his clerkship. He ended up going to the large law firm and working there until he began the clerkship. That experience was valuable and showed him that he would not like to work for one of the giant law firms. During the last months of his clerkship, he began interviewing for public sector jobs and was hired into his first government position, one with the district attorney's office he had set his sight on. He worked for a very prominent district attorney, and this position in state prosecution had the prestige and career value of the assistant US attorney positions that he also could have taken. Still, he noted that the state lawyers thought that he would take the federal position: they could not believe that he would want to work for the district attorney when he could obviously go to the US attorney's office. As noted in chapter 3, elite lawyers such as Fred now compete more than they have in the past with local law school graduates for many of these high-level state and local positions.

Eventually, Fred was assigned to a unit in which he had some experience. After leaving the district attorney's office, he went to work for the compliance department of a major corporation in an executive position. He stayed for five years. He left and in 2016 joined the C-suite of another major corporation, where he is the principal architect of the company's compliance strategy. His wife is an associate at a prestigious law firm in the same city.

There are also fast-track programs in some states that encourage promising local graduates to join respected state offices rather than be tempted to leave the state or join local corporate firms. Interviewed only at wave 1, Heather—a White woman—was a government lawyer for a state department of justice in the Pacific Northwest. She graduated from a local tier 4 law school and had a two-year clerkship with the presiding judge of the state supreme court before being hired by the state in an "honors attorney" position. She had just started her second year in that job when we interviewed her. She said that she wanted to stay local and that that was why she applied for both the clerkship and the honors position. Her husband ran a business in the area. She did not actually know that she wanted a government position; rather, she applied for the position because of its location. She was working in the appellate section when we talked to her. She is married and has two adopted children. When we interviewed her, the youngest was nine months old. Her father is a retired professor, and her mother is a secretary. From Internet resources, we see that she joined a small firm and became a named partner. The firm specializes in municipal and insurance defense, personal injury and commercial litigation. Her relatively high state position helped her find a good niche in private practice in her preferred location.

Philip, a White man who graduated from a law school ranked from 51 to 100, had a similar trajectory. He attended local schools; his father was a business manager. He was also an honors attorney in the same state as Heather. He graduated from a local law school and was at the appellate division of the state department of justice when we interviewed him at wave 1. He is still a lawyer at the same state department and still doing appellate work. In contrast to Heather, Philip had thought that he would like to work as a lawyer for the government before finishing law school. He also had a two-year experience away from his undergraduate school working for a residential treatment counseling facility for children. He told us that he had friends who were working for law firms, none of whom were happy with their workplace. His workday runs from 8:00 A.M. to 5:00 P.M., and he occasionally works from home. He noted that people tend to stay working for the state department of justice for a long time, doing arguments about twice a month: "It's the perfect job for me. And I have a hard time understanding why it wouldn't be the perfect job for everyone." He especially enjoys the cooperative environment.

On the surface, Caroline appears to be that rare case of an attorney who started in a large law firm and eventually took a position in state government law practice. Yet, in many respects, she represents an elite corporate career as she capitalized on elite law school credentials and experience in a corporate law firm to become a university counsel at a prestigious public university. She started her career like many graduates of top-10 law schools, going to work for a large corporate law firm. After a few years, she quit that job, moved to a smaller town closer to family, and had children. She was working part-time for small local law firms that practiced defending debtors in foreclosure actions and in construction cases. Her sister-in-law told her about a part-time position in a university legal counsel's office just before it was about to be posted. Her top law degree and large-firm corporate experience made her an attractive candidate, despite her detour. She took the job, has gradually moved to full-time, and has moved up to a higher position in the university counsel's office. Although she came to the position through a circuitous route, Caroline is fully committed to her job. When we asked her whether she was glad she went to law school, she responded: "I'm glad now . . . since I've found a job that's so great. . . . It's really a privilege to be able to work for the university because I just really believe in the university's mission." Even though she did not plan a public sector career, she has found a job that is professionally challenging and mission driven.

GENERAL STATE GOVERNMENT POSITIONS

Several of the interviewees who worked for state and local government had a decidedly local, pragmatic approach to getting a job. Most did not seriously consider a job in private practice, saying that they did not see themselves fitting into that world. We see the operation of gender, race, and class hierarchies in these narratives of pragmatic choice, which essentially enact the state government set of sequences outlined in chapter 3. These interviewees define their satisfaction in some instances in terms of ideals but most often in terms of the lifestyle of a state government employee. They did not have access to large law firm positions, but they also made a point of explaining that they did not want such a position.

Laura, a White woman in a regional market city that is also a state capital, was a nontraditional law student—going to law school at night after taking some 15 years to obtain her undergraduate degree, a period of time that included a stint in the military immediately after high school. After obtaining her JD from a tier 4 law school, she took a series of government jobs—moving from one job to the next within the state employment system. As she commented about her job search after law school: "[I was] not interested in firm work, and I'm sure they weren't interested in me either." She described how she had "forged [her] own way," consciously pursuing a "nontraditional" career path: "I always said I wanted to practice the kind of law where I could wear Birkenstocks, and I kind of stuck to that. . . . I think my friends are all in very traditional kinds of law. I think, in terms of salary, I'm on the very low end. I think, in terms of career satisfaction, I'm on the high end." At wave 3, Laura was only three years from being able to retire with a defined-benefit pension and reported that she was in her "end of career" job.

Karina, also a White woman, presents a case similar to Laura's, hailing from the same area, also attending a tier 4 law school, and also saying that she never saw herself in a law firm. She also knew when she went to law school that she wanted to be a public interest lawyer. She chose her law school on the basis of the city in which she wanted to live and whether the school had a public interest law program. The school she chose had a public service project that was recognized on her diploma when she graduated. She worked for the local legal aid office during law school. Her first job after law school was with a foundation that tried to match volunteers with agencies so that they could do some public interest law. Like several respondents working in government and nonprofits, Karina started working for the organization at which she got her first job while still in law school. After a few years at that nonprofit, Karina moved to another nonprofit, and after five years took a job in a state agency as an attorney who does background checks. She explained that she switched because she was pregnant and needed to make more money. She also had student loans that she was paying off. She told us that she did not want to have to work in a private firm. She also liked the state position because, when she went home, she felt like she had "made a difference." At the time of the wave 3 interview, she had been at the state agency for seven years, and our web search shows that she is still working there. Her husband worked in human resources, and they had children aged five and eight when we interviewed her.

Luci, a Latina working in a major law market where she has lived her entire life, also never pursued a job in private practice. Like Laura, she attended the night law school program of a tier 3 school, which took four years to complete. She came from a modest middle-class background: her father was a police officer, her mother a teaching assistant. During law school, she gained an internship in a compliance position in a government agency through the agency of a high school friend. As she approached graduation, the only jobs she considered were in public interest or government. Yet the public interest jobs paid only between $30,000 and $40,000, and she could not afford to take one of them. Her parents both had become very ill and required considerable care. As a result, she needed a nine-to-five job that would, if necessary, allow her to attend to her parents' medical emergencies. She was offered a full-time compliance position at the agency where she was interning and took it for the practical reasons of salary and a fixed schedule despite the fact that it was not a law job.

Luci remained and advanced in large county bureaucracies. As with her early career planning centering around the need for a nine-to-five job, she has been strategic about applying for the right kinds of jobs for her and has relied on personal relationships to enhance her credentials and learn of new opportunities within the track she was now on. In her wave 1 interview, she told us of a mentor who was concerned that, if she remained full-time in compliance work, she would not establish her credentials as a lawyer. Getting employment as a lawyer is often part of enhancing prestige and pay in a government (and often business) position. The mentor succeeded in creating a part-time assistant general counsel position for Luci so that she could split her time between working in compliance and building a law portfolio. She considered a higher-paying job in another government body but had heard that the law department at the other agency was "a den of vipers" and decided to stay where she was: "I have a home here now. I'm not making as much money as I'd like to, but I'm comfortable, and people understand my situation."

When we interviewed her at wave 2, some nine years into her career, Luci had moved to another large county law department. Again, her entrée came through a personal connection, her sister-in-law, who told her of the opportunity and suggested she apply. She took a pay cut in making the move, but she wanted more interesting, legally substantive work. The larger organization offered more opportunities for upward mobility. Working in a subunit with 15 other lawyers, she spoke of the stress of her responsibilities in her first year and expressed hope that things would calm down or that she would move to a less intense subunit. After describing the possibilities for promotion in her unit, she said that she was not interested in trying for division chief as it was very competitive but would like to get a promotion to principal, which would put her on a pay scale that "goes up in steps automatically." Job security was the most important aspect of her job. Her personal financial situation had improved. Her parents had died and left her their home. She remained unmarried and without children. She spoke of her network of friends from college and law school who enjoyed traveling together.

When we interviewed Luci in wave 3, she had been promoted to principal counsel and still was working in the counsel's office but had changed divisions. She told us during the interview that she had been sexually harassed by her boss and ended up changing sections to avoid him. She appears to have a safe and secure job. She developed her career by building up her experience as a lawyer and moving into law positions. But she did not express any ambition to change jobs or seek a higher position in the county bureaucracy.

ATTORNEYS GENERAL AND PUBLIC DEFENDERS

State government jobs that sometimes blur the boundary between law practice and nonlaw work can offer a path of upward mobility for women of color. Isabel, Ellie, and Molly are African American women who exemplify the statistical tendency we found for African American women to launch nontraditional careers in government. Isabel attended a historically Black university as an undergraduate and was encouraged by a professor to apply to law school. She decided to take the LSAT and see how she scored. She did well but described her application process as "haphazard"—applying to just two law schools, one in the top 10, one in the top 25. She was accepted by both and chose the lower-ranked school, which was closer to home. In her first semester of law school, she attended a Christmas party at a law firm and "just really felt out of place and weird": "I knew right then this is not for me. . . . The personalities of the people that I met . . . I just thought they're so fake, so phony. Why are you sitting here talking to me about golf? I already told you . . . I've never played golf." In her third year of law school, she interned at the public defenders' office and was hired for a regular position after passing the bar. She left law school with $150,000 in debt. She expected to remain at the public defender's office for the next four years. Our web search in 2019 showed that she had stayed in the public defender's office for 13 years. After that, she moved to a small criminal defense law firm and also works as a county magistrate. This trajectory is common both for local prosecutors and for defenders. It is not as lucrative as the fast track we see for those from assistant US attorneys' offices.

Ellie is the daughter of working-class parents. She graduated from a tier 4 law school that historically served nontraditional students from underserved populations. She had considerable experience before going to law school. She established her own business and had had two children before law school and a third after passing the bar. After two years working in a small immigration law firm, she realized that she did not want to deal with the time demands imposed by private practice and took a position as a clerk to local judges. Owing to strong recommendations from the judges for whom she worked, she was hired as an assistant district attorney. Her survey responses indicate that she stayed in government positions through waves 1 and 2 but had left to run the business she had established early in her career by wave 3. She had reported that, when she began her legal career, she trained her husband to operate the business. Web searches indicate that in 2019 she maintained an active law license but was also running the business.

Molly is an African American woman who graduated from a top-25 undergraduate university with a BA and an MBA. She attended a tier 3 law school. A single mother during graduate school, she took a nonlaw job in an economic development agency in her home state and attended law school at night. Her position at the time of the interview (2004) was largely nonlegal, and she spoke of her desire to make use of her law degree. She was in the process of applying for a position in the state attorney general's office. She told us (referring to state employees) that in her state you were not considered a real lawyer unless you worked for the attorney general's office. She in fact joined the attorney general's office in 2005 as a deputy. Molly said that she occasionally insisted on following her interpretations of state policy even if her superiors disagreed. She would not "brownnose" even though that might limit her chances for promotion. In response to our question about whether she faced bias as a woman of color, she said:

MOLLY: I think people, even now in this century, . . . are very surprised when I come to a meeting and I open my mouth that I'm articulate, that I'm intelligent.

INTERVIEWER: Is that insulting?

MOLLY: It's disappointing, It's never insulting because I hope that at the end of the day, when we leave a meeting, that they can say, OK, she had it together. And I assume that there's more out there like her. You know whether I agree with Condoleezza Rice or not, I'm proud when I hear her speak because she's so articulate, she's so together. When I hear Hillary Clinton speak, I'm proud, so to me it's the more you bombard the masses . . . then hopefully it will change.

Molly has now been a deputy attorney general for more than fifteen years. A profile on the Internet reports that she has held a variety of key leadership positions and that she has an exceptional success rate for hundreds of child abuse/neglect cases, some of which have involved very complex legal matters. Internet sources also indicate that she joined a class action lawsuit alleging discrimination on the basis of race and sex by her state government employer.

Joanna, a White woman who attended a liberal arts college and law school in the Northwest, exemplifies a circuitous route to the state attorney general's office by a public interest–oriented lawyer. When she decided to go to law school, she was not convinced that she would come out and be a practicing attorney. After college, she had managed a subsidized housing project for two and a half years. She worked with senior and disabled people, many of them mental health clients who had been deinstitutionalized. After law school, she began in a regional market with a space-sharing arrangement that provided her with referrals to support a solo practice.

After a year, Joanna moved to the state department of human services, working within an agency on aging and a Medicaid unit. She was hired into a coordinator position in which she managed federal grants totaling more than $15 million. She had other program managers, but she headed up the entire project. When other top managers left, she quickly assumed other responsibilities, such as hearing coordinator, contract manager, and coordinator for interpreter services, transportation vendors, and in-home services. Her position might be classified as JD preferred since it did not require bar membership, but she said that the law does figure into what she is doing. She was the only lawyer in her office. She told us that she would like to be making more money but that she really appreciated the autonomy she had.

We know from Internet sources that Joanna moved up within the department, staying in various positions until she took a leadership position focused on health information technology at the state level. Interestingly, during various times in her government career, she also conducted a private practice as a solo practitioner.

Richard became a public defender later in life and used his PD experience to move into private practice. A White man, Richard graduated from a service academy, spent seven years in the military, then went to work for a Fortune 500 company and attended law school at night. The company paid his law school tuition. He graduated from law school at the age of 40. His uncle had been the chief public defender in a large midwestern city, and Richard was impressed by his uncle and knew he would like to do similar work. He had introduced himself to the public defender's office while a law student and was hired on graduation. He came up through the ranks, beginning with misdemeanors, then juvenile crimes, and finally all major crimes (including murder and rape cases). He told us that he loved the work. By the time we interviewed him, his was carrying 30 cases, primarily because he was handling major felonies. He told us that the job completely met his expectations as far as providing meaningful work. He viewed his role as: "We've got to be the 'check' against this big machine, and unfortunately it means representing people that are in a lot of cases guilty of some pretty terrible things."

Richard felt the same public purpose he felt in the army but not when he worked for the Fortune 500 company. He told us during the interview: "I really can't envision doing anything but criminal defense work right now." He really enjoyed being in the courtroom and being in front of a jury. He thought his desire to do the work he was doing would not have arisen had he graduated from law school at the age of 25. He was married, his wife is an assistant principal, and they have two sons. When we interviewed him, the sons were ages 13 and 10. Despite his expressed enthusiasm for his public defender job, he is now in private practice in a large midwestern city. It appears that Richard was a public defender for four years and then an associate in a law firm for a year before opening his own office in 2005. His firm now apparently has six attorneys.

Ryan is a White man who attended a law school ranked from 51 to 100 in a national law market city and spent his entire third year working in a public defender's office, a job he "loved." Having accumulated $100,000 in law school debt, he considered going to work for a large corporate law firm. But he was repulsed by the interviewing process and withdrew his application. Owing to the medical needs of a parent, he moved home to a regional market city and pursued a position in a 501(c)(3) that contracted with the state to provide all public defender services. He very much enjoyed his work, amassing significant trial experience. Although he was under financial strain owing to his debt load, he described the compensation in his organization as good for the area in which he lived. Still, his objective was to move to California and practice in a large criminal defense law firm, which would afford him a comfortable income. The timing of when he would move depended on the circumstances of his family, but his eventual intention was clear. Our 2019 web search found that he was working at the same organization in the same regional city where he had grown up.

Our last two state prosecutors and defenders come from top-20 schools, suggesting that these are not typical positions of first choice for relatively elite law school graduates with corporate law options. Only particular sets of circumstances led to these jobs. On graduation, Scott, an African American man, landed a position in a corporate law department practicing entertainment law, seemingly a dream job for his law school cohort. Yet the job proved far less glamorous than he had expected, a constant grind of contract review work: "It was not fun at all, and I hated what I was doing. It felt like when I worked at Kmart when I was in high school. I dreaded going to work in the morning. . . . The first six months were great because I was learning something new, but after that. . . . I told a friend I hate what I'm doing." The friend worked in the public defender's office and suggested he come watch a trial. Scott applied for an opening in the office and had been there 12 years at the time of our interview: "It doesn't feel like a job. I enjoy what I do. I'm not sitting around looking at the clock, trying to figure out what time I am getting off. Friday comes, and it's like, Wow, Friday's already here." Scott already had moved up in a series of promotions in the public defender's office by wave 3, and our 2019 web search found that he was still practicing there.

Pamela, an Asian American woman whom we introduced in chapter 6, had left a megafirm after nearly 10 years, took some years off from active practice to have a child, and then engaged in volunteer work for small municipalities as part of a strategy to retool as a prosecutor. At the time of her wave 3 interview, she had just accepted a full-time position prosecuting misdemeanors in a municipality with a small prosecution staff. In contrast to what we found for other respondents who used their large-firm experience as a credential to obtain different employment, Pamela observed that local government employers viewed ex-members of big law firms with suspicion: "They had a slight bias toward people who had salaries of $300,000, [that they] did not really need the money, or perhaps [they were] just doing the job for a little while to get trial experience and then [would] go back to a big firm." Instead, they hired her because she had been developing relationships with them for many years in her volunteer and part-time work. Asked whether she would ever go back into private practice, she answered: "Oh lord no. No. Never. Done." As we saw in chapter 4, the least frequent transition for attorneys who begin in large law firms is to move to state government by wave 3. Pamela had followed an unusual path after the crushing disappointment of being terminated by a large law firm when she might have been on the cusp of gaining an equity partnership.

Pamela talked about the significance of prosecuting misdemeanors and how important the prosecution was in the lives of people charged with these crimes. But she also indicated that her dream job was to be a prosecutor in felony cases in a larger jurisdiction. A government website shows that as of 2019 she had indeed moved to a prosecutor's office in a large county and is prosecuting felonies.

Conclusion

The government, nonprofit, and public interest sectors are defined by the legal literature as the places for those who retain their ideals despite the temptations of the big money of private practice in large corporate law firms. We see this image, not surprisingly, most dramatically in the graduates of the elite schools, who tend to be the most privileged and to have had to confront the choice. Within the group we interviewed, again not surprisingly, we find more women than men. And these public interest lawyers who are graduates of elite schools show considerable resilience: most have stayed in public interest law. This group, for the most part, had access to loan forgiveness programs not available to other public sector lawyers.

There is also an elite track in the government, but it is more complex than the literature suggests. To be sure, we see again the idealism and appreciation of the public service component. These lawyers, at least for a time, reject the rewards of corporate law, finding the position they have more meaningful. At the same time, however, especially within the federal government and certain state governments, there are fast tracks that can convert lawyers with corporate law beginnings or the credentials of corporate lawyers from top law schools into very desirable lateral recruits into private practice. Most obvious here is the assistant US attorney position, which builds prestige, skills, and relationships that translate into criminal defense and regulation positions in business and, especially, corporate law firm white-collar defense positions. Other federal government positions, in contrast, are not as elite but, as with positions involving immigration law, may turn out to open up opportunities in corporate law practice. Advancement comes from inside, for example, through promotion to immigration judgeships or supervisory positions in large public defenders' offices, rather than from private marketability.

In both the public interest and the government tracks, there are common themes despite these differences. One is the theme of rejection of corporate law, which often goes with a desire to "have a life." This is true of the most elite paths and the more accessible career trajectories into government and public interest law. Indeed, throughout the interviews of respondents in government and public interest organizations, we find expressions of sentiments about life balance that are absent from the literature on the choice between idealism and greed. Within the assistant US attorney setting, Carrie celebrated the fact that there were no "demands to work weekends for no apparent reason." We also see concerns about salary. Careers in state government and the nonelite public interest settings provide a mix of pragmatism and idealism. A number of positions in state government are slightly better paying than are those in public interest law and in many segments of private practice.

The prosecutors and defenders at the state level are somewhat in their own category. They present unique paths of mobility, sometimes into the judiciary, sometimes into a stable private practice. There are complaints about the pay and the workload, but most of those we interviewed enjoyed their work. We also see that a combination of burnout and the lure of more pay and control does lead a number of these lawyers into private practice, though not in the lucrative large law firm setting. For most of these lawyers, it is not a matter of depression owing to a failure to reform criminal justice. Instead, it is the goal of finding a position that is respected and valued and uses their legal skills. Again, the ideal of the academic description does not do justice to the real life of building a legal career.

For those calling for more law school graduates to take up careers in government or public interest law, these interviews are essentially success stories, with only a relatively few dropouts. But the narratives are not only or even mostly about persisting with idealism. They are about many other features of these positions, such as work/life balance, a supportive community, options in private practice, family resources, personal networks, and career opportunities after public service positions. Until scholars recognize these realities, they will not be able to build a more robust model of the public sector of the legal profession.

PART 4

Inequalities of Race and Gender

White Spaces: The Enduring Racialization
of American Law Firms

WITH VITOR M. DIAS

In this chapter, we examine the racial dynamics of careers in law firms—arguably still the dominant institution in the American legal profession—using data on respondents' career moves from 2000 through 2019. These data afford new insights into how American law firms are fundamentally racialized organizations. It is not that law firms merely undermine the careers of minority lawyers in general and African American lawyers in particular. They are White spaces, created by and run for the benefit of White lawyers, typically White men. Applying critical race theory, we reject the view of law firms as race-neutral organizations that merely host the prejudices of its individual members and clients (Ray 2019). To be sure, such individual-level processes are part of the story. But, rather than viewing the organizational processes that create and legitimate cognitive schemas and shared, taken-for-granted beliefs about who fits in a law firm, who has the right stuff, who has leadership potential, who is attractive to big clients, and thus who is partner material as somehow exogenous to law firms, we view law firms as active agents of racialization processes. Racialization is not just a bug or a minor design flaw in law firms. It is a design feature baked into law firms.

As we discussed in chapter 2, the corporate law firm sector was almost exclusively composed of White men until large firms began adopting diversity programs in the 1970s. This formal commitment to diversity has facilitated a substantial increase in the representation of racial and ethnic minorities in law firms, yet the partnership ranks remain overwhelmingly occupied by Whites. In their classic articles, David Wilkins and Mitu Gulati (1996, 1998) chronicled the plight of African American lawyers in corporate law firms and identified its institutional roots. Notwithstanding the pervasive lip service given to diversity, equity, and inclusion (Wilkins and Kim 2016), little has changed two decades later. Minority lawyers remain systematically underrepresented in the legal profession as a whole and in law firms in particular (Gorman and Kay 2010; Rivera 2012). Even when they do recruit minority lawyers for entry-level associate positions, law firms systematically deny them the opportunities and resources necessary to stay and succeed (Payne-Pikus et al. 2010; Woodson 2014). At the heart of the institutional features of law firms rewarding Whiteness is the up-or-out tournament for partnership described in chapter 2 and in the narratives of chapter 7. Although many firms have created partnership tiers (e.g., nonequity partner) and retain associates who do not make partner (e.g., permanent associate, of counsel), equity partnership remains the prized Holy Grail of law firms. By design, equity partnership is improbable; making equity partner remains a low-probability event. Equity partners—the vast majority of whom are White—exercise enormous discretion with respect to whom to groom and mentor. High associate-to-partner ratios, particularly in large law firms, limit promotion opportunities for associates and force partners to pick and choose the associates in whom they will invest.

Without powerful patrons, the equity partnership prospects of associates are low to nil. Equity partners mentor associates informally and formally. Informally, by spending time socializing over meals and during recreational activities, mentors make their mentees feel welcome and valued. Informal mentoring helps mentees cement personal relationships and accumulate relational capital that confers important professional benefits. Formally, mentors assign work and clients to mentees. In so doing, they also signal to other partners mentees' value to the law firm. As one recent study found:

> Most successful diverse attorneys credited their success, at least in part, to having strong mentors. . . . One woman of color emphasized that the mentoring program cannot simply be "a lunch a month." Instead, "it needs to be that you are responsible for getting this person into the partner ranks." One attorney noted that, at her big firm, it was "years before a White male partner took me out to lunch" even though "they would take largely male associate groups out to lunch." (Dunlop and Gassman-Pines 2021, 157)

Study after study shows that African American lawyers in law firms are typically shunted to the "dead-end track" and assigned routine paperwork, whereas their White counterparts are more often put on the "training track" and assigned challenging work for important clients (Briscoe and Kellogg 2011; Kay and Gorman 2012; Pearce et al. 2015). As a result, African American lawyers lead the exodus out of law firms; their risk of exiting far exceeds that of any other racial or ethnic group. Part of the story is the durability of the up-or-out

Cravath System; another is that, palpably aware of the dearth of meaningful opportunities for career development, African American lawyers exit law firms preemptively.

Through at least the 2010s, law firms stubbornly failed to integrate minorities. They remain predominantly White spaces, racially segregated and far from welcoming to non-Whites. African American lawyers find themselves to be second-class citizens, separate and unequal, and unable to gain a foothold. The symbolic and economic rewards—status and money—conferred by partnership remain mostly monopolized by White men.

We base this argument on data from some 4,000 respondents who participated in either wave 2 or wave 3. The questionnaires collected career data in two ways. First, they collected *complete employment histories* at each wave: start date, end date, job type, practice setting, full-time or part-time, location, and reason for leaving for every position held since passing the bar (excluding judicial clerkships). Second, they collected detailed information about respondents' *current job* at the time of each survey. We analyze both types of career data.

We focus our empirical scrutiny on two outcomes: (1) exits from the law firm sector and (2) promotion to equity partner. We find that enormous racial disparities with respect to both outcomes are substantially accounted for by corresponding racial disparities with respect to mentoring and perceived discrimination.

This chapter is roughly divided into two sets of tasks. We first present descriptive overviews of the changing racial and ethnic composition of law firms over time and racialized patterns of exit and promotion. We then turn to the task of explaining why law firms remain overwhelmingly White spaces. Our explanation for stark racial and ethnic differences in exits from and promotions within law firms rests with similarly stark racial and ethnic differences in promotion aspirations, perceived promotion prospects, mentoring, and experiences of discrimination. Third, we summarize results from (omitted) multivariate models to ensure that descriptive patterns persist net of a variety of control variables that might offer alternate explanations for the racial disparities we observe.[1] Fourth, we probe racial patterns in the reported importance of mentoring for career changes. Fifth, we examine respondents' answers to questions about why they accepted offers of employment and why they thought legal employers offered them jobs.

Before launching our analysis, we need to discuss why in this chapter we primarily focus on race without an extended discussion of gender or the intersection of race and gender. As we saw in chapter 4, there are significant differences in the gender composition of racial and ethnic groups in the legal profession, most notably the much higher percentage of women among African Americans than among other groups. To some extent, therefore, gender is a proxy for race and ethnicity. In several chapters of this book, including the narrative chapters, and in other AJD Project publications, we find that women of color are uniquely positioned in the legal profession and their workplaces. These analyses are very important but are not the focus of the analysis here. The examination of race in legal careers poses several challenges, both due to the small numbers of respondents in racial/ethnic categories and the complexity of the mechanisms that produce racial disparities in career outcomes. We did our utmost to isolate racial effects from gender effects. Multivariate regression models we omit from this chapter assure us that what appear to be differences between racial and ethnic groups are not an artifact of an overrepresentation of women among African American respondents. Gender inequality is not secretly driving our story of racial and ethnic inequality. We will see in chapter 12 that patterns of gender inequality in career trajectories present different analytic challenges, but these are supported both by much larger numbers of women than men and women of color in the sample and by the very robust engines of inequality we observe in the production of gender inequality. Chapter 12 does undertake an analysis of the intersection of race and gender in the earnings of lawyers. And chapter 11 examines intersectional issues related to education debt.

A Descriptive View of Law Firm Racialization

We start with the big picture to justify our empirical focus on law firms. Law firms remain central in the careers of law school graduates. Three-quarters (75%) of the AJD Project sample worked in a law firm at some point in the first 13 years of their careers. Whites were the most likely (76%), with Latinx and Asian Americans close behind (75% and 73%, respectively). African Americans (67%) were the least likely to report work experience in a law firm. Of all respondents we observed over the full 13-year period, White respondents spent the most time in law firms, averaging 6.6 years, or 51% of their work histories. African American respondents spent the least time in law firms, averaging 5.6 years, or 42% of their work histories. One-quarter (25%) of White respondents spent the entirety of their 13-year work histories in law firms. These include the "big law lifers" from chapter 3 (Dinovitzer and Garth 2020). Asian American and Latinx respondents were similarly likely to have worked exclusively in law firms (21% and 24%, respectively). African American respondents, by contrast, were far less likely to have worked exclusively in law firms (14%).

Compared to respondents in other racial and ethnic groups, African Americans were the least likely to begin their careers in law firms. Overall, almost two-thirds of all respondents (66%) reported working in a law firm at some point in the 2000–2003 time period. White respondents were the most likely to begin their careers in law firms (68%), followed by Asian American and Latinx respondents (64% and 63%, respectively). African American respondents, by contrast, were the least likely to so do (53%). They were instead the most likely to start their careers in federal or state government (29%, compared to 22% of Whites), legal services, a public defender's office, or a public interest organization (12%, compared to 7% of Whites), and education (8%, compared to 3% of Whites).

African Americans were also the most likely to leave law firms. By 2012, law firms accounted for 40% of all respondents. At this point in time, the share of respondents in law firms was highest among Whites (42%), followed closely by Latinx and Asian American respondents (41% and 39%, respectively), and lowest among African Americans (29%).[2] Among respondents who left law firms, African Americans were the least likely to join another law firm and the most likely to move to federal or state government, legal services, a public defender's office, a public interest organization, or an education institution. Among respondents who changed positions within law firms, African Americans were far less likely than Whites to move into equity partner positions (11% and 21%, respectively) and far more likely than Whites to move into non-equity partner positions (28% and 14%, respectively) and contract attorney positions (11% and 6%, respectively).

A shocking proportion of law firms were all White. Combining all three survey waves, almost 30% of respondents in law firms reported that 0% "of the lawyers in [their] workplace are members of racial-ethnic minority groups." Law firm Whiteness is particularly pronounced in small firms of 2–20 lawyers, which account for more lawyers than any other law firm size category. Here, almost 60% of lawyers were in all-White firms. Further limiting the sample to metropolitan areas with populations below 1 million, over three-quarters of respondents in small firms of 2–20 lawyers (76%) reported having no minority lawyer colleagues.

In 2000, 89% of all respondents in law firms were associates, with virtually no variation by race and ethnicity. By 2012, almost two-thirds of respondents who remained in law firms were not working as associates. Among respondents working in law firms in 2012, White respondents were the least likely to be working as associates (33%), followed by African American respondents (38%), Latinx respondents (41%), and Asian American respondents (46%). White respondents were correspondingly the most likely to be working as equity partners (34%), followed by African American and Latinx respondents (24%) and Asian American respondents (19%); the least likely to be working as contract attorneys/of counsel (11%), followed by Asian American respondents (15%) and African American and Latinx respondents (17%); and the least likely to be working as staff attorneys (4%), followed by African American, Asian American, and Latinx respondents (8%).

In 2012, African Americans and Whites accounted for 7% and 72%, respectively, of respondents working in law firms. However, they accounted for 5% and 80%, respectively, of all equity partners in law firms in the same year. Just as African Americans were underrepresented among equity partners, they were similarly overrepresented in lower-status positions in law firms. African Americans and Whites accounted for 9% and 62%, respectively, of all respondents working as contract attorneys/of counsel, staff attorneys, and supervising/managing attorneys in law firms in 2012.

Between 2000 and 2006, the gap in equity partnership between African Americans and Whites was consistently small (as were rates of making partner for all respondents). It then doubled in 2007 and continued to widen from 3 percentage points in 2007 to 11 percentage points in 2012. An exodus of African Americans from law firms coincided with a rapid increase in Whites making equity partner. Given that the partnership track is typically in the range of six to eight years, no one should be surprised that both exits from the law firm sector and promotions to equity partner increased after 2007 (recall that our sample is limited to lawyers admitted to a state bar in the year 2000).

Among 2,961 lawyers who had ever worked in a law firm (i.e., those at risk of exiting law firms or making equity partner), 8% were African American (n = 249), and 71% were White (n = 2,092). Twenty percent had made equity partner by 2012. However, Whites were more than twice as likely as African Americans to have made equity partner (23% vs. 11%). Within this general pattern is a conspicuous spike in exits among African American respondents and in promotions to equity partner among White respondents between 2007 and 2008. At every point in the first 13 years of their careers, African American lawyers were more likely than lawyers in any other racial or ethnic group to exit the law firm sector. The gap widened considerably after 2007. Naturally, exits from the law firm sector were fueled by the up-or-out Cravath System.

Cross-sectional information about respondents' current job at each survey wave reaffirms the foregoing descriptive findings. Exiting the law firm sector is an utterly common experience. At the same time, it is far more of a career-defining event for African American lawyers than it is for White lawyers. Meanwhile, making equity partner is far more of a career-defining event for White lawyers than it is for African American lawyers.

An alternative analytic approach to measuring exits and promotions is as follows. With respect to exits from the law firm sector, respondents who were in law firms at wave 1 and in nonfirm practice settings at wave 2 are considered to have exited the law firm sector at wave 2. Likewise, respondents who were in law firms at wave 2 and in nonfirm practice settings at wave 3 are considered to have exited the law firm sector at wave 3. With respect to promotion to equity partner, respondents employed by law firms at wave 1 in positions other than equity partner who either reported in their employment histories making equity partner between wave 1 and wave 2 or reported themselves as equity partners at wave 2 are considered to have been promoted to equity partner at wave 2. Likewise, respondents employed by law firms at wave 2 in positions other than equity partner who either reported in their employment histories making equity partner between wave 2 and wave 3 or reported themselves as equity partners at wave 3 are considered to have been promoted to equity partner at wave 3. We use job information gathered from web searches conducted in November 2019 to analyze both types of changes between wave 3 and 2019.

Between wave 1 and wave 2, all lawyers in law firms were similarly likely to exit the law firm sector (an overall average of one-third did so). But, between wave 2 and wave 3, African American lawyers were nearly twice as likely as White lawyers were to exit the law firm sector: 48% and 25%, respectively. Similarly, between wave 3 and 2019, African American lawyers remained dramatically more likely than White lawyers to exit the law firm sector: 57% and 40%, respectively. These racial differences are statistically significant at wave 3 and in 2019.

Across every time period, White lawyers were about twice as likely as African American lawyers to make equity partner. Between wave 1 and wave 2, 5% and 14% of African American and White lawyers, respectively, made equity partner. Between wave 2 and wave 3, 13% and 27% of African American and White lawyers, respectively, made equity partner. Finally, between wave 3 and 2019, 20% and 37% of African American and White lawyers, respectively, made equity partner. These differences are statistically significant. The number of African Americans promoted to partner at each of these three points of transition is strikingly small: 4, 10, and 11, respectively.

To what extent are these patterns driven by self-selection, namely, differences in the probability of voluntarily opting out? To what extent are they driven by racialized treatment of associates, namely, differences in mentoring, access to and relationships with partners, and bias and discrimination? To what extent are they driven by human capital, namely, differences in qualifications and skills? We next consider the self-selection explanation before turning to the racialized treatment explanation. Finally, we will consider the human capital explanation.

Selectivity of Lawyers: Declaring the Intent to Leave Law Firms Preemptively

In this section, we report racial and ethnic differences with respect both to the desire to leave one's law firm and to aspirations and perceived prospects of attaining equity partner.

Our measure of the desire to leave one's law firm comes from answers to the following question: "If the decision were up to you, approximately how much longer would you like to stay with your current employer?" This question was asked of all three waves. Respondents' declining desire to leave law firms at each successive wave—25%, 20%, and 15%, respectively—itself reflects self-selection. Those who stayed in law firms did so undoubtedly because their desire to leave was weaker than that of respondents who had already left. At each wave, African American lawyers were almost twice as likely as White lawyers were to indicate a desire to leave their law firms within one year (either "I am already looking for another position" or "less than a year"): 38% vs. 21% at wave 1, 32% vs. 19% at wave 2, and 23% vs. 12% at wave 3. The differences are statistically significant at the .05 level at waves 1 and 2 and the .10 level at wave 3.

Our measure of aspirations to make equity partner comes from answers to the following question: "How strongly do you aspire to attain each of the following positions within your firm?" Response categories ranged from 1 ("not at all") to 10 ("very high aspirations"). Our measure of prospects of attaining equity partner comes from answers to the following question: "How would you rate your chances, as a percentage ranging from 0 to 100, of attaining each of the following positions in your firm?" Respondents were asked to answer each question with respect to four positions: equity partner, nonequity partner, of counsel, and contract lawyer. These questions were asked only in wave 2.

No racial group exhibited either resounding determination to make equity partner or resounding confidence about their prospects of doing so. At the same time, African American respondents were far below White respondents in terms of both aspirations and perceived prospects of attaining equity partnership. Every racial and ethnic group aspired to make equity partner more than they aspired to make nonequity partner. However, only White lawyers rated their chances of attaining equity partnership above their chances of attaining other positions. Members of every other racial or ethnic group rated their chances of making nonequity partner above their chances of making equity partner. Aspirations to become (and hence also perceived chances of becoming) of counsel and contract attorneys were low across the board.

With respect to equity partner, African American and White respondents reported average aspirations of 4.5 and 6.5, respectively, and average perceived prospects of 47% and 58%, respectively. Both differences are statistically significant. African Americans were similarly less bullish than were Whites about becoming nonequity partners (statistically significantly so only with respect to aspirations). However, African Americans were more likely than were Whites to view of counsel and contract attorney as attainable positions (even though differences were not statistically significant).

As we will see next, the foregoing patterns of selecting into and out of law firms were shaped by corresponding patterns of employer treatment in the form of work opportunities, mentoring, and bias.

Treatment of Lawyers: Suffering from Neglect within Law Firms

At all three waves, respondents were asked whether they did the following "on a recurring basis": (1) join partners for breakfast or lunch and (2) spend recreational time with partners. Among respondents in law firms who were not equity partners, White lawyers were more likely than were African American lawyers to respond in the affirmative to both questions at all three points in time (but differences were statistically significant only at wave 1). The proportions of African American and White respondents reporting joining partners for breakfast or lunch on a recurring basis were 43% and 61%, respectively, at wave 1, 47% and 54%, respectively, at wave 2, and 49% and 55%, respectively, at wave 3. With respect to spending recreational time with partners on a recurring basis, respective proportions were 22% and 35% at wave 1, 26% and 33% at wave 2, and 31% and 34% at wave 3.

At all three waves, respondents were asked to check boxes on a list following the question: "What changes would you most like to see in your job?" We analyzed the likelihood of checking "more and/or better mentoring by senior attorneys, coworkers, and partners" and "more and/or better training." Among law firm lawyers who were not equity partners, African American lawyers were statistically significantly more likely than were White lawyers to check the first box at waves 2 and 3 and statistically significantly more likely than were White lawyers to check the second box at waves 1 and 2.

At all three waves, respondents were asked to indicate sources of support they received in various aspects of their job: (1) acquiring technical aspects of the job, (2) learning firm/office protocols and customs, (3) devising specific strategies for achieving career goals, (4) receiving support and encouragement in stressful times, (5) getting informal feedback on performance, (6) gaining valuable networking opportunities, and (7) having a personal advocate within the firm or office. Among the various sources of support that respondents could choose was "informal mentors at your firm or office." We constructed our measure of "received support from informal mentors at your firm" according to whether any aspect of a respondent's job was supported by any informal mentors. Among law firm lawyers who were not equity partners, African American lawyers were less likely than were White lawyers to report such support at all three waves: respectively, 43% and 48% at wave 1, 39% and 53% at wave 2, and 39% and 54% at wave 3. Differences are statistically significant at wave 2 only.

The wave 2 questionnaire includes a question asking, "Are there any of the firm's preexisting clients (not including new clients you brought in) for whom you are the primary responsible attorney?" In wave 3, the question was slightly reworded as, "Do you have primary responsibility for relations with one or more of the major clients of the firm?" At wave 2, African American law firm lawyers who were not equity partners were far less likely than were their White counterparts to answer in the affirmative: 42% and 56%, respectively (a statistically significant difference). This difference did not extend to wave 3.

The wave 2 questionnaire also asked respondents to indicate reasons why they may have experienced "difficulties in meeting your billables in 2006." We analyze the likelihood of checking boxes for "did not get enough assignments" and "partner discounted hours (or did not give full credit)." With respect to both measures, African American law firm lawyers without equity partnership were almost two times more likely than were their White counterparts to check the box: 39% and 22%, respectively, for the first item and 21% and 11%, respectively, for the second item (both differences were statistically significant).

Finally, respondents were asked about discrimination: "During the last two years, have any of the following ever happened to you in your place of work by virtue of your race, religion, ethnicity, gender, disability, or sexual orientation?" Questionnaires from all three waves included the following items: (1) experienced demeaning comments or other types of harassment, (2) missed out on a desirable assignment, (3) had a client request the someone else handle a matter, and (4) experienced one or more other forms of discrimination. Waves 2 and 3 included an additional item: (5) had a colleague or supervisor request someone else to handle a matter. African American respondents were statistically significantly more likely than White respondents to report (1) experiencing demeaning comments or another type of harassment (28% and 12%, respectively, at wave 1, 18% and 13%, respectively, at wave 2, and no differences at wave 3), (2) missing out on a desirable assignment (respectively, 24% and 9% at wave 1, 20% and 8% at wave 2, and 19% and 7% at wave 3), (3) experiencing another form of discrimination (respectively, 28% and 7% at wave 1, 16% and 6% at wave 2, and 11% and 4% at wave 3), and (4) having a colleague or supervisor request someone else handle a matter (10% and 6%, respectively, at wave 2, and no differences at wave 3). (For an extended analysis of AJD Project data on perceived discrimination by race, gender, and sexual orientation, see Nelson et al. [2019].)

Do Selectivity and Treatment Explain Law Firms' Racialization?

So far, we have established that, compared to their White counterparts, African American respondents left law firms at higher rates and made equity partner at lower rates. We have also established that African Americans exhibited greater selectivity than did their White counterparts insofar as they reported stronger desires to leave law firms, weaker aspirations to make equity partner, and slimmer perceived chances of success in the associate-to-partner tournament. Compared to their White counterparts, African Americans also reported receiving poorer treatment within law firms. To what extent do these racial and ethnic differences in the selectivity and treatment of lawyers explain racial and ethnic differences in our outcomes of interest, namely, exiting law firms and making equity partner? To find out, we ran multivariate regression models for both exits from law firms and making equity partner between wave 1 and wave 2 and between wave 2 and wave 3 (omitted to conserve space).

Our panel survey, conducted at three points in time, affords a rare and valuable opportunity to assess the impact of something reported at one point in time on something reported at a subsequent point in time. In more concrete terms, we assess the effects of our measures of selectivity and treatment reported at *wave 1* on exits and promotions reported at *wave 2*. Likewise, we assess the effects of selectivity and treatment reported at *wave 2* on these exits and promotions reported at *wave 3*. Doing so reduces the likelihood that respondents' answers to questions about selectivity and treatment were their post hoc rationalizations for a career setback or failure in the eyes of those who view equity partnership as the pinnacle of career success in the legal profession and the essence of what it means to make it as a lawyer. When respondents answered questions about their desire to leave law firms, their aspirations to make equity partnership, and their treatment at work, they had no crystal ball through which to see their future, even if many of them had a reasonably accurate sense of their prospects for equity partnership. Had we assessed relationships between pieces of information respondents reported at the same survey wave, we would have had more trouble ruling out the possibility that respondents reported sour grapes about the law firms at which they were not promoted to equity partner and from which they departed.

In our models for exits from the law firm sector, we found no significant differences by race/ethnicity in exits between the first two waves. This should come as no surprise given that making equity partner was improbable for all law school graduates in the first seven or eight years of their careers. However, several other variables had significant effects, including whether respondents received support from informal mentors, spent recreational time with partners, and desired to leave the firm within a year. Women were more likely to exit net of other effects. Those relatively few respondents who made equity partner at this stage were far less likely to exit. Notably, human capital variables such as law school grades, LSAT scores, and law school selectivity either had no significant effects or did not decrease the probability of exiting a law firm, with the exception that graduates of less selective law schools were less likely to exit law firms at this stage.

The time between wave 2 and wave 3 was when the rubber met the road. Exits in this more critical time period tell a different story with regard to race. Among respondents who had otherwise seemingly identical levels of human capital (law school grades, LSAT scores, and law school rank), African Americans were 20 percentage points more likely than were Whites to exit the law firm sector (a statistically significant difference between the model's predicted probabilities of 44.4% and·24.7%, respectively). After adding treatment variables to the model, the gap between African Americans and Whites shrunk to 13 percentage points (also a statistically significant difference between the model's predicted probabilities of 38.2% and 25.3%, respectively). The gap shrunk further, to 11 percentage points, after we added our measure of selectivity: the desire to leave one's law firm within the next year. At this point, the gap between the predicted probabilities of 36.9% and 25.4%, respectively, was only marginally statistically significant. The gap shrunk to 9 percentage points (predicted probabilities of 34.7% and 25.9%, respectively) and lost all statistical significance after we added whether a lawyer made equity partner. Informal mentors and gaining primary responsibility for existing firm clients—key measures of the treatment of lawyers within law firms—significantly reduced the probability of exit. Desire to leave within a year statistically significantly increased the probability of exit by 22 percentage points in the final model (from 20.5% to 42.1%). None of the human capital variables had significant effects. We can therefore be confident that all racial differences we observe are among lawyers in seemingly identical contexts with seemingly identical backgrounds. To sum up, African Americans' greater tendency, relative to their White counterparts, to exit law firms is largely accounted for by their poorer treatment in law firms, their greater desire to leave law firms, and their lower probability of making equity partnership.

Our models for promotion to equity partner include only 83 African American respondents at waves 1 and 2, only 4 of whom (5%) made equity partner, and 819 White respondents, 122 of whom (15%) made equity partner. Models for making equity partner between wave 2 and wave 3 include 74 African American lawyers and 648 White lawyers, 12% and 27% of whom, respectively, made equity partner. Once again, because so few lawyers made equity partner between wave 1 and wave 2, African Americans were not statistically significantly less likely than were Whites to do so at this stage. Between wave 2 and wave 3, however, among law firm lawyers with otherwise seemingly identical levels of human capital, African Americans were 12 percentage points less likely than were Whites to make equity partner (a statistically significant difference between the model's predicted probabilities of 26.4% and 14.8%, respectively). When aspirations were added to the model, the gap shrunk to 10 percentage points (a marginally statistically significant difference between predicted probabilities of 26.2% and 16.2%, respectively). Mentorship, gaining responsibility for clients, and the desire to leave reduced the gap between African Americans and Whites to 7 percentage points (predicted probabilities of 25.7% and 19.2%, respectively), below the threshold of even marginal statistical significance. Aspirations figured prominently in promotions to partnership as those with moderate and high aspirations of making partner were 6 and 17 percentage points more likely to do so, respectively, than were those with low aspirations. The addition of perceived chances of making partner to the model reduced the gap between African Americans and Whites to only 5 percentage points (predicted probabilities of 20.1% and 24.9%, respectively), also statistically insignificant. Respondents were apparently good at estimating their prospects for promotion as those who gave themselves a 75%–89% and a 90%–100% chance of making equity partner were 17 and 42 percentage points more likely to do so, respectively, than were those who gave themselves no chance at all. Women were significantly less likely to make partner at both points of transition. Meanwhile, human capital variables had no significant effects on the probability of making partner. The data fail to support the notion (espoused by certain economists) that racial disparities with respect to either outcome stem from racial differences in qualifications or skills. The probability of making equity partner between wave 1 and wave 2 was higher for smaller firms, but this difference faded between wave 2 and wave 3.

In separate models for the desire to leave law firms, we found gaps between African Americans and Whites of 8 percentage points at wave 1 (marginally statistically significant) and 13 percentage points at wave 2 (statistically significant) among respondents with otherwise seemingly identical levels of human capital. These gaps were almost entirely erased after adding our treatment variables, which were powerful predictors of the desire to leave law firms. Lawyers who received support from informal mentors were statistically significantly less likely to report that they wanted to leave their law firm between wave 1 and wave 2. Lawyers who perceived that they were targets of discrimination were significantly more likely to report that they desired to leave their firm between wave 1 and wave 2 and between wave 2 and wave 3. As noted above, desire to leave the law firm was a significant predictor of exits and of promotion to partner.

Finally, in models for aspirations for and perceived prospects of attaining equity partnership, statistically significant gaps between African Americans and Whites of 15 and 6 percentage points, respectively, among respondents with otherwise seemingly identical levels of human capital mostly disappeared after controlling for mentoring and discrimination, which in turn are powerful predictors of future exits from the law firm sector (at subsequent waves) and of future promotion to equity partner (at subsequent waves). Spending recreational time with partners significantly increased both aspirations for an equity partnership and perceived chances of making equity partner after wave 2. Lawyers with high aspirations for making partner and lawyers who gave themselves good chances of making equity partner were significantly more likely to gain an equity partnership by wave 3.

Taken together, the results of our multivariate regression analyses can be summarized in the form of the following (admittedly crude) path model: treatment in law firms → desire to leave law firms → aspirations and perceived chances of making equity partner → exits from law firms and promotions to equity partner. In plain language, outcomes with respect to exiting the law firm sector and promotion to equity partner were far worse for African American lawyers than they were for White lawyers. An important reason for these divergent outcomes is that African American and White lawyers in law firms were operating on a highly uneven playing field. African American lawyers were hugely disadvantaged with respect to mentoring and bias. By controlling for mentoring and bias in our multivariate regression models, we statistically (or artificially) leveled the playing field. In other words, we created a parallel world in which African American and White lawyers enjoyed seemingly identical levels of mentoring and bias. In this alternate universe, narrowing the racial gap in mentoring and bias *directly* narrowed the racial gap with respect to our two outcome measures, namely, exiting the law firm sector and promotion to equity partner. Narrowing the racial gap in mentoring and bias also *indirectly* narrowed the racial gap with respect to our two outcome measures by both weakening the desire to leave law firms and strengthening aspirations and perceived prospects to attain equity partnership.

One important takeaway from these findings is that lawyers accurately predicted their futures. Those who reported an intention to leave their firms at either wave 1 or wave 2 were a lot more likely than those who did not report such an intention to have left the law firm sector by the subsequent survey wave. Likewise, those who reported high prospects of making equity partner at wave 2 were a lot more likely than those who did not report such high prospects to have made equity partner by wave 3. Lawyers clearly can read the writing on the wall.

Perceptions of the Importance of Mentoring for Career Support

So far, we have seen the consequential nature of mentoring. We can see this in yet another way, that is, by examining answers to an additional question on mentoring introduced in wave 3: "Thinking of all the mentors (both formal and informal) you have had since being admitted to the bar, how important have the following forms of support been to your career?" Lawyers who had attained equity partnership by wave 3 were statistically significantly more likely than those who had not attained equity partnership to report that mentoring had been extremely important (65% vs. 54%). African American lawyers in law firms, who we know were less likely than White lawyers in law firms to receive mentoring, were also statistically significantly more likely than were White lawyers to say that mentors were extremely important in their careers (68% vs. 55%). This somewhat paradoxical pattern suggests that African American lawyers recognized the importance of the mentoring that they received but of which many of their fellow African American lawyers were deprived.

Hiring Considerations by Job Candidates and Law Firms

Given their relatively grim prospects of succeeding in law firms, what motivates African American lawyers to join law firms when they embark on their careers, and what motivates law firms to recruit African American lawyers in the first place? In this final set of analyses, we consider answers to two batteries of questions. The first asks respondents to assess the importance of each item on a list of factors influencing the choice to accept their current jobs. The second asks respondents to assess the perceived importance of each item on a list of factors influencing their law firms' decision to offer them their current jobs.

Far more than White respondents, African American respondents were motivated by financial considerations to join law firms. At wave 1, only two or three years after graduating from law school, the most important reason both African American and Latinx respondents identified for joining law firms was "paying off law school debts" and "salary/compensation." Meanwhile, among Asian American respondents, law school debt was only the tenth most important reason for joining a law firm. Among White respondents, law school debt was the sixth most important reason for joining a law firm. In chapter 11, we compare debt burdens across race and ethnicity, law school selectivity, and wave of the survey. The responses about the importance of compensation in part reflect racial and ethnic differences in debt loads, which remain persistently high for African American lawyers.

The emphasis African American law firm lawyers who were not equity partners attached to financial considerations does not mean that they are not interested in social values in the law firm context. They attached more importance than did respondents of any other racial or ethnic group to "opportunity to do socially responsible work," "diversity of the workplace," and "pro bono opportunities." Compared to other respondents, White lawyers attached by far the least importance to "diversity of the workplace."

Respondents' perceptions of why law firms recruited them also dramatically varied by race and ethnicity. African American respondents were far more likely than were White respondents to believe that they were hired because of their "law school reputation" (as we saw in chapter 4, African American respondents are overrepresented among graduates of elite law schools), "race/ethnicity," and "physical appearance." By contrast, White lawyers were more likely than were those in any other racial or ethnic group to believe that they were hired on the basis of their "law school grades" and "law school faculty recommendations." African American lawyers are perceived to be in law firms less because of their qualifications and more because of the color of their skin. Taken together, these empirical patterns reflect African American lawyers' sense of tokenism in law firms and their perception that the fix is in against them.

Conclusion

This chapter provides definitive evidence about the enduring racialization of American law firms. We documented the extent to which many law firms— some 30%—contain no attorneys of color. These proportions are even higher among small law firms and in less populated areas. Employment history data reveal that African American lawyers are differentially affected by the up-or-out system that continues to dominate American law firms. For the first seven years of their careers, African Americans and Whites had similar and steady patterns of exit from law firms. But, after year 7, at the threshold of equity partnership, we see the career trajectories of African Americans and Whites diverge. African Americans increasingly exit the law firm sector. Whites increasingly gain an equity partnership.

Contrary to what many law firm leaders state, this pattern is not the result of African Americans seeking better opportunities elsewhere. Nor does it reflect differences in the human capital profiles of African American and White lawyers. Rather, it is produced by the discrimination that many African American lawyers experience and the lower levels of mentorship, training, and client inheritance that they receive in law firms. As a result of this disparate treatment, African American lawyers in law firms are far more likely to indicate that they desire to leave their law firm employers in the next year, that they do not aspire to equity partnership with the same intensity as their counterparts, and that they view their chances of making equity partner as lower than their White counterparts view their chances. These processes are at the heart of the racialization of law firms. Because these processes are at the heart of the law firm career system, they will not be easily changed.

Student Debt and Cumulative
(Dis)Advantage in Lawyers' Careers

I'm still sitting on about $50,000 worth of debt. . . . It's just a miserable, miserable thing. . . . That debt has caused real problems in my life, real problems. Really. That was a huge mistake I made . . . taking on that debt. (Stewart, wave 3)

Stewart, an African American man whom we met in chapter 7, attended a historically Black undergraduate institution and a top-20 law school. He did not receive financial support from his parents and graduated with $60,000 in student debt. Spending his early career in a small law firm and in state government, he had repaid only $10,000 toward his principal by wave 3. In contrast, James, a White man whom we met in chapters 1 and 7, graduated from an Ivy League university and a top-10 law school before joining the prestigious law firm where he became an equity partner. His parents helped pay for law school, and he borrowed $60,000 from Stafford and Perkins loans. He repaid all his student debt by wave 3 with additional help from his parents.

Although James and Stewart began their careers with equal amounts of student debt, their repayment trajectories are remarkably different. This divergence is partly a function of earnings differences that, as we will see in chapter 12, tend to accumulate over time. At wave 1, Stewart earned $48,000, while James earned $180,000. By wave 3, Stewart earned $102,000—57% of James's *wave 1* earnings. Although James did not report his wave 3 earnings, his promotion to equity partner suggests that his earnings had grown by a significant margin. Moreover, his wife, who is also a lawyer but had no student debt because her parents funded her education, earned more than double what Stewart's wife earned at wave 3 ($110,000 compared to $50,000). Thus, in addition to the vast differences in their personal incomes and the levels of financial support they received from family, James and Stewart had different stocks of household wealth to draw on to repay their debt.[1]

James's story illustrates how even attorneys working in corporate law firms benefit from early advantages related to social class background, specifically in the form of elite education credentials and financial support from family.

These advantages accumulate over the course of lawyers' careers. Stewart's story illustrates how student debt is associated with cumulative *disadvantage* for African Americans from all social backgrounds.

This chapter analyzes student debt as an aspect of race and social class inequality. We demonstrate how inherited social differences are reproduced and exacerbated through processes of cumulative (dis)advantage in lawyers' careers. These patterns are not unique to lawyers. Social science research finds a wealth gap between African Americans and Whites that is maintained across generations and over the life course (Conley 1999; DiPrete and Eirich 2006; Killewald 2013; Killewald and Bryan 2018; Oliver and Shapiro 1995; Pfeffer and Killewald 2019). The AJD Project allows us to examine the relationship between race, social class background, and student debt among individuals from a single occupation. Although AJD Project respondents are a heterogeneous group, they come from relatively privileged social backgrounds (Dinovitzer et al. 2004; Heinz and Laumann 1982; Heinz et al. 2005) and share comparable education and professional credentials.

Law School Debt

The cost of American legal education skyrocketed in the two decades before AJD Project respondents graduated from law school,[2] increasing more than sevenfold. By 1997, the average tuition was $19,000 for private law schools, $12,500 for out-of-state public law schools, and $6,000 for in-state public law schools (Olivas 1999, 333). Mirroring this steep increase in law school tuition was a rise in law school debt and the share of legal education costs covered by loans (Kornhauser and Revesz 1995, 877).

In the 1996–97 academic year, the government underwrote most of the cost for legal education, with the federal government contributing 42% and states covering 15% of the roughly $3.4 billion dollars spent that year in the form of loans. Family and personal resources financed 31%, followed by law schools and other private sources, which contributed 13% combined. Although families and students themselves financed nearly one-third of these costs, this share "grows substantially as they repay government loans over time, reflecting the reality that personal finance is the major underwriter of legal education" (Olivas 1999, 336).

Student Debt and Inequality

Parents' contributions are an important source of law school financing, yet the availability of this form of financial support is a function of parents' means, which are not equally distributed (Kornhauser and Revesz 1995). In addition to material resources, parents' and relatives' financial support reflects cultural norms and expectations around supporting children's postsecondary education, which may vary by race/ethnicity, class, and gender. Research shows that African Americans, Latinx, and individuals from low-socioeconomic-status backgrounds borrow more money to fund their postsecondary education than do Whites, Asian Americans, and individuals from higher-income and higher-wealth families (Addo et al. 2016; Huelsman 2015; Pyne and Grodsky 2020; Schneider et al. 2018). In addition to racial and social class differences in student debt, women borrow more than do men (Dwyer et al. 2013; Pyne and Grodsky 2020), and African American women borrow the most (American Association of University Women 2021).

These disparities are mirrored in law school debt. African American, Latinx, and first-generation college-educated law students are more likely to rely on loans than are Whites, Asian Americans, and law students with college-educated parents and expect higher levels of debt on graduation (Taylor 2018). Women borrow more than do men, and African American women and Latinas are especially likely to graduate with high levels of debt (Deo 2021).

Student Debt and Cumulative (Dis)Advantage

Longitudinal research indicates that African Americans, Latinx, and college graduates from lower-income backgrounds are at significantly greater risk of having high student debt four years after graduation than are Whites and graduates from higher-income families (Price 2004). Research on the first two waves of the AJD Project found that, seven years into their careers, African American and Latinx respondents and lower-tier law school graduates—who tend to come from less privileged social class backgrounds—were significantly more likely than were White and Asian American respondents and elite law school graduates not only to *have* student debt but also to have *more* debt (Dinovitzer et al. 2013). Moreover, the Black-White student debt gap widens in early adulthood, something that Houle and Addo (2019, 573) attribute to "hardship and discrimination experienced at different stages of the life course: family resources when young, postsecondary experiences and credit market access as students, and social and financial success as young adults." Building on these longitudinal studies, we examine how early (dis)advantages accumulate over lawyers' early careers.

The Consequences of Law School Debt

While much scholarship on law school debt focuses on *who* has debt and *how much*, other studies examine the impact of student debt. One important avenue of research interrogates the popular assumption that student debt steers law school graduates away from careers in public service and has gleaned mixed results. Although qualitative studies have identified student debt as an important factor shaping law students' decision-making process surrounding which job to take after law school (Bliss 2018; Granfield 1992; Schleef 2006), quantitative analyses indicate the absence of a causal relationship between student debt and starting sector. While Chambers (1992, 199) found that student debt was "mildly and weakly" associated with starting sector, Kornhauser and Revesz (1995) identified as factors driving entry into public service careers law school performance, early commitment to nonprofit work, and higher earnings in the for-profit sector. Similarly, McGill's (2006) analysis of individual and law school–level data suggests that law school graduates are drawn to the private sector not because of debt but because law firm jobs are more lucrative and prestigious than are jobs in public service, which are relatively scarce. Thus, in addition to analyzing the predictors of student debt, we examine whether student debt predicts entry into public service careers.

Findings

Using the subsample of AJD Project respondents who participated in all three waves of the study ($N = 2,023$),[3] we analyze respondents' student debt at two points in time: when they graduated from law school and at midcareer. We rely on two measures of student debt: a binary measure of whether respondents had any debt and a continuous measure of amount of debt for respondents with any debt ("debtors"). Nearly all respondents (87.4%) graduated from law school with debt, and 50.5% had debt at wave 3. Thus, while 42% of respondents who graduated from law school with debt repaid their loans by midcareer, the majority remained indebted by this stage. The mean amount of debt among debtors was $70,921 at graduation ($n = 1,687$) and $56,163 by midcareer ($n = 998$).

Table 11.1 illustrates the bivariate relationship between student debt by race/ethnicity, revealing stark racial differences in student debt at graduation. African American and Latinx respondents are the most likely to graduate with debt and borrow the most among debtors. Asian American respondents are the least likely to graduate with debt, and Native Americans incur the least debt among debtors. By midcareer, African Americans are the least likely to be debt free (28.2%) and have the highest mean debt among debtors. While the average debt for African Americans decreases by less than $4,000 over time, the student debt profiles of Latinx respondents more closely resemble those of other racial/ethnic groups by midcareer than they do those of African

TABLE 11.1 Race/ethnicity of respondents by student debt at graduation and at midcareer

	Respondents without student debt (%)		Amount of student debt (respondents with student debt only) (mean)	
Race/ethnicity	At graduation	At midcareer	At graduation	At midcareer
African American	3.0	28.2	$76,029	$72,201
Latinx	5.7	41.2	$82,352	$57,136
Native American	14.3	45.7	$60,833	$53,684
Asian American	16.8	64.9	$71,340	$50,557
White	14.1	51.2	$68,827	$53,756
Total	12.6	49.5	$70,921	$56,163
Total (N)	244	978	1,687	998
χ^2, F-value of difference	27.0***	55.1***	6.95***	6.08***

*** $p \leq 0.001$. ** $p \leq 0.01$. * $p \leq 0.05$.

Americans. Asian Americans are the most likely to be debt free at midcareer (64.9%) and have the lowest mean debt among debtors.

Nearly identical proportions of men and women have student debt at graduation and at midcareer. Female debtors have significantly more debt than do male debtors at graduation ($p \leq .01$), but the actual difference is small ($73,149 compared to $68,712) and shrinks below conventional levels of statistical significance by midcareer. However, we find that racial/ethnic differences in student debt are gendered. African American men are more than three times more likely than are African American women to graduate without debt but are no more likely to be debt free at wave 3. And, with the exception of Latinos, who graduate with the highest levels of debt in the entire sample, men borrow less on average than do women from the same racial/ethnic group. By midcareer, African American men have the highest debt among debtors and Asian American women the lowest.

We also find significant differences in student debt by social class background. Both at graduation and at midcareer, the proportion of debt-free respondents increases with higher levels of parents' education and with law school ranking. Amount of debt at graduation also varies by parents' education, and the patterns are generally well ordered, with debt increasing as parents' education decreases. One exception, however, is that debtors whose parents are high school educated report less debt than do debtors whose parents attended college. This pattern may reflect the allocation of need-based scholarships to students from lower socioeconomic backgrounds as respondents with high school–educated parents report the highest proportion of financial support from scholarships. Among debtors, debt is highest among respondents who attended top-10 law schools and decreases in a linear fashion with law school rank at graduation, yet we find the inverse pattern at midcareer. Graduates of private law schools report significantly more debt than do graduates of public schools, with private school graduates having 40% greater debt at graduation than do public school graduates and 32% more at midcareer. Additionally, greater proportions of respondents working in more remunerative practice settings at midcareer are debt free compared to respondents working in settings like solo practice and state government. Respondents working in midsize and large law firms at wave 3 have the lowest midcareer debt by practice setting, and solo practitioners have the highest.

Next, we examine the relationship between debt-income ratio[4] and the personal and career characteristics of AJD Project respondents, particularly race/gender.[5] With the exception of Latinos, men from all racial/ethnic groups have debt-income ratios below 1 at graduation.[6] In contrast, women from all racial/ethnic groups have ratios above 1, indicating that their average debt burden exceeds their annual income regardless of their race/ethnicity. African American women report the highest debt-income ratios at both graduation and midcareer. Latinos have the highest ratios of any racial/ethnic group of men at graduation, but their ratio decreases by the greatest margin of any group over time (65%). By midcareer, Latinos' ratios are lower than those of Asian American and White men. In contrast, African American men's ratios decrease by only 1% (compared to 36% for the sample overall), leaving them with the highest ratio for men at midcareer.

Debt-income ratios also vary by law school rank and by practice setting. Top-10 law school graduates reduce their debt-income ratios by nearly three-quarters (72%) between wave 1 and wave 3, which is the highest reduction achieved by any group of respondents in the sample. Respondents working in the largest firms at midcareer reduce their ratios by the second greatest margin (67%%), and solo practitioners at wave 3 reduce their ratio by the least (2%). These longitudinal patterns highlight the financial rewards of elite status (Dinovitzer 2011).

Table 11.2 displays the percentage of financial support that respondents received for law school from law school grants and scholarships and from parents and other relatives. Both these sources of support vary by race/ethnicity ($p \le .001$). African Americans received by far the highest percentage of support from scholarships (14% compared to 7% overall) but the lowest percentage of support from family (4% compared to 13% overall). Asian Americans received the lowest proportion of support from scholarships (5%) and the highest proportion of support from family (22%). These differences in support

TABLE 11.2 Mean financial support for law school from law school grants, scholarships, and parents/relatives by social characteristics of respondents (%)

Social characteristics	Law school grants and scholarships	Parents/relatives
Race/ethnicity		
African American	14.0	4.2
Latinx	6.5	10.6
Native American	9.1	7.8
Asian American	4.6	21.5
White	6.9	13.0
F-value of difference	6.7***	7.0***
Parent education		
Graduate/professional school	15.7	16.8
Bachelor's degree	16.0	12.6
College	12.2	5.8
High school or less	17.9	6.2
F-value of difference	1.5	14.0***
Law school ranking		
Top 10	7.6	21.6
11–20	7.6	14.7
21–50	7.3	14.1
51–100	6.1	12.3
Tier 3	8.3	8.2
Tier 4	10.0	7.7
F-value of difference	1.5	5.8***
Total	7.4	12.6
Total (N)	1,387	1,387

*** $p \leq 0.001$. ** $p \leq 0.01$. * $p \leq 0.05$.

from family may reflect both racial/ethnic differences in household wealth and cultural differences in how families manage support for their children's post-secondary education.

As we saw in chapter 4, law school rank operates as a proxy for social background as respondents with more highly educated parents are the most likely to attend elite law schools. However, disaggregating this relationship by race/ethnicity reveals that law school ranking is a reliable indicator of the social background of White respondents only, reflecting in part the use of affirmative action and other race-conscious policies and practices in law school admissions and law firm hiring (see chap. 2). The amount of support received from family varies by both parents' education and law school rank. Respondents with more highly educated parents and graduates of higher-ranked law schools receive greater proportions of financial support from parents and other relatives. Highly educated parents may place a greater value on professional education for their children and are likely to have greater incomes and wealth to support them financially. Additionally, parents might be willing to contribute more money or to stretch their finances if their children get into more selective schools owing to the material and symbolic value of elite education credentials (Zaloom 2019).

We find something of a curvilinear relationship between law school rank and support from scholarships, with graduates of the highest- and the lowest-ranked law schools receiving the greatest proportions of financial support from this source. (This difference is not statistically significant.) This pattern may reflect the awarding of need-based scholarships by highly ranked schools offering places to less privileged and traditionally marginalized students and the use of merit scholarships by lower-ranked schools to attract students with stronger applications.

We also find notable patterns when comparing law school funding sources and wave 1 practice setting. Respondents working in the largest law firms report the highest proportion of financial support from both scholarships and family. Respondents working in solo practice and small firms report the lowest percentage of financial support from scholarships, and respondents working in government received the least support from family. Given the strong association we found in chapter 4 between law school rank and practice setting, the association between debt and practice setting may be attributable to differences in law school status, which for White respondents is closely related to social background.

PREDICTING DEBT AT GRADUATION AND AT MIDCAREER

We turn next to a set of multivariate analyses predicting debt at graduation and at midcareer so that we can isolate the effects of variables of interest while holding the others constant at their means.[7] Because many respondents reported zero debt, we estimated a pair of two-part models composed of logistic regression models predicting the probability of having any debt at graduation and at midcareer and linear regression models predicting the amount of debt held by debtors at these stages (Belotti et al. 2015). To retain cases with missing data, we imputed fifty data sets using chained equations, dropping cases that were missing data on the dependent variable before running the multivariate analyses (von Hippel 2007; White et al. 2011).

Both two-part models examine the predictive value of social background, race/ethnicity and gender, law school characteristics, GPA, and financial support from family members and scholarships. The models predicting debt at midcareer also include midcareer practice setting, household earnings at

TABLE 11.3 Logistic regression models predicting having any student debt at graduation and at midcareer

	At graduation (N = 1,930)			At midcareer (N = 1,975)					
	Odds ratio	Coeff.	SE	Odds ratio	Coeff.	SE	Odds ratio	Coeff.	SE
Constant	7.626	2.032***	0.279	3.292	1.192***	0.241	0.643	−0.442	0.281
Parent high school or less	1.284	0.250	0.283	1.007	0.007	0.153	1.141	0.132	0.170
Parent graduate/professional school	1.045	0.044	0.197	0.806	−0.216	0.115	0.862	−0.148	0.128
African American man	1.718	0.541	0.644	2.413	0.881**	0.329	2.429	0.888*	0.363
Latino	1.736	0.551	0.528	1.878	0.630*	0.261	1.134	0.126	0.290
Native American man	1.773	0.573	0.926	0.875	−0.133	0.508	0.874	−0.135	0.548
Asian American man	1.357	0.305	0.437	0.622	−0.475	0.275	0.482	−0.730*	0.316
African American woman	5.517	1.708*	0.747	2.536	0.931***	0.243	1.849	0.615*	0.264
Latina	3.186	1.159*	0.539	1.135	0.127	0.241	0.698	−0.359	0.264
Native American woman	0.677	−0.391	0.740	1.240	0.215	0.576	1.322	0.279	0.636
Asian American woman	1.194	0.177	0.380	0.714	−0.337	0.242	0.485	−0.723**	0.274
White woman	1.302	0.264	0.195	1.066	0.064	0.120	0.815	−0.204	0.137
Top-10 law school	2.337	0.849*	0.364	0.486	−0.721***	0.219	0.144	−1.935***	0.264
Law school ranked 11–20	1.701	0.531	0.325	0.722	−0.325	0.188	0.372	−0.988***	0.215
Law school ranked 21–50	2.580	0.948***	0.290	0.813	−0.207	0.160	0.553	−0.592***	0.181
Law school ranked 51–100	1.485	0.395	0.250	0.919	−0.085	0.142	0.669	−0.402*	0.161

Private law school	2.074	0.729***	0.199	1.360	0.308**	0.117	0.559	-0.582***	0.139
3.75–4.0 undergraduate GPA	0.555	-0.590*	0.237	0.734	-0.310*	0.151	0.973	-0.027	0.169
Support from scholarships	0.982	-0.018***	0.005	0.985	-0.016***	0.004	0.999	-0.001	0.004
Support from parents/relatives	0.957	-0.044***	0.003	0.972	-0.029***	0.003	0.995	-0.005	0.004
Married at midcareer				0.726	-0.321*	0.154	0.810	-0.211	0.172
Has children at midcareer				1.225	0.203	0.123	1.211	0.192	0.138
Solo practice at midcareer				1.044	0.043	0.218	1.237	0.213	0.245
Law firm 21–100 at midcareer				0.808	-0.213	0.216	0.849	-0.163	0.239
Law firm 101+ at midcareer				0.873	-0.136	0.194	1.002	0.002	0.218
Business at midcareer				0.677	-0.390*	0.174	0.717	-0.333	0.197
Federal government at midcareer				0.666	-0.406	0.242	0.753	-0.284	0.267
State government at midcareer				1.005	0.005	0.195	1.182	0.167	0.217
Nonprofit/education at midcareer				0.907	-0.098	0.204	1.102	0.097	0.226
Midcareer household earnings ($1,000)				0.998	-0.002***	0.000	0.997	-0.003***	0.000
Amount of debt at graduation ($1,000)							1.037	0.036***	0.002
Pseudo R^2	0.284			0.140			0.284		

Note: Reference categories include parent college or undergraduate degree, white men, tiers 3 and 4 law school, public law school, 3.74 or lower under-graduate GPA, not married, no children, and law firm 2–20.

*** $p \leq 0.001$. ** $p \leq 0.01$. * $p \leq 0.05$.

midcareer, whether respondents have children at midcareer, and the amount of respondents' debt at graduation. Controlling for debt at graduation allows us to estimate change in debt over lawyers' early careers, net of unmeasured variation in background and prior experiences (Dinovitzer and Hagan 2014). We turn to these longitudinal analyses in the next section.

The first part of the multivariate models predicts the probability of having any student debt at graduation and at midcareer (table 11.3). African American women are the only race/gender group that is consistently more likely to have student debt than are White men, although the relative magnitude of the difference shrinks over time from 5.5 times greater odds at graduation to 2.5 times greater odds at midcareer. Latinas have 3.2 times greater odds of having debt than do White men at graduation but not at midcareer, and African American men and Latinos have 2.4 and 1.8 times greater odds of being indebted at midcareer than do White men.

Law school rank has an inverse impact on debt at graduation and at midcareer; respondents who attended law schools ranked in the top-10 or in the range from 21 to 50 are more than twice as likely to graduate with student debt than are those who graduate from bottom-tier law schools. However, the direction of these effects of law school ranking flip by midcareer such that graduates of top-10 law schools are about half as likely to be indebted as are graduates from bottom-tier law schools. Graduating from a private law school increases the odds of having debt at graduation and at midcareer, and financial support from scholarships and family decreases these odds. At midcareer, household earnings is a negative predictor of having debt.

The second part of the models estimates the amount of debt held by debtors (table 11.4). Net of all predictor variables, Latinos and Latinas graduate with $16,087 and $10,298 higher debt, respectively, than do White men, African American and White women with $8,685 and $7,191 more, respectively. By midcareer, only African American debtors have significantly higher debt than do White men, with a debt premium of $25,452 for African American men and $19,298 for African American women. Graduating from a top-20 law school or law school ranked from 51 to 100 significantly increases debt at graduation compared to graduating from tier 3 and tier 4 schools, while graduating from a law school ranked from 21 to 50 reduces debt at midcareer. Financial support from scholarships and family is associated with lower debt at graduation and at midcareer, and private law schools are associated with greater debt at both junctures. Respondents working in midsize and large law firms and in federal government at midcareer have significantly less debt than do debtors working in small firms of 2–20 lawyers.

TABLE 11.4 OLS regression models predicting amount of student debt for respondents with any debt at graduation and at midcareer

	At graduation (N = 1,930)		At midcareer (N = 1,975)			
	Coef. ($)	SE	Coef. ($)	SE	Coef. ($)	SE
Constant	57,604***	2,476	66,849***	5,486	26,555***	5,444
Parent high school or less	−3,579	2,209	−1,227	3,369	310	2,945
Parent graduate/ professional school	−2,641	1,715	−2,940	2,713	−388	2,390
African American man	4,028	4,455	25,452***	6,294	24,868***	5,535
Latino	16,087***	3,640	3,035	5,493	−3,424	4,812
Native American man	−6,628	7,511	−2,777	12,639	4,078	11,060
Asian American man	1,569	4,075	2,798	7,539	−2,676	6,651
African American woman	8,685**	3,197	19,298***	4,737	16,635***	4,193
Latina	10,298**	3,542	4,852	5,612	572	4,967
Native American woman	7,580	8,669	−6,933	12,002	−8,106	10,672
Asian American woman	6,668	3,589	−5,395	6,499	−8,294	5,656
White woman	7,191***	1,836	2,640	2,927	−1,383	2,571
Top-10 law school	22,972***	3,130	−10,152	5,856	−29,497***	5,327
Law school ranked 11–20	11,945***	2,738	−6,341	4,500	−15,028***	3,963
Law school ranked 21–50	3,145	2,352	−8,727*	3,800	−12,621***	3,318
Law school ranked 51–100	4,703*	2,125	1,857	3,238	−1,002	2,830
Private law school	24,671***	1,721	14,875***	2,795	−2,720	2,683
3.75–4.0 undergraduate GPA	−7,547***	2,202	−7,341	3,798	−1,851	3,246
Support from scholarships	−499***	56	−393***	97.3	−80	88
Support from parents/ relatives	−703***	49	−390***	101	25	99
Married at midcareer			−4,539	3,380	−3,137	2,945
Has children at midcareer			−2,314	2,857	−1,026	2,492
Solo practice at midcareer			6,597	4,846	5,666	4,285
Law firm 21–100 at midcareer			−11,288*	5,168	−11,770**	4,472
Law firm 101+ at midcareer			−9,730*	4,876	−8,585*	4,281
Business at midcareer			−4,308	4,188	−5,100	3,728
Federal government at midcareer			−14,620*	5,804	−10,222*	5,130
State government at midcareer			−3,010	4,348	−3,393	3,843
PI/nonprofit/education at midcareer			−6,730	4,948	−5,427	4,271
Midcareer household earnings ($1,000)			−23*	10	−32***	9
Student debt at graduation ($1,000)					626***	39
R^2	0.296		0.172		0.363	

Note: Reference categories include parent college or undergraduate degree, white men, tiers 3 and 4 law school, public law school, and 3.74 or lower undergraduate GPA.

*** $p \leq 0.001$. ** $p \leq 0.01$. * $p \leq 0.05$.

PREDICTING CHANGE IN STUDENT
DEBT OVER TIME

After examining the predictors of student debt at two discrete points in time, we exploited the longitudinal nature of the AJD Project data by estimating the change in debt between law school graduation and midcareer. We reran the two-part model predicting debt at midcareer but controlling for debt at graduation (Dinovitzer and Hagan 2014). (These models are shown in the last two columns of tables 11.3 and 11.4.) Strikingly, African American women experience significant increases compared to White men in both the odds of having any debt and the amount of debt among debtors, and these patterns are even more accentuated for African American men. Asian American women and men have a significant decrease in the odds of having debt over time. Thus, indebted African American respondents are the only group to experience a relative increase in amount of debt from graduation to midcareer when controlling for amount of debt at graduation.

We find an orderly relationship between law school ranking and change in student debt. Compared to tier 3 and tier 4 graduates, the graduates of higher-ranked law schools experience a significant decrease in the odds of being indebted and in amount of debt. This pattern holds across all groups of schools ranked in the top 100 and increases in magnitude with ranking. Working in federal government, business, or a law firm of 21 or more lawyers is associated with a significant decrease in amount of debt compared to working in a firm of 2–20 lawyers. Household earnings are associated with a decrease over time in both the odds of having debt and the amount of debt.

Fitting the parameter estimates from the models illustrates how racial differences grow over time. Figure 11.1 shows the predicted values of student debt by race/gender and law school ranking, holding all other variables at their means. Among debtors, African American men and women graduate with levels of debt that are virtually identical to those of their White counterparts. However, the mean amount of debt decreases by the smallest margin for African American women, while debt *increases* over time for African American men. In contrast, mean debt decreases by substantial amounts among all other groups by midcareer, particularly for Latinos—who started out with the highest debt—and Asian American and Native American women. As a result, both African American women and African American men have far higher debt burdens than do members of other racial groups by midcareer net of social class background, law school and family characteristics, midcareer earnings, and practice setting ($65,567 and $71,208, respectively, compared to $51,121 or less for all other groups).

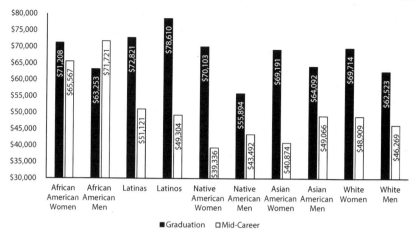

FIGURE 11.1. Predicted value of student debt at graduation and at midcareer by race/gender

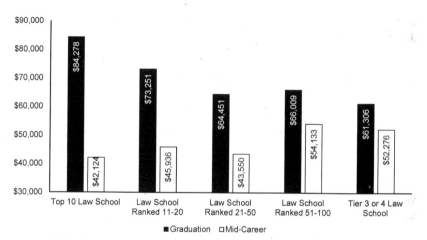

FIGURE 11.2. Predicted value of student debt at graduation and at midcareer by law school ranking

Another striking observation is the relatively well-ordered and inverse relationship between law school status and amount of debt at graduation and midcareer (figure 11.2). Graduates of higher-ranked law schools generally graduate with higher debt than do graduates of lower-ranked schools, but we observe the opposite pattern at midcareer. Although the variation in debt by law school ranking at graduation and at midcareer is more constrained than what we observed by race/gender, the relative differences in change over time between these groups is notable. While the mean debt for debtors who graduated from top-10 law schools is reduced by half, the mean debt for tier 3 and tier 4 graduates shrinks by only 15%.

The Impact of Student Debt

Wave 2 included a battery of questions about the influence of debt on various career and personal decisions, including what job to take, what sector to work in, where to live, whether and when to have children, home ownership, and exiting the profession. In general, respondents assigned relatively low scores to the influence of debt on decision-making, which is unsurprising given the myriad factors guiding these complex decisions. Notably, however, respondents working in midsize and large law firms assign the highest influence scores to which sector to take and job to work in. Given this finding, we investigate whether debt is related to job and career satisfaction by examining scores for three groups at midcareer: respondents with no debt, respondents with any debt, and respondents with high debt (which we define as the 90th percentile, or $100,000 more).[8]

We find that, for each measure of career satisfaction (including satisfaction with the decision to go to law school, whether respondents consider a law degree to be a good investment, and whether respondents would still go to law school if they could do it over again), respondents with no debt report the highest scores and respondents with high debt the lowest. However, although career satisfaction is lower among debtors, mean scores on career satisfaction are relatively high, even among the most indebted.

Although job satisfaction tends to decrease as debt increases, it also reflects the practice settings in which debtors are situated. For example, respondents with no debt are the most satisfied with compensation but are also more likely than respondents with high debt to be working in high-status and highly remunerative settings. The most indebted respondents are more likely to work in state government and solo practice, where both compensation and satisfaction along this dimension tend to be lower. But the higher levels of satisfaction with work/life balance and the value of lawyers' work to society reported by debtors—and particularly by respondents with high debt—reflect the trade-offs involved in working in these settings and demonstrate the desirability of a law degree for graduates of lower-tier law schools and lawyers working outside corporate law firms (Dinovitzer et al. 2013).

To investigate whether student debt steers law school graduates away from starting careers in public service, we conducted a logistic regression analysis using the career history data described in earlier chapters. The mean amount of starting debt among student loan borrowers is similar between starting sectors, at $62,921 in the private sector (which we define as law firms and business) and $60,853 in the public sector (including government and public service). Using the same imputation approach as earlier, we estimated a model predicting the odds of taking a first job in public service[9] on the basis of the following predictors: amount of debt at graduation; race/gender (with White men as the comparison group); top-10 law school (compared to law school ranked 11 or lower); law school grades in the top 11%–25%, second quartile, third quartile, or fourth quartile of the class (with grades in the top 10% of the class as the comparison group); and a binary measure indicating whether helping society was an important factor motivating the decision to go to law school.[10] Modeling McGill's (2006) approach, we included values of zero in our continuous measure of debt.[11]

Like McGill, we do not find empirical support for the assumption that student debt diverts law school graduates from public service careers. While student debt does not have a statistically significant effect on starting sector, we find that an early commitment to public service increases the odds of taking a first job in the public sector, with respondents who desire to help society having 1.6 times greater odds of starting a public service career than do those who do not place importance on this value. We also find that African American women are 2.4 times more likely than are White men to take a first job in the public sector, net of debt, law school ranking, law school grades, and early public service commitment.

Discussion and Conclusion

This chapter examines the determinants and consequences of student debt for law school graduates, documenting race- and class-based differences that accumulate over time. We find growing disparities in debt by law school tier suggesting that cumulative (dis)advantage accrues along lines of social class, with early advantages accumulating for individuals from privileged social backgrounds. Yet we also find that race has a significant effect on student debt for African American lawyers net of social class and a myriad of controls. While most studies of student debt focus on initial debt levels, the longitudinal analysis of AJD Project data indicates that racial disparities both emerge and grow over time. It is clear from our analysis that growing racial disparities in student debt reflect cumulative disadvantage for African Americans.

On average, African American and Latinx respondents come from less privileged social backgrounds, receive less financial support from parents and relatives, and graduate with higher debt levels than do White and Asian American respondents. African American men graduate from law school with near average student debt levels but reduce their debt by a negligible margin over time and by midcareer stand out as the most indebted of any group. African American women encounter disparities earlier on—graduating with the highest mean debt after Latinx respondents and with the highest odds of being in-debted of any race/gender group—and this disparity grows over time.

In contrast, Latinx respondents as a group are much more successful in repaying their debt—which is enabled in part by their earnings.[12] African American respondents' high debt at midcareer is due in part to their concen-tration in public service organizations rather than law firms, which are White spaces and inhospitable to African Americans in general and African Ameri-can women in particular (see chap. 10). Starting salaries in the public sector are lower than those in the private sector and increase by a smaller margin over time (see chaps. 5 and 12). Thus, the sorting of African Americans into lower-status and lower-paying settings exacerbates early disadvantages by im-peding their ability to repay debt. Survey data also suggest that the higher mid-career debt of African American men compared to African American women may be attributable in part to differences in the loan repayment strategies they deploy and the sources of financial support to which they have access. Re-spondents were asked to rate the importance of a variety of resources in help-ing manage the repayment of their student loans. Among African American respondents, women rated the importance of loan repayment assistance, loan forgiveness programs, and financial support from parents and spouses more highly than did men, while men rated the importance of flexible repayment options, refinancing through debt consolidation, and postponing repayment through deferments or forbearance more highly than did women. However, none of these differences meet the threshold for conventional levels of statis-tical significance.

Although we find evidence of racial disparities in debt that persist net of social background, law school ranking, practice setting, household earnings, and other important covariates, it is important to highlight the role of agency in borrowing money to finance a law degree as it is an important strategy of upward mobility and wealth accumulation. Indeed, African American respon-dents rate the desire for eventual financial security as more important in mo-tivating their decision to go to law school than does any other racial or ethnic group. From a policy perspective, however, it is vital to examine the longer-term student debt trajectories of African American women and men. The anal-yses in this chapter suggest that, although African Americans are no longer formally excluded from the legal profession, over time they may pay a higher price for admission. This evidence of cumulative (dis)advantage is particu-larly troubling given that debt loads and racial disparities in law school bor-rowing have increased over the past two decades (Law School Survey of Stu-dent Engagement 2020).

Analyzing lawyers' debt trajectories demonstrates the deeply stratified character of lawyers' careers by revealing the long-term cost of admission to the profession. Importantly, the results show that, even among members of an elite profession who come from relatively privileged social backgrounds, African Americans are uniquely burdened by education debt over the course of their early careers. Yet even respondents with the highest levels of debt are satisfied with their decision to go to law school and tend to consider a law degree to be a good investment, complicating assumptions of widespread buyers' remorse among lower-tier law school graduates and lawyers working in the public sector (Dinovitzer et al. 2013). Moreover, student debt does not keep law school graduates from entering public service careers. Together, these findings depict law school debt both as a means for upward mobility and as a mechanism that reproduces—and amplifies—inequality.

Hegemonic Masculinity, Parenthood, and Gender Inequality

WITH ANDREEA MOGOSANU

RBG: I had three strikes against me: One, I was Jewish. Two, I was a woman. But the killer was I was a mother of a four-year-old child.

HOST: You graduated first in your class. Didn't that say something about your ability to be both a mother and the best?

RBG: It should have.[1]

When the women in the AJD study entered law school, they had every reason to be optimistic. Half their law school peers were also women, cresting a trend that had been in the making for over a quarter century. Indeed, not only were women well represented in their law schools; they also were equally successful. On average, women's attainments were equal to or better than those of men on the metrics of LSAT scores and law school GPA (Clydesdale 2004; see also chap. 4). The women of the class of 2000 entered the legal labor force as the modern legal profession had reached its pinnacle: large firms were hiring unprecedented numbers of associates, offering generous salaries whose rise was breathlessly covered in the media, and law firms were signing onto proclamations affirming gender equity (Reichman and Sterling 2004). The status of women as lawyers thus appeared well established. Not only did their gender represent half their law school class, but women were also almost as likely as men to begin their careers in the most coveted setting: the large law firm.

Yet fissures in the veneer of gender equality were quickly apparent even within the law school context. Women were less likely than were men to make the prestigious selection into law review (Kolodinsky 2014), they were less likely to be called on in class (Mertz 2007), only 11% of law school deans were women, and only 22% of full professors were women (Neumann 2004). Once women graduated from law school, the gender divide only became more apparent, especially by one important metric: earnings. Our data show that, at the start of their careers, women earned 88% of men's average incomes. The gender gap grows over time: by wave 2, which is about seven years into their careers, women earn 76% of men's earnings, and, by wave 3 (13 years after the initial study), we see the largest gap, with women's earnings reaching only

71% of men's. We argue that careers in the contemporary American legal profession continue to reflect what other scholars refer to as *hegemonic masculinity*. Women's careers are disadvantaged because they work within a gendered social order that is deeply embedded in organizational structures and legitimates unequal gender relations (Messerschmidt 2018).

Overview

One of the most common explanations for the gender wage gap, especially when it is analyzed over time, is marriage and childbearing. It seems only logical that the transition to parenthood is largely to blame for the gender wage gap. Studies confirm that women in professional and highly paid positions devote more time to child-rearing than do same-status men (Juhn and McCue 2017; Percheski 2008; Saye et al. 2004). Data show that male lawyers report half as much time dedicated to household chores as their female colleagues do (see Kay 2002). It is thus not surprising that most working mothers experience a motherhood penalty, earning less than their male counterparts or childless women (Dixon and Seron 1995; Gough and Noonan 2013; US Bureau of Labor Statistics 2016). Motherhood is reflected in other homologous patterns, including women reducing their work hours or working part-time (sometimes characterized as a lack of commitment) and taking positions in settings that allow them to balance their work and personal lives (such as the public sector). For example, Hewlett and Luce (2005) estimate that 42% of female lawyers take time off for children at some point in their careers, and they do so for on average 2.2 years. These career interruptions prove detrimental. Career breaks are linked with income penalties, loss of prestige, and difficulty finding mentors or employment when returning to the labor market (Weisshaar 2018; Williams et al. 2013).

Yet the data on the motherhood penalty for professional women and women with higher skills are less definitive. England et al. (2016) find that mothers with high skills and wages suffer the largest motherhood penalties, with fathers with a college degree earning the highest premiums (Hodges and Budig 2010). But, when focusing explicitly on women in the professions, Buchmann and McDaniel (2016) conclude that the story of inevitable motherhood wage penalties does not hold for all professions. Examining wage differences among midcareer professionals from 1980 to 2010, they find a high level of diversity in parenthood penalties and premiums across different professions. Women in female-dominated professions (such as teachers or social workers) continued to experience a motherhood penalty, while mothers in STEM fields, medicine, and law earned a motherhood premium.

There are reasons to expect to find that gendered income trajectories among professional parents might be minimized: professional women start off with training, skills, and preferences similar to those of their male colleagues (England et al. 2016; Percheski 2008). Professional women are also more likely to delay motherhood to advance their careers, which has helped equalize early career earnings among men and women (Byker 2016; England et al. 2016). They are also more likely to maintain high levels of workforce participation compared to other working mothers (Goldin 2006; Percheski 2008; Wilde et al. 2010).

As we demonstrate in this chapter, the transition to parenthood is an important contributor to the gendered wage gap, but it is not the sole cause. In fact, we find that motherhood may *benefit* women financially as they outearn women who do not have children when all else is considered.[2] Moreover, that we find a wage gap even at the start of lawyers' careers, in wave 1, suggests that the mechanisms underlying earnings *precede* the transition to parenthood (see also Dinovitzer et al. 2009b). From the data emerges the well-known story about social and organizational logics that undermine the interests, progress, and aspirations of women. But the bigger story is about the logic of patriarchy that supports and values men's careers at the expense of women's. Men get ahead and earn more to a significant extent thanks to the support of their spouses who work part-time or not at all.[3] This pattern is one side of hegemonic masculinity. Our analyses point to processes of hegemonic masculinity woven into the fabric of the legal profession that idealize, value, and promote masculinity, of which fatherhood is an important component, and that consider women to be of lesser value than are men.

Gender and Earnings: The Descriptive Pattern

We begin our analysis of earnings by outlining some basic patterns, highlighting the trajectory of the gender gap over time. We then present our analysis of earnings by income quantile, followed by our analysis of the relationship between parenthood, gender, and earnings.

SETTINGS

Practice settings are a key driver of earnings in the legal profession, and these effects vary by career stage, but we note from the outset that women earn less than men in nearly every setting at all points in time. Table 12.1 compares median earnings for women and men working full-time across practice settings by each wave. The overall picture for women in law firms is that the gen-

TABLE 12.1 Median earnings by wave 3 practice setting and gender (full-time workers only)

Wave 3 practice setting	Women ($)	Men ($)	Women/men (%)	Gap (%)
Solo practice	66,000	70,000	94	6
Law firm 2–20	80,000	100,000	80	20
Law firm 21–100	110,000	135,000	81	19
Law firm 101–250	135,000	139,000	97	3
Law firm 251+	150,000	185,000	81	19
Public sector	89,000	87,000	102	−2
Business	110,000	130,000	85	15
Overall	100,000	120,000	83	17

der wage gap grows over time, but this varies somewhat by size of firm. In the smallest (2–20 lawyers) and largest (251 more) private law firms, women begin their careers with smaller wage gaps that double over time to almost 20%, and, in midsize firms (21–100), there is more variance over time, but by wave 3 the wage gap is also 20%. In contrast, women almost closed the earnings gap in large law firms (101–250 lawyers). There is far more equity in the public sector (including government, legal services, and public interest organizations), where women even outearn men by a small margin at wave 3. The business sector includes a wide range of workplaces, encompassing lawyers both practicing and not practicing law, and here, too, the wage gap ultimately grows over time.

CHILDREN

Rates of childbearing vary by practice setting in some counterintuitive ways: among women working full-time, the highest rates of parenthood are in the largest (69%) and midsize (71%) firms, while women working in state government have some of the lowest rates of parenthood (only 56% have a child). For those working part-time, the findings are striking: women with no children are more likely to be working in state government, legal services, and nonprofits.

This differential pattern of parenthood by setting translates into earnings in important ways. Across the sample, among women working full-time, women with children earn *more* than do women with no children ($158,885 vs. $127,150; $p \leq .05$). In private law firms, mean earnings are almost equivalent between these two groups of women, and, in almost every other setting, women with children who work full-time earn *more* than do their female counterparts who do not have children. The analysis offered below will help elucidate this relationship.

The Earnings Distribution: Quantile Analysis

The descriptive discussion identified a significant gender wage gap, but we need to explore the data systematically in order to better understand the mechanisms that produce this gap. Recent research on earnings has suggested that researchers consider the relationship between gender and earnings at various points along the income distribution. Analyses have typically considered wages as a single distribution, with regular regression methods modeling the mean returns of gender for earnings. The conventional approach is not able to tell us the extent of the gender gap for highly paid women compared to women whose earnings are at the bottom of the distribution, for example (Budig and Hodges 2010). Yet it may be that the mechanisms undergirding the gender wage gap vary depending on earnings levels: highly paid women may be working in settings that are able to provide them with parental leave and part-time policies that support the balance of work and family, but they may also demand excessive hours or hold higher expectations for work commitment and penalize women who take a family leave. Lower-wage positions may be the result of working in sectors or organizations that are more regulated (such as the public sector), resulting in a smaller gender gap because there is less discretion in the wage structure and a greater acceptance of maternity leaves.

To date, research has tended to focus on the effects of motherhood on the gender wage gap, yet this line of research has not yet settled which earnings group faces higher penalties (Budig and Hodges 2010; Doren 2019; England et al. 2016). Budig and Hodges (2014) report an earnings penalty for mothers at the lower end of the income distribution and a motherhood premium for high-earning mothers. On the other hand, England et al. (2016) find that, among Whites, women with high skills and wages suffer the largest motherhood penalty.

In this analysis, we embrace the approach of quantile regression for understanding the gender wage gap in our data. We find a wide range of earnings: respondents in the bottom 25th quantile earn around $50,000, while the top 75th quantile of lawyers earns over $110,000. There is relatively little movement across earnings quantiles by individual respondents, who are most likely to remain near their original quantile as earnings increase over time. Moreover, women tend to fall in the lower earnings quantiles compared to men. By wave 3, 28% of women are in the bottom quantile, compared to only 13% of men. The proportion of women in the higher earnings quantiles decreases in a linear fashion, with only 13% of women in the 90th quantile of earners, compared to 26% of men. This general pattern is replicated at each wave of the study.

DATA AND METHODS

To explore these research questions, we consider all respondents, including those who are working or have worked part-time or who are or have been unemployed. Owing to the longitudinal and layered nature of the research questions, we investigate earnings using unconditional quantile regression (England et al. 2016). Our analyses use Powell's (2020) method for quantile regression for panel data (QRPD) with nonadditive *fixed effects* (for persons across time). The baseline and the full models are each run at the 25th, 50th, 75th, and 90th income percentiles. Powell's unconditional quantile regression accounts for fixed effects and controls for time-stable characteristics that are not included in our model but may bias our results (e.g., personality factors). The resulting coefficients reflect an average of how different factors affect the arc of individuals' income trajectories over the entire period of study (years 3–12 of their careers). These coefficients for each model can be compared within and across the tables to ascertain the relative contribution of each factors' effect on respondents' income trajectories. To minimize the impact of a nonnormal earnings distribution, and to make our results easier to interpret, our analyses predict log earnings. For individuals reporting unemployment, missing salary values were recoded as earning $1.00 (or 0 logged dollars). Since the study spans a 13-year period, we tested additional models relying on constant dollars, and, since the results were similar, we show the original reported data.

To ensure confidence in our approach, we examined the wage ranks of women across the waves of the study (termed *rank invariance*). We find that there is a good deal of stability in how a given woman's wage ranks relative to the wages of her peers across the years. This gives us confidence that referring to wage *groups* and comparing these groups' earnings penalties is sensible.

ANALYTIC PLAN

The analysis will examine the gender income gap while controlling for demographic factors, technical competence (GPA), prestige (law school rank), and practice setting. These measures are included in the model because they are key drivers of income, helping set the initial wage trajectory on which male and female lawyers embark. The model will also account for the mechanisms typically hypothesized to affect earnings, including personal characteristics (the importance attached to wealth and career advancement, whether more children are planned), work history (seniority, ever working part-time or being unemployed, ever working in a large firm, taking parental leave), job status (whether workers are full-time, equity partners, or occupy supervisory positions), a variety of work characteristics (hours billed, organizational ties, work/life conflict, whether respondents are overworked, whether they experienced discrimination at work), and family factors (spouse's income and employment status, number of children, years having been a parent, having two children or more, and the proportion of household chores assumed). In order to account for the fact that the mechanisms predicting earnings vary for men and women, we also consider separate models by gender and report on those results as necessary.[4] The results reported in table 12.2 reflect regression models with full controls.

TABLE 12.2 Coefficients for unconditional quantile regression models predicting income (full models)

	25th quantile	50th quantile	75th quantile	90th quantile
Female	−0.073***	−0.094***	−0.098***	−0.114***
Age	0.514***	0.979***	1.316***	1.436***
City of 2 million +	0.099***	0.106***	0.114***	0.117***
Race/ethnicity				
African American	0.066***	0.063*	0.029	0.026
Latinx	0.053*	0.067**	0.080*	0.055
Asian American	0.107***	0.119***	0.115***	0.129***
Other race/ethnicity	0.009	0.047	0.068	0.022
Law school GPA	0.124***	0.148***	0.154***	0.163***
Law school ranking				
Top-10 law school	0.209***	0.251***	0.292***	0.300***
Law school ranked 11–20	0.128***	0.176***	0.193***	0.203***
Law school ranked 21–50	0.068**	0.118***	0.130***	0.148***
Law school ranked 51–100	0.015	0.035	0.050	0.056
Tier 3 law school	−0.013	0.016	0.028	0.033
Practice setting and firm size				
Solo practice	−0.476***	−0.301***	−0.170***	−0.009
Law firm 2–20	−0.219***	−0.162***	−0.105***	−0.038
Law firm 101–250	0.002	−0.055	−0.092*	−0.070
Law firm 251+	0.164***	0.086***	0.059	0.048
Public sector	−0.329***	−0.325***	−0.302***	−0.267***
Business	−0.040	0.089**	0.179***	0.294***
Work history				
Ever unemployed	−0.183***	−0.234***	−0.173***	−0.136***
Ever worked part-time	0.048*	0.207***	0.130***	0.093***
Ever worked in a large firm of 100+	0.213***	0.297***	0.316***	0.322***
Ever took parental leave	0.076***	0.105***	0.101***	0.086***
Job status				
Full-time	10.760***	10.078***	0.804***	0.552***
Seniority	1.367***	1.437***	1.290***	1.110***
Supervisory index score	0.034*	0.036	0.055***	0.073***
Equity partner	0.109***	0.132***	0.220***	0.313***
Worker characteristics				
Work effort				
Hours billed	1.573***	1.598***	1.502***	1.581***

TABLE 12.2 (*continued*)

	25th quantile	50th quantile	75th quantile	90th quantile
Overwork	0.053***	0.051***	0.074***	0.114***
Work-life conflict	0.024	0.026	0.043*	0.060*
Has experienced discrimination	0.026*	0.025*	0.049***	0.057***
Organizational ties				
Meals with partners/senior attorneys	0.014	0.011	0.014	−0.002
Organizational committee member	0.028*	0.030*	0.035*	0.047*
Personal preferences				
Importance of wealth	0.037**	0.050***	0.066***	0.075***
Importance of career	0.001	−0.016	0.007	0.009
Family factors				
Plans to have more children	0.012	0.022	0.030	0.052*
Married	−0.014	−0.020	−0.005	0.010
Spouse's income (log)	0.005**	0.006**	0.006*	0.005
Spouse employed full-time	−0.047***	−0.044*	−0.051*	−0.065**
One child	0.017	0.023	0.043	0.066*
Two children or more	0.093***	0.119***	0.111***	0.121***
Years parent	−0.001	−0.003	−0.002	−0.003
Proportion of chores	−0.039	0.013	−0.089	−0.052

Note: Reference categories include male, city less than 2 million, white, tier 4 law school, law firm 21–100, never unemployed, never worked part-time, never worked in a large firm of 100+, never took parental leave, part-time, not an equity partner, no overwork, does not often experience work-life conflict, has not experienced discrimination, does not share meals with partners/senior attorneys, not an organizational committee member, does not plan more children, not married, spouse not employed full-time, and does not have children.

*** $p \leq 0.001$. ** $p \leq 0.01$. * $p \leq 0.05$.

RESULTS

We begin by noting that men earn significantly more than women do at all income levels. This gender gap persists even though we account for job status, work history, and work- and family-related factors. Looking across the earnings distribution, we find that women's disadvantage increases as income increases. Specifically, in models with all controls included, at the 25th percentile of the income distribution women earn 7% less than men do, and this difference grows with women earning 11% less than men do at the 90th percentile of the income distribution. This pattern signals the importance and entrenched nature of the gender divide in the legal profession.

Demographic Background and City Size

As expected, we find a positive relationship between age and earnings at all quantiles, with the coefficient increasing in the higher earnings categories, indicating that age matters more among the higher earners. We also find that working in a large city (over 2 million residents) significantly increases earnings. The results for race are perhaps surprising. Respondents who are African American, Latinx, or Asian American all report significantly higher earnings than do Whites at the bottom two quantiles. Asian American lawyers report significantly higher earnings than do Whites across all the quantiles, while Latinx attorneys report higher earnings than do Whites at all but the highest quantiles. These results hold even after all controls. We will return to the issue of race later in this chapter.

Law School Tier

Law school attended confers a persistent advantage in earnings across the distribution. At all earnings levels, graduates of the most elite law schools (the top 10) earn significantly more than do graduates of tier 4 law schools (the reference group), and the premium grows with the earnings quantile. Thus, at the 25th quantile, they earn 23% more than do tier 4 law school graduates, and, at the 90th quantile, they earn 35% more. Graduates of top-20 and top-50 schools also experience an earnings advantage across the entire distribution, though not quite as large, and, again, the earnings premium attributed to law school is even greater at the higher quantiles. The results reinforce the step-graded nature of law school rank: graduates of top-10 schools earn the largest advantage, followed by graduates of top-20 schools and then graduates of top-50 schools, *in that order* in every earnings quantile. This finding reinforces the importance of symbolic capital in the legal profession, with the prestige of law schools translating directly into higher earnings. It is also equally important to recall that law school attended is correlated with social background, acting as an important mechanism in the reproduction of social advantage.

Law school performance remains an important predictor of earnings, again across the full earnings distribution. The magnitude of the effect also increases across the quantiles, but in a much more constrained range (each increment in GPA increases earnings from 13% at the lowest quantile to 18% at the 90th).

Sector and Firm Size

Practice settings are key drivers of lawyers' earnings. Earnings generally track firm size: lawyers working in solo practice tend to earn significantly less than does the reference group of small firms of 2–20 lawyers. On the other hand, those working in firms of 21–100, 101–250, and 251 or more all earn more than lawyers in the reference group, though the increase is not statistically significant at every quantile. Lawyers working in the largest law firms (251 or more) earn the highest premiums. For example, at the 50th percentile, lawyers working in firms of more than 250 lawyers earn 28% more than do lawyers in firms of 2–20 lawyers, and, at the 90th percentile, they earn 10% more, after all controls. It is important to note that these models account for a range of factors underlying earnings, including equity partnership, which is a strong and positive predictor of earnings. When we do not account for these factors in the control model (which includes only gender, age, region, race, GPA, and law school attended), we find that the premiums associated with firm size are about double and more consistently result in earnings premiums. This pattern confirms that earnings are higher in larger firms not because of their size but because they are associated with practices (such as equity partnerships, long workdays, billings) that drive these earnings.

Across the board, respondents who work in the public sector have significantly lower earnings across all quantiles compared to the reference category of firms with 2–20 lawyers. Finally, working in business settings (both practicing and not practicing law) results in significantly higher earnings than those seen by the reference group at all quantiles, demonstrating the rising importance of business in the modern legal profession. The premiums are substantial: 29% at the 50th quantile up to 40% at the 90th quantile. While it may seem that working in business is more lucrative than working in a large firm is, recall again that the large-firm earnings coefficient in our model is independent of the premium of being an equity partner.

Work History

Work history includes variables such as ever working part-time or being unemployed, ever working in a large firm, or ever taking parental leave. Men are less likely than are women to work part-time or be unemployed at all three waves. At wave 1, 93% of women and 96% of men were working full-time. At wave 2, we observe a large transition out of the full-time labor force for women, with 13% working part-time and 7% unemployed, compared to only 2% of men working part-time and 1% unemployed. By wave 3, there is a slight increase in the proportion of women who are working part-time (16%) and who are unemployed (9%) and a small increase in the proportion of unemployed men (2% part-time and 2% unemployed). Yet we find that working part-time and being unemployed are not necessarily permanent statuses, especially for men. Among respondents who worked part-time at wave 1 or wave 2, 34% of women and 79% of men worked full-time at a subsequent wave. And, among respondents who were unemployed, 64% of women and 87% of men returned to the workforce at a later wave. Although 80% of men who were unemployed subsequently returned to full-time work, only 42% of women did so, with the other 22% returning to part-time employment.

We also find that the proportion of respondents who return to the labor force varies by parental status at wave 3, with 67% of previously unemployed respondents with children returning to work, compared to 78% of respondents who did not have children. However, these patterns diverge by gender, with all previously unemployed men who had children by wave 3 returning to the labor force in a subsequent wave. Among women who were unemployed at wave 1 or wave 2 who report having children at wave 3, 30% went on to work full-time, and 28% worked part-time at a subsequent wave. By comparison, 69% of previously unemployed women who did not have children at wave 3 subsequently worked full-time, and 10% returned to part-time work.

All work history measures are significantly related to earnings across the distribution. The indicator for whether a respondent has ever been unemployed depresses earnings across the distribution. In contrast, ever having worked part-time or ever having taken parental leave are both positively related to earnings across the distribution. Amuedo-Dorantes and Kimmel (2005, 2008) suggest that this could be due to more generous benefits and policies among employers of professional women in the private sector. The fact that professional women have access to an institutionalized transition back to work after childbirth may be central in protecting their earnings (Doren 2019; Yu and Kuo 2017). Padavic et al. (2020) mention that family-friendly policies are a way for employers to maintain that they are on the employees' side while also preserving the unequal status quo of generally lower earnings for women. Part-time work, parental leave, and long-term positions in nonequity partnerships are some of the main mechanisms law firms use to accommodate the needs of their female employees while at the same time limiting women's advancements. These arguments would also explain why, in our case, having taken parental leave or part-time work are both associated with positive effects across the earnings distribution, a finding also supported by Kay et al. (2016).

We also find that ever having worked in a large firm increases respondents' earnings across the distribution, which supports our discussion of the new role of the corporate law firm in the careers of lawyers discussed in chapter 3 (Dinovitzer and Garth 2020). The growth of the large law firm in the late twentieth century meant that the women and minorities who had been formally excluded from this setting were now embraced in entry-level positions. And, while the firms generally did not retain these individuals in equity partnerships, the prestige of having begun in this setting provided an income boost over their life course.

Job Status

The indicators of job status are important across the earnings distribution because they highlight basic features of labor force participation that are key to earnings. Working full-time is a strong and significant predictor of earnings across the distribution, with a larger boost at lower quantiles (likely because individuals at the high end are less likely to be working part-time). Both seniority and supervisory status increase earnings across the distribution, with both indicating that more senior positions are related to higher earnings. As expected, being an equity partner is a strong and significant predictor of earnings across the distribution. Equity partners earn a premium of 11% at the 25th quantile and up to 38% more at the 90th quantile. We should note that this is a gendered finding: for women, equity partnership is significant only at the 90th quantile, whereas, for men, it is significant at all quantiles. This is perhaps because the rates of equity partnership for women are so low that there is insufficient power in the models or because female equity partners do not get as large a draw as their male counterparts do.

Work Effort

Work effort reflects the hours worked in any sector and hours billed in private law firms, and both increase income as expected across the distribution. Hours billed (in private law firms) significantly increase earnings fairly consistently at every quantile. Overwork—that is, working over 40 hours per week—significantly increases earnings as the quantiles increase, suggesting larger payoffs for more working hours at the top of the earnings scale (from a 5% premium at the 25th quantile to a 12% premium at the 90th quantile). In line with these findings, we find that reports of work/life conflict also significantly increase earnings at the 90th quantile. The intensification of work and the concomitant hours required in high-paying positions are certainly apparent in these findings.

Organizational Ties

There are features of work beyond sheer hours that are also important for earnings. We find that individuals who sit on key firm/organizational committees report significantly higher earnings, and this relationship is positive in all quantiles. We do not find any significant patterns for socializing with senior attorneys.

Personal Preferences

Orientations and aspirations are also related to earnings. Respondents who express that the accumulation of wealth is important to them also earn significantly more in all earnings quantiles. On the other hand, career importance is not significantly related to earnings. Planning to have more children is significant only at the 90th quantile and is positively related to earnings.

Discrimination

A perhaps unexpected finding is that individuals who report an experience of discrimination (including sexual harassment) also report significantly higher earnings at all quantiles. This counterintuitive finding is supported by research that finds that women in positions of leadership are more likely to experience harassing behaviors and sexual harassment and that they likely earn more than other women (McLaughlin et al. 2012, 2017). Research by Kay (2019) finds a similar positive relationship between experiences of discrimination and earnings. In addition, we also know that lawyers who are women and minority group members tend to report higher levels of discrimination (Nelson et al. 2019), which is further evidence of dysfunctional organizational climates marked by hegemonic masculinity contests, harassment, and bullying (Berdahl et al. 2018).

Family Factors

Understanding the role of family factors in earnings is important, especially because they are often thought to be a primary source of the gender wage gap. We find that marital status is nonsignificant but that spouse's earnings are related to a small but significant net positive gain from the lowest and up to the 75th quantile. We expected to find a positive relationship since couples tend to come from similar social classes (Mare 2016). However, this small effect is eclipsed by the fact that we also find that having a spouse who works full-time significantly depresses earnings in every quantile. This is perhaps not surprising: given the work hours required to succeed financially in the modern legal profession, it is beneficial to have a spouse who does not work full-time and can instead devote his or her time to taking care of the home and the children. This is also a very gendered relationship. In separate models, we find that, for women, spouse's income is a strong and positive predictor of their own earnings in every quantile, but we find no significant effect of their spouse's labor force participation in any quantile. For men, it is the opposite: spouse's earnings have no significant relationship in any quantile, but having their spouse working full-time significantly depresses their earnings in every quantile.

Following this pattern, we also find that respondents' reports of the proportion of household chores for which they are responsible are not significant predictors of earnings in the full model but do significantly reduce earnings for women at all quantiles in the gender-only model. We again see a continuation of a very traditionally gendered pattern in the legal profession, whereby men benefit financially by having a spouse who stays home, yet women do not benefit from having a spouse who does not work full-time. As we have seen in other chapters, the legal profession continues to bestow financial rewards and advancement on those whose lives are structured conventionally—most often White men with wives at home.

Becoming a parent is considered to be a major source of the gender wage gap. It is therefore important to reiterate that we find a significant gender wage gap at all quantiles even though we control for the presence of children. In the full sample, which considers both men and women together, having one child compared to no children results in a significant earnings premium for all respondents only at the 90th quantile, and having two children compared to no children provides an earnings boost at all quantiles (from 10% to 13%). Further analyses reveal that these are gendered results. We find that any positive relationship of children to earnings is reserved for male respondents only. For fathers, having two or more children compared to no children results in positive and significant earnings across the distribution. For mothers, there tends to be no significant effect of having children (either one child or two or more) on earnings. The exception is a significant earnings drop at the 50th percentile for mothers with one child compared to women without children. These results confirm yet again the way in which normative masculinity is celebrated and rewarded in the modern legal profession. This also upends many popular assumptions by demonstrating that having children is not the main driver of the gender gap in earnings. The gender wage gap persists despite controlling for the presence of children and despite controlling for a full range of measures that are typically thought of as driving earnings in the legal profession, from law school attended, to practice settings, work hours, and many others. We elaborate on the relationship between parenthood and earnings below.

Gender, Race, and Earnings

Given the distinct patterns of racial inequality that we find in other chapters in this book, including chapter 10 on law firm exits and promotions and chapter 11 on debt, we posit that women's earnings are further shaped by the intersections between their gender and their racial identity.

Table 12.3 presents median and mean earnings for the combined categories of race/ethnicity and gender. The results demonstrate that, within every racial/ethnic group, men earn more than their female counterparts do and that all women (except Asian American women at wave 1) have earnings that are below the mean of the sample.

In regression models similar to those reported above, we begin with a baseline model (not shown). There are no significant differences by race either as direct effects or as interaction effects with gender. We then add in controls for personal characteristics, work history, job status, work characteristics, and family factors (as above). This final model demonstrates patterns of disadvantage for women of different racial groups. African American women earn significantly less than White men do at the 75th and 90th percentiles, and in these quantiles their earnings disadvantage compared to White men is the largest of all race/gender groups. Latinas earn significantly less at the 25th, 50th, and 75th quantiles, with coefficients that indicate larger penalties than those experienced by White women. White women earn significantly less than White men at every earnings quantile. We note that there are some significant coefficients for racialized men that demonstrate an earnings premium compared to White men: Latinos earn significantly more than White men do at the 25th

TABLE 12.3 Earnings by gender*race/ethnicity and wave (full-time workers only)

	Wave 1			Wave 3		
Gender*race/ethnicity	n	Mean ($)	Median ($)	n	Mean ($)	Median ($)
African American men	47	91,450	82,500	51	140,932	118,000
Latinos	80	89,241	75,000	75	179,098	146,000
Native American men	16	98,182	93,000	18	174,500	153,500
Asian American men	7	100,599	88,000	67	169,641	135,000
White men	711	84,937	75,000	681	169,658	150,000
African American women	109	78,613	67,000	96	128,318	104,000
Latinas	89	81,370	64,000	82	137,065	130,000
Native American women	16	60,601	52,500	14	73,854	65,375
Asian American women	98	85,511	75,000	82	134,250	120,000
White women	597	74,776	64,000	535	127,251	108,000
Total	1,836	81,996	70,550	1,701	149,526	125,750

and 75th quantiles, and Asian American men earn significantly more than White men at all but the 90th quantile.

That the race/gender effects emerge only after controls suggests a suppression effect, meaning that were it not for the distribution of women and men of different racial and ethnic groups across these variables—such as their participation in full-time work, their representation in various practice settings, and characteristics of their work and personal lives—we would see greater disparities in earnings across the wage distribution. Taken together, the results confirm that both race and gender—and especially the combination of race and gender—produce disadvantage in the legal profession. Exploring the full relationship between race and earnings is beyond the scope of this chapter, and we hope to continue to explore these relationships in future work.

These findings suggest that inequalities are produced in different ways across the legal profession. We again see the salience of gender inequality as women of different racial and ethnic groups earn less than White men do and often experience earnings penalties that are greater than those experienced by White women (who also earn less than White men do). These results also reinforce the importance of intersectional approaches to inequality. African American women, Latinas, Asian American women, Native American women, and White women bring different experiences and are treated differently in the legal workplace. Some of these differences are obvious in statistical differences across groups. For example, a larger proportion of African American lawyers are women than is the case for other groups. A larger percentage of African American women practice full-time than do women in other racial and ethnic groups (86%), especially White women (72% of whom practice full time), which of course raises their earnings profile. Other differences are revealed in the in-depth interviews as we hear the narratives of men and women who occupy different race and class positions describing the unique challenges they face. Our findings are consistent with emerging lines of research that reveal the racialized character of professional occupations (Wingfield 2019).

THE MOTHERHOOD PENALTY

It is clear that motherhood is an important transition in the working lives of women, one that destabilizes the linear trajectory of full-time work that men experience and is well rewarded in the legal profession. The consequences of parenthood are gendered, with financial rewards for men who are parents. To explore the relationship between parenthood and earnings further, we ran models that rely on the same set of variables used above and replace the variables for gender and children with variables for mothers, fathers, nonmothers, and nonfathers.[5] It is important to emphasize that, because we are interested in zeroing in on the relationship between gender and parenthood, the base of comparison in these analyses is women with no children.

In the baseline models, having children benefits only men; there is no significant difference between mothers and women with no children. In the full models, our results demonstrate a parenthood premium for both men and women, but the premium is strongly gendered. For men, the fatherhood premium is present at the 50th and 90th quantiles prior to any controls—and no other group earns a premium. After we add all controls to the model, we continue to find a fatherhood premium. Men with children outearn—by a large margin—childless men, childless women, and women with children, from 17% more at the 25th quantile up to 32% more at the 90th. Importantly, we also find that women with children earn significantly more than do women with no children at all quantiles but the 25th but that their premiums are more modest, ranging from 11% to 13%. Men with no children also earn significantly more than do women with no children at all quantiles (the premium is similar to that of mothers). In other words, it is women with no children, in all settings and all quantiles, who earn the least.

In line with other research, when we compare women with children to women with no children, we do not find evidence of a strong motherhood penalty when all factors are considered (Amuedo-Dorantes and Kimmel 2005). That mothers earn significantly more than nonmothers only after all controls demonstrates that the positive relationship of motherhood with income is masked by variation in the various dimensions of engagement with the workforce that idealize a devotion to work through long hours, full-time work, an orientation to wealth accumulation, seniority within the organization, and having a spouse at home. We conclude that, in order to receive the parenthood premium, mothers have to manage their careers and families in a way that fathers do not as men receive the parenthood premium regardless of these factors.

Our finding of a hierarchy of normative masculinity, with fathers at the top and women without children at the bottom, is important. Mothers' wage premium does not significantly surpass the male premium of childless men in the private sector. Much of the literature on the gender wage gap among lawyers assumes that women without children would be able to pursue the same career path as their male colleagues do and therefore earn similar wages (Azmat and Ferrer 2017; Hagan and Kay 2010; Robson and Wallace 2001). Instead, we find that they earn less than all other parent-gender categories. This points to a strong bias against nonnormative pathways in the legal profession, reinforcing and maintaining the male exclusivity of the work devotion schema (Acker 1990; Berdahl et al. 2018; Blair-Loy 2003).

GENDERED NORMS IN THE LEGAL PROFESSION

Women in the legal profession have made extraordinary advancements over the past half century, and it is important to celebrate the many accomplishments they have achieved. Yet it is equally important to document the barriers they face. The analyses presented in this chapter lay out a clear story of inequality in earnings that is anchored in the gendered nature of the modern legal profession. From the beginning of their careers, female lawyers earn less than their male counterparts do (Dinovitzer et al. 2009b). This gender gap in earnings in the legal profession has been carefully documented by others (e.g., Hagan and Kay 1995; Sterling and Reichman 2016), but our contribution here is to establish that this wage gap begins early in careers and persists across the life course, that it persists across the earnings distribution, that it persists despite accounting for all obvious explanations, and that it persists—and even worsens—when women do not have children.

Despite the weak empirical connection between women's role as mothers and women's lower earnings in the legal workforce, the popular narrative remains one that focuses on women and family. Why does it persist? In seeking to explain the stagnation of women in high-level professional positions, Padavic et al. (2020, 98) have recently explained that the work-family narrative explanation persists because it "allowed the firm to deflect responsibility for women's stalled advancement": "Firm leaders' diligent efforts to solve the problem gave them an airtight alibi against any accusation that women's failure to advance might be their fault. The narrative also justified the gender imbalance at senior levels: if women themselves prefer to be with their families, as the work-family narrative has it, leaders cannot be accountable for the glaring gender inequality in their senior ranks."

The tenacity with which business leaders adhere to the work-family conflict as the source of women's stalled advancement despite evidence to the contrary is important because it speaks to the extent to which gendered norms are embedded in organizational structures and assumptions. The experience of one of our interviewees, Penelope, sheds light on how the processes that we describe and empirically document work in practice. Penelope worked at a law firm that she described as a setting of "rampant misogyny and gender biases." She says that she was overlooked at the time of promotion despite having brought in more clients and having done more firm service than the man who was promoted and that she was denied the credit for clients she developed.

At the same time, this was a firm that had a "women's initiative" headed by Penelope that formulated antibias training and maternity leave policies.

Penelope's interview highlights a setting that was explicitly discriminatory, but her comments equally highlighted the perhaps less subtle processes through which the association between women and motherhood results in the devaluation of women and ultimately translates into reduced earnings through lack of promotion and credit for clients. When asked whether she had children, Penelope explained that she does not have children by personal choice, noting: "I'm the closest thing to a man that these people have." She elaborated: "I mean, I don't have to be home, I don't have to pick up kids, I don't have that second job pulling at me, and I still couldn't succeed." She also commented that retention of women at the firm was problematic. Yet, when the women would leave, she elaborated, the firm would say: "Well, they just want to spend more time with their family." She explained that, when faced with the departure of women, the firm was not held accountable because the conflation of work and family let it "off the hook." Her conclusion is similar to that of Padavic (2020, 81): that the work-family script is "a hegemonic narrative" that "is a pervasive, uncontested, seemingly natural account that makes singular sense of an array of personal experiences and is resilient to countervailing evidence": "It is an overarching strategic story that preserves dominant cultural meanings and power relations and reproduces them."

Penelope's experience as a woman without children and the experiences of women in her firm more broadly shed light on the ways in which the implicit association of women with children permeate all interactions. Of course, that there is a very strong cultural association between women and family is not new, nor is it confined to the legal profession. For example, the gender-career Implicit Association Test (see https://www.projectimplicit.net) empirically establishes this relationship more generally (Nosek et al. 2002). Despite these strong cultural proscriptions, however, it is worth reiterating that we find the greatest earnings penalty for women with no children. As we note above, this is likely because of workplace policies (such as part-time and maternity leave policies) in higher-earning organizations that the earnings of women with children have been somewhat protected. Yet, at the same time, these policies and practices maintain women's position in the lower tiers of earnings. At the end of the day, it is men—specifically men with children—who earn the most.

We propose that, in order to understand this valuation of fathers, we need to refocus on the celebration of masculinity in the legal profession. That masculinity is rewarded in the legal profession is the result, of course, of broader societal and cultural norms and processes that many have described as *hegemonic masculinity* (Connell and Messershmidt 2005), something that is heightened within the professions in part because of their processes of social closure and exclusivity (Schleef 2010; Sommerlad 2002). These processes play out in many different arenas. Here, we focus on the organizational manifestations of masculinity, while others highlight the importance of professional education socialization in the normalization, institutionalization, and legitimation of masculinity in the professions more broadly (Schleef 2010).

Building on the work of Epstein (1981), who identified the legal profession as a "male establishment," that of Hagan and Kay (2010), who identified a "masculine mystique," Sommerlad's (2016) "hyper-masculine work cultures," and Pierce's (1996) "Rambo litigator," we find evidence of a gendered hierarchy that promotes masculinity (cf. Schleef 2010). We identify several features of masculinity for which both male and female lawyers are financially rewarded, including what is often referred to as the "work devotion schema" (Acker 1990; Blair-Loy 2003) of long hours, high billings, an uninterrupted work history, and membership in organizational committees, all of which assume a spouse primarily responsible for domestic work and childcare. In addition, while men with children are the paradigmatic example of the ideal worker, we find that, under certain conditions, women too may receive some financial reward (when compared to women with no children) for being parents when all else is considered.

At the same time, the full income inflation that is due to masculine privilege remains the exclusive domain of men. Masculinity is defined in part by asserting male dominance over other expressions of gender and sexuality (Connell 1995). Recent research by Berdahl et al. (2018, 30) demonstrates the ways in which masculinity—along with a process that they identify as "masculinity contest cultures"—is expressed through work norms that conflate top performance with masculine gender performance, with the result that "masculinity and workplace success are often treated as synonymous." In our results, these processes are visible in that men outearn women from the very start of their careers, that men without children also outearn mothers, and that nonmothers pay the highest penalty for their nonconforming lifestyle.

The experience of Pamela, an Asian American woman whom we profiled in chapters 6 and 9, highlights the masculinity embedded within legal organizations and the struggles that women face in this context. Pamela began her career on what many would describe as the fast track. Although she was the child of immigrant parents, she attended a top-15 law school and was in high demand as she searched for her first job, ultimately selecting a position at a large elite law firm. During our first interview, she exemplified all the features of a future star, easily billing long hours, and finding her place within the firm. Yet, as she progressed, she began to experience "a little bit of a paternalistic attitude towards women," an attitude that came with rigid gender roles. These gender roles manifested at several levels. First, they created a set of differential "performative criteria" for men and women (Haynes 2012). Pamela described the men as "comfortable swearing and dropping the F-bomb here and there," but, when she broke the expected "submissive" role and become more assertive, she found that "it scares them a little . . . so you feel like you can't win." She further described the workplace as a game of *Survivor*, fitting perfectly into Berdahl et al.'s (2018) definition of a masculinity contest culture. Gender norms also permeated interpersonal interactions, solidifying the role of women as wives and mothers, and continuing to establish a work devotion schema that conflates masculinity with long work hours. Pamela's male colleagues commented to her that they could not imagine their wives doing the work that she does and that "there's only one person who can wear the pants in the family and that's got to be me": "I've got to be the breadwinner and . . . work long hours." Gender roles were further reinforced when making social plans, with partners saying to each other, "Why don't you have your wife call my wife." Finally, the organizational commitment to masculinity also translates into tangible negative workplace outcomes for women. Because she was never considered an equal contributor, the work Pamela was given was low level and routine. When she "leaned in" (Sandberg 2015) and asked for better work, she was told to be a "team player." This was a process that played out repeatedly, with Pamela eventually being let go from the firm after attaining nonequity partner status because she had not done enough substantive work.

Pamela's story is also notable in that it does not include her role as a mother—she was let go before she had her first child. There were no obvious "competing devotions" (Blair-Loy 2003) for her law firm to blame. The bias and the negative workplace dynamics that she faced are thus an almost ideal typical instantiation of masculinity. Her experiences highlight the ways in which masculinity is defined in opposition to femininity, with the roles so rigid that only (certain) men could embody ideal masculinity and women penalized both when they breach the norms and when they play by the rules. It is equally important to note that Pamela is a woman of color, and, while we cannot adequately reflect on her intersectional status here, it undoubtedly played a role.

Conclusion

Our analyses of lawyers' earnings paint the very clear picture that traditional masculinity is the framework that identifies how rewards are distributed in the legal profession. This norm produces and legitimates a set of practices such as the valuation of prestige, fatherhood, and traditional gender relations that financially reward married men with spouses at home. Male lawyers build their careers and their roles as parents through the career sacrifices of their spouses. Female lawyers lag behind men in earnings and advancement not so much because they are mothers as because they are women, with women of color experiencing the double burden of gender and race. This is precisely what is described by Ridgeway in her analysis of the mechanisms behind social inequality. As she states: "Cultural status beliefs about which groups are 'better' constitute group differences as *independent* dimensions of inequality that generate material advantages due to group membership itself" (Ridgeway 2014, 1). Both prestige and masculinity bestow an esteemed social status that is "woven into organizations of resources and power." This social status becomes embedded in organizations through a range of processes (Ridgeway 2014) that create strong boundaries between groups of individuals, with some considered categorically better than others (Bourdieu 1984; Lamont 2012; Tilly 1998). Despite the vast transformations in the legal profession since Ruth Bader Ginsburg graduated first in her class at Columbia Law School, patterns of male dominance persist in the contemporary legal profession.

PART 5

Public Roles and Private Lives

13

Dualities of Politics, Public Service, and Pro Bono in Lawyers' Careers

WITH IOANA SENDROIU

In February 2020, a group of New York University law students staged a protest in Manhattan outside a posh recruiting event hosted by Paul Weiss, a preeminent Wall Street law firm. The students were decrying a victory Paul Weiss had won for ExxonMobil in a lawsuit filed against it by the attorney general of the state of New York, a victory the students viewed as contributing to climate change. As one of the student leaders proclaimed: "Together Harvard, Yale, and NYU law students make up a significant portion of Paul Weiss's recruiting pool, and many of us are saying we refuse to join a firm that defends major players causing the climate crisis" (Queen 2020). The Paul Weiss chairman responded to the press: "We are proud of the outstanding work we do for a range of commercial and pro bono clients in their most challenging and high-profile matters, including our recent defense of ExxonMobil." The law students were asserting that politics mattered when it came to climate change and that Paul Weiss could not claim it was playing a neutral professional role in the ExxonMobil case. The firm legitimated its professional role by highlighting not only its zealous advocacy on behalf of well-paying clients but also its pro bono activities.

In this chapter we present AJD Project data on the politics, public service activities, and pro bono efforts of lawyers—not limited to the elite described in the Paul Weiss story—but across the American legal profession. These data reveal that the tensions between lawyers' liberal politics, their representation of powerful business interests, and their embrace of pro bono service is not a contradiction or a paradox. Rather, they reflect a duality, an inherent aspect of the American legal profession. The politics and public service activities of lawyers help to sustain and legitimate inequalities in the delivery of legal services. We demonstrate this duality both at the level of system and at the level of individual career.

Lawyers' Politics

Bonica et al. (2016, 320) suggest:

> Lawyers occupy an extremely prominent role in American politics and society. As a result, how the bar operates—its partisan inclinations and ideological proclivities—is especially important. In total, lawyers control two-thirds of the three branches of the federal government. Understanding how this population as a whole behaves is not only descriptively interesting, but also illuminating in terms of understanding the influence wielded by this very significant group.

From Tocqueville's (1840/2009) characterization of lawyers as the American aristocracy, to Gordon's (1984, 2009, 2017) analyses of the relationship between prominent lawyers' private practices and public roles as the American republic developed, to Dezalay and Garth's (2008) research on corporate legal statesmen, to work on emerging groups of lawyers at such pivotal moments in American history as the New Deal (Irons 1993; Shamir 1995), the civil rights movement (Kluger 1975; Schmidt 2019), and the rise of conservative legal movements (Hollis-Brusky 2011; Southworth 2008; Teles 2008), to Eulau and Sprague's (1964) analysis of lawyer-legislators, there has been a long-standing interest in the political role of lawyers. But there has been much less research conducted on the political ideologies or affiliations of ordinary lawyers. As the quote from Bonica et al. (2016) illustrates, much of the scholarship has centered on the political process itself rather than the relationship of politics to professional practices and hierarchies. Here, we examine the politics of a national sample of lawyers, comparing their politics to society's more generally, examining the relationship between their politics and their professional practices, and analyzing how their politics evolve over their careers.

PRIOR RESEARCH

National polls indicate that registered voters are evenly divided between independents, Democrats, and Republicans (Pew Research Center 2020) but that women, the college educated, African Americans, Latinx, and Asian Americans are more likely to identify with the Democratic Party. Lawyers as an educated group encompassing large numbers of women and people of color can be expected to identify with Democrats at a higher rate than voters overall do. The two Chicago lawyer studies (Heinz and Laumann 1982; Heinz et al.

2005) support this expectation, although Chicago has a long history of Democratic dominance that became even more pronounced in the years of the AJD Project study. Bonica et al.'s (2016) more recent and nationwide study based on patterns of campaign contributions by lawyers confirms that lawyers are more liberal and Democratic than some professionals—medical doctors, bankers, financial workers, accountants—but less so than academics, journalists, and technology workers. Bonica et al. (2016) characterize the legal profession as having bimodal politics, with a large center-left cluster and a smaller center-right cluster.

But Heinz and Laumann (1982), Heinz et al. (2005), and Bonica et al. (2016) all find considerable variation within the legal profession. Political divisions in the Chicago bar were shaped by religion, client type, and practice setting, with Jewish lawyers voicing more liberal positions than Protestant lawyers and large-firm attorneys representing business clients expressing more conservative positions than small-firm and government attorneys (Heinz et al. 2005, 190). Bonica et al. (2016) find that personal attributes and professional attributes correlate with lawyer politics. For example, they find that women are more liberal than men, that lawyers who have been practicing longer are more conservative than are junior lawyers, that graduating from a top-14 law school is associated with being more liberal, and that attending a law school ranked lower than the top 100 is associated with being more conservative. They suggest that at least part of the relationship between law school and political affiliation is explained by geography as the most conservative law schools are located in the South.

Bonica et al. (2016) also find that practice setting is an important predictor. Lawyers working in government are more liberal than lawyers who do not work in government. Prosecutors are not as left leaning as public defenders are, but they are more liberal than the profession as a whole is. Law professors and public defenders are more liberal than average. And working in big law is associated with conservativism. Additionally, they find differences in the political leanings of lawyers working in big law that are based on the size of the law firms in which they work. Lawyers working in the 25 largest law firms are the most liberal, though Bonica et al. (2016, 34) argue that there may be a geographic dimension to this finding as 22 of these firms are headquartered in states Barack Obama won in the 2012 presidential election. They also found that partners are more conservative than associates are but that this pattern "can likely be explained at least in part by the fact that partners are more likely to be older, richer, male, and white than the associates at their firms" (Bonica et al. 2016, 42).

While these studies are suggestive, they lack the kind of longitudinal data collected by the AJD Project that allow us to examine changes in political orientation over career. AJD Project respondents entered the legal profession as George W. Bush was elected president and were surveyed for the third time when Barack Obama was reelected. The careers of the AJD Project cohort unfolded alongside both Republican and Democratic federal governments and during a time of increasing polarization along partisan lines (Pew Research Center 2012). The AJD Project cohort was in law school in a period after the rise of the conservative legal movement, which left a significant imprint on the legal profession, legal culture, and legal doctrine (Hollis-Brusky 2011; Southworth 2008; Teles 2008).

DESCRIPTIVE PATTERNS

At all three waves, the AJD Project collected data on political party affiliation, social conservatism, and economic conservatism. Table 13.1 reports the breakdown of these measures across waves.

Democrats indeed predominate in the AJD Project sample, constituting about 50% of the sample, compared to only about 25% who identify as Republican. The balance is made up of independents and the unaffiliated and a small "other" group that includes Libertarians and Green Party affiliates—thus a very heterogeneous mix. There is a high degree of consistency in party affiliation over the course of careers. Only 12% of respondents changed party affiliation in any direction between wave 1 and wave 2, and only 11% changed party affiliation in any direction between wave 2 and wave 3. If a respondent

TABLE 13.1 Political party affiliation (%) and mean economic and social conservatism score by wave

	Wave 1	Wave 2	Wave 3
Party affiliation			
Democrat	47.1	51.2	50.0
Republican	27.4	24.2	23.4
Independent	10.0	11.9	15.1
Unaffiliated	12.4	10.6	8.8
Other	3.2	2.1	2.7
Total (*N*)	1,974	1,735	1,971
Conservatism score			
Social conservativism	3.22	2.97	2.97
Economic conservativism	3.92	4.00	4.23
Total (*N*)	2,014	1,727	2,035

Note: Conservativism is measured on a scale of 1 (liberal) to 7 (conservative).

identified as a Democrat at wave 1, the probability of his or her identifying as a Democrat at wave 2 was 92%. If a respondent identified as a Democrat at wave 2, the probability of his or her identifying as a Democrat at wave 3 was 89%. If a respondent identified as a Democrat at wave 1, the probability of his or her identifying as a Democrat at wave 3 was 88%.

We measured social and economic conservatism by asking respondents to place themselves on seven-point scale from liberal (value of 1) to conservative (value of 7) to indicate their "political leaning on 'social issues' and on 'taxation, spending, and social welfare issues.'" Lawyers are more liberal on social issues than they are on economic issues. By wave 3, roughly two-thirds of the sample responded on the liberal end of the social conservatism scale, but only a little more than one-third fell on the liberal end of the economic conservatism scale. Again, we see strong consistency in political orientation across waves. For social conservatism, there is a .69 correlation between wave 1 and wave 2 and a .83 correlation between wave 2 and wave 3. We see almost identical correlations across waves for economic conservatism: .68 between wave 1 and wave 2 and .82 between wave 2 and wave 3.

We pursue further analyses with the simpler metric of percentage Democrat.[1] Women are consistently more likely to identify as Democrats, 60% vs. 41% men at wave 3. People of color are more likely to be Democrats than are Whites, led by African Americans at 70%, Latinx at 61%, and Asian Americans at 57% vs. 44% for Whites. Thus, on gender and race, lawyers mirror national patterns.

Similar to what Bonica et al. (2016) found, we found a very clear association between law school selectivity and percentage of Democrats. By wave 3, top-10 law school graduates are 68% Democrat, a figure declining slightly to 62% among graduates of law schools ranked from 11 to 20, to between 50% and 45% among graduates of law schools ranked from 21 to 50 and tier 3 schools, to just 35% among graduates of tier 4 law schools. Law school differences may in part reflect regional variations in politics. In analyses not shown here, we find modest variation by region, with the South at 48% Democratic at wave 3, the Midwest at the sample mean of 50%, the Northeast at 52% Democratic, and the West at 55% Democratic. Clearly, law school status is more influential on party identification than region is.

Practice settings show considerable variation in the percentage of Democrats.[2] Nonprofits (which include the academy and public interest organizations) have the highest proportion—some 64% at wave 3—followed closely by the federal government sector at 62%. But other settings fall within the narrow range of between 44% and 53% Democratic. Strikingly, large law firm attorneys are 53% Democratic, a figure that is slightly higher than it is among state government lawyers. The least Democratic are solos and attorneys working in firms of 21–250 lawyers and business, at 44% to 45%, respectively. Thus, the segment of the bar that is least associated with business clients and elite status is the least liberal politically.

MULTIVARIATE MODELS: A FOCUS ON CHANGE AND BUSINESS REPRESENTATION

What is the relative influence of these cross-cutting relationships, and how do they change over the course of careers? One of the key issues in previous studies is whether the observed relationship between business representation and more conservative political orientations is a phenomenon of self-selection—that lawyers with more conservative politics gravitate to and stay in business representation—or whether serving business clients moves lawyers' politics to the right, or some combination of both processes (Cummings 2004; Heinz et al. 2005, 180). We developed a measure of the percentage of time lawyers spend on business clients, which we defined as time spent on high-income individuals, Fortune 500 corporations, other large and midsize businesses, and insurance companies. We included the business representation variable along with several other personal and professional variables: gender, race/ethnicity, parents' education, social and economic conservatism, partnership status, working in a large law firm (101 or more attorneys), graduating from a top-50 law school, residing in a blue state (i.e., one typically carried by Democratic candidates in recent presidential elections), working in private practice, the public sector, or business, membership in a political party, and membership in a political advocacy group.

We first included these variables in a logistic regression model predicting whether a respondent identified as a Democrat at wave 3.[3] This model confirmed that respondents who lived in blue states or who identified as Democrats in the previous wave are more likely to be Democrats at wave 3 and, not surprisingly, that social and economic conservatives are less likely to be Democrats. Members of political parties also are more likely to be Democrats. Surprisingly, other variables do not achieve statistical significance, including the key variable of representing business clients.

Such a cross-sectional model does not take advantage of the longitudinal nature of our data. A hybrid fixed-effects model allows us to examine the effects of changes in independent variables across waves on changes in our outcome measure of interest—the odds of identifying as a Democrat (see Firebaugh et al. 2013). The model includes the mean value of variables across waves ("between-person changes") and changes in those variables across waves

("within-person changes"). In this model, only change variables have significant effects on change in Democratic Party affiliation across waves. Becoming
more conservative on social or economic conservatism scales decreases the
propensity to be a Democrat across waves. Those who joined political parties,
however, become more likely to identify as Democrats. On the key question
of the effect of business representation, we find that, if lawyers represent an
increasing percentage of business clients across waves, they become less likely
to identify as Democrats.[4] If a respondent went from 0% to 100% representation of business, the estimated effect would be comparable to the effect of
moving up two points on the seven-point social conservatism scale or one
point on the seven-point economic conservatism scale.

But what is the direction of the effect between business representation and
politics? It still is possible that Democratic affiliation leads to less business representation. We tested for this possibility with structural equation models that
looked at the lagged effects of political affiliation on business and found no
significant effect. This is strong evidence that the link between business representation and politics runs from business to politics and not from politics
to business.

Lawyers' politics are not monolithic. As in American society, gender and
race/ethnicity are powerful determinants of lawyers' political identification.
Within the profession, we see that graduates of elite law schools are far more
liberal than are graduates of tier 4 law schools. Most lawyers in elite law firms
embrace both Democratic politics and the representation of business, a duality illustrated in our opening story of law student protests against Paul Weiss.
Yet, within this apparently stable constellation of elite practice and Democratic politics, our analysis of change over time reveals that, if attorneys represent an increasing proportion of business clients over their careers, their
propensity to identify as Democrats declines.

Participation in Political, Professional, and Community Organizations: The Disappearance of the Citizen-Lawyer?

Robert Putnam's *Bowling Alone* (2000)—which was developed from Putnam
(1995)—raised the concern that the lack of community association among
Americans reflected a weakening of social bonds that contributed to the decline of democracy. A version of this concern has been raised over the years by
legal elites with regard to the waning participation of lawyers in American civic
institutions and the corresponding decline in the role of the citizen-lawyer,
a lawyer who promotes the public good both in private practice and by participating in civic and community organizations (see Heinz et al. 2005; and

Kronman 1993). Much of the literature on the citizen-lawyer or lawyer-statesman emphasizes iconic individuals who held prominent roles in private practice and in public affairs, such as Elihu Root, John W. Davis, Henry Stimson, and Warren Christopher (Dezalay and Garth 2016; Gordon 2009, 2017). And the biographies of law firms in major cities enumerate many corporate lawyers who served as mayor or held other positions of prestige and influence (Lipartito and Pratt 2011).

Much less attention is given to the community roles of ordinary lawyers. Justice Robert Jackson (1944) spoke of the critical functions that lawyers played in small-town America, not just as legal advisers and courtroom advocates, but as leaders in churches, schools, and other civic organizations. A prominent thread in critiques of the contemporary American legal profession is that specialization and demands for long hours have undercut this traditional role. With limited exceptions, these critiques have been mounted without the benefit of data on the public service activities of lawyers (but see Heinz et al. 2005).

A less idealistic view recognizes that participation in voluntary organizations may also be a way for lawyers to build their careers, gaining visibility and network connections that may generate clients or lead to positions of perceived stature and influence that benefit their practice (Seron 1996). As Wilkins (2004a) suggests, these activities may be especially valuable for outsiders like African American lawyers who need the added visibility and contacts even more than Whites do.

We collected data on memberships and leadership roles among the sample across all three waves. We ranked the 16 organizations in which lawyers participate from most frequent to least frequent at wave 3 and also determined the rate at which respondents held leadership positions in these organizations and their membership rates in those organizations in earlier waves.[5] The results rebut the notion that lawyers have withdrawn from community and association activities. Leading the list are state and local bar associations at 60%, which may in part be a product of mandatory membership requirements maintained by some 60% of state bars (Lawyer Legion 2022). Almost 50% of lawyers participate in charitable organizations. As we discussed above, a significant proportion (42%) belong to a political party. More than one-third belong to religious organizations. Similarly, more than one-third belong to sections of bar associations or to the ABA. Lawyers are somewhat more likely to belong to their undergraduate alumni association (32%) than to their law school alumni group (26%). About a quarter of lawyers are members of a parent teacher association (a proportion that grows from earlier waves as more respondents have school-age children by wave 3).

From the list of 16 possible sources of organization membership, we calculated the number of different types of organizations to which respondents belonged. There is a full range from 0 to 16 in each wave. The median number of types of membership is 5 in each wave. Only a relatively small proportion of respondents belonged to no organizations, with a range from 3% at wave 1, to 16% at wave 2, to 10% at wave 3. Fewer than one-quarter of cases have seven or more types of membership in any wave.

A much smaller proportion of the sample maintains leadership roles in community organizations. The most common is a leadership position in a charitable organization, held by one in five members of the sample. Leadership in religious organizations is the next most frequent (1 in 10 lawyers). There is a significant drop off in leadership rates in other organizations: 5.2% are leaders in organized sports, 3.8% lead political party organizations, 3.2% lead race/ethnicity-based organizations, 2.9% lead political advocacy groups, and so on.

The AJD Project cohort reflects patterns in American society more broadly. A survey conducted in 2017 found that almost 6 in 10 Americans participate in some kind of community group or organization, and 1 in 10 say they participate in 4 or more community groups (Sandstrom and Alper 2019). In wave 3, more than half of AJD Project lawyers participated in 5 or more organizations. Lawyers may no longer be the aristocracy Tocqueville described in the nineteenth century, but they appear to be more active than other members of their communities.

The AJD Project cohort also appears at least as active as the Chicago lawyer samples of 1975 and 1995 (see Heinz and Laumann 1982; and Heinz et al. 2005). Indeed, there are some striking similarities in the level of participation in certain types of organizations: 34% in religious organizations in Chicago in 1995 vs. 36% in wave 3 of the AJD Project, 25% in civic organizations in Chicago in 1995 vs. 23% in wave 3 of the AJD Project, 23% in education organizations in 1995 Chicago vs. 26% in wave 3 of the AJD Project, and 8% in ethnic organizations in 1995 Chicago vs. 12% in race/ethnicity-based organizations in wave 3 of the AJD Project. There are much higher levels of political party membership in AJD Project wave 3 (42%) than in 1995 Chicago (15%).

The literature on voluntary associations suggests that dominant social groups tend to have higher levels of participation (Smith 1994, 246). Our analyses by gender, race/ethnicity, and law school status do not support this thesis.

Instead, we see the clustering of lawyers in different types of organizations on the basis of their political orientations, race/ethnicity, and practice settings, all of which are interrelated. Members of religious organizations, organized sports and private clubs, and service organizations are more conservative on both social and economic conservatism. Members of political advocacy groups are more liberal on the economic conservatism scale. Members of gender-based and race-based organizations are more liberal on social and economic scales. Some of these political affinities reflect the demographics of membership. Men predominate in organized sports, producing more conservative scores for members of those groups. Women and people of color predominate in gender- and race-based organizations, and these produce more liberal scores.

While only 2% of Whites belong to race/ethnicity-based organizations, 44% of African American, 28% of Latinx, 17% of Native American, and 35% of Asian American attorneys do. Graduates of top-10 law schools are more likely to belong to racial/ethnic organizations, 20% vs. 12% for the sample overall. Membership in the ABA is connected to practicing in large law firms, where 50% of attorneys are ABA members, compared to 35% for the sample overall. State government attorneys are especially unlikely to belong to the ABA—only 21% do.

Thus differences in organization memberships correspond to and possibly contribute to cleavages among American lawyers.

CAREER BENEFITS TO INVOLVEMENT IN COMMUNITY ORGANIZATIONS

In casual cocktail party conversation between one of our coauthors and an African American attorney who was a partner in a major law firm, the subject turned to service on the boards of nonprofits. The attorney recounted that the best move he had made to grow a book of business was to serve on the board of a prominent community organization. There, he met and interacted with leaders of the business community, was approached to serve on other prestigious boards, and established client relationships with several of the businesses whose leaders sat on the boards. The story exemplified how community service can become a form of social capital that leads to professional success.

Community activities may not simply reflect the altruism of lawyers. They may also reflect and reinforce efforts to build the kind of social capital that advances careers. Given the rich data we possess on involvement in community organizations over the course of lawyers' careers, we were able to examine whether there was a link between participation in community organizations and career advancement. We focused on the prospects for making partner in a private law firm. Building on the analyses in previous chapters of the determinants of making partner, we estimated simultaneous equation models of the odds of making partner at wave 2 and wave 3 that included participation in specific types of community and professional organizations and key control variables.[6] We produced two sets of models: one including membership in a charitable organization and one including ABA membership. We found that participating in a charity and belonging to the ABA at wave 2 each are positively associated with having made partner at wave 3. The models are somewhat complex in that we see that there is a reciprocal relationship between being a partner at wave 2 and belonging to the ABA at wave 2 and that ABA membership at wave 2 predicts both being a partner at wave 3 and being a member of the ABA at wave 3. Also, when we allow the model to include the reciprocal relationship between participating in a charity at wave 2 and making partner at wave 2, the effect of charity work at wave 2 on partnership at wave 3 is no longer significant. Still, the coefficients in the models suggest that membership in the ABA and doing charity work are as influential as gender, race, and hours worked in predicting who makes partner by wave 3. In the next section, we will discuss similar findings for doing pro bono service.

These results are the very definition of doing good and doing well. Attorneys who have the wherewithal to engage in charity work and participate in the ABA also have the wherewithal to make partner. Our finding of the reciprocal relationship between partnership and ABA membership captures the duality of this relationship. These are mutually reinforcing kinds of social capital. Certainly, not everyone who joins the ABA will make partner in a law firm, and, certainly, not all partners will join the ABA. Rather, stature in a law firm as signified by partnership facilitates participation in the ABA, just as membership in the ABA is a marker of the kind of professional stature that gets recognized in law firms.

The Pro Bono Efforts of Lawyers over Their Careers

We now turn to one of the defining elements of law as a profession: providing professional service to people who cannot otherwise afford it. For lawyers and other professionals, such work is referred to with the Latin phrase *pro bono publico* (for the public good), or simply *pro bono*. In the context of the American legal profession, which is organized as a private market and has a relatively small publicly or charitably funded legal services sector compared to other advanced societies (Cummings et al. 2022; Sandefur 2009), the pro bono efforts of lawyers may be critical to meeting the legal needs of moderate and low-income groups. In addition to defending government support for the Legal Services Corporation, the ABA's Model Rules of Professional Conduct (rule 6.1) establishes the aspirational goal that all lawyers spend 50 hours a year doing pro bono service. As of 2015, the chief judge of New York instituted a requirement that bar applicants must complete 50 hours of pro bono service (see https://www.nycourts.gov/ctapps/520rules10.htm#B16). Pro bono programs have become institutionalized in large law firms, which promote them widely as an expression of their commitment to public service and a channel for law firm members to engage in socially meaningful work (see Adediran 2020; Boutcher 2009, 2017; Cummings 2004). *The American Lawyer* provides annual rankings of large law firms that are based on the scale and monetary contributions of their pro bono programs (see Faith-Slaker 2018, 4), which is yet another indication of professional concern about pro bono efforts.

While there has been a substantial amount of policy research on the pro bono efforts of lawyers, such as national surveys by the ABA (Faith-Slaker 2018), a large-scale survey of more than 3,000 lawyers (Rhode 2005), and sociological research on the pro bono programs of law firms (see Adediran 2020; and Boutcher 2009, 2017), we are in a position to examine how the pro bono efforts of lawyers evolve over the course of their careers and relate to the social organization of the legal profession. We build here on the theoretical and empirical insights of our colleagues Dinovitzer and Garth (2009) and Sandefur (2009), who employed AJD Project data from wave 1.

OVERALL PATTERNS: WELL BELOW ABA GOAL

The AJD Project sample reports time spent on pro bono work as being on average well below the ABA's goal of 50 hours per year. There is slight variation from early to midcareer, with between 45% and 53% of lawyers reporting that they did any pro bono work. The mean level of effort, counting the zeros, falls between 25 and 28 hours per year. For those who spend some time, the commitments are quite large on average: 51 hours in their early careers, rising to 58 hours at midcareer. These numbers are very skewed as a relatively small number of lawyers spend 1,000 hours or more a year on pro bono work. The top quantile provided more than 118 hours in wave 1, 106 hours in wave 2, and 175 hours in wave 3. Our measure includes both forms of pro bono work we inquired about in our survey, work for charities and work for people with low or moderate incomes. In wave 1, we did not ask respondents to make this distinction. In wave 2 and wave 3, we did and found that pro bono work for the poor predominated: 39% for the poor vs. 23% for charities and 38% for "other" in wave 2 and 48% for the poor vs. 40% for charities and 12% for "other" in wave 3. We inspected the "other" responses. They contain a range of comments that might be reclassified or dropped from the count of pro bono hours. The most frequent was "helping out family members" (without an indication of whether the family member could not otherwise afford a lawyer) and serving on the board of a nonprofit (without an indication of what the organization does). We decided not to change the pro bono counts, which means that we may have slightly exaggerated the total amount of pro bono efforts.[7]

PRO BONO COMPARED TO LAWYERS'
TOTAL EFFORT FOR CLIENTS

We can put the amount of hours spent on pro bono work in perspective by comparing it to the total effort lawyers devote to different types of clients. Figure 13.1 displays the percentage of lawyers' total effort by type of client at wave 3, adding an illustration of what total pro bono hours would contribute. (The figure is an elaboration on what we presented in chap. 5.) The largest piece of the pie is for large to midsize business clients at 41%, another 10% for small business, 17% for government, 6% for high-income individuals, 3% for nonprofits and public interest organizations, and 23% for middle- to low-income individuals, the category in which pro bono clients reside. In this analysis we treat all pro bono hours as serving middle- to low-income individuals even if a significant portion of reported pro bono hours served charities or other organizations that do not necessarily serve the poor. Even with our generous method of counting, pro bono effort makes up only 1% of this 23% (or 4% of the total for middle- and low-income clients).

Despite the importance that leaders of the bar and large law firms attach to pro bono efforts, total pro bono work is a small drop in the bucket of lawyers' total work. It does not come close to ameliorating inequality in representation resources for middle- and low-income groups in any significant way.

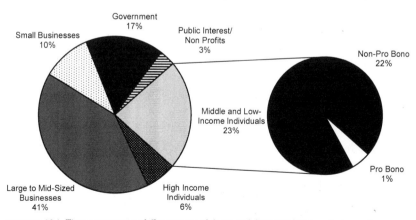

FIGURE 13.1. Time spent serving different types of clients and doing pro bono work at wave 3

IS PRO BONO AN ELITE CAREER STRATEGY?

Bourdieu suggested that seemingly disinterested activity, such as pro bono service, may at the same time be interested. Because certain fields of social action may require actors to engage in seemingly altruistic acts, actors who have internalized those rules may not question whether or even be aware that their participation serves to maintain hierarchies within the field (Bourdieu 1998, 76–77, 83). Yet, by conforming to norms of disinterestedness, they may also profit in the process (Bourdieu 1998, 89).

Dinovitzer and Garth (2009, 117–18) draw on this perspective to suggest (1) that the legal profession is structured to reward those who work to sustain the legitimacy of the legal profession as a whole, with pro bono helping legitimate a system in which the overwhelming proportion of resources sustains business and economic interests; (2) that elites take the lead in promoting the ideals of the profession but also reap the rewards of advancing those ideals, as illustrated in the competition among major law firms to be recognized as leaders in providing pro bono services; (3) that nonelite lawyers see pro bono as a way to build their practices at the same time as it conforms to a professional ideal; and (4) that, given the hierarchical structure of the legal profession, a strategy of investing in professional virtues is more available to those at the top of the hierarchy both because they have been socialized into a system of noblesse oblige and because they see public service as a way of distinguishing their work from the mere pursuit of economic gain. Thus, they predicted and found in the wave 1 data that lawyers in larger law firms and lawyers from more elite law schools were more likely to do pro bono service. They also predicted that lawyers who did pro bono would be rewarded materially and symbolically. We tested these hypotheses across the three waves of AJD Project data.

Table 13.2 presents the social correlates of pro bono efforts by waves. In their early careers, lawyers from top-10 and top-20 law schools report much higher levels of pro bono than do graduates of other tiers of law school— more than 60% compared to 50% or less. Yet that leadership ends by wave 2. Indeed, tier 3 and tier 4 graduates post the highest rate of pro bono service at wave 3.

Another way to consider the elite nature of pro bono effort is to consider the practice settings in which it is conducted. Lawyers working in the largest law firms report high rates of doing pro bono. And they report the highest mean hours devoted to pro bono at all waves (not shown), which is consistent with an elite thesis and with what we know about the institutionalization of

TABLE 13.2 Social characteristics and practice setting of
respondents doing any pro bono by wave (%)

	Wave 1	Wave 2	Wave 3
Gender			
Women	52.7	40.4	50.7
Men	52.5	50.5	55.5
t-value of difference	0.1	−4.6***	−2.0*
Race/ethnicity			
African American	47.5	44.9	52.5
Latinx	44.7	43.7	47.3
Asian American	48.5	40.6	44.4
White	54.1	46.5	55.1
F-value of difference	1.7	0.9	3.2*
Law school ranking			
Top 10	61.9	41.5	51.9
11–20	63.0	41.3	53.2
21–50	51.2	47.3	51.7
51–100	50.6	42.9	50.3
Tier 3	44.5	50.2	57.2
Tier 4	49.6	49.6	54.5
F-value of difference	3.3**	1.9	0.8
Practice setting			
Solo practice	84.9	76.1	76.9
Law firm 2–20	55.5	68.1	72.3
Law firm 21–100	43.4	61.8	59.0
Law firm 101–250	72.8	65.4	81.2
Law firm 251+	73.7	71.1	67.0
Business	50.9	22.9	41.1
Federal government	22.0	20.2	27.3
State government	19.4	21.6	31.0
Nonprofit/PI/education	23.1	19.8	42.1
F-value of difference	29.0***	69.1***	31.6***
Total (N)	*1,166*	*2,033*	*1,705*

*** $p \leq .001$. ** $p \leq .01$. ** $p \leq .05$.

pro bono in large firms. But also striking is the higher rate at which pro bono
work is conducted by solo attorneys, the group that historically is depicted as
at the bottom of the profession's status hierarchy. One possible explanation for
the high rate of pro bono work by solos is that they are more likely to count as
pro bono work that falls outside the standard definition, such as unpaid fees.
Yet we find no evidence of that in what solos reported in the "other" category
of types of pro bono work. We regard this as a valid finding, one that likely
reflects the proximity of solos to lower- and middle-income clients. Given all

the attention given to the pro bono programs of large law firms, these data are a reminder of the importance of small-firm practitioners in providing pro bono representation.

We find quite striking differences between private practice and attorneys working for business or in the public sector. At each wave, more than 60% of private practitioners do some pro bono work, compared to as little as 22% by the business lawyers and 21% by the public sector lawyers in wave 2. In wave 3, almost 70% of lawyers in private practice do some pro bono work and spend an average of 34 hours on pro bono matters, while 39% of lawyers in business do some pro bono and average 17 hours a year. Only 31% of public sector lawyers do some pro bono work, but those who do do a lot. They average 31 hours a year, close to the figure for private practitioners.

This striking contrast raises interesting questions for scholars of the legal profession. The private practice sector is governed by lawyers, whereas the business and public sectors are not. It is in this realm of governance by professionals that we see the most fealty to the professional ideal of public service. It may also be that for-profit practice settings most clearly define pro bono effort as a distinct kind of professional work. Business lawyers may work for corporations that have their own very substantial public service activities. Business lawyers may participate in those activities, but not as a traditional form of pro bono practice (Bliss and Boutcher 2022). Public sector lawyers work for organizations that are themselves dependent on public social spending or private philanthropy. Therefore, they may see what they do in practice as serving the public good, or they may not have an opportunity for pro bono projects given public sector rules about avoiding conflicts of interest.

Organizational policies that allow lawyers to count their pro bono time as billable hours have a strong effect on pro bono effort. Over half of pro bono hours at each wave are reported by respondents as being billable to their firms.

To examine the relationship between elite status and pro bono more fully, we conducted multivariate analyses that considered a wide range of personal and professional variables as determinants of pro bono activity. Our analysis included social background characteristics (gender, race/ethnicity, and parents' occupation), law school selectivity, whether respondents participated in pro bono programs in law school, whether they reported a desire to help others as one of the reasons they went to law school, what sector they practiced in (private, business, or public), whether their employer allowed them to count pro bono hours as billable hours, their total number of billable hours, how they scored on a scale of economic conservatism, whether they were a partner (either equity or nonequity), whether they were a participant or leader in

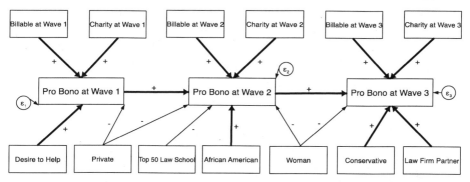

FIGURE 13.2. Stylized structural equation model of equations 1, 2, and 3 predicting pro bono effort

a charitable organization, and whether they had done pro bono work at the time of the previous wave of the survey.

Figure 13.2 presents a simplified schematic of a simultaneous equation model that predicts pro bono across waves.[8] (This model predicts whether a lawyer does any pro bono work. Models that estimate the number of pro bono hours produced similar results.)

Three variables stand out in the final model: whether the employer counts pro bono hours as billable, whether a lawyer is active in a charitable organization, and whether a lawyer did pro bono work in an earlier wave. If lawyers said that they joined the profession because of a desire to help others, that has a positive effect at wave 1. Working in private practice, as opposed to business or the public sector, has a positive effect at wave 1 and wave 2 but drops below significance at wave 3. Women are somewhat less likely to do pro bono work, both at wave 2 and at wave 3, that is, later in their careers. We examined whether the gender effect was due to women having children but found that it was not. Interestingly, social conservatives are more likely to do pro bono work both at wave 1 and at wave 3. Thus, pro bono is not associated with more liberal politics, all else being equal. Neither law school selectivity nor race yield consistent effects in the final model. Graduating from a top-50 law school has, in fact, a negative relationship with pro bono at wave 2 but not in other waves. African Americans are more likely to do pro bono at wave 2 but not in other waves.

Figure 13.2 demonstrates the importance of individual engagements in pro bono work over a career that cannot be reduced to group characteristics. At each wave, we see that participating in charitable organizations predicts more pro bono work. We investigated whether this was purely a function of doing charitable forms of pro bono. It was not. Then, in waves 2 and 3, we see that having done pro bono service in the previous wave increases the likelihood of doing pro bono service in the current wave. That is, once lawyers start doing pro bono service, they continue to do so over the course of their careers. Getting started in pro bono service is related to expressing a desire to help others as a reason for taking an early career job. But, interestingly, doing pro bono in law school has no carryover effect even into doing pro bono at wave 1.

Organizational policies that encourage pro bono by allowing lawyers to count pro bono time as billable hours have a significant effect at each wave. And this effect is independent of total hours worked, which has no significant relationship to pro bono at any wave. Working in the public sector is associated with fewer pro bono hours at waves 1 and 2 but loses significance by wave 3.

CAREER BENEFITS TO DOING PRO BONO

As in our analysis of the career benefits of participating in community organizations, we sought to determine whether doing pro bono work could also function as a way to build social capital and promote one's career. We estimated a set of simultaneous equation models that included controls for key variables.[9] Of critical importance is that we found that doing pro bono work at wave 2 was significantly related to having made partner by wave 3. The size of the effect of doing pro bono at wave 2 on making partner at wave 3 is as high as that of being a woman, nearly as high as that of graduating from a top-50 law school, and about two-thirds as high as that of being White.

We can summarize the results from the multivariate models as indicating that the lawyers who are most likely to do pro bono service are the committed, the engaged, and the powerful. Their commitment is reflected in the carryover in pro bono work at each wave of the survey, from early to midcareer. Their engagement is reflected in the consistent association between working for charitable organizations and doing pro bono work. And that they are powerful is reflected in the greater propensity of those who did pro bono work at wave 2 to become a partner at wave 3. Although women are somewhat more likely to do charity work, when controlling for other variables, they are less likely to do pro bono work at waves 2 and 3. We could not readily predict who would be committed or engaged. Thus, individual biography plays an important role in explaining differences in pro bono effort.

Yet individual biographies are embedded in social structure. The power of partners who are more likely to do pro bono is very much a reflection of position within the social structure. And it is obvious that organizational policies have an impact on pro bono, as employers who allow their attorneys to count pro bono time as billable time have the predictable effect of increasing pro bono hours.

It is striking that our statistical data found a significant link between pro bono effort at wave 2 and making partner at wave 3. This demonstrates that the anecdote related earlier about building a clientele by joining the boards of prestigious nonprofits reflects a broader pattern of how public service can reproduce social advantage. The statistical result may invite an instrumental interpretation of this relationship—that those who provide pro bono service increase their odds of making partner. That likely is too simplistic an interpretation. The capacity to do pro bono work reflects an understanding of the politics surrounding pro bono in a law firm context. It likely corresponds to the capacity to succeed in navigating the politics of making partnership.

The in-depth interviews reveal the various ways in which pro bono engagements fit into career development. James, whose narrative we included in the introduction, exemplifies the connection between elite law firm practice and pro bono engagements. A White graduate of an elite law school, James made partner quickly (by wave 2) in an elite law firm known for its litigation practice. His firm has a standing arrangement with a county public defender's office to provide pro bono representation to some criminal indigents. James characterized the relationship as "a wonderful way to get people experience." He reported doing pro bono criminal defense work at each wave of interviews, including a trial and appeals on an attempted murder case. His pro bono work complemented and deepened his expertise in criminal defense work, which he also provides to white-collar clients. James embodies noblesse oblige. While early in his career he may have been interested in doing pro bono work to get trial experience, by wave 2, when he was already a partner, he seemed to take for granted that he should apply his expertise in criminal defense to the representation of an indigent client.

Two other interviewees who started in large law firms offer different perspectives on careers and pro bono. Lynden, the African American graduate of a top-20 law school whom we met in chapter 6, began his career in a large elite litigation firm. Early in his career, he spent considerable time on pro bono cases, something the firm encouraged as a way for him to gain trial experience. Yet, as he approached the eight-year mark in the firm in the midst of the economic downturn, he found himself without connections to any of the firm's practice groups. He was forced to leave, moving to a government position. Pro bono by itself is not a ticket to partnership.

Pamela, whom we met in chapter 9, also the graduate of a top-20 law school, was terminated by a large law firm 10 years into her career, when she was seemingly on the cusp of an equity partnership. She had done a significant amount of pro bono work, but, when she suddenly found herself unemployed, she stepped away from practice and had a child. She made her way back into practice by performing pro bono services for municipalities as a volunteer prosecutor. That pro bono work allowed her to cultivate relationships she ultimately drew on to become a public prosecutor. She observed that her history with a large law firm hurt her with city governments "because they have a slight bias toward people who had salaries of $300,000 . . . [and] perhaps are just doing the job for a little while to get trial experience and then going back to a big firm." Pamela was genuinely interested in moving into work as a criminal prosecutor, and the 2019 web search reports that she has become a prosecutor for a large county government. Her pro bono work provided the bridge from her former career in a large law firm to her job as a criminal prosecutor. She self-consciously did pro bono work as a way to advance her career.

Engagement in pro bono service as a pragmatic, career building process is illustrated by the cases of Jacob and Alejandro, both graduates of tier 4 law schools who never practiced in large law firms. We met both Jacob and Alejandro in chapter 7. By wave 3, Jacob had built a successful plaintiffs' personal injury practice, drawing on relationships with the Armenian community and referrals by former clients. Most of his income came from contingency fee cases, but other small matters he would handle for free. At wave 2, he reported 200 hours of pro bono service. His interviews suggested that his pro bono matters just came with his clients, that they were favors he could not refuse and were not worth billing for.

By wave 3, Alejandro had built a thriving criminal/immigration practice. He traced the roots of his business-generating success to the free advice he gave at Latinx law fairs and the profile he developed as a law commentator on Spanish-language media. He reported pro bono hours at all three waves of the survey. His public service work was part of the entrepreneurialism through which he established his small-firm practice.

Conclusion

This chapter provides insights into the relationships between lawyers' politics, their community roles, and their pro bono efforts. In all three arenas, lawyers do not constitute a unitary profession. As with many other aspects of lawyers' work and careers, it is necessary to consider what segment they are operating in and, often, where they are situated in the hierarchies of the bar. The legal profession as a whole is far more likely to identify with the Democratic

Party than with the Republican Party or independents. But it is the elites of the profession—the graduates of more selective law schools and those who practice in large law firms—who are more likely to be Democrats than are the graduates of lower-tier law schools and practitioners working as solos.

Contrary to the rhetoric of some supreme court justices, bar leaders, and legal scholars, we do not see that lawyers have withdrawn from active participation in political, professional, and community organizations. Indeed, it seems that the AJD Project cohort is even more active in community roles than are other Americans with college or graduate educations and high earnings and perhaps even the cross sections of lawyers in Chicago discussed in Heinz and Laumann (1982) and Heinz et al. (2005). But, again, we see segmentation in the patterns of community involvement as women and people of color belong to different kinds of organizations than do White men. We see the career benefits that some of these community involvements confer. Those who participate in charitable organizations or the ABA are more likely to make partner in a succeeding wave.

The pro bono efforts of lawyers also reveal divisions within the bar. Overall, the bar fails to meet the goal the ABA sets for the amount of time spent on pro bono matters per year. The total amount of time American lawyers spend on pro bono makes up only 1% of the total time lawyers spend on clients and thus falls far short of what is needed to redress the inequality in the provision of legal services or close the justice gap for underrepresented groups. But there are major differences in pro bono efforts across segments of the bar. Lawyers employed by business and government put in much lower levels of pro bono hours than do private sector lawyers. Within the private sector, we see two distinct practice segments that lead in providing pro bono service: solo and small-firm attorneys and attorneys working in large corporate law firms that have well-institutionalized pro bono programs. Pro bono efforts have career benefits as we find that those who do pro bono at wave 2 are more likely to have made partner by wave 3. Our qualitative interviews underscore the different ways in which pro bono service is connected to career advancement, with elite lawyers seeing pro bono as a form of noblesse obliges while some lawyers in the personal client sphere do pro bono to build their reputation and practice and others consider it a necessary aspect of doing favors for less resourceful clients.

In all three arenas of the public roles of lawyers, we see the dualities of public service and professional gain. Lawyers are liberals but overwhelmingly represent business interests. Lawyers are active members of community organizations but belong to different organizations depending on their race and gender. Lawyers and law firms pay lip service to and often engage in pro bono service, yet pro bono does not come close to making up the justice gap that characterizes the American legal system. Participation in community and professional organizations and pro bono service pays off in higher rates of partnership, but it is apparent that these payoffs occur less frequently for women and people of color.

These are the dualities that were very much on display in our opening story of elite law student protests at Paul Weiss. Those students or their peers will start their careers at Paul Weiss or other elite law firms. They will continue to embrace liberal politics, but they will reap the rewards of representing powerful corporations. They will engage in pro bono programs that will help legitimate the large law firms in which they work and satisfy their own passion for serving justice. Their work and careers are thus supporting the dual character of the American legal profession, a profession that espouses equal justice but sustains a legal system built on market-based inequalities.

Lawyers' Satisfaction and the Making of Lawyers' Careers

WITH IOANA SENDROIU

Job satisfaction often serves as a lightning rod for researchers and observers of the legal profession. It is often taken as a measure of the desirability, health, and worth of the profession, and, for many, seeking job satisfaction is as important a career goal as is seeking a high income, while inequality in job satisfaction may be as important a marker as inequality in earnings is. The distribution of job satisfaction can tell us far more than whether law is a worthy career because job satisfaction is a reflection and expression of an individual's response to his or her circumstances. It is constructed within a context of possibilities, circumstances, aspirations, and expectations. As a result, it provides a unique and complex window into the lives of lawyers and the structure of the legal profession.

This chapter offers a unique analysis of the evolution of job satisfaction over the course of lawyers' careers and the relationship of satisfaction to the social hierarchies of law. It not only counters reports about widespread dissatisfaction among lawyers but also provides a multivariate examination of the workplace circumstances that affect job satisfaction and the role that satisfaction plays in job change. We draw on the in-depth interviews to illustrate the trade-offs that women make to achieve a satisfying work/life balance. Our discussions with lawyers about the worth of their law degree reflect their personal values and morality and thus their broader social class aspirations and expectations.

Patterns of Satisfaction: Descriptive Results

At all waves, respondents were asked whether they were satisfied with their decision to become a lawyer (scores ranging from 1 to 5, i.e., from extremely

TABLE 14.1 Respondents who are moderately or
extremely satisfied with their decision to become a
lawyer by gender and race/ethnicity (%)

	Wave 1	Wave 2	Wave 3
Gender			
Woman	76.5	75.3	75.7
Man	80.5	78.5	79.4
χ^2	4.4*	2.8	4.0*
Race/ethnicity			
African American	85.2	74.9	78.4
Latinx	77.7	82.0	84.7
Native American	77.1	72.2	77.8
Asian American	75.3	76.8	75.4
White	78.2	76.8	76.8
Other race/ethnicity	90.0	70.0	83.3
χ^2	6.1	3.8	6.7
Total (N)	1,869	1,951	2,029

* $p \leq .05$.

dissatisfied to extremely satisfied). Satisfaction is generally quite high, just below 4 for all three waves, corresponding to "moderately satisfied." Satisfaction scores are strongly correlated across waves: $r = .47$ between wave 1 and wave 2 and .59 between wave 2 and wave 3. While these are relatively high correlations, they indicate that satisfaction levels are not merely a reflection of individual dispositions.

Table 14.1 presents the percentage of respondents indicating that they were "moderately" or "extremely" satisfied with their decision to become a lawyer, broken down by wave, gender, and race/ethnicity. Overall, about 78% of the sample are moderately or extremely satisfied at each wave. We see that men are consistently more satisfied with the decision to become a lawyer, while the effects of race are inconsistent across the waves and not statistically significantly different. Respondents in the other race/ethnicity category and African Americans have the highest satisfaction with the decision to become a lawyer at wave 2, while Latinx have the highest satisfaction in waves 2 and 3. These are striking results given what we observed about the career disadvantages faced by women and people of color.

Alongside race and gender, law school attended creates some of the strongest lines of demarcation in the legal profession and, as we saw in chapter 4, is strongly correlated with social class. Some commentators suggest that potential law students should pursue a legal career only if they gain entry to a relatively selective law school, one that offers access to higher-paying positions (Tamanaha 2012). At least with respect to career satisfaction, figure 14.1

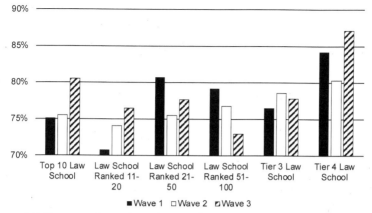

FIGURE 14.1. Percentage of respondents who are moderately or extremely satisfied with their decision to become a lawyer by law school ranking and wave

rebuts that assertion. There, we see interesting patterns over time. The proportion of graduates from schools ranked from 1 to 10 and from 11 to 20 who are moderately to extremely satisfied with their decision to become a lawyer increases dramatically across waves, while the proportion of graduates of schools ranked from 21 to 50 and from 51 to 100 decreases between wave 1 and wave 3. Interestingly, graduates of tier 3 and tier 4 schools also become more likely to express career satisfaction by wave 3, and tier 4 graduates report the highest levels of satisfaction at all three waves. These findings add important complexity to conceptions of job satisfaction. As we saw in chapters 3 and 4, the graduates of top-20 law schools and the graduates of tier 4 law schools have very different career trajectories. Top-20 graduates predominantly start in large law firms and then either move up in those firms or move to smaller firms, business, or the federal government. As they make these moves, they become more satisfied. The graduates of tier 4 law schools predominantly work in small law firms, state government, or businesses where they often are not practicing law. From the outset, and over the course of waves, they report satisfaction with becoming a lawyer, suggesting that they appreciated the opportunity set offered by a law degree. The graduates of law schools that fall between the top 20 and tier 4 appear to have started their careers with more promise than they realized by wave 3. These patterns of change in satisfaction across status categories of law schools correspond to the analyses of satisfaction by law school rank based on wave 1 data presented by Dinovitzer and Garth (2007). They found that elite graduates are more reserved in expressions of satisfaction at wave 1 both because their comparison group is other elites who are pursuing careers in investment banking and because they are

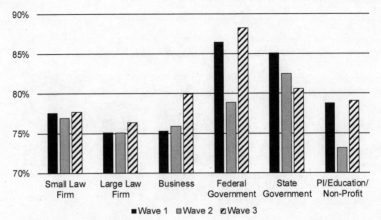

FIGURE 14.2. Percentage of respondents who are moderately or extremely satisfied with their decision
to become a lawyer by practice setting and wave

experiencing the intense work demands of being an associate in a large law firm. They found that tier 4 graduates are the happiest because they hail from more modest social backgrounds and their alternative career is running their own business or working in a nonprofessional job.

In figure 14.2, we display career satisfaction by practice setting by wave. The dominant feature of the figure is that satisfaction levels are high across all practice settings and all waves. The lowest but still high satisfaction levels are in large law firms and business at wave 1. The highest levels are for federal government attorneys at waves 1 and 3, levels followed closely by those of state government attorneys at all three waves.

In addition to the measure of satisfaction with the decision to become a lawyer, respondents were also asked a battery of 16 more specific satisfaction questions. These dimensions of satisfaction span from satisfaction with compensation and levels of responsibility to satisfaction with diversity and amount of travel. In their analysis of lawyer satisfaction based on AJD Project wave 1, Dinovitzer and Garth (2007) used principal components analysis to reduce the 16-item satisfaction battery to four factors. These four variable groupings are our focus across waves. The first represents job setting satisfaction and includes work/life balance, job security, control over work, and relationships with colleagues. The second is substance of work satisfaction, including satisfaction with work area, skill-building opportunities or tasks performed, level of responsibility, and perceived value of work to society. The third composite satisfaction score is social index satisfaction and includes pro bono opportunities and workplace diversity. Finally, power track satisfaction includes items regarding compensation, advancement opportunities, recognition for work, and performance evaluation. The four factors are only weakly correlated with each other and with the decision to become a lawyer at waves 1 and 2 but register stronger correlations among themselves and with the career decision variable at wave 3 (most correlation coefficients range between .4 and .6 and are statistically significant).

As we found in chapter 4, and as reported in earlier AJD Project publications (e.g., Dinovitzer et al. 2014), different practice settings offer different levels of satisfaction with these factors. Figure 14.3, which displays these differences at wave 3, reveals some patterns we might expect but also some surprises. Respondents working in public interest and nonprofit settings and in law firms score the highest on the social index, reflecting the social justice orientation of public interest work, the institutionalization of pro bono work in large law firms, and the freedom of solos and small-firm practitioners to devote time to pro bono work and to choose with whom they work. (Recall from chapter 13 that solos spend as many hours on pro bono work as large-firm attorneys do.) Reflecting the substantial attrition from law firms across waves, attorneys working in large and small firms at wave 3—or the relative few who remain in these settings—report the highest levels of satisfaction with the power track. Federal government attorneys report the highest levels of satisfaction with their job setting by far, followed by lawyers working in small firms and state government. Large-firm attorneys are the least satisfied with their job setting. In terms of satisfaction with the substance of their work, government and small-firm attorneys report high levels, bested only by lawyers working in public interest, nonprofits, and education institutions. Lawyers

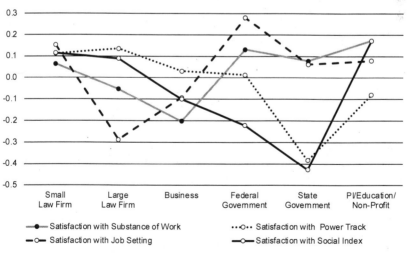

FIGURE 14.3. Mean scores for job satisfaction factors by wave 3 practice setting

working in state government report the lowest levels of satisfaction with both the power track and social index, presumably because of their relatively low pay and because they are prevented from doing pro bono work. These results make apparent that different practice settings offer different kinds of satisfactions.

Patterns of Satisfaction: Multivariate Results

While these bivariate patterns are very suggestive, we require multivariate analysis to understand these relationships fully. In multivariate analyses, we controlled for gender, race, law school rank, relationship status, and education debt so that we might isolate the effects of experiences at work on career satisfaction.[1] Although we ran these models on each of the four factors as separate dependent variables, we focus on overall satisfaction with the decision to become a lawyer.

The multivariate models of career satisfaction by wave largely support the bivariate patterns we discussed above, with some important added findings. In all waves of the study, African Americans are significantly more satisfied than are Whites. Latinx also are statistically more satisfied than are Whites at waves 2 and 3. While the bivariate results showed a relationship between law school selectivity and satisfaction, here we find only a significant difference in the contrast between tier 4 law school graduates and top-10 law school graduates. Tier 4 graduates are more satisfied than are their elite counterparts at every wave. We also find that job settings matter: federal and state government attorneys report statistically significantly higher satisfaction levels than does the reference category of solo and small-firm (fewer than 100 lawyers) attorneys. Working in the public interest sector and in business also results in significantly higher levels of satisfaction (compared to solo and small firms), but only in later waves as more lawyers move into these settings.

Economic factors prove significant in the multivariate models. Earnings has a significant positive relationship to satisfaction at waves 1 and 2 but becomes nonsignificant at wave 3. Higher levels of education debt significantly reduce satisfaction, all else equal, which is significant in waves 1 and 3.

Conditions of work shape levels of satisfaction, but the results are inconsistent. Hours worked significantly reduces satisfaction, but only at wave 2. Networking (operationalized as joining senior partners for meals or recreational activities) has positive effects on satisfaction, but it is significant only at wave 2. Experiencing discrimination in the workplace significantly reduces satisfaction at all three waves. This is particularly interesting because, while

African Americans report higher career satisfaction, it is African American women who also report the highest levels of discrimination (Nelson et al. 2019). Our results suggest that people can find satisfaction in their career choice even if their proximate environment is discriminatory. Practicing law (as opposed to not practicing) has significant positive effects at all three waves. Equity partners are significantly more satisfied than are others, but their numbers do not reach statistical significance until wave 3. Both measures of autonomy at work increase career satisfaction.

Turning to mentorship, we note that this was measured only at waves 2 and 3 and the question varied over time.[2] Consistent with previous research, we see that having more mentors is associated with higher satisfaction. At both wave 2 and wave 3, mentorship increases overall career satisfaction. We should note that, while we see the effects of mentorship while controlling the effects of other variables, it is important to ask about the mentors themselves. The career narratives revealed that getting the right kind of mentor was critical to success in law firms, business, and government. The narratives suggest that this is especially problematic for women and people of color.

These results reflect how the role of elite law school credentials in reproducing job satisfaction shifts over the course of careers. In early careers, law school attended is the most salient symbol of eliteness, and it translates directly into pecuniary and nonpecuniary rewards. By wave 3, after that form of capital has been transformed multiple times over and exchanged for practice settings, a book of business, networks, clients, spouses, children, houses, and vacations, it is somewhat more amorphous. In later careers, then, we no longer observe the direct translation of law school eliteness into various rewards, and instead practice settings and positions are the primary markers of differentiation. Still, as we have seen, the law school credential is important to achieving those positions even later in careers.

Our data also highlight the ways in which job satisfaction works in counterintuitive ways. Our research finds—as do many other studies—that individuals whom we would expect to have lower satisfaction, such as women and minorities, in fact express fairly high levels of satisfaction (Hull 1999; Markovic and Plickert 2019). Such seeming contradictions highlight that job satisfaction is produced in myriad ways: it is a response to proximate work conditions, but it is also a reflection of how expectations and aspirations align with reality. And, of course, job satisfaction can also be produced as a virtue of necessity, a concept on which Dinovitzer and Garth (2007) rely to explain the relatively high levels of satisfaction among lower-tier law school graduates in their early careers.

Probing the Changing Meaning of Satisfaction

Our interview data provide a unique opportunity for understanding how job satisfaction is produced. The interviews with two women—Marcia and Wendy—discussed below exemplify the changing circumstances of careers and career goals and the ways in which these can then produce different forms of satisfaction and dissatisfaction. In particular, these stories highlight the careers of two women who worked in law firms and sought out partnership positions. Each encountered different obstacles along the way so that by their later careers we hear them expressing a satisfaction with their work/life balance that was never expressed at an earlier point in time. A focus on lifestyle satisfaction sometimes emerges only after lawyers face blocked opportunities for partnership.

Marcia is a graduate of a midwestern state law school who worked in litigation for a regional firm in a major market. Her husband, a graduate of the same law school, worked in an elite law firm. She was thinking of children and as an associate "vocal" about having the possibility of reduced hours. A partner with whom she had discussed this formed a committee—on which she served—to create a policy: "We basically drafted an . . . arrangement that, ultimately, I was not happy with, but it was better than nothing." The policy allowed reduction from 2,000 hours to 1,600 hours for a two-year period. She knew that it would be a problem for her. She was then a sixth-year associate for partnership purposes, which was awarded at nine years. She had her son in 2006, and she took an extra month off because of postpartum issues. She went back after four months. She wanted to work 60% to stay home two days a week, but the firm said the policy was 80% if she wanted to stay on the partnership track. "I was the first person to ever use the policy," she said, "the policy that I knew was gonna do this to me, and they said, 'You go 60%, then you stall in partnership.'" She agreed even though it meant she was in "limbo land." Her first review—in December 2007—was conducted by a demanding senior male partner and a female partner who had said, "Either you're a mother, or you're a lawyer. What's your priority?" Marcia had not had a secretary since coming back from maternity leave. She was doing the work, the clients loved her, but her "files were a mess." Consequently: "They lit out at me in my review." Essentially, they argued that she should work more hours: "You need to spend more time on your filing." She had already billed 250 hours over her requirement, and she was miserable, working five days a week, and pumping milk at work, where they would not put a lock on her door. She decided she had had enough. She asked a supportive partner, who had spoken against the negative review, if she could do contract work for him: "I wrote up the proposal; he pitched it. [The firm's partners] were very, very unhappy." In fact: "They really had hoped that I would come back onboard and go toward partnership." Her response was: "What is it to be a partner in a firm and be miserable and hate your life and have your kids prefer the nanny?" She saw the decision as a death knell for her career but also the "best move [she] ever made."

Wendy was also committed to trying to pursue a partnership position after returning from a maternity leave. She said: "Well, . . . when I was on leave, I . . . thought about this a lot, and I figured . . . I have to come back and at least try for partnership." She planned to attend "a fifth-year training coming up that tells you, OK, this is what you need to start doing . . . if you're going to be on partnership track": "Everybody flies out to this year it's in San Francisco, and a bunch of presentations . . . about billing or business development." At the time of the second interview, she had returned from her second maternity leave. Her perception was that she had slowed: "It has been eight years; most firms have an eight-year track. . . . I've been held back a year . . . well, they say due to the structure of my department . . . but also because . . . I've taken leave and I've been reduced schedule. . . . So I'm . . . on a slower track generally."

These stories show the script of a preference for work/life balance and a choice of family over work being produced in response to the workplace. Marcia, for example, wanted to work with her firm to find a way to make her commitment to the partner track succeed under difficult conditions that pitted work against family ("Either you're a mother, or you're a lawyer"). Ultimately, circumstances led her to value her children over her career. We heard similar stories from many of the women we interviewed in depth.

THE LAW DEGREE AS AN INVESTMENT

With law and lawyers playing a central role in the state and the economy, it is not surprising that many—even among its own ranks—seek to challenge law's position by questioning its value (Garth 2013). Thus, in addition to a purported crisis in satisfaction, many commentators have seen a questioning of the value of a law degree itself. As with job satisfaction, considerations of the value of law school involve more than economic factors. In this section, we move beyond the strictly financial debates about the value of the law degree and instead examine how lawyers think about a career in law as having been a good investment and whether they would still go to law school if they could do it all over again. Of course, relative success will always shape assessments, but here we can observe reflections on the trade-offs made and challenges faced in order for law to have been a worthwhile investment. And so it can be true that people can think that law was a good investment and would do it again but at the same time hope for recognition that it was a difficult pathway. When lawyers reflect on the totality of their careers, which includes the sacrifices and hard work that underwrote their success, this inevitably raises the question of worth, values, and morality.

We begin by considering responses from wave 3 of the survey, in which respondents were asked to rate their agreement with these items on a scale of 1 (strongly disagree) to 7 (strongly agree). Respondents tended to be positive in their assessments of the value of a law degree, with a mean score of 5.6, and somewhat lower on their responses to the question about going to law school again, with a mean score of 5.0. The first, of course, is a more direct reflection of their personal success, while the second is the result of their lived experience watching many succeed even without a law degree—and, indeed, for the 20% or so who no longer practice law, a reflection of their own careers.

To probe the determinants of these attitudes, we analyzed a pair of OLS regression models predicting whether respondents consider law school to be a good investment and whether they would still go to law school.[3] We find remarkably similar patterns across the two models. Perhaps not surprisingly, the results show the general pattern that markers of career success and having experienced support result in positive assessments of the value of a law degree. Economic factors loom large here as a higher income and less education debt increase the rating of the value of a law degree. Networking also has significant positive effects on both dependent variables. Process autonomy, satisfaction with the work setting, and satisfaction with work substance also have significant positive effects. As with satisfaction, we find that African Americans are more positive about getting a law degree and would do it again. But experiencing discrimination has negative effects on these valuations.

MORAL BOUNDARIES: COMPETITION, AMBITION, AND HARD WORK IN LAWYERS' CAREERS

While the survey data suggest a fairly straightforward interpretation of how respondents assess the value of their legal careers, our interview data include discussions with respondents about whether they would recommend law school to their children and/or others more generally. In the process of giving this advice, our respondents reflected on their careers more holistically, with many remembering how hard they have worked and exposing a desire to shield their children from a difficult life. Notably, many of these interviews also took place at the height of the crisis rhetoric, when questions about the value of a law degree were ubiquitous.

Michèle Lamont's (1992) work on professionals and managers provides unique traction in understanding the accounts of our interviewees. It highlights the importance of moral character in understanding people's descriptions of their working lives. For American professionals, Lamont (1992, 85) explains, it is not sufficient to be socioeconomically successful. It is also necessary to demonstrate that this success was the result of ambition, a strong work ethic, and competition. In many of the responses reported below, these character traits are front and center as respondents describe the challenges, sacrifices, and uncertainty involved in building their careers:

> I don't regret going to law school, I'm glad to have that legal education, but coming out with the amount of debt you have at the end of the day and what I do . . . it's hard. Unless you put in the work I think the perception, general perception of attorneys is they're rich, they live in big houses and drive fancy cars, and not at all. I mean most of us aren't. Most of us aren't going to be that way practicing residential real estate law in [his midwestern state]. (Jackson, White man, tier 3 law school, solo practitioner)

When Stewart—an African American man we met in several earlier chapters who went to a law school ranked from 11 to 20 and works in state government—was asked what he advises people considering going to law school, he responded: "Well in [his midwestern city in a regional market] they are graduating over and over again, and they're not getting jobs, and that is a really hard, hard thing. And so even my daughter I caution her against going to law school because of that."

In part reflecting the crisis rhetoric, and in part reflecting his own experience, Austin—a Latino who attended a law school ranked from 11 to 20 and is now an equity partner in a large law firm of 251 or more attorneys—noted the importance of attending a highly ranked school and the level of commitment that is required to have a lucrative and satisfying career as a lawyer. Despite the focus on credentials, his comments—like the others—serve to highlight the hard work that it takes to succeed in the legal profession:

> If he [his son] came to me, it would depend on a variety of things. One is it would depend on how good his grades were. To me if you go to a law school . . . if you're able to get into the top law schools, great. If you're able to get into the best law school or two in your state, fine. But after that you're going to struggle, it's going to be very difficult, and so if it's just something you just love and you're willing to do it for $50,000 a year then great. But this notion of the pot of gold at the end of the rainbow is there for a very select few, and, if you're not in those [law school] categories, it's very difficult to get there. And then I think it would also depend on what he wants to do with life. If he's very into sort of

recreation and outside activities and things like that, you're going to have to get rid of those for a number of years at least.

Like Austin, Rufus, whom we met in chapter 6, also made equity partner in a large firm of 251 or more lawyers. While privileged as a White man who graduated from a top-10 law school, his journey to this apex was not straightforward. The seemingly guaranteed path to equity partnership in his first firm was derailed by the recession, and it took a series of lateral moves to get his career back on track. When asked whether he would advise others to go to law school, he conveyed satisfaction with his own decision to become a lawyer, which he connected to his enjoyment of law school and his eventual promotion to partnership. However, he also reflected on the challenges he encountered along the way:

> I think it depends on what they're looking for. You know I certainly am happy with my choice. I had a great time at [his law school]. I thought it was a great school, and it certainly, my career isn't finished yet certainly at all, but in terms of you know the story so far it definitely had some twists and turns I wasn't expecting, but I sort of ultimately ended up where I had hoped to end up. It's not for everybody, I'll put it that way.

Despite being among the select few respondents who attained an equity partnership, Rufus expressed that he would not want his child to follow in his footsteps because of the vast amount of support and sacrifice that was required to achieve this benchmark of success. When reflecting on whether he would recommend law school to his son, he described the burden that his career had placed not only on he himself but also on his family, and he underscored the importance of having a supportive spouse at home for achieving a successful career in a law firm:

> Maybe the better question would be would I want my child to go to law school, and the answer would be no. . . . Because this is a great way to make a decent living, but you work for every penny. I mean you really work hard for every penny, and so I think a lot of people don't realize that, and they don't realize how hard we work. . . . So, if I was choosing for my children, I wouldn't have them be in a profession that requires you to work this hard. . . . Not that I don't want them to work hard, but there's like working hard, and then there's working so hard that it's affecting your health and . . . your social life. I lucked out. I met a woman who is ridiculously understanding, and I met her when I was like a second-year associate, and we're still together, but that doesn't happen for everyone, and it can be really hard on relationships.

In contrast to Rufus, Kareem—a South Asian tier 3 law school graduate whom we met in chapter 6—expressed enthusiasm and certainty when asked whether he would recommend law school: "I for sure tell them to [go to law school]. I think [law is] a great field. . . . I really enjoy it. I'm happy I did it." Kareem's family immigrated to the United States from India when he was a young child. He worked for a series of increasingly larger and more elite law firms before deploying his elite firm credentials and connections to develop an intellectual property practice serving the Indo-Pakistani entrepreneurial community in the Bay Area. During law school and his early career, mentors encouraged him to specialize in intellectual property because it was a lucrative field and complemented his undergraduate training in biology. Over the course of his career, he learned that his practice area was not recession proof, and he advised finding a specialization that provided a steady flow of work: "I'm telling my son to be a tax attorney . . . because, I mean, taxes, they are always going to tax you. . . . It's a great little practice. . . . It's a good field. . . . So, yeah, absolutely." He also praised the flexibility of a law degree: "You know, even if you don't use it, it's a great degree to have." Kareem's story and law school advice highlight the importance of both capital assets and strategy in building satisfying careers.

In the advice they offer, these quotes reveal respondents' priorities for their children. They want their children to enjoy the benefits that their hard work secured for them: to work hard but not too hard, to be flexible, and to be interested in their work. This resonates with Lamont's (1992, 168) finding that the child-rearing values of the "established" (third-generation) professional class stress "self-actualization, intellectual curiosity, and aesthetic pursuit over more material and practical goals." Respondents also highlighted the demands of a career in law (e.g., long hours, hard work, constant availability). Both men and women drew on this theme in articulating their responses, suggesting that long hours and the work-family conflict associated with lawyers' careers are not only women's issues (Ely et al. 2014; Padavic et al. 2020).

Some respondents' hesitancy to recommend law as a career is decoupled from their own satisfaction and instead demonstrates the many—sometimes opposing—considerations involved in assessing the desirability of and satisfaction to be derived from a career in law, including value to society, professional ethics, and financial security:

> You know, my own daughter, would I want her to be a lawyer? The answer is no. I would rather her be a doctor or an engineer. Not because I don't honor the profession and I don't think she would be a wonderful lawyer. I just think that I, myself, the practice of law is only as good as the state in which I'm in. I don't have a value to the world at large. Whereas, if my daughter were to be a doctor or engineer, she can contribute to society on a much larger level than I do. (Jacob, White man, tier 4 law school, solo practitioner)

The in-depth interviews reveal some of the complexity underlying our high satisfaction statistics. Lawyers recognize (and perhaps even admire) the challenges they faced in the pursuit of career satisfaction. They draw clear moral boundaries that highlight the lauded features of the professional class: ambition, hard work, and competitiveness.

The Effects of Satisfaction

INTENT TO LEAVE AND JOB CHANGES

As we noted in chapter 2, it is widely assumed that lawyers now change jobs far more often than was the case in the golden age of law firms. Yet we possess relatively little systematic data on the number of job changes in the profession outside the Chicago lawyer studies of the 1970s and 1990s (see Heinz and Laumann 1982; and Heinz et al. 2005). Heinz et al. (2005, 141) found for both the 1975 and the 1995 surveys that lawyers averaged 2.5 jobs and that, for those in practice fewer than 20 years, the average was 1.6 moves. As we saw in previous chapters, we find a higher rate of job changes in the AJD Project cohort even though we are looking at only the first 12 years of respondents' careers. On average, AJD Project lawyers have had between two and three employers by wave 3: 16% have one, 30% have two, 25% have three, 16% have four, and 13% have five or more, for an average of 2.8 jobs. Given the new structure of lawyers' careers—in which first jobs (especially in large law firms) serve as an apprenticeship—it is not surprising to find the highest rates of mobility in early careers. Almost 50% of lawyers change[4] employers between wave 1 and wave 2, but the rate remains relatively high in succeeding waves: 38% between waves 2 and 3 and 39% between wave 3 and the 2019 web searches. To put things in historical perspective, these are much higher rates of changing employers than have been found in earlier studies, but they may be lower than what is reported in the popular media. It is important to note, however, that these data reflect changes in employers[5] only and do not account for other employment events, including spells of unemployment, leaves, and position changes within employing organizations.

Kay et al. (2016, 2013) have analyzed patterns of attrition in Canadian law firms. They find that women have higher rates of attrition than do men owing in part to discriminatory experiences in the workplace and inflexibility of work demands. Interestingly, the attrition of women continues after they make partner and is not associated with taking parental leave.

Lacking information on actual job changes, we often analyze intent to leave as a measure of commitment to or satisfaction with an employer (Dinovitzer

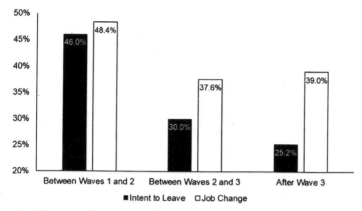

FIGURE 14.4. Percentage of respondents who intend to leave their jobs and who actually change jobs by wave

and Garth 2007; Wilkins et al. 2015). Here, we possess direct measures of both intent and behavior, which affords us more insight into the plans and adaptive behaviors of lawyers than previous research allowed. The relationship between expressed intention and behavior is a fundamental question in several spheres of social action, whether we are examining choices people make in intimate relationships (Swidler 2001), how expressed commitment to equal opportunity in employment practices compares to the actual hiring decisions of employers (Pager 2007; Pager and Quillian 2005; Quillian et al. 2017), or how the attitudes of Whites about African Americans contrast with Whites' decisions about the racial composition of the neighborhoods in which they choose to live (Quillian and Pager 2001; Sampson and Raudenbush 2004).

Figure 14.4 reveals that many fewer lawyers say they intend to change employers than actually do, and the gap between intent and movement grows across waves. At wave 1, some 46% of respondents plan to leave their employer within three years, and almost half change employers by wave 2. By wave 2, the figure for those changing drops dramatically, to 30%. A significantly larger proportion, 38%, actually change employers by wave 3. At wave 3, only a quarter of respondents plan to leave, but an even greater percentage, 39%, did so by 2019. Through a combination of being pushed out and pursuing other opportunities, lawyers move far more often than they expect from wave 2 on. This suggests that intentions to change jobs are likely tapping into something far more amorphous than plans for the future.

Intent to move and actual moves reflect the opportunities and adaptations that differently selective law schools present to their graduates. Figure 14.5 presents these data by law school rank and wave. Consistent with Dinovitzer and Garth's (2007) work on wave 1 data, we see that the graduates of top-10

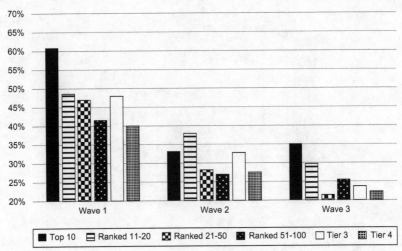

FIGURE 14.5A. Percentage of respondents who intend to leave their jobs by law school rank and wave

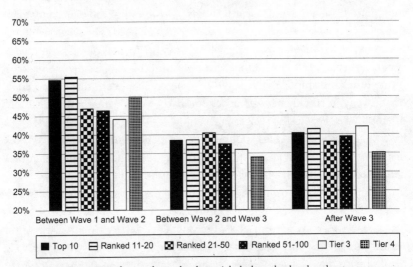

FIGURE 14.5B. Percentage of respondents who change jobs by law school rank and wave

law schools are the most likely to say they plan to move, and these plans are borne out by the movement of more than half of top-10 and top-20 law school graduates to different employers between wave 1 and wave 2. Yet, by wave 2, the percentage of top-10 graduates who intend to move has dropped by almost half, from 61% to 33%, reflecting perhaps a better match between their expectations and their reality. This is perhaps especially true for the many who began in large law firms simply because they were collecting an important credential and understood their first positions to be temporary.

At the opposite end of the status spectrum, tier 4 graduates at every wave are the least likely to say they intend to change jobs and the least likely actually to change jobs between wave 2 and wave 3 and after wave 3. This pattern rebuts the notion that the careers of lower-status graduates are more subject to change than are the careers of graduates from higher-ranked law schools.

These patterns vary by practice setting in some expected and some surprising ways. Here, we highlight the dominant trends. Figure 14.6 shows that jobs in business and in large law firms continue to see relatively high levels

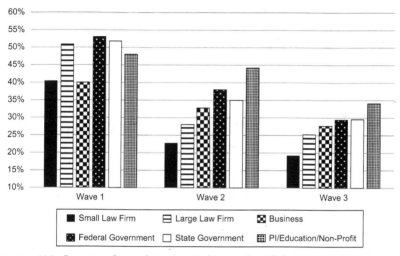

FIGURE 14.6A. Percentage of respondents who intend to leave their jobs by practice setting and wave

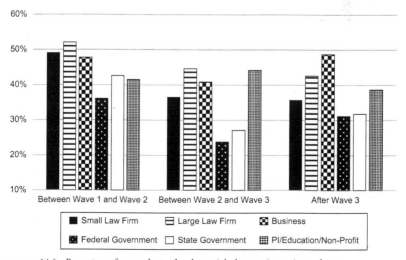

FIGURE 14.6B. Percentage of respondents who change jobs by practice setting and wave

of movement well into midcareer, which marks a significant change from the golden age for large law firm attorneys and even higher rates of mobility for lawyers in business. Movement is not limited to the private sector, however, with public interest lawyers also experiencing consistently high rates of job change intentions and actual mobility.

Patterns of intention to move and actual moves are gendered particularly at the start of lawyers' careers.[6] At wave 1, more women (60%) than men (just under 50%) expect to be leaving their employer. It is also meaningful that at wave 3 more women than men expect to be changing jobs. As our data suggest, job outcomes for women are generally less successful than they are for men, and these expressions of expected mobility likely reflect that dissatisfaction.

These patterns play out differently by race and ethnicity as well.[7] Most groups follow the general pattern for the sample of changing employers at higher rates than they say they intend. Most notable are Native Americans, who move at substantially higher rates than their intentions would predict and, indeed, have the highest rates of job changes at all three points of transition. At all three transitions, African Americans are the most likely to report an intention to move. And, indeed, African Americans experience high levels of actual job mobility after waves 1 and 2, though at slightly lower rates than we would predict given their intentions.

MULTIVARIATE ANALYSIS OF INTENT TO LEAVE AND JOB CHANGES

We again turn to multivariate analyses to examine the relative impact of satisfaction and other variables on intent to move and actual moves. For these models, we include a simplified suite of control variables.[8] Our goal across these analyses is to focus on the relationships among satisfaction with the decision to become a lawyer, intent to leave, and job mobility.[9]

Across all three waves, logistic regression models demonstrate that satisfaction is closely related to wanting to leave one's job. More specifically, higher satisfaction with the decision to become a lawyer is a consistent predictor of wanting to stay in one's workplace. An equally important finding is that perceptions of discrimination significantly increase the intent to leave one's job, controlling for all other factors. Also notable is that, in contrast to the suggestive bivariate findings, gender is not a significant predictor of intent to move, while race appears to be significant in early careers, with White respondents significantly less likely than are African Americans and Latinx to be thinking of leaving their jobs at wave 1.

Consistent with Dinovitzer and Garth's (2007) argument that higher-status law degrees increase mobility intentions, we see that those coming from top law schools were more likely to intend to leave their jobs. This pattern holds at the start of lawyers' careers (at wave 1) and at wave 3. As we noted above, at the start of their careers, many top-tier law school graduates obtain positions (especially in large law firms) simply because they are accumulating capital. By wave 3, job mobility intentions may reflect disappointment with one's outcomes, the realization that one may have better mobility elsewhere, or a lack of fit.

Our data also highlight the importance of social embeddedness, which appears to matter more at midcareer and later: measures of networking and mentoring (at wave 2 only) both significantly reduce job mobility intentions. This is very much in harmony with other work on the AJD study highlighting the importance of "finding the love" in lawyers' careers (e.g., Garth and Sterling 2009) and the analysis of the role of race in law firm exits and promotions offered in chapter 10. We find varying effects for autonomy across the waves, but, in all instances, it is a positive resource that reduces mobility intentions. Finally, it is not surprising that status matters: making partner significantly reduces mobility intentions. Yet we find no relationship between earnings and intent to move.

While satisfaction is strongly associated with intent to leave, its role in prompting job turnover among lawyers is unknown. Here, we predict job changes between wave 1 and wave 2, between wave 2 and wave 3, and after wave 3. These binary variables do not distinguish between voluntary and involuntary mobility, so the implications of our models are suggestive rather than definitive. Nonetheless, they allow us to better complete the picture of how satisfaction shapes how lawyers navigate their careers. The models we discuss here have the same independent variables as those discussed above, where we predict mobility intent. We introduce satisfaction with the decision to become a lawyer in a stepwise fashion and add a third step where we control for intent to leave.

The findings establish a strong empirical connection between intent to move and actual mobility. In each wave, intent to move is a positive and significant predictor of actual mobility. On the other hand, job satisfaction acts as a buffer: at wave 1, and partially at wave 2, career satisfaction reduces turnover. By waves 2 and 3, job changes are unrelated to job satisfaction, a decoupling that suggests that moves in later careers might be more about opportunities, positioning, and upward career mobility than about finding fit.

The models are also demonstrating that what drives job turnover varies by career stage. Between wave 1 and wave 2, many lawyers left law firms for business, which may be why we do not see a specific effect for large law firms, why there is no independent effect for top law school graduates, and even why there is no effect for networking. Simply put, everyone was moving (except for those working in the federal government), and moves were not necessarily happening because of negative conditions in the firm. They were happening because these were first jobs—apprenticeships of a sort. People of color were, however, more likely to change jobs after wave 1 than were Whites, with all controls in the model. This too is consistent with what we reported in chapter 10.

After wave 2 the patterns are quite similar, and, here, we see a connection to the patterns in the career sequences and the bifurcation in the career patterns of lawyers. On the one hand, we observe job changes related to precarity: lawyers who are practicing law are significantly less likely to experience a job change (before we control for intentions). In other words, lawyers who leave the practice of law change jobs as they shift the direction of their careers. We also see higher turnover for non-Whites, which again suggests an experience of lack of fit at the start of their careers. On the other hand, income is positive and significant, which may suggest that high-earning lawyers are also changing jobs, perhaps as they search for more lucrative positions and are seeking promotions and partnerships.

Taken together, the models for job changes are also instructive in that they demonstrate the difference between intent to move and actual moves: for example, discrimination is a significant predictor of intent to leave but not of actual mobility. This is important because negative experiences in the workplace cannot always translate into action, especially if one's options are limited. In this way, job mobility intentions are a more accurate reflection of lawyers' experiences than are actual changes. And, thus, evidence of turnover is not necessarily an indicator of dissatisfaction, and churn is not necessarily negative. Changes can signal upward mobility, while lack of change can signal being trapped in one's position. This is certainly the case with a number of the women we interviewed who are working in nonequity positions in large law firms. As we saw in the career narratives, lawyers plan their career moves but cannot see around every corner and often make changes they did not anticipate. The structures of law school status, practice setting, workplace experience, gender, and race shape the next step in a career path but are not completely determinative.

SATISFACTION, DEPRESSION, AND GENDER

Research suggests that job satisfaction (or dissatisfaction) may be a catalyst for negative mental health outcomes. This is especially true for women. Hagan and Kay (2007) use a sample of Toronto lawyers to argue for a gendered relationship between mental health and satisfaction. Taking on the puzzle of women facing less desirable working conditions but reporting levels of satisfaction similar to those of their male peers, a pattern echoed in the findings we presented above, they show that women *internalize* their career dissatisfaction, sometimes to the point that their mental health is affected.

Plickert et al. (2017) build on this research by demonstrating how lawyers' mental health is conditioned by career stage and the life course, with mental health outcomes improving over time as lawyers establish their careers. Job satisfaction has a particularly strong effect on depressive symptoms in early careers—which may be particularly stressful for young professionals—as do career commitment, authority, a sense of control in the workplace, and being married or in a cohabiting relationship. Net of these factors, however, women are slightly more likely than men are to report depressive symptoms, reflecting workplace constraints that uniquely burden women in their early careers. As Plickert et al. (2017, 31) suggest: "It is during the early years of building a career and investing in one's personal life (i.e., marriage/cohabitation and having children), a phase in which women face greater challenge in efforts to balance these two domains, that depressed feelings are more common and distinctively gendered." They go on to argue that the long hours culture of law firms and traditional law practice—coupled with inadequate accommodations for family responsibilities and cognitive bias from superiors who may doubt women's job and career commitment—may produce work/life conflict, which may in turn cause stress and mental health deterioration.

The AJD Project included measures of mental health at waves 2 and 3, specifically a seven-item version of the Center for Epidemiological Studies Depression Scale (Mirowsky and Ross 2003), which asks on how many days per week respondents reported a range of symptoms (which we summed and then averaged to produce a value out of 7). At wave 2, the depression score has an average of 1.12 days (SD = 1.29), while, at wave 3, the average is 1.23 days (SD = 1.43). Both scores are well below the standard cutoff for clinical depression, which, calculated as an average, would be roughly 2.28 days per week,[10] suggesting that our study population is not meaningfully depressed. At the same time, at wave 2, 404 individuals or almost 20% of the sample would qualify as clinically depressed, while, at wave 3, this increases to 487 respondents or roughly 24% of the sample.

Additional models (available on request) show a strong relationship between satisfaction and mental health at these waves. Depression is a consistent predictor of all our satisfaction variables. Meanwhile, satisfaction also

predicts depression. For example, at wave 3, overall satisfaction is a significant predictor of lower rates of depression. The relationship is thus bidirectional cross-sectionally. It is also bidirectional longitudinally, meaning that
satisfaction at wave 2 predicts mental health at wave 3 and that mental health
at wave 2 predicts satisfaction at wave 3.

We also briefly considered the gendered dimensions of the relationship
between mental health and satisfaction. In line with Hagan and Kay (2007),
Plickert et al. (2017), and the literature on gender and depression more generally, we find that female lawyers report higher depression scores at both
waves than do male lawyers (1.21 days vs. 1.02 days at wave 2, and 1.31 days
vs. 1.14 days at wave 3). We also find a significant interaction between gender
and depression when predicting overall satisfaction at wave 3, meaning that
women who are depressed report higher levels of satisfaction than do men
who are depressed. The result is that men and women appear to have similar
levels of satisfaction, but this is in part due to the different effects of depression on the two genders. Taken together, these complex patterns point to the
need for further study of lawyers' satisfaction and mental health.

Conclusion

This chapter has provided a unique analysis of the evolution of job satisfaction over the course of lawyers' careers and the relationship of satisfaction to
the social hierarchies of law. It counters reports about widespread dissatisfaction among lawyers, finding instead that three-quarters of young lawyers are
moderately or extremely satisfied with their decision to attend law school and,
if given the opportunity, would do so again. We have added considerable nu-
ance to the analysis of satisfaction, showing that workplace conditions (practice setting, support from mentors, partnership status, income, the experience of discrimination) shape levels of satisfaction. Satisfaction in turn affects
intention to change employers, but intention to change employers does not
necessarily correspond to actual job changes. Actual job changes can occur
despite expressed lack of intent to move, and job continuity can occur despite
expressed intent to move. Sometimes an opportunity comes up; sometimes
people get stuck in their jobs. Beneath the rosy overall numbers on satisfaction, the in-depth interviews exhibit the more complex views of lawyers about
the value of their law degrees: they achieved success through hard work. They
thus express the social position of their professional class. But they would not
necessarily wish it for their children.

While we have demonstrated the great variability in the career paths of
lawyers and in the positive and negative aspects of their work lives, we come

back to the basic finding that most lawyers in most practice contexts in different stages of their careers express high levels of satisfaction. We find these positive assessments among traditionally marginalized groups whose professional penalties we have documented throughout this book. Despite the vast and growing inequalities we observe in the careers of American lawyers, most lawyers find a path to satisfaction in their profession.

PART 6

Conclusion

Conclusion: Structure and Agency in the Making of Lawyers' Careers

This book has examined structure and agency in the making of lawyers' careers. Through a combination of survey data and in-depth interviews collected at three points in time that has been supplemented by more recent web-based data, we have developed a comprehensive profile of the careers of American lawyers. Lawyers' careers are heavily shaped by social and professional hierarchies and therefore largely reflect and reproduce larger structures of inequality in law and in society. Yet these hierarchies are not fully determinative of the course of individual careers, nor are the hierarchies static. Through the lens of lawyers' careers, we see contestation and competition among law schools, law firms, business entities, government agencies, bar associations, and bar regulatory authorities. Despite the dynamic character of these processes and the reinvention of careers in some contexts, we see surprising resilience in the social organization of the American legal profession and the inequalities it contains. As individual lawyers exercise agency in their decisions about where to go to law school, where to start their careers, what legal specialty to pursue, what mentors to seek out, and if and when to marry and have children, they are both making their careers and making the legal profession. While scholars have long recognized the segmented and highly stratified character of the American legal profession, this book reveals the growing inequality in the profession across segments of the bar and the enduring inequalities of race and gender that seem to be not just aberrations from an ideal but baked into the very structure of law firms and other legal employers. The implications for equal justice in society are profound. A profession granted a monopoly in our courts that pledges to purge discrimination within its ranks and aspires to level the playing field among repeat players and one-shotters in the legal system has made little progress toward these noble goals. We have found that most lawyers consider themselves to have successful careers despite these inequalities. Job satisfaction is just one mechanism among many that we uncover contributing to the ongoing reproduction of inequality in law.

In this concluding chapter, we lay out notable findings from the AJD Project to date and consider their implications for theory and policy.

Theory and Method in the Study of Lawyers' Careers

This book has sought to push the boundaries of social science research on the legal profession. While the chapters reflect the scholarly orientations of individual authors, a core theory of our effort has been the field sociology of Pierre Bourdieu and his students working on law (Bourdieu 1977, 1987; Dezalay and Garth 1996, 2010). We have examined the issue of change and continuity in the legal profession from this explicitly sociological perspective.

A central concept in Bourdieu's theory is social capital, wherein actors in a social field strive to obtain valued forms of social capital or to promote the value of the kind of capital they possess. An important dimension of this conception is that what is valued can change over time, sometimes in response to demands by those within or outside the profession. For example, demands for greater diversity in law schools and law firms gave a form of social capital to traditionally disadvantaged groups. Women and people of color who were admitted to the profession in response to these demands were then able to use their newfound access to increase the value of their once-discredited social capital and press for changes in the profession's norms and practices. But, as Bourdieu's framework underscores, hierarchy runs deep (and sometimes silent and deep), shaping the very perception of opportunities and inequalities. Habitus is Bourdieu's concept about how class, race, and gender become embodied in individuals. Because individuals have internalized certain values, certain styles of speech and dress, and consumption patterns, they often reproduce existing social systems even as they make what appear to be autonomous choices. Time and time again, we see them operate as autonomous entities. Yet they fit into and reproduce a given social system. And we see struggle play out as lawyers try to determine whether they fit in a particular work organization or type of practice. From the other side, we see the governing group in the legal workplace make judgments about who fits—at the entry level and over the course of career development.

These are the micro-level dynamics we saw play out in four narratives showcased in chapter 1: Alicia's rejection for partnership, Paula's decision to leave corporate law firm practice, James's seamless rise to partnership, and

Constance's lateral move into a law firm partnership that prized her specialty but probably would not have hired her as an entry-level associate or promoted her to equity partner. In this project, we have recorded and analyzed the stories of young lawyers in all major sectors of the profession. These narratives come together to display the operation of hierarchies in different contexts and how young lawyers reacted to and sometimes remade them. But our project also collected survey data from a large random sample of this cohort. We obtained data on the types of social capital with which they entered the profession and the types of social capital they accumulated over the course of the first 20 years of their careers. In the same way that Bourdieu (1984) made use of survey data to develop a theory of class and culture, we have been able to map the role of different kinds of social capital in the career trajectories of young lawyers.

As we described in chapter 1, the AJD Project employed an unusually strong research design. We constructed a large national sample of lawyers who passed the bar in the year 2000, stratified by the number of new lawyers in a jurisdiction, and then interviewed them three times—in 2003, in 2007, and in 2012. In 2019, we conducted web searches on the 2012 respondents and found basic career data on 85% of them. The original sample included a minority oversample to increase statistical power in examining the careers of people of color. In addition to the survey data, we conducted 216 in-depth interviews with selected members of the sample, interviewing several respondents three times. Longitudinal studies are rare in the social sciences but are especially powerful in the study of lawyers' careers, for they allow systematic analysis of how careers evolve over the life course. This design, coupled with in-depth career narratives, is well suited to a Bourdieusian examination of the interaction of structure and agency

Key Findings

THE SEQUENCES OF LAWYERS' CAREERS: INDIVIDUAL VARIATION MAKING UP STRUCTURAL PATTERNS

Using the technique of sequence analysis, which was developed to match strands of DNA, we examined the career moves of lawyers. From the thousands of career changes, we identified distinct clusters of career trajectories: large-firm starters, small- and midsize-firm starters, business, and the public sector. Within the broad clusters, we see trajectories that follow social scripts and reflect the accumulation of different kinds of social capital. Graduating from a top-20 law school is a requirement for most but not all lawyers who start in large law firms, but then experience in large corporate law firms typically is required to move into inside counsel positions in business organizations. This is part of what Dinovitzer and Garth (2020) refer to as the new role of the corporate law firm—rather than being an end in itself, experience in a large law firm becomes a credential for career moves into business or smaller law firms. While this reflects a shift in careers in corporate law firms, we find continuity with the past as the predominant group among equity partners in law firms comprises White men with wives at home. It is useful to focus on this pattern. At wave 3, there are 300 equity partners in our sample. Fifty-eight percent of this group are White men. Ninety-six percent of White male equity partners are married, 45% of whom have spouses who do not work. Married men of color who are equity partners, a much smaller group ($n = 32$), are slightly less likely to have spouses who do not work (40%). Married women who are equity partners—both women of color and White women—are much less likely to have spouses who are not working (9% for women of color, 13% for White women). Within sectors, we also find specific social scripts. State government careers less often begin from selective law schools, more often begin and remain in government, and contain larger percentages of women and people of color. In contrast, lawyers employed by the federal government often have elite law school credentials and worked for a period in large corporate law firms before making the move to government, often returning to become an equity partner in a law firm.

NARRATIVES OF LAWYERS' CAREERS

The sequence analysis invites us to infer the social scripts that guide lawyers along different paths. The narrative chapters of the book make these scripts explicit, offering them in the words of the lawyers themselves. Following the results of the sequence analysis, we organize these narratives by broad sector: larger law firms, solo and small firms, business, and the public sector. We again find considerable differentiation within each sector: the differences between careers in midsize and large law firms, solos who inhabit the personal client hemisphere in contrast to those in the business client sector, lawyers working in business who came in through the front door of a large corporate law firm compared to those who came in through the side door by working their way up in the business, and the differences between the relatively more elite tracks in public service and government (such as highly selective public interest organizations and the federal government) and positions in state government and nonprofits. As these lawyers articulate their career strategies, we hear their own assessment of their preferences, opportunities, and constraints. As we saw in the sequence analysis, where lawyers begin shapes their career paths going forward, so lawyers' opportunities and strategies at the beginning of their careers are significant. Yet almost all lawyers alter their plans and adapt to the changes in their opportunities and life preferences. To the individual lawyers, their careers may seem like the result of serendipity or individual choice. Yet we once again see that they follow distinct patterns.

RESILIENCE OF RACE, GENDER, AND CLASS INEQUALITY

Race

The legal profession is now more diverse in terms of race and ethnicity than it has been at any time in its history. Yet it remains racialized in its structure. Some one-third of the AJD Project cohort are people of color. This is in part a function of diversity outreach by law schools, efforts that continue to be under legal threat from claims of reverse discrimination and other laws that ban the use of race by public bodies. Within the profession, the leaders of the organized bar, inside counsel to business, and the managers of large law firms have issued calls to action to increase racial and ethnic diversity (see Headworth et al. 2016). Yet we continue to find significant evidence of racial inequality in lawyers' careers. In our analysis of job history data, which includes an extensive set of controls, we see that African Americans are far more likely to exit law firms and far less likely to make equity partner than are their White counterparts. We find that several contexts within the legal profession remain White spaces in which people of color are notably absent or positions of power are held primarily by White men.

Since the AJD Project cohort graduated from law school, there have been significant increases in law school tuition and, correspondingly, student debt levels. Even in 2000 there was a significant debt load for graduating law students. Only 13% of our sample graduated with no debt. The mean education debt among those with debt was $70,921. By wave 3, half the sample had paid off their debt, and the mean debt for those with debt was $56,163. But we found significant and previously unreported differences by law school status and race. While a slightly higher proportion of graduates of top-10 law schools had no debt compared to the sample overall (15% vs. 12%), those with debt led the sample with $88,511 in debt at graduation. By wave 3, this pattern had reversed. Graduates of top-10 law schools had the highest percentage with no debt (70%), and the mean among those with debt was $42,397, the lowest of all law school categories and well below the overall mean for the sample of $56,066. Also striking are the differences we observe in debt levels by race and ethnicity, specifically for African Americans. Over 40% of other racial and ethnic groups had paid off their debt by wave 3, but only 28% of African Americans had. The mean debt levels for African Americans barely declined from graduation to wave 3, from a mean of $76,029 at graduation to $72,201 at wave 3. Significant differences for African Americans remain in multivariate models that control for other predictors of debt, including law school selectivity. This pattern reflects the cumulative economic disadvantages African Americans face within the legal profession, as within society at large.

Gender

Although women make up roughly half of lawyers under the age of 40 and almost half of our AJD Project sample, they occupy a distinctly disadvantaged position in the profession, reflecting a structure that remains deeply gendered. They are far more likely to work part-time or be unemployed than are men. A job history analysis that parallels that of race finds that women also are far more likely to exit law firms and far less likely to make equity partner than are men, controlling for relevant variables. One of the shocking findings of the AJD Project has been the consistent gender gap in pay between men and women, starting from the first wave of the study. At wave 3, we see women making on average 80% of what men make (even when the sample is limited to full-time workers), with larger gaps in law firms and business and smaller gaps in government and nonprofits. A comprehensive analysis of earnings in this book that examined differences at different quantiles of the earnings distribution confirmed these patterns. Importantly, it showed that the earnings penalty was not derived from a motherhood penalty as women without children earned even less than did the mothers in our sample. The inference we drew was that these patterns reflected a masculine hegemony in which patriarchal values devalued women's work, even that of women who did not have children, while it awarded a fatherhood premium to men.

Class

American lawyers tend to have parents who are professionals or managers rather than members of the working class. This pattern holds in the AJD Project sample, although African Americans and Latinx are more likely to come from lower socioeconomic origins than are Asian Americans and Whites. Class is a fundamental, if somewhat invisible, determinant of lawyers' career trajectories. In our statistical analyses, we find that social class (measured as parents' education and occupation) shapes the schools that lawyers attend, both at the undergraduate level and at the law school level. There is a linear relationship between occupational status of AJD Project parents and the selectivity of the law schools their children attend. Class becomes invisible in statistical models that include law school selectivity as the more proximate variable of law school renders social background variables insignificant. The model suggests that an apparent meritocracy is at work through the influence of law school status on career paths. Yet we should note that no one has ever determined whether graduates of select law schools are objectively better lawyers than are those who graduate from less select law schools. While selectivity is a proxy for some things that are arguably connected to being a good lawyer (like intelligence and hard work), other factors like grit, common sense, and empathy may not correlate with selectivity. Yet law school selectivity has a profound influence on where lawyers begin their careers, which in turn affects where they end up practicing. Importantly, law school selectivity continues to have an effect over the course of lawyers' careers as it shapes earnings at later stages and also law school debt. The graduates of top law schools make more money net of other variables in their later careers. And, even though the graduates of top law schools begin their careers with more debt, by wave 3 they have less debt than other lawyers.

Class also enters the narratives of careers and is a factor that quantitative indicators may capture only in crude fashion. The narratives describe how having parents who knew a federal judge led to a clerkship, how a wealthy aunt helped pay for law school, or how not playing golf or knowing about sailing off the coast of France made a young Latinx associate feel uncomfortable at his law firm and eventually led him to leave.

The Intersectionality of Race, Gender, and Class

Not only is the legal profession stratified along lines of gender, race, and class, but the opportunities and rewards that are available to lawyers are also shaped by their unique position along these overlapping axes. Recall from chapter 3 our conclusion that the top of the hierarchy remains the equity partners of corporate law firms, who tend to be White male graduates of elite law schools with wives at home. This group embodies the intersecting advantages of race, gender, and class. Our findings thus reflect the observations of a substantial body of scholarship (see, e.g., Carbado and Gulati 2013; Chung et al. 2017; Crenshaw 1989, 1991; García López 2008; and Wilkins and Gulati 1996) that hierarchies of race, gender, and class do not operate independently of each other but rather are part of a matrix of domination (Collins 2000) in which these hierarchies intersect to produce unique and situated patterns of advantage and disadvantage. We see the significance of these intersections in both the quantitative and the qualitative data. For example, the proportion of women in racial and ethnic categories varies significantly from a high of 65% for African Americans to 57% for Asian Americans to rough parity for other groups. While men of all racial and ethnic groups are likely to work full-time, women are less likely to do so. But there are notable differences within women on the proportion working full-time. African American women post the highest rate of full-time work among women, some 86% at wave 3, compared to 72% of White women. The magnitude of earnings differences between men and women varies by race and ethnicity. Native American women earn less than half of what Native American men make at wave 3, compared to an earnings difference of 20% between men and women in the sample overall. Our analysis of education debt, discussed above, finds significant racial disparities for African Americans compared to other groups. But of particular interest are the high debt levels among African American men compared to men of other races, even after an extensive set of controls. This is one example among many of important differences at the intersection of race and gender that call out for further analysis.

The narratives capture other notable aspects of intersectionality, often involving how individuals confront stereotypes about men and women of different racial and ethnic groups, such as whether an Asian American woman of small stature was tough enough to handle litigation, or bias against Middle Eastern men after 9/11, or whether a White woman was pretty enough to make partner, or whether an African American woman was capable of heading a major state agency. Ricardo's narrative of making a self-conscious effort to brand his boutique law firm as providing "high-quality legal service" rather than as a potential recipient of "affirmative action" preferences exemplifies some of the complicated strategies that lawyers of color face in determining whether and how to embrace their racial and ethnic identity in the legal marketplace.

Class also is an important intersecting axis of difference. Ricardo's story of being from working-class roots, a background more common for African American and Latinx respondents in our sample, explained why he did not feel he fit in the corporate law firm context.

THE TWO HEMISPHERES REVISITED:
RISING SPECIALIZATION AND FRAGMENTATION

Heinz and Laumann (1982) introduced the concept of the two hemispheres to capture a fundamental aspect of the social organization of the legal profession in their 1975 study of Chicago lawyers. They asserted that stratification in the legal profession can be understood by the division between lawyers who represent business clients (the corporate client hemisphere) and those who represent personal clients (the personal client hemisphere). The two hemispheres practiced different legal specialties (with different levels of prestige), attended different law schools, were from different ethnoreligious groups, and had different relationships with clients. Ironically, lawyers in the more prestigious corporate client sector had less autonomy from their sophisticated corporate clients than did lawyers in the personal client sector, who dealt with largely unsophisticated one-shot clients. Heinz et al. replicated the Chicago survey in 1995 and asserted that the two hemispheres conception was still important but had to be revised in light of further differentiation within the legal profession (see Heinz et al. 2005). Nonetheless, the binary concept of two hemispheres has continued to be widely cited in work on the legal profession.

Through the AJD Project surveys, we collected similar sorts of data on fields of practice, specialization, and client type as those that underlay the two hemispheres analysis. We found that specialization by field of practice has grown beyond that observed in the Chicago studies. Moreover, we found similar fragmentation among fields of practice. There are clear lines of demarcation among fields of law, with the result that most lawyers confine their practices to a small set of fields of law, often specializing in only one. As was seen in the 1995 study, we too see the continued decline in the kind of ethnoreligious segregation of fields reported in 1975 Chicago. Instead, we find that there are a small number of fields numerically dominated by women (family law) and Latinx or Asian American lawyers (immigration).

The similarity in the structure of fields of practice from 1975 to 1995 to 2012 is striking. Even as we move across decades and from one city to a national sample, we see very similar patterns of fragmentation among lawyers. Some fields have grown, some have declined, but there remains a fundamental divide between the fields of practice of lawyers serving corporate clients and those serving personal clients. Analyses of patterns of copractice among fields of law reveal that, just as in 1975 and 1995, lawyers who practice in personal client fields such as personal injury plaintiffs, family law, and criminal defense do not also practice in corporate fields such as securities and intellectual property. One change within the corporate hemisphere that we see in our 2012 data is the eclipsing of large law firms as the predominant specialists in corporate fields. Large-firm attorneys are not more numerous as specialists than inside counsel in any corporate field.

THE DOMINANCE OF BUSINESS REPRESENTATION

An important finding reported in Heinz et al. (2005) was the significant increase in the proportion of lawyers' effort devoted to business clients compared to personal and government clients from 1975 to 1995, from rough parity to a two-thirds to one-third balance in 1995. Using the same methods as Heinz et al. did, we examined the relative balance between business and personal client representation among our sample. While we replicated the Chicago finding of a 2:1 ratio of business over personal client representation, given the growth of large law firms we expected the imbalance to have grown even more. Further analysis indicates that part of the lack of change overall is the result of the fact that the AJD Project sample includes lawyers outside major urban areas. The proportion of business representation as a share of lawyers' total effort is smaller in less populous areas. In urban markets, business representation has grown beyond the levels reported in 1995 in Chicago. We saw in our data on geographic mobility that there is dramatic movement into the most populated areas from wave 1 to wave 3. This trend may add to the relative imbalance between the representation of business and the representation of personal clients. Another factor that may affect these results is the growth of nonlawyer leverage in large law firms. If nonlawyers' effort were added to these calculations, there might be a more pronounced shift to business representation.

THE PROMINENCE OF INSIDE COUNSEL

We already have alluded to the transformation in the status of inside counsel in corporations. This phenomenon bears emphasis. Statistically speaking, the percentage of lawyers in our sample working in business (both those who are practicing and those who are not) doubled from wave 1 to wave 3, growing from 10% of the sample to 20%—a percentage that is twice as large as lawyers working in large law firms by wave 3. Large-firm partners still lead the profession in earnings at wave 3, but inside counsel constitute the second most highly compensated group and in some quantiles earn more than large-firm attorneys do. The increasing importance of inside counsel highlights the interplay between larger macroeconomic and political changes and the institutional structures and dynamics of the profession. Responding to the legalization of business—and the growing use of law as a weapon in business—corporations have increasingly sought both to reduce costs, by utilizing employed lawyers rather than ones who bill by the hour, and to improve outcomes, by integrating lawyers into business operations. At the same time, the in-house lawyers who assume these positions are increasingly utilizing their positions of power and authority to press the law firms that companies continue to use to reduce costs and provide more business-focused services, further destabilizing traditional law firm structures and norms. Both these trends are likely to diminish the autonomy that corporate lawyers—whether located in internal legal departments or outside firms—have from their clients as well as the overall power of the corporate hemisphere (Galanter and Henderson 2008; Nelson and Nielsen 2000; Wilkins 2009). They also contribute to the instability of legal careers, and the growing economic gap between lawyers in the corporate and individual hemispheres (Wilkins and Gulati 1998).

GROWING EARNINGS INEQUALITY OVER THE COURSE OF CAREERS

The legal profession historically has had high levels of earnings inequality, with lawyers working in large law firms making far more than lawyers in small firms, state government, and public interest organizations (Heinz et al. 2005). AJD Project data demonstrate that this inequality grows over the course of careers. The highest-earning quartile at wave 1 commanded 42% of total earnings, with median earnings of $150,720, compared to the fourth quartile of earners, who were paid 13% of total earnings for the sample at a median of $41,975, or a 3.6:1 ratio. By wave 3, the top quartile earned 52% of total earnings at a median income of $395,117, compared to the bottom quartile, who were paid 9.0% of total earnings at a median income of $66,741, or a 5.9:1 ratio. These earnings differences are generated at the level of practice setting. At wave 3, we find attorneys in large law firms commanding 25% of total earnings while making up 15% of lawyers. Attorneys in state government are paid 6.7% of total earnings while making up 13.7% of lawyers. Rising inequality among lawyers is not surprising in a market-driven profession that provides only weak support to public sector lawyering.

LOW LEVELS OF PRO BONO EFFORT

Despite the ABA's recommendation that all lawyers spend at least 50 hours a year on pro bono work for disadvantaged clients, the median across all three waves falls below 30 hours. Close to half of lawyers spend no time on pro bono cases. Thus, pro bono work makes up only about 1% of lawyers' total effort. In large law firms where pro bono has been institutionalized, allowing lawyers to count pro bono effort as part of billable hours, we see more pro bono work, particularly among associates who are paid their full salaries regardless of the amount of pro bono they do (although those who do too much often suffer other adverse career consequences, including being asked to leave the firm). Solos and small firms, however, provide as much pro bono effort as large law firms do, notwithstanding the fact that for the most part these lawyers have to self-fund their pro bono work. While pro bono effort is associated with commitments to other kinds of charitable work and endures over the course of a career, it also is associated with making partner in a law firm, suggesting the career benefits of such work, at least within acceptable limits.

The in-depth interviews suggest that pro bono activities can be personally very meaningful for individual attorneys. Some solos spoke of pro bono service as a way of building their reputation in the community; other solos spoke of pro bono as just an inherent aspect of serving low-income clientele. Other attorneys referred to their pro bono cases as a rare career-affirming effort, an intervention in the lives of otherwise underrepresented poor people of which they were very proud. For corporate elites—considered both as individuals and as law firms (i.e., as institutions)—pro bono provides some legitimation of their more usual role in representing clients with significant resources. It also helps with recruitment and is a way to provide training to junior lawyers. But our quantitative data reveal the small part that pro bono work plays in legal representation overall.

THE POLITICAL ORIENTATIONS OF LAWYERS

Despite representing predominantly business clients, lawyers tend to affiliate with the Democratic Party, with roughly half the sample identifying as Democrats vs. only about one-quarter identifying as Republicans. Indeed, more elite segments of the profession, such as graduates of more selective law schools and lawyers working in large law firms and the federal government, are more likely to identify as Democrats than are graduates of less selective law schools and solo and small-firm practitioners. Consistent with national patterns, women and people of color are more likely to identify as Democrats. Representing business clients over the course of a career does, however, have a modest effect in moving lawyers in a conservative political direction. Lawyers are far more conservative on economic issues than they are on social issues, and this divergence grows over the course of careers as they become more liberal on social issues and more conservative on economic issues. Lawyers who occupy less privileged positions within the profession—the graduates of less selective law schools who tend to work as solos and in small law firms—are more conservative politically than are other lawyers.

HIGH LEVELS OF CAREER SATISFACTION SHAPED BY WORKPLACE EXPERIENCES

At all three waves, three-quarters of our sample report being extremely or moderately satisfied with their decision to become a lawyer. Despite the profound levels of inequality and discrimination by race, gender, and class that we have found, satisfaction levels are comparable across gender and race, with some variation by law school selectivity. Beneath this important uniformity, however, are important differences. Thus, lawyers working in different practice settings report different levels of satisfaction with various aspects of their jobs. For example, state government lawyers are less satisfied with their compensation than are large-firm attorneys, and large-firm attorneys are less satisfied with their work/life balance than are most other lawyers. Moreover, positive and negative experiences in the workplace affect career satisfaction: having mentors and making partner increase satisfaction; discrimination reduces it. The relationship between job changes and satisfaction is more complex. Satisfaction is a significant predictor of intent to leave a job within the next three years, but it is not a significant predictor of job changes, while intent to leave is. Indeed, we see a pattern in which, in their later careers, lawyers actually change jobs more frequently than they reported intending to. This gap is particularly pronounced for lawyers in business, almost half of whom change jobs in their later careers, while many fewer said that they expected to. This finding connects nicely to lawyers' narrative accounts about their plans for the future. There, they often suggest an openness to making a job change or even positioning themselves for a job change, but an actual job change depends on circumstances. Overall, these findings also reinforce both the increasing salience of mobility in the strategies of AJD Project lawyers and the complex structural factors that constrain and guide whether lawyers are willing or able to act on these strategies.

We probed job satisfaction in greater depth in the interviews and asked whether respondents would advise their children or the children of friends to go to law school. While the answers we received largely supported what we see in the survey data, lawyers' advice to others invokes moral boundaries about professional careers. To succeed as they have, others will have to be ambitious, work hard, and compete in challenging situations. Our respondents do not necessarily wish this for their children, but they are proud of their own accomplishments.

THE REPRODUCTION OF HIERARCHY IN LAW AND IN SOCIETY

Our data say much about the reproduction of hierarchy in the operation of law in American society. American law and American lawyers operate at the intersection of spheres of power: the market, the state, and civil society. We demonstrated that lawyers' efforts mostly serve business interests, including helping businesses to fight other businesses. If we look at which careers are rewarded financially in the legal profession, we see only very weak investments in the government and public interest sector. The pro bono programs that large law firms have institutionalized and tout as showing their commitment to equal justice are just a drop in the bucket of lawyers' total effort. Bar associations have defended the funding of the Legal Services Corporation (LSC) as opponents have attempted to defund it, but in real dollars the support for the LSC has declined. Moreover, rules about what kinds of cases and clients the LSC can take have limited its capacity to act as an agent of social change.

Efforts by law schools to enhance the public interest wing of the profession also are weak in practical effect. Loan forgiveness for public interest jobs does show up in the career histories of our public interest lawyers, but it yields very few attorneys working in the public interest. Our analysis of student debt supported previous research that showed little impact of debt on choice of careers in government or public interest. Specialized public interest programs in law schools do seem to shape a commitment to that kind of work that can persist over the course of careers (Albiston et al. 2021), but again the number of graduates produced by these programs is very limited. As we saw in our analysis of the determinants of who does pro bono work, participation early in a career carries over into later phases of careers. But law school programs requiring pro bono work has no appreciable effect on pro bono efforts. When we look at the public sector of our sample, we find a preference for elite law school credentials in hiring for the small number of public interest jobs. Thus, even the public interest sector reaffirms the significance of elite law school credentials.

The plaintiffs' bar and public interest law organizations have had some success in advancing the interests of consumers, tort victims, and environmental groups, among others. As Haltom and McCann (2009) suggest, these efforts are under sustained attack from business interests, who have successfully limited the reach of such lawsuits through damage caps and other techniques.

Yet this form of class action litigation remains as one form of redress and redistribution in American law.

No group needs to be at the controls for the reproduction of hierarchy in the legal profession and in law. We do not need to look for a conspiracy between business, law schools, bar associations, conservatives, and liberals to argue that the current social organization of the legal profession reproduces the hierarchical character of the legal profession. The tendency to reproduce hierarchy is anchored in history and reinforced by the practices of law schools, legal employers, and lawyers. We have seen notable interventions that have sought to level the playing field in legal representation, such as the landmark case *Gideon v. Wainwright* (1963), which guaranteed the right to counsel in criminal cases that could result in incarceration. Yet the mandate in *Gideon* is subject to the hierarchical distribution of legal talent and legal resources. As Galanter (1974) famously noted, a change in legal rules without a fundamental change in the organization of representational resources will have limited practical effect.

The reproduction of hierarchy within the American legal profession has profound implications for the reproduction of hierarchy in American society. The social organization of the legal profession does not just reflect broader patterns of inequality; it reinforces those patterns. While the profession may hold out the ideals of equality of opportunity and equal access to justice, the opportunities it affords are not equally available to all segments of society. And the rewards and resources it provides valorize career paths in ways that increase inequality in the distribution of legal representation.

Prospects for the Future

Our findings have important implications both for contemporary debates about the legal profession and for the future prospects of the legal profession. Most fundamentally, we demonstrate that the legal profession continues to be structured by inequalities of race, gender, and class and that these divisions widen over the course of careers. Our data demonstrate that the selectivity of law school attended has far-reaching effects. Where lawyers begin in practice is significantly influenced by law school attended. And where lawyers begin their careers heavily shapes their later career paths. Controlling for other variables, law school attended has significant effects on career earnings and education debt. Thus, policies regarding law school admissions are critical to the shape of inequality in the profession. Those who advocate the elimination of affirmative action in law school admissions as a way to aid traditionally marginalized groups are fundamentally misguided.

Our findings also show that the current commitments that law firms and other employers are making toward diversity are not sufficient because they fail to intervene in practices (both institutional and attitudinal) that reproduce existing hierarchies. Similarly, existing commitments to pro bono engagement and the provision of low-cost legal services are unlikely to produce meaningful access to justice in a world in which the incentive structures of legal careers continue to lead more and more lawyers to devote more and more effort to serving corporate clients.

At the same time, our findings belie the popular narratives that all lawyers are miserable and that only lawyers from top law schools can have successful and satisfying careers. Lawyers across the spectrum of law school selectivity and practice settings report high levels of career satisfaction. It is especially striking that, despite relatively lower rewards and more discriminatory experiences, graduates of less selective law schools and women and people of color express among the highest levels of satisfaction with their decision to become a lawyer.

As this book goes to press, America may be emerging from a global pandemic and has recently experienced a year of protest over racial and social injustice in the wake of the murder of George Floyd by a police officer. Many are predicting that these events are creating a "new normal" in which existing ways of working will be fundamentally upended by technology and generational change. Our analysis suggests that we should be cautious in making these predictions. While there will undoubtedly be many changes in the way in which lawyers live and work, our findings underscore that the social structure of the bar can adapt to these changes in ways that replicate existing hierarchies even as they create new strategies for individual lawyers to manipulate and challenge these structures. While we cannot predict exactly how these processes will play out, we submit that in-depth quantitative and qualitative examination of the careers of the lawyers who will navigate this complex intersection of structures and strategies will shed valuable light on just how new this new normal really is.

Acknowledgments

Many institutions and individuals contributed to the creation of this book. Foremost is the American Bar Foundation (ABF) and its leadership over two decades, including directors Bryant Garth, Robert Nelson, and Ajay Mehrotra. Standing with the ABF is its major funder, the American Bar Endowment.

The National Association for Law Placement (NALP) and its foundation deserve special mention. The idea for a study of lawyer turnover was conceived in 1999 by Paula Patton, president and CEO of the NALP Foundation, and Abbie Willard, assistant dean for career services at Georgetown Law. James Leipold and Tammy Patterson, executive directors of NALP and the NALP Foundation, respectively, provided further support over the course of the project.

At various phases of the project, the following organizations provided major grants: the American Bar Foundation, the National Science Foundation (grants SES-0115521, SES-0550605, SES-102306), the Law School Admissions Council, the Access Group and AccessLex, the Montgomery Foundation, the Open Society Institute, and the National Conference of Bar Examiners.

We have had the great fortune to have three superb project managers who oversaw the data collection in three waves, the production of initial reports for each wave, and the building of an elaborate longitudinal data set. First was Ronit Dinovitzer, who managed waves 1 and 2 of data collection before moving to the Department of Sociology at the University of Toronto. Second was Gabriele Plickert, who managed wave 3 before moving to the Department of Sociology at Cal Poly Pomona. And third was Meghan Dawe, who administered the data analysis and writing while in residence at the ABF. (She is now at Harvard University's Center on the Legal Profession.)

The heart of this project has been the team of scholars who have collaborated on it, some for the duration. As stated in the note on authorship, this includes Ronit Dinovitzer, Bryant Garth, Robert Nelson, Joyce Sterling, and

David Wilkins. We were joined more recently by Ethan Michelson and Meghan Dawe. Other important academic contributors were Terry Adams, John Hagan, Gita Wilder, Gabriele Plickert, Rebecca Sandefur, and Richard Sander. Research assistants who provided significant contributions on specific chapters include Vitor Dias, Andreea Mogosanu, and Ioana Sendroiu. Several authors have published with us collaboratively from AJD Project data, including Nancy Reichman and Monique Payne Pikus.

Over the years, we have had many talented research assistants and editorial associates. These include Tony Love, Chantrey J. Murphy, Sarah Babbitt, Travis Patrick Colburn, Joseph Krupnick, Milti Leonard, Josiah Evans, Leslie Greer, Rachel Cook, Sabra Thorner, Curtiss Cobb III, JeeYoon Park, Skyler Nielsen-Sorensen, Laura Fagbemi, Kelsey Rydland, and other undergraduate and summer fellowship students working at the ABF.

The National Opinion Research Center, the Institute for Social Research (ISR), and Leo Shapiro and Associates were the contractors for data collection at different waves. Terry Adams and Sarah Parikh led data collection and cleaning efforts at ISR and Leo Shapiro and Associates, respectively. We are indebted to bar authorities in several jurisdictions who provided us with the lists of attorneys who entered the bar in the year 2000 from which we drew our sample. We benefited from guidance by an advisory group that included Richard Geiger, Jeffrey Hanson, David Hill, and representatives from major donor organizations noted above.

Colleagues at our respective institutions have provided important support and advice. Jack Heinz was not only an inspiration for this book through his and Edward Laumann's research but also an insightful reader of earlier drafts of various chapters. Laura Beth Nielsen, Ann Southworth, Beth Mertz, Carole Silver, and others provided helpful comments throughout the project. Two anonymous reviewers for the University of Chicago Press gave careful and thoughtful comments on the entire book manuscript. Chuck Myers encouraged the development of this manuscript at the University of Chicago Press, and Sara Doskow has helped us bring it home.

On a personal level, we have been fortunate to have loving families and friends for the last two decades. Indeed, our families have grown with new children and grandchildren. We cannot say we are totally done with the AJD Project, but we know our families will be relieved to know we are done with this phase and the seemingly endless Zoom calls, project meetings, and conference presentations needed to finish this book.

Finally, we thank the 5,000 attorneys who gave their time and attention to respond to our surveys and interviews. Without their participation, we would not have been able to tell the stories of the making of lawyers' careers.

Notes

Chapter One

1. Constance never mentioned this part of her identity and her ethnicity was not apparent to our interviewers. We know her ethnicity from her survey responses.

2. This section draws on Garth and Sterling (2018).

3. The sequence analysis we describe in chap. 3 highlights these flows, which ultimately demonstrate both the stability in the structures of inequality and the spaces of change.

4. For a more detailed sampling memo as well as other supplementary materials, see the online appendix.

5. For the original text of all three surveys, see the online appendix.

Chapter Two

1. To be sure, theory is not the same as practice, and Galanter and Palay (1991) document that Paul Cravath himself was no real believer in equal compensation or democratic governance.

Chapter Four

1. While the earlier sources count Latinx as a distinct racial group, BLS data consider Latinx an ethnicity that falls into different racial categories. Thus, Latinx constitute 5.8% of the legal profession, divided among Whites, African Americans, and Asian Americans.

2. Given the longitudinal analysis, we restrict the sample to respondents of all three waves ($N = 2,035$).

3. In the weighted sample, African Americans constitute 5.5%, Latinx 3.7%, Asian Americans 6.7%, and Whites 84.0% (Dinovitzer et al. 2009a). That there are additional people of color in our sample allows more analysis within and across groups, but, owing to the differences from other population estimates, we counsel against using our data to make estimates about the relative presence of racial/ethnic groups in the profession.

4. See table 4A.1 in the online appendix.

5. National universities offer a broad range of undergraduate majors and graduate degree programs.

6. We ranked undergraduate institutions in March 2018 using the most recent *US News*

undergraduate rankings (https://www.usnews.com/best-colleges?int=994d08). *US News* ranked 1,801 different undergraduate institutions/campuses in four different categories (national universities, liberal arts schools, regional universities, regional colleges). (Methodology: https://www.usnews.com/education/best-colleges/articles/how-us-news-calculated-the-rankings.) We combined the top 25 national universities and liberal arts colleges ($n = 50$) into our top ranked category, we combined national universities and liberal arts colleges ranked 26–100 into our second ranked category ($n = 150$), and we combined all other undergraduate institutions into our lowest-ranked category, including national universities and liberal arts colleges ranked 101 and higher, regional universities, colleges, and unranked US and foreign institutions. Among respondents who attended foreign undergraduate institutions, nearly half ($n = 35$) obtained a degree from a school in Asia, 20 from Canada, 19 from Europe, 7 from Africa, 2 from Latin America, and 1 from New Zealand, and 2 did not disclose the name or location of their undergraduate institution. Of the 55 foreign graduates who attended undergraduate schools included in the most recent *US News* list of global rankings, 3 attended schools ranked in the top 20 globally, 11 attended schools ranked 21–50, 4 attended schools ranked 51–100, and the remaining 37 attended schools ranked 101 and higher.

7. In 2003, *US News* published individual rankings for the top 100 law schools. Schools ranked 101 and higher were divided among tier 3 (schools ranked from 101 to 137) and tier 4 (schools ranked 138 and higher). We use 2003 rankings for commensurability with past AJD Project analyses. The report is no longer available online, but a copy is available from the authors on request.

8. See table 4A.2 in the online appendix.

9. See table 4A.3 in the online appendix.

10. We exclude parents' occupation because it is highly correlated with parents' education.

11. See table 4A.4 in the online appendix.

12. See figures 4A.1 and 4A.2 in the online appendix.

13. See table 4A.5 in the online appendix.

14. See table 4A.6 in the online appendix.

15. See table 4A.7 in the online appendix.

16. See tables 4A.8–4A.10 in the online appendix.

17. At wave 3, lower-tier (what we call *other*) undergraduates compose 47.2% of respondents in solo practice or small firms and 41.0% of those in state government, representing the highest proportions in any sector. Graduates of these schools also have a higher probability of working in solo/small firms than in any other sector (33.8%). Similarly, respondents with the lowest undergraduate GPAs are the most highly represented group in solo/small firms (31.6%), and respondents in this sector have the second lowest mean LSAT score after state government (0.004 and 0.055, respectively). Graduates of tier 3 and tier 4 law schools are the most likely to work in solo/small firms at midcareer (34.1%) and account for the largest proportion of respondents in this sector (34.6%). Respondents with the lowest law school GPAs are the most likely to work in solo/small firms and state government (33.7% and 20.1%, respectively) and compose the largest shares of the respondents in these settings at wave 3 (27.6% and 34.2%, respectively).

Chapter Five

1. See table 5A.1 in the online appendix.

2. See table 5A.2 in the online appendix.

3. We calculated the number of working hours spent on each client type by multiplying the number of hours worked in the last week by the percentage of time spent serving that type of client, then reported the sum by client type.

4. In wave 1, we see a larger share of effort goes to middle- to low-income personal clients, a somewhat lower share to large business, and very similar shares to other client types. These differences may be due to lower levels of specialization at wave 1.

5. See table 5A.3 in the online appendix.

6. That Jewish lawyers are less populous in the AJD study compared to the Chicago studies may be due to its national scope; 40% of Jewish respondents were sampled from the four major markets compared to 34% of the sample overall.

7. See table 5A.4 in the online appendix.

8. See table 5A.5 in the online appendix.

9. See table 5A.6 in the online appendix.

10. See table 5A.7 in the online appendix.

11. See table 5A.8 in the online appendix.

12. Only a small number of respondents reported that they had retired, 0 at wave 1, 5 at wave 2, and 12 at wave 3.

13. There is no difference in city size between practicing and nonpracticing lawyers, suggesting that the higher proportion of nonpracticing lawyers in the AJD Project sample is not merely an artifact of its national scope.

14. See table 5A.9 in the online appendix.

15. See table 5A.10 in the online appendix.

16. See table 5A.11 in the online appendix.

Chapter Nine

1. Academic institutions with tenure track faculty are up-or-out systems.

Chapter Ten

1. For additional details, please refer to supplementary online material.

2. We arrived at these estimates using work history data reported at wave 3 and supplemented with work history data reported at wave 2. According to information on current employer reported at wave 1, 66% and 51%, respectively, of White and African American respondents, respectively, were working in law firms. By wave 2, 50% and 37% of White and African American respondents, respectively, reported law firms as their current employer. Finally, by wave 3, only 39% and 25% of women and men, respectively, reported law firms as their current employer.

Chapter Eleven

1. On average, 6.7% of White and 2.6% of African American respondents' legal education is funded by their spouses.

2. AJD Project respondents graduated from law school between 1998 and 2000 (Dinovitzer et al. 2004).

3. Owing to the small number of respondents identifying as "other race/ethnicity" ($n = 12$), we exclude this group from the analyses.

4. The term *debt-to-income ratio* technically refers to the ratio of one's debt payments to one's earnings in the same period (Schrag 2013). Given that we do not know the size of respondents' debt payments, we use a simplified debt-income ratio that compares the value of respondents' total education debt to their annual earnings. The earnings data have been bottom-coded at $10,000. Since this ratio compares respondents' debt to their annual income, the analysis includes debtors only.

5. See table 11A.1 in the online appendix.

6. What we refer to as the *debt-income ratio at graduation* is the ratio of debt at graduation to income at wave 1; thus, this figure is likely to be somewhat inflated given that wave 1 was fielded two to three years into respondents' careers. However, this measure still effectively demonstrates differences in the early debt-income distribution across different social groups.

7. For descriptive information on independent variables, see table 11A.2 in the online appendix.

8. See table 11A.3 in the online appendix.

9. We define public service jobs as employment in government, legal services or public defense, public interest, and nonprofit and education (McGill 2006).

10. Respondents were asked to measure the importance of these motivations along a scale ranging from 1 (irrelevant) to 5 (very important).

11. As a robustness check, we tried excluding zeros from our debt measure, but the findings were similar.

12. It is also important to note the heterogeneity of Latinx individuals. We consider Latinx respondents to be those who identified as Hispanic in the survey and adopt this terminology to include non-Spanish-speaking individuals of Latin American origin. According to Vickers and Isaac (2012, 27): "Hispanics are less homogeneous than African Americans. While they have speaking Spanish in common, the US census assigns them to different racial categories. But . . . they are a racialized group. Many are mestizo or mixed race; many others are European culturally. So it is difficult to determine whether the exclusion and oppression of Hispanics is produced by race or by language or by some combination of the two; or how much the unauthorized migrant status of some Hispanics plays a role."

Chapter Twelve

1. CBS News interview with Ruth Bader Ginsberg (October 16, 1999).

2. There is a long history of academic debate on statistical modeling of the motherhood penalty (England et al. 2016). Specifically, this chapter relies on quantile regressions and examines earnings trajectories across the three waves of the study. Furthermore, the base of comparison in the models is women with no children. Thus, alternative specifications of these statistical models may offer other insights into additional dimensions of gender and professional outcomes.

3. About 3% of our sample responded that they identify as LGBTQ. The questions we included about having children were asked of all respondents. While we have not conducted separate analyses on LGBTQ respondents and parenthood, we make no heteronormative assumptions about who is married or a parent.

4. For a detailed description of our variables, see table 12A.1 in the online appendix.

5. See table 12A.3 in the online appendix.

Chapter Thirteen

1. See table 13A.1 in the online appendix.

2. See table 13A.2 in the online appendix.

3. See table 13A.3 in the online appendix.

4. See table 13A.4 in the online appendix.

5. See table 13A.5 in the online appendix. The phrasing of the questions about organization membership changed across the three waves. Wave 1 asked whether respondents were not a member, a member, previously an active participant or officer, and currently an active participant and officer. Wave 2 asked whether they were not a member, a member, or currently active or an officer. Wave 3 asked whether they were not a member, a member, or had a leadership role.

6. See table 13A.6 in the online appendix.

7. Defining pro bono service is a vexing issue for any attempt to enumerate pro bono hours. The ABA study states: "The definition of pro bono is subjective and personal for many attorneys." Thus: "Establishing a definition for survey purposes was one of the greatest challenges [for the study]" (American Bar Association 2018, 4). The ABA definition does not include work for friends and family members who are not impoverished, or for clients who fail to pay, or for nonprofits who do not provide services to persons of limited means. We did not elaborate on the definition of pro bono in our survey. Yet our results are quite similar to those found in the ABA's national survey, which reported that 52% of respondents spent some time on pro bono work, with a mean of 40 hours per year for those who did any pro bono work.

8. See table 13A.7 in the online appendix.

9. See table 13A.8 in the online appendix.

Chapter Fourteen

1. See table 14A.1 in the online appendix.

2. Moreover, wave 2 asked respondents to report on their total number of formal mentors, while wave 3 asked about formal and informal mentors. Mentorship levels ranged broadly at the two waves, with substantial portions of the sample reporting having no mentors (15% at wave 2 and 17% at wave 3) and some respondents reporting as many as 50 or 60 mentors. To avoid skewing our findings with the more extreme values in our multivariate models, we top-coded these measures at wave 4.

3. See table 14A.2 in the online appendix.

4. To measure job changes, we used job history data from the surveys, the same data that underlie the sequence analysis in chap. 3 and the analysis of law firm careers in chaps. 10 and 12. We compared the employers for whom respondents were working during the years in which the surveys were conducted (2003, 2007, 2012). If the employers were different, we coded a respondent as having changed jobs. Thus, to determine whether respondents had changed jobs between wave 1 and wave 2, we compared employers in 2003 and in 2007; for job changes between wave 2 and wave 3, we compared employer in 2007 with the last employer reported in the job histories of the wave 3 surveys; and, for job changes after wave 3, we compared the last employer reported in the wave 3 job histories with the current employer identified in our 2019 web searches.

5. We define different government agencies as different employers.

6. See figure 14A.1 in the online appendix.

7. See figure 14A.2 in the online appendix.

8. The controls are race (White = 1, non-White = 0), gender (female = 1, male = 0), income, hours worked, marital status (married = 1, else = 0), practicing and practice setting, law school rank, networking in law firm, and discrimination. At waves 2 and 3, we also add partner status, mentorship, and structural and process autonomy.

9. See tables 14A.3 and 14A.4 in the online appendix.

10. This is based on the standard 16-day cutoff (Henry et al. 2018; Vilagut et al. 2016), which refers to the summed number of days respondents feel each of the seven symptoms in the scale. To make this comparable with our depression measure, we therefore divided the total number of days (i.e., 16) by seven, as we also did for the depression scores we tabulated for our sample.

References

Abbott, Andrew. 1988. *The System of Professions: An Essay on the Division of Expert Labor.* Chicago: University of Chicago Press.

Abel, Richard L. 2010. "Law and Society: Project and Practice." *Annual Review of Law and Social Science* 6 (1): 1–23.

———. 1989. *American Lawyers.* Los Angeles: Oxford University Press.

———. 1982. *The American Experience.* Vol. 1 of *The Politics of Informal Justice.* New York: Academic.

Abramson, Leigh McMullan. 2014. "The Only Job with an Industry Devoted to Helping People Quit." *The Atlantic.* July 29. https://www.theatlantic.com/business/archive/2014/07/the-only-job-with-an-industry-devoted-to-helping-people-quit/375199.

Acker, Joan. 1990. "Hierarchies, Jobs, Bodies: A Theory of Gendered Organizations." *Gender and Society* 4 (2): 139–58.

Addo, Fenaba R., Jason N. Houle, and Daniel Simon. 2016. "Young, Black, and (Still) in the Red: Parental Wealth, Race, and Student Loan Debt." *Race and Social Problems* 8 (1): 64–76.

Adediran, Atinuke O. 2020. "Solving the Pro Bono Mismatch." *University of Colorado Law Review* 91 (4): 1035–79.

Aiken, Juliet, and Milton Regan. 2016. "Gendered Pathways: Choice, Constraint, and Women's Job Movements in the Legal Profession." In *Diversity in Practice: Race, Gender, and Class in Legal and Professional Careers,* 301–27. Cambridge: Cambridge University Press.

Aisenbrey, Silke, and Anette E. Fasang. 2010. "New Life for Old Ideas: The 'Second Wave' of Sequence Analysis Bringing the 'Course' Back into the Life Course." *Sociological Methods and Research* 38 (3): 420–62.

Albiston, Catherine, Scott L. Cummings, and Richard L. Abel. 2021. "Making Public Interest Lawyers in a Time of Crisis: An Evidence-Based Approach." *Georgetown Journal of Legal Ethics* 34:223–94.

Ambrogi, Bob. 2020. "The Decade in Legal Tech: The 10 Most Significant Developments." LawSites, January 1. https://www.lawnext.com/2020/01/the-decade-in-legal-tech-the-10-most-significant-developments.html.

American Association of University Women. 2021. "Deeper in Debt: 2021 Update." https://www.aauw.org/app/uploads/2021/05/Deeper_In_Debt_2021.pdf.

American Bar Association. 2018. *Supporting Justice: A Report on the Pro Bono Work of America's Lawyers*. Chicago: Standing Committee on Pro Bono and Public Service. https://www.americanbar.org/content/dam/aba/administrative/probono_public_service/ls_pb_supporting_justice_iv_final.pdf.

———. 2016. "2016 Standard 509 Information Report Data Overview." American Bar Association. https://www.americanbar.org/content/dam/aba/administrative/legal_education_and_admissions_to_the_bar/statistics/2016_standard_509_data_overview.pdf.

Amuedo-Dorantes, Catalina, and Jean Kimmel. 2008. "New Evidence on the Motherhood Wage Gap." IZA Discussion Paper 3662. https://www.ssrn.com/abstract=1251030.

———. 2005. "The Motherhood Wage Gap for Women in the United States: The Importance of College and Fertility Delay." *Review of Economics of the Household* 3 (1): 17–48.

Arewa, Olufunmilayo B., Andrew P. Morriss, and William D. Henderson. 2014. "Enduring Hierarchies in American Legal Education." *Indiana Law Journal* 89 (3): 941–1068.

Auerbach, Jerold S. 1976. *Unequal Justice: Lawyers and Social Change in Modern America*. New York: Oxford University Press.

Azmat, Ghazala, and Rosa Ferrer. 2017. "Gender Gaps in Performance: Evidence from Young Lawyers." *Journal of Political Economy* 125 (5): 1306–55.

Bader, Hans. 2011. "Mind-Boggling Increase in Tuition since 1960 Even as Students Learn Less and Less." Competitive Enterprise Institute, May 25. https://cei.org/blog/mind-boggling-increase-in-tuition-since-1960-even-as-students-learn-less-and-less.

Baćak, Valerio, Sarah Lageson, and Kathleen Powell. 2020 "The Stress of Injustice: Public Defenders and the Frontline of American Inequality." Ninth Judicial Circuit Historical Society. https://www.njchs.org/wp-content/uploads/Stress-of-Injustice-article.pdf.

Ballakrishnen, Swethaa S. 2021. *Accidental Feminism*. Princeton, NJ: Princeton University Press.

Barsky, Robert, John Bound, Kerwin Kofi Charles, and Joseph P. Lupton. 2002. "Accounting for the Black-White Wealth Gap: A Nonparametric Approach." *Journal of the American Statistical Association* 97 (459): 663–73.

Barton, Benjamin H. 2015. *Glass Half Full: The Decline and Rebirth of the Legal Profession*. New York: Oxford University Press.

Becker, Gary S. 1957. *The Economics of Discrimination*. Chicago: University of Chicago Press.

Bell, Derrick A., Jr. 1970. "Bakke, Minority Admissions, and the Usual Price of Racial Remedies." *California Law Review* 67 (1): 3–20.

Belotti, Federico, Partha Deb, Willard G. Manning, and Edward C. Norton. 2015. "twopm: Two-Part Models." *Stata Journal* 15 (1): 3–20.

Berdahl, Jennifer L., Marianne Cooper, Peter Glick, Robert W. Livingston, and Joan C. Williams. 2018. "Work as a Masculinity Contest." *Journal of Social Issues* 74 (3): 422–48.

Bianchi, Suzanne M., Melissa A. Milkie, Liana C. Sayer, and John P. Robinson. 2000. "Is Anyone Doing the Housework? Trends in the Gender Division of Household Labor." *Social Forces* 79 (1): 191–228.

Blair-Loy, Mary. 2003. *Competing Devotions: Career and Family among Women Executives*. Cambridge, MA: Harvard University Press.

———. 1999. "Career Patterns of Executive Women in Finance: An Optimal Matching Analysis." *American Journal of Sociology* 104 (5): 1346–97.

Bliss, John. 2018. "From Idealists to Hired Guns? An Empirical Analysis of 'Public Interest Drift' in Law School." *UC Davis Law Review* 51: 1973–2032.

Bliss, John, and Steven A. Boutcher. 2022. "Rationalizing Pro Bono: Corporate Social Responsibility and the Reinvention of Legal Professionalism in Elite American Law Firms." In *Global Pro Bono: Causes, Context, and Contestation*, ed. Scott L. Cummings, Fabio de Sa e Silva, and Louise G. Trubek. Cambridge: Cambridge University Press.

Bonica, Adam, Adam S. Chilton, and Maya Sen. 2016. "The Political Ideologies of American Lawyers." *Journal of Legal Analysis* 8 (2): 277–335.

Bosvieux-Onyekwelu, Charles. 2018. "Multinacionais do direito, escritórios de advocacia e pro bono: Elementos para uma análise comparativa dos campos jurídicos francês e americano." *Revista Debates* 12 (3): 33–52.

Bourdieu, Pierre. 1998. *Practical Reason: On the Theory of Action*. Cambridge: Polity.

———. 1987. "The Force of Law: Toward a Sociology of the Juridical Field." *Hastings Law Journal* 38: 814–53.

———. 1984. *Distinction: A Social Critique of the Judgement of Taste*. Cambridge, MA: Harvard University Press.

———. 1977. *Outline of a Theory of Practice*. Cambridge: Cambridge University Press.

Bourdieu, Pierre, and Loïc J. D. Wacquant. 1992. *An Invitation to Reflexive Sociology*. Chicago: University of Chicago Press.

Boutcher, Steven A. 2017. "Private Law Firms in the Public Interest: The Organizational and Institutional Determinants of Pro Bono Participation, 1994–2005." *Law and Social Inquiry* 42 (2): 543–64.

———. 2009. "The Institutionalization of Pro Bono in Large Law Firms: Trends and Variation across the AmLaw 200." In *Private Lawyers and the Public Interest: The Evolving Role of Pro Bono in the Legal Profession*, ed. Robert Granfield and Lynn Mather, 135–53. Oxford: Oxford University Press.

Briscoe, Forrest, and Katherine C. Kellogg. 2011. "The Initial Assignment Effect: Local Employer Practices and Positive Career Outcomes for Work-Family Program Users." *American Sociological Review* 76 (2): 291–319.

Briscoe, Forrest, and Andrew von Nordenflycht. 2014. "Which Path to Power? Workplace Networks and the Relative Effectiveness of Inheritance and Rainmaking Strategies for Professional Partners." *Journal of Professions and Organization* 1 (1): 1–16.

Brock, David, C. R. Hinings, and Michael Powell, eds. 1999. *Restructuring the Professional Organization: Accounting, Health Care and Law*. London: Routledge.

Brockman, Joan. 2001. *Gender in the Legal Profession: Fitting or Breaking the Mould*. Vancouver, BC: University of British Columbia Press.

Buchmann, Claudia, and Anne McDaniel. 2016. "Motherhood and the Wages of Women in Professional Occupations." *RSF: The Russell Sage Foundation Journal of the Social Sciences* 2 (4): 128–50.

Budig, Michelle J., and Melissa J. Hodges. 2014. "Statistical Models and Empirical Evidence for Differences in the Motherhood Penalty across the Earnings Distribution." *American Sociological Review* 79 (2): 358–64.

———. 2010. "Differences in Disadvantage: Variation in the Motherhood Penalty across White Women's Earnings Distribution." *American Sociological Review* 75 (5): 705–28.

Burk, Bernard A. 2019. "The New Normal Ten Years In: The Job Market for New Lawyers Today and What It Means for the Legal Academy Tomorrow." *FIU Law Review* 13 (3): 341–82.

Byker, Tanya. 2016. "The Opt-Out Continuation: Education, Work, and Motherhood from 1984 to 2012." *RSF: The Russell Sage Foundation Journal of the Social Sciences* 2 (4): 34–70.

Campos, Paul. 2012. *Don't Go to Law School (Unless): A Law Professor's Inside Guide to Maximizing Opportunity and Minimizing Risk*. Seattle, WA: Amazon Electronic Books.

Carbado, Devon W., and Mitu Gulati. 2013. *Acting White? Rethinking Race in Post-Racial America*. Oxford: Oxford University Press.

Carlin, Jerome E. 1994. *Lawyers on Their Own: The Solo Practitioner in an Urban Setting*. San Francisco: Austin & Winfield.

———. 1966. *Lawyers' Ethics: A Survey of the New York City Bar*. New York: Russell Sage.

———. 1962. *Lawyers on Their Own: A Study of Individual Practitioners in Chicago*. New Brunswick, NJ: Rutgers University Press.

Carr-Saunders, Alexander M., and Paul A. Wilson. 1933. *The Professions*. Oxford: Clarendon.

Carson, Clara N., and JeeYoon Park. 2012. *The Lawyer Statistical Report: The U.S. Legal Profession in 2005*. Chicago: American Bar Foundation.

Chambers, David L. 1992. "The Burdens of Educational Loans: The Impacts of Debt on Job Choice and Standards of Living for Students at Nine American Law Schools." *Journal of Legal Education* 42:187–231.

Chambliss, Elizabeth. 2019. "Evidence-Based Regulation." *Washington University Law Review* 97 (2): 297–350.

———. 2009. "New Sources of Managerial Authority in Large Law Firms." *Georgetown Journal of Legal Ethics* 22 (63): 63–95.

Chambliss, Elizabeth, and David B. Wilkins. 2002. "A New Framework for Law Firm Discipline." *Georgetown Journal of Legal Ethics* 16:335–52.

Chayes, Abram, and Antonia H. Chayes. 1985. "Corporate Counsel and the Elite Law Firm." *Stanford Law Review* 37 (2): 277–300.

Chetty, Rah, David Grusky, Maximillian Hell, Nathaniel Hendren, Robert Manduca, and Jimmy Narang. 2017. "The Fading American Dream: Trends in Absolute Income Mobility since 1940." *Science* 356 (6336): 398–406.

Chetty, Raj, Nathaniel Hendren, Patrick Kline, Emmanuel Saez, and Nicholas Turner. 2014. "Is the United States Still a Land of Opportunity? Recent Trends in Intergenerational Mobility." *American Economic Review* 104 (5): 141–47.

Chung, Eric, Samuel Dong, Xiaonan April Hu, Christine Kwon, and Goodwin Liu. 2017. "A Portrait of Asian Americans in the Law." Yale Law School and National Asian Pacific American Bar Association. https://static1.squarespace.com/static/59556778e58c62c7db3fbe84/t/596c f0638419c2e5a0dc5766/1500311662008/170716_PortraitProject_SinglePages.pdf.

Clark, Robert C. 1992. "Why So Many Lawyers? Are They Good or Bad?" *Fordham Law Review* 61 (2): 275–302.

Clydesdale, Timothy T. 2004. "A Forked River Runs through Law School: Toward Understanding Race, Gender, Age, and Related Gaps in Law School Performance and Bar Passage." *Law and Social Inquiry* 29 (4): 711–69.

Collins, Patricia Hill. 2000. "Gender, Black Feminism, and Black Political Economy." *Annals of the American Academy of Political and Social Science* 568 (1): 41–53.

Conley, Dalton. 1999. *Being Black, Living in the Red: Race, Wealth, and Social Policy in America*. Berkeley and Los Angeles: University of California Press.

Connell, R. W. 1995. *Masculinities*. Sydney: Allen & Unwin.

Connell, R. W., and James W. Messerschmidt. 2005. "Hegemonic Masculinity: Rethinking the Concept." *Gender and Society* 19 (6): 829–59.

Coquillette, Daniel R., and Bruce A. Kimball. 2015. *On the Battlefield of Merit: Harvard Law School, the First Century.* Cambridge, MA: Harvard University Press.

Cornwell, Benjamin. 2015. *Social Sequence Analysis: Methods and Applications.* Cambridge: Cambridge University Press.

Crenshaw, Kimberlé. 1995. "The Intersection of Race and Gender." In *Critical Race Theory: The Key Writings That Formed the Movement,* 357–83. New York: New Press.

———. 1991. "Mapping the Margins: Intersectionality, Identity Politics, and Violence against Women of Color." *Stanford Law Review* 43 (6): 1241–99.

———. 1989. "Demarginalizing the Intersection of Race and Sex: A Black Feminist Critique of Antidiscrimination Doctrine, Feminist Theory and Antiracist Politics." *University of Chicago Legal Forum* 1989 (1): 139–68.

Cummings, Scott L. 2004. "The Politics of Pro Bono." *UCLA Law Review* 52:1–149.

Cummings, Scott L., and Deborah L. Rhode. 2010. "Managing Pro Bono: Doing Well by Doing Better." *Fordham Law Review* 78 (5): 2357–2442.

Cummings, Scott L., Fabio de Sa e Silva, and Louise G. Trubek. 2022. *Global Pro Bono: Causes, Context, and Contestation.* Cambridge: Cambridge University Press.

Daly, Mary C. 1997. "The Cultural, Ethical, and Legal Challenges in Lawyering for a Global Organization: The Role of the General Counsel." *Emory Law Journal* 46 (3): 1057–1112.

Dau-Schmidt, Kenneth G., Marc Galanter, Kaushik Mukhopadhaya, and Kathleen E. Hull. 2009. "Men and Women of the Bar: An Empirical Study of the Impact of Gender on Legal Careers." *Michigan Journal of Gender and Law* 16 (1): 49–145.

Dau-Schmidt, Kenneth G., and Kaushik Mukhopadhaya. 2021. "Men and Women of the Bar: A Second Look at the Impact of Gender on Legal Careers." *International Journal of the Legal Profession* 46 (1): 1–104.

Dawe, Meghan, and Robert L. Nelson. 2021a. "The Geography of Opportunity: Mapping Lawyer Careers." https://themakingoflawyerscareers.org.

———. 2021b. "Markets and Lawyer Careers." https://themakingoflawyerscareers.org.

Deo, Meera. 2021. "Student Debt Is a raceXgender Issue." Law School Survey of Student Engagement. Blog post, July 9. https://lssse.indiana.edu/uncategorized/student-debt-is-a-race xgender-issue/?utm_source=rss&utm_medium=rss&utm_campaign=student-debt-is-a-race xgender-issue.

Derber, Charles. 1983. "Managing Professionals: Ideological Proletarianization and Post-Industrial Labor." *Theory and Society* 12 (3): 309–41.

———. 1982. "The Proletarianization of the Professional: A Review Essay." In *Professionals as Workers: Mental Labor in Advanced Capitalism,* ed. Charles Derber, 13–34. Boston: G. K. Hall.

Dezalay, Yves, and Bryant G. Garth. 2021. *Law as Reproduction and Revolution: An Interconnected History.* Oakland: University of California Press.

———. 2016. "'Lords of the Dance' as Double Agents: Elite Actors in and around the Legal Field." *Journal of Professions and Organization* 3 (2): 188–206.

———. 2010. *The Internationalization of Palace Wars: Lawyers, Economists, and the Contest to Transform Latin American States.* Chicago: University of Chicago Press.

———. 2008. "Law, Lawyers, and Empire." In *The Cambridge History of Law in America,* ed. Michael Grossberg and Christopher Tomlins, vol. 3, *The Twentieth Century and After (1920–),* 718–58. Cambridge: Cambridge University Press.

———. 1996. *Dealing in Virtue: International Commercial Arbitration and the Construction of a Transnational Legal Order.* Chicago: University of Chicago Press.

Dinovitzer, Ronit. 2011. "The Financial Rewards of Elite Status in the Legal Profession." *Law and Social Inquiry* 36 (4): 971–98.

Dinovitzer, Ronit, and Bryant G. Garth. 2020. "The New Place of Corporate Law Firms in the Structuring of Elite Legal Careers." *Law and Social Inquiry* 45 (2): 339–71.

———. 2009. "Pro Bono as an Elite Strategy in Early Lawyer Careers." In *Private Lawyers and the Public Interest: The Evolving Role of Pro Bono in the Legal Profession*, ed. Robert Granfield and Lynn Mather, 115–34. Oxford: Oxford University Press.

———. 2007. "Lawyer Satisfaction in the Process of Structuring Legal Careers." *Law and Society Review* 40 (2): 445–80.

Dinovitzer, Ronit, Bryant G. Garth, Robert L. Nelson, Gabriele Plickert, Rebecca Sandefur, Joyce S. Sterling, and David B. Wilkins. 2014. "After the JD III: Third Results from a National Study of Legal Careers." Chicago: American Bar Foundation and NALP Foundation for Law Career Research and Education.

Dinovitzer, Ronit, Bryant G. Garth, Richard Sander, Joyce Sterling, and Gita Z. Wilder. 2004. "After the JD: First Results of a National Study of Lawyer Careers." Chicago: NALP Foundation for Law Career Research and Education and American Bar Foundation.

Dinovitzer, Ronit, Bryant G. Garth, and Joyce S. Sterling. 2013. "Buyers' Remorse? An Empirical Assessment of the Desirability of a Lawyer Career." *Journal of Legal Education* 63 (2): 211–34.

Dinovitzer, Ronit, and John Hagan. 2014. "Hierarchical Structure and Gender Dissimilarity in American Legal Labor Markets." *Social Forces* 92 (3): 929–55.

Dinovitzer, Ronit, Robert L. Nelson, Gabriele Plickert, Rebecca Sandefur, and Joyce S. Sterling. 2009a. "After the JD II: Second Results from a National Study of Legal Careers." Chicago: American Bar Foundation and NALP Foundation.

Dinovitzer, Ronit, Nancy Reichman, and Joyce Sterling. 2009b. "The Differential Valuation of Women's Work: A New Look at the Gender Gap in Lawyers' Incomes." *Social Forces* 88 (2): 819–68.

DiPrete, Thomas A., and Gregory M. Eirich. 2006. "Cumulative Advantage as a Mechanism for Inequality: A Review of Theoretical and Empirical Developments." *Annual Review of Sociology* 32:271–97.

Dixon, Jo, and Carroll Seron. 1995. "Stratification in the Legal Profession: Sex, Sector, and Salary." *Law and Society Review* 29:381–412.

Doren, Catherine. 2019. "Which Mothers Pay a Higher Price? Education Differences in Motherhood Wage Penalties by Parity and Fertility Timing." *Sociological Science* 6:684–709.

Dunlop, Sybil, and Jenny Gassman-Pines. 2021. "Why the Legal Profession Is the Nation's Least Diverse (and How to Fix It)." *Mitchell Hamline Law Review* 47 (1): 129–61.

Dwyer, Rachel E., Randy Hodson, and Laura McCloud. 2013. "Gender, Debt, and Dropping Out of College." *Gender and Society* 27 (1): 30–55.

Elder, Glen H. 1974. *Children of the Great Depression: Social Change in Life Experience.* Chicago: University of Chicago Press.

Ely, Robin J., Pamela Stone, and Colleen Ammerman. 2014. "Rethink What You 'Know' about High-Achieving Women." *Harvard Business Review*, December 1, 100–109.

Elzinga, Cees. 2006. "Turbulence in Categorical Time Series." Unpublished manuscript, Vrije University.

England, Paula, Jonathan Bearak, Michelle J. Budig, and Melissa J. Hodges. 2016. "Do Highly Paid, Highly Skilled Women Experience the Largest Motherhood Penalty?" *American Sociological Review* 81 (6): 1161–89.

Epstein, Cynthia Fuchs. 1981. *Women in Law*. New York: Basic Books.

Epstein, Cynthia Fuchs, Robert Saute, Bonnie Oglensky, and Martha Gever. 1995. "Glass Ceilings and Open Doors: Women's Advancement in the Legal Profession." *Fordham Law Review* 64 (2): 291–449.

Epstein, Cynthia Fuchs, Carroll Seron, Bonnie Oglensky, and Robert Saute. 1999. "The Part-Time Paradox: Time Norms, Professional Life, Family, and Gender." London: Routledge.

Espeland, Wendy Nelson, and Michael Sauder. 2007. "Rankings and Reactivity: How Public Measures Recreate Social Worlds." *American Journal of Sociology* 113 (1): 1–40.

Eulau, Heinz, and John D. Sprague. 1964. *Lawyers in Politics: A Study in Professional Convergence*. Indianapolis: Bobbs-Merrill.

Faith-Slaker, April. 2018. "Supporting Justice: A Report on the Pro Bono Work of America's Lawyers." Chicago: American Bar Association. https://www.americanbar.org/content/dam/aba/administrative/probono_public_service/ls_pb_supporting_justice_iv_final.pdf.

Falconbridge, James, and Daniel Muzio. 2008. "Organizational Professionalism in Globalizing Law Firms." *Work, Employment and Society* 22 (1): 7–25.

Firebaugh, Glenn, Cody Warner, and Michael Massoglia. 2013. "Fixed Effects, Random Effects, and Hybrid Models for Causal Analysis." In *Handbook for Causal Analysis for Social Research*, ed. Stephen L. Morgan, 113–32. Dordrecht: Springer.

Flood, John. 2011. "The Re-Landscaping of the Legal Profession: Large Law Firms and Professional Re-Regulation." *Current Sociology* 59 (4): 507–29.

Fourcade, Marion. 2006. "The Construction of a Global Profession: The Transnationalization of Economics." *American Journal of Sociology* 112 (1): 145–94.

Freidson, Eliot. 1986. *Professional Powers: A Study of the Institutionalization of Formal Knowledge*. Chicago: University of Chicago Press.

———. 1970. *Profession of Medicine*. New York: Dodd, Mead.

Galanter, Marc. 1996. "Lawyers in the Mist: The Golden Age of Legal Nostalgia." *Dickinson Law Review* 100 (3): 549–62.

———. 1986. "The Day After the Litigation Explosion." *Maryland Law Review* 46 (1): 3–39.

———. 1974. "Why the 'Haves' Come Out Ahead: Speculations on the Limits of Legal Change." *Law and Society Review* 9 (1): 95–160.

Galanter, Marc, and William D. Henderson. 2008. "The Elastic Tournament: The Transformation of the Big Law Firm." *Stanford Law Review* 60 (6): 1867–1929.

Galanter, Marc, and Thomas Palay. 1991. *Tournament of Lawyers: The Transformation of the Big Law Firm*. Chicago: University of Chicago Press.

Ganzeboom, Harry B. G., and Donald J. Treiman. 1996. "Internationally Comparable Measures of Occupational Status for the 1988 International Standard Classification of Occupations." *Social Science Research* 25 (3): 201–39.

García-López, Gladys. 2008. "'NUNCA TE TOMAN EN CUENTA [THEY NEVER TAKE YOU INTO ACCOUNT]': The Challenges of Inclusion and Strategies for Success of Chicana Attorneys." *Gender and Society* 22 (5): 590–612.

Garth, Bryant G. 2017. "Notes on the Future of the Legal Profession in the United States: The Key Roles of Corporate Law Firms and Urban Law Schools." *Buffalo Law Review* 65 (2): 287–328.

———. 2013. "Crises, Crisis Rhetoric, and Competition in Legal Education: A Sociological

Perspective on the (Latest) Crisis of the Legal Profession and Legal Education." *Stanford Law and Policy Review* 24:503–32.

Garth, Bryant G., and Joanne Martin. 1993. "Law Schools and the Construction of Competence." *Journal of Legal Education* 43 (4): 469–509.

Garth, Bryant G., and Joyce S. Sterling. 2018. "Diversity, Hierarchy, and Fit in Legal Careers: Insights from Fifteen Years of Qualitative Interviews." *Georgetown Journal of Legal Ethics* 31:123–74.

———. 2009. "Exploring Inequality in the Corporate Law Firm Apprenticeship: Doing the Time, Finding the Love. Symposium: Empirical Research on the Legal Profession: Insights from Theory and Practice." *Georgetown Journal of Legal Ethics* 22 (4): 1361–94.

George, Tracey, and Albert H. Yoon. 2014. "The Market for New Law Professors." *Journal of Empirical Legal Studies* 11 (1): 1–38.

Gilson, Ronald J. 1990. "The Devolution of the Legal Profession: A Demand Side Perspective." *Maryland Law Review* 49 (4): 869–916.

Glater, Jonathan D. 2008. "Even Lawyers Are Getting Laid Off." *New York Times*, November 12.

Glendon, Mary Ann. 1996. *A Nation under Lawyers: How the Crisis in the Legal Profession Is Transforming American Society*. Cambridge, MA: Harvard University Press.

Goldin, Claudia. 2006. "The Quiet Revolution That Transformed Women's Employment, Education, and Family." Working Paper 11953. Cambridge, MA:. National Bureau of Economic Research. https://www.nber.org/papers/w11953.

Goode, William J. 1957. "Community within a Community: The Professions." *American Sociological Review* 22 (2): 194–200.

Gordon, Robert W. 2017. "The Return of the Lawyer-Statesman Essay." *Stanford Law Review* 69 (6): 1731–64.

———. 2009. "The Citizen Lawyer—a Brief Informal History of a Myth with Some Basis in Reality." *William and Mary Law Review* 50 (4): 1169–1206.

———. 1984. "'The Ideal and the Actual in the Law': Fantasies and Practices of New York City Lawyers, 1880–1910." In *The New High Priests: Lawyers in Post–Civil War America*, ed. Gerard W. Gawalt, 51–74. Westport, CT.: Greenwood.

Gorman, Elizabeth H. 2006. "Work Uncertainty and the Promotion of Professional Women." *Social Forces* 85 (2): 865–90.

Gorman, Elizabeth H., and Fiona M. Kay. 2020. "Skill Development Practices and Racial-Ethnic Diversity in Elite Professional Firms." In *Professional Work: Knowledge, Power and Social Inequalities*, ed. Elizabeth H. Gorman and Steven P. Vallas, 115–45. Research in the Sociology of Work, vol. 34. Bingley: Emerald.

———. 2010. "Racial and Ethnic Minority Representation in Large U.S. Law Firms." In *Special Issue: Law Firms, Legal Culture, and Legal Practice*, ed. Austin Sarat, 211–38. Studies in Law, Politics, and Society, vol. 52. Bingley: Emerald.

Gough, Margaret, and Mary Noonan. 2013. "A Review of the Motherhood Wage Penalty in the United States." *Sociology Compass* 7 (4): 328–42.

Granfield, Robert. 1992. *Making Elite Lawyers: Visions of Law at Harvard and Beyond*. New York: Routledge.

Hadfield, Gillian K. 2016. *Rules for a Flat World: Why Humans Invented Law and How to Reinvent It for a Complex Global Economy*. New York: Oxford University Press.

Hagan, John, and Fiona Kay. 2010. "The Masculine Mystique: Living Large from Law School to Later Life." *Canadian Journal of Law and Society* 25 (2): 195–226.

———. 2007. "Even Lawyers Get the Blues: Gender, Depression, and Job Satisfaction in Legal Practice." *Law and Society Review* 41 (1): 51–78.

———. 1995. *Gender in Practice: A Study of Lawyers' Lives.* New York: Oxford University Press.

Haltom, William, and Michael McCann. 2009. *Distorting the Law: Politics, Media, and the Litigation Crisis.* Chicago: University of Chicago Press.

Hanlon, Gerard. 1999. *Lawyers, the State and the Market: Professionalism Revisited.* London: Palgrave Macmillan.

Haynes, Kathryn. 2012. "Body Beautiful? Gender, Identity and the Body in Professional Services Firms." *Gender, Work and Organization* 19 (5): 489–507.

Hazard, Geoffrey C., Susan P. Koniak, Roger C. Cramton, George M. Cohen, and W. Bradley Wendel. 2017. *The Law and Ethics of Lawyering.* University Casebook Series. 6th ed. St. Paul, MN: Foundation.

Headworth, Spencer, Robert L. Nelson, Ronit Dinovitzer, and David B. Wilkins, eds. 2016. *Diversity in Practice: Race, Gender, and Class in Legal and Professional Careers.* Cambridge Studies in Law and Society. Cambridge: Cambridge University Press.

Heineman, Benjamin W. 2016. *The Inside Counsel Revolution: Resolving the Partner-Guardian Tension.* Chicago: American Bar Association.

Heinz, John P., and Edward O. Laumann. 1982. *Chicago Lawyers: The Social Structure of the Bar.* Chicago: American Bar Foundation.

Heinz, John P., Robert L. Nelson, Rebecca Sandefur, and Edward O. Laumann. 2005. *Urban Lawyers: The New Social Structure of the Bar.* Chicago: University of Chicago Press.

Henderson, William D. 2014. "From Big Law to Lean Law." *International Review of Law and Economics* 38 (June): 5–16.

———. 2011. "Three Generations of U.S. Lawyers: Generalists, Specialists, Project Managers." *Maryland Law Review* 70 (1): 373–89.

———. 2005. "An Empirical Study of Single-Tier versus Two-Tier Partnerships in the Am Law 200." *North Carolina Law Review* 84:1691–1750.

Henderson, William D., and Arthur S. Alderson. 2016. "The Changing Economic Geography of Large U.S. Law Firms." *Journal of Economic Geography* 16 (6): 1235–57.

Henderson, William D., and Leonard Bierman. 2009. "An Empirical Analysis of Lateral Lawyer Trends from 2000 to 2007: The Emerging Equilibrium for Corporate Law Firms." *Georgetown Journal of Legal Ethics* 22:1395–1430.

Henry, Samantha K., Merida M. Grant, and Karen L. Cropsey. 2018. "Determining the Optimal Clinical Cutoff on the CES-D for Depression in a Community Corrections Sample." *Journal of Affective Disorders* 234:270–75.

Herrera, Luz E. 2007. "Reflections of a Community Lawyer." *The Modern American* 3 (2): 39–45.

Hewlett, Sylvia Ann, and Carolyn Buck Luce. 2005. "Off-Ramps and On-Ramps: Keeping Talented Women on the Road to Success." *Harvard Business Review*, March 1. https://hbr.org/2005/03/off-ramps-and-on-ramps-keeping-talented-women-on-the-road-to-success.

Hinings, C. R. 2006. "The Changing Nature of Professional Organizations." In *The Oxford Handbook of Work and Organization*, ed. Stephen Ackroyd, Rosemary Batt, Paul Thompson, and Pamela S. Tolbert, 404–24. Oxford: Oxford University Press.

Hodges, Melissa J., and Michelle J. Budig. 2010. "Who Gets the Daddy Bonus? Organizational Hegemonic Masculinity and the Impact of Fatherhood on Earnings." *Gender and Society* 24 (6): 717–45.

Hollis-Brusky, Amanda. 2011. "Support Structures and Constitutional Change: Teles, Southworth, and the Conservative Legal Movement." *Law and Social Inquiry* 36 (2): 516–36.

Houle, Jason N., and Fenaba R. Addo. 2019. "Racial Disparities in Student Debt and the Reproduction of the Fragile Black Middle Class." *Sociology of Race and Ethnicity* 5 (4): 562–77.

Hovenkamp, Herbert, Mark Janis, and Mark A. Lemley. 2003. "Anticompetitive Settlement of Intellectual Property Disputes." *Minnesota Law Review* 87:1719–54.

Huelsman, M. 2015. "The Debt Divide: The Racial and Class Bias behind the 'New Normal' of Student Borrowing." https://www.demos.org/sites/default/files/publications/Mark-Debt%20divide%20Final%20%28SF%29.pdf.

Hughes, Everett C. 1963. "Professions." *Daedalus* 92 (4): 655–68.

———. 1958. *Men and Their Work*. Glencoe, IL: Free Press.

Hull, Kathleen E. 1999. "The Paradox of the Contended Female Lawyer Changing Employment Statuses in the Practice of Law: Research Note." *Law and Society Review* 33 (3): 687–702.

Irons, Peter H. 1993. *The New Deal Lawyers*. Princeton, NJ: Princeton University Press.

Jackson, Robert H. 1944. "Tribute to Country Lawyers: A Review." *Texas Bar Journal* 7 (5): 146–63.

Jeffreys, Brenda Sapino. 2021. "Profits Surged at Am Law 100 Firms in 2020: Can They Keep It Up in 2021?" *The American Lawyer*, April 20. https://www.law.com/americanlawyer/2021/04/20/profits-surged-at-am-law-100-firms-in-2020-can-they-keep-it-up-in-2021.

Johnson, Terence J. 1972. *Professions and Power*. New York: Routledge.

Juhn, Chinhui, and Kristin McCue. 2017. "Specialization Then and Now: Marriage, Children, and the Gender Earnings Gap across Cohorts." *Journal of Economic Perspectives* 31 (1): 183–204.

Kahlenberg, Richard D. 1999. *Broken Contract: A Memoir of Harvard Law School*. Amherst: University of Massachusetts Press.

Kan, Man Yee, Oriel Sullivan, and Jonathan Gershuny. 2011. "Gender Convergence in Domestic Work: Discerning the Effects of Interactional and Institutional Barriers from Large-Scale Data." *Sociology* 45 (2): 234–51.

Kawamoto, Dawn. 2012. "There's No Need to Hire a Lawyer When These Sites Let You Do It Yourself." *Business Insider*, May 2. https://www.businessinsider.com/diy-legal-sites-could-make-you-the-only-lawyer-you-need-2012-5.

Kay, Fiona M. 2019. "Social Capital, Relational Inequality Theory, and Earnings of Racial Minority Lawyers." In *Race, Identity and Work* (Research in the Sociology of Work, vol. 32), ed. Ethel L. Mickey and Adia Harvey Wingfield, 63–90. Bingley: Emerald Group.

———. 2002. "Crossroads to Innovation and Diversity: The Careers of Women Lawyers in Quebec." *McGill Law Journal* 47 (4): 699–746.

———. 1997. "Flight from Law: A Competing Risks Model of Departures from Law Firms." *Law and Society Review* 31 (2): 301–35.

Kay, Fiona M., Stacey L. Alarie, and Jones K. Adjei. 2016. "Undermining Gender Equality: Female Attrition from Private Law Practice." *Law and Society Review* 50 (3): 766–801.

———. 2013. "Leaving Private Practice: How Organizational Context, Time Pressures, and Structural Inflexibilities Shape Departures from Private Law Practice." *Indiana Journal of Global Legal Studies* 20 (2): 1223–60.

Kay, Fiona M., and Elizabeth H. Gorman. 2012. "Developmental Practices, Organizational Culture, and Minority Representation in Organizational Leadership: The Case of Partners in Large U.S. Law Firms." *Annals of the American Academy of Political and Social Science* 639:91–113.

Kay, Fiona M., and Jean E. Wallace. 2009. "Mentors as Social Capital: Gender, Mentors, and Career Rewards in Law Practice." *Sociological Inquiry* 79 (4): 418–52.

Kidder, William C. 2001. "Does the LSAT Mirror or Magnify Racial and Ethnic Differences in Educational Attainment: A Study of Equally Achieving Elite College Students." *California Law Review* 89:1055–1124.

Killewald, Alexandra. 2013. "Return to Being Black, Living in the Red: A Race Gap in Wealth That Goes Beyond Social Origins." *Demography* 50 (4): 1177–95.

Killewald, Alexandra, and Brielle Bryan. 2018. "Falling Behind: The Role of Inter- and Intragenerational Processes in Widening Racial and Ethnic Wealth Gaps through Early and Middle Adulthood." *Social Forces* 97 (2): 705–40.

Kluger, Richard. 1975. *Simple Justice: The History of Brown v. Board of Education and Black America's Struggle for Equality*. New York: Knopf.

Kolodinsky, Lynne. 2014. "The Law Review Divide: A Study of Gender Diversity on the Top Twenty Law Reviews." Cornell Law Library Prize for Exemplary Student Research Papers. Ithaca, NY: Cornell University Law Library. https://scholarship.law.cornell.edu/cllsrp/8.

Kornhauser, Lewis A., and Richard L. Revesz. 1995. "Legal Education and Entry into the Legal Profession: The Role of Race, Gender, and Educational Debt." *New York University Law Review* 829 (4): 829–964.

Kritzer, Herbert M. 2002. "From Litigators of Ordinary Cases to Litigators of Extraordinary Cases: Stratification of the Plaintiffs' Bar in the Twenty-First Century." *DePaul Law Review* 51:219–40.

Krivo, Lauren J., and Robert L. Kaufman. 2004. "Housing and Wealth Inequality: Racial-Ethnic Differences in Home Equity in the United States." *Demography* 41:585–605.

Kronman, Anthony T. 1993. *The Lost Lawyer: Failing Ideals of the Legal Profession*. Cambridge, MA: Harvard University Press.

Ladinsky, Jack. 1963. "Careers of Lawyers, Law Practice, and Legal Institutions." *American Sociological Review* 28 (1): 47–54.

Lamont, Michèle. 2012. "Toward a Comparative Sociology of Valuation and Evaluation." *Annual Review of Sociology* 38:201–21.

———. 1992. *Money, Morals, and Manners: The Culture of the French and American Upper-Middle Class*. Chicago: University of Chicago Press.

Larson, Magali Sarfatti. 1977. *The Rise of Professionalism: A Sociological Analysis*. Berkeley and Los Angeles: University of California Press.

Law School Survey of Student Engagement. 2020. "The Changing Landscape of Legal Education: A 15-Year LSSSE Retrospective." Indiana University Center for Postsecondary Research. https://lssse.indiana.edu/wp-content/uploads/2015/12/LSSSE_Annual-Report_Winter 2020_Final-2.pdf.

Law School Transparency. 2019. "Law School Costs." https://data.lawschooltransparency.com /costs/tuition.

Lawyer Legion. 2020. State Bar Associations. https://www.lawyerlegion.com/associations/state-bar.

Lazega, Emmanuel. 2000. "Rule Enforcement among Peers: A Lateral Control Regime." *Organization Studies* 21 (1): 193–214.

Leipold, James G., and Judith N. Collins. 2016. "The Stories behind the Numbers: Jobs for New Grads over More Than Two Decades." *NALP Bulletin*, December. https://www.nalp.org/1216 research.

Lempert, Richard, David Chambers, and Terry Adams. 2001. "Myths and Facts about Affirmative Action." *Arizona Attorney* 38 (10): 27–29.

Leonard, Walter J. 1977. *Black Lawyers: Training and Results, Then and Now.* Boston: Senna & Shih.

Leslie, Christopher R. 2011. *Antitrust Law and Intellectual Property Rights: Cases and Materials.* Oxford: Oxford University Press.

Li, Miranda, Phillip Yao, and Goodwin Liu. 2020. "Who's Going to Law School? Trends in Law School Enrollment since the Great Recession." *UC Davis Law Review* 54 (2): 613–62.

Linowitz, Sol M. 1994. *The Betrayed Profession: Lawyering at the End of the Twentieth Century.* New York: Scribner.

Lipartito, Kenneth J., and Joseph A. Pratt. 2011. *Baker and Botts in the Development of Modern Houston.* Austin: University of Texas Press.

Macaulay, Stewart. 1963. "Non-Contractual Relations in Business: A Preliminary Study." *American Sociological Review* 28 (1): 55–67.

Mare, Robert D. 2016. "Educational Homogamy in Two Gilded Ages: Evidence from Inter-Generational Social Mobility Data." *The Annals of the American Academy of Political and Social Science* 663 (1): 117–39.

Markovic, Milan, and Gabriele Plickert. 2019. "The Paradox of Minority Attorney Satisfaction." *International Review of Law and Economics* 60 (December): 1058–59.

Mawdsley, John, and Deepak Somaya. 2015. "Strategy and Strategic Alignment in Professional Service Firms." In *The Oxford Handbook of Professional Service Firms*, ed. Laura Empson, Daniel Muzio, Joseph Broschak, and Bob Hinings, 213–37. Oxford: Oxford University Press.

McGill, Christa. 2006. "Educational Debt and Law Student Failure to Enter Public Service: Bringing Empirical Data to Bear." *Law and Social Inquiry* 31 (3): 677–708.

McLaughlin, Heather, Christopher Uggen, and Amy Blackstone. 2017. "The Economic and Career Effects of Sexual Harassment on Working Women." *Gender and Society* 31 (3): 333–58.

———. 2012. "Sexual Harassment, Workplace Authority, and the Paradox of Power." *American Sociological Review* 77 (4): 625–47.

Menkel-Meadow, Carrie. 1986. "The Comparative Sociology of Women Lawyers: The 'Feminization' of the Legal Profession." *Osgoode Hall Law Journal* 24 (4): 897–918.

Merritt, Deborah Jones. 2015. "What Happened to the Class of 2010? Empirical Evidence of Structural Change in the Legal Profession." *Michigan State Law Review* [2015] (3): 1044–1123.

Mertz, Elizabeth. 2007. *The Language of Law School: Learning to "Think Like a Lawyer."* Oxford: Oxford University Press.

Messerschmidt, James W. 2018. *Hegemonic Masculinity: Formulation, Reformulation, and Amplification.* Lanham, MD: Rowman & Littlefield.

Mirowsky, John, and Catherine Ross. 2003. *Social Causes of Psychological Distress.* 2nd ed. New York: Aldine de Gruyter.

Monahan, John, and Jeffrey Swanson. 2019. "Lawyers at the Peak of Their Careers: A 30-Year Longitudinal Study of Job and Life Satisfaction." *Journal of Empirical Legal Studies* 16 (1): 4–25.

Neely, Meghan Tobias. 2022. *Hedged Out: Inequality and Insecurity on Wall Street.* Oakland: University of California Press.

Nelson, Robert L. 1988. *Partners with Power: The Social Transformation of the Large Firm.* Berkeley and Los Angeles: University of California Press.

Nelson, Robert L., Ronit Dinovitzer, Bryant G. Garth, Joyce S. Sterling, Gita Z. Wilder, and Terry K. Adams. 2006. "Observations from the After the Bar Survey of the Bar Class of 2000." *Quinnipac Law Review* 24:539–53.

Nelson, Robert L., and Laura Beth Nielsen. 2000. "Cops, Counsel, and Entrepreneurs: Constructing the Role of Inside Counsel in Large Corporations." *Law and Society Review* 34 (2): 457–94.

Nelson, Robert L., Ioana Sendroiu, Ronit Dinovitzer, and Meghan Dawe. 2019. "Perceiving Discrimination: Race, Gender, and Sexual Orientation in the Legal Workplace." *Law and Social Inquiry* 44 (4): 1051–82.

Nelson, Robert L., and David M. Trubek. 1992. Introduction to *Lawyers' Ideals/Lawyers' Practices: Transformations in the American Legal Profession*, 1–27. Ithaca, NY: Cornell University Press.

Neumann, Richard K. 2004. "Women in Legal Education: A Statistical Update." *UMKC Law Review* 73 (2): 419–42.

New York State Bar Association. 2000. *Preserving the Core Values of the American Legal Profession: The Place of Multidisciplinary Practice in the Law Governing Practice*. Albany, NY.

Nosek, Brian A., Mahzarin R. Banaji, and Anthony G. Greenwald. 2002. "Harvesting Implicit Group Attitudes and Beliefs from a Demonstration Web Site." *Group Dynamics: Theory, Research, and Practice* 6 (1): 101–15.

Offer, Shira, and Barbara Schneider. 2011. "Revisiting the Gender Gap in Time-Use Patterns: Multitasking and Well-Being among Mothers and Fathers in Dual-Earner Families." *American Sociological Review* 76 (6): 809–33.

Olivas, Michael A. 1999. "Paying for a Law Degree: Trends in Student Borrowing and the Ability to Repay Debt." *Journal of Legal Education* 49 (3): 333–41.

Oliver, Melvin L., and Thomas M. Shapiro. 1995. *Black Wealth/White Wealth: A New Perspective on Racial Inequality*. New York: Routledge.

Padavic, Irene, Robin J. Ely, and Erin M. Reid. 2020. "Explaining the Persistence of Gender Inequality: The Work-Family Narrative as a Social Defense against the 24/7 Work Culture." *Administrative Science Quarterly* 65 (1): 61–111.

Pager, Devah. 2007. *Marked: Race, Crime, and Finding Work in an Era of Mass Incarceration*. Chicago: University of Chicago Press.

Pager, Devah, and Lincoln Quillian. 2005. "Walking the Talk? What Employers Say versus What They Do." *American Sociological Review* 70 (3): 355–80.

Parikh, Sara, and Bryant Garth. 2005. "Philip Corboy and the Construction of the Plaintiffs' Personal Injury Bar." *Law and Social Inquiry* 30 (2): 269–304.

Paterson, Alan A. 1982. *The Law Lords*. Toronto: University of Toronto Press.

Payne-Pikus, Monique R., John Hagan, and Robert L. Nelson. 2010. "Experiencing Discrimination: Race and Retention in America's Largest Law Firms." *Law and Society Review* 44 (3): 553–84.

Pearce, Russell G., Eli Wald, and Swethaa S. Ballakrishnen. 2015. "Difference Blindness vs. Bias Awareness: Why Law Firms with the Best of Intentions Have Failed to Create Diverse Partnerships." *Fordham Law Review* 83 (5): 2407–55.

Percheski, Christine. 2008. "Opting Out? Cohort Differences in Professional Women's Employment Rates from 1960 to 2005." *American Sociological Review* 73 (3): 497–517.

Pew Research Center. 2020. "Democratic Edge in Party Identification Narrows Slightly." June 20. https://www.people-press.org/2020/06/02/democratic-edge-in-party-identification-narrows -slightly.

———. 2012. "Partisan Polarization Surges in Bush, Obama Years: Trends in American Values, 1987–2012." June 4. https://www.people-press.org/2012/06/04/partisan-polarization-surges-in-bush-obama-years.

Pfeffer, Fabian T., and Alexandra Killewald. 2019. "Intergenerational Wealth Mobility and Racial Inequality." *Socius: Sociological Research for a Dynamic World* 5 (January): 237802311983179.

Pierce, Jennifer L. 1995. *Gender Trials: Emotional Lives in Contemporary Law Firms.* Berkeley and Los Angeles: University of California Press.

Piketty, Thomas, and Emmanuel Saez. 2003. "Income Inequality in the United States, 1913–1998." *Quarterly Journal of Economics* 118 (1): 1–39.

Plickert, Gabriele, Fiona Kay, and John Hagan. 2017. "Depressive Symptoms and the Salience of Job Satisfaction over the Life Course of Professionals." *Advances in Life Course Research* 31 (March): 22–33.

Powell, David. 2020. "Quantile Treatment Effects in the Presence of Covariates." *Review of Economics and Statistics* 102 (5): 994–1005.

Price, Derek V. 2004. "Educational Debt Burden among Student Borrowers: An Analysis of the Baccalaureate and Beyond Panel, 1997 Follow-Up." *Research in Higher Education* 45 (7): 701–37.

Putnam, Robert. 2000. *Bowling Alone: The Collapse and Revival and American Community.* New York: Simon & Schuster.

———. 1995. "Bowling Alone: America's Declining Social Capital." *Journal of Democracy* 6 (1): 65–78.

Pyne, Jaymes, and Eric Grodsky. 2020. "Inequality and Opportunity in a Perfect Storm of Graduate Student Debt." *Sociology of Education* 93 (1): 20–39.

Queen, Jack. 2020. "NYU Law Students Disrupt Paul Weiss Event over Exxon Win." Law360, February 11. https://www.law360.com/articles/1243046/nyu-law-students-disrupt-paul-weiss-event-over-exxon-win.

Quillian, Lincoln, and Devah Pager. 2001. "Black Neighbors, Higher Crime? The Role of Racial Stereotypes in Evaluations of Neighborhood Crime." *American Journal of Sociology* 107 (3): 717–67.

Quillian, Lincoln, Devah Pager, Ole Hexel, and Arnfinn H. Midtbøen. 2017. "Meta-Analysis of Field Experiments Shows No Change in Racial Discrimination in Hiring over Time." *Proceedings of the National Academy of Sciences* 114 (41): 10870–75.

Rampell, Catherine. 2013. "Law School Applications Decline, Especially from Graduates of Elite Colleges." *New York Times,* August 23.

Ray, Victor. 2019. "A Theory of Racialized Organizations." *American Sociological Review* 84 (10): 26–53.

Regan, Mitt. 2004. *Eat What You Kill: The Fall of the Wall Street Lawyer.* Ann Arbor: University of Michigan Press.

Regan, Mitt, and Lisa H. Rohrer. 2021. *BigLaw: Money and Meaning in the Modern Law Firm.* Chicago: University of Chicago Press.

Reichman, Nancy J., and Joyce S. Sterling. 2004. "Sticky Floors, Broken Steps, and Concrete Ceilings in Legal Careers." *Texas Journal of Women and the Law* 14 (1): 27–76.

Remus, Dana. 2017. "Hemispheres Apart: A Profession Connected." *Fordham Law Review* 82 (6): 2665–82.

Rhode, Deborah L. 2011. "From Platitudes to Priorities: Diversity and Gender Equity in Law Firms." *Georgetown Journal of Legal Ethics* 24:1041.

———. 2005. *Pro Bono in Principle and in Practice: Public Service and the Professions*. Stanford, CA: Stanford University Press.

———. 1991. "The 'No-Problem' Problem: Feminist Challenges and Cultural Change." *Yale Law Journal* 100 (6): 1731–93.

Ribstein, Larry E. 2010. "The Death of Big Law." *Wisconsin Law Review* [2010] (3): 749–816.

Ridgeway, Cecilia L. 2014. "Why Status Matters for Inequality." *American Sociological Review* 79 (1): 1–16.

Rivera, Lauren A. 2016. *Pedigree: How Elite Students Get Elite Jobs*. Princeton, NJ: Princeton University Press.

———. 2012. "Hiring as Cultural Matching: The Case of Elite Professional Service Firms." *American Sociological Review* 77 (6): 999–1022.

Robson, Karen, and Jean E. Wallace. 2001. "Gendered Inequalities in Earnings: A Study of Canadian Lawyers." *Canadian Review of Sociology and Anthropology* 38 (1): 75–95.

Rosen, Robert Eli. 1989. "The Inside Counsel Movement, Professional Judgement and Organizational Representation." *Indiana Law Journal* 64 (3): 479–553.

Sampson, Robert J., and Stephen W. Raudenbush. 2004. "Seeing Disorder: Neighborhood Stigma and the Social Construction of 'Broken Windows.'" *Social Psychology Quarterly* 67 (4): 319–42.

Sandberg, Sheryl. 2015. "Lean in—Women, Work and the Will to Lead." *NHRD Network Journal* 8 (2): 137–39.

Sandefur, Rebecca L. 2014. "Bridging the Gap: Rethinking Outreach for Greater Access to Justice." *University of Arkansas at Little Rock Law Review* 37 (4): 721–40.

———. 2009. "Access to Justice: Classical Approaches and New Directions." *Sociology of Crime, Law and Deviance* 12:ix–xvii.

———. 2001. "Work and Honor in the Law: Prestige and the Division of Lawyers' Labor." *American Sociological Review* 66 (3): 382–403.

Sandstrom, Aleksandra, and Becka A. Alper. 2019. "Americans with Higher Education and Income Are More Likely to Be Involved in Community Groups." Pew Research Center, February 22. https://www.pewresearch.org/fact-tank/2019/02/22/americans-with-higher-education-and-income-are-more-likely-to-be-involved-in-community-groups.

Sayer, Liana C., Suzanne M. Bianchi, and John P. Robinson. 2004. "Are Parents Investing Less in Children? Trends in Mothers' and Fathers' Time with Children." *American Journal of Sociology* 110 (1): 1–43.

Schleef, Debra. 2010. "Identity Transformation, Hegemonic Masculinity and Research on Professionalization." *Sociology Compass* 4 (2): 122–35.

———. 2006. *Managing Elites: Professional Socialization in Law and Business Schools*. Lanham, MD: Rowman & Littlefield.

Schmidt, Christopher. 2019. *The Sit-Ins: Protest and Legal Change in the Civil Rights Era*. Chicago: University of Chicago Press.

Schneider, Daniel, Orestes P. Hastings, and Joe LaBriola. 2018. "Income Inequality and Class Divides in Parental Investments." *American Sociological Review* 83 (3): 475–507.

Schrag, Philip G. 2013. "Failing Law Schools—Brian Tamanaha's Misguided Missile." *Georgetown Journal of Legal Ethics* 26 (3): 387–422.

Scott, W. Richard. 1965. "Reactions to Supervision in a Heteronomous Professional Organization." *Administrative Science Quarterly* 10 (1): 65–81.

Segal, Geraldine R. 1983. *Blacks in the Law: Philadelphia and the Nation*. Philadelphia: University of Pennsylvania Press.

Seron, Carroll. 1996. *The Business of Practicing Law: The Work Lives of Solo and Small-Firm Attorneys.* Philadelphia: Temple University Press.

Shamir, Ronen. 1995. *Managing Legal Uncertainty: Elite Lawyers in the New Deal.* Durham, NC: Duke University Press.

Sloan, Karen. 2021. "'A Year Like No Other': Top Law Schools Are Inundated with Strong Applications." Law.Com, March 4. https://www.law.com/2021/03/04/a-year-like-no-other-top-law-schools-are-inundated-with-strong-applicants/?slreturn=20210517101830.

Slovak, Jeffrey S. 1981. "The Ethics of Corporate Lawyers: A Sociological Approach." *Law and Social Inquiry* 6 (3): 753–94.

———. 1979. "Working for Corporate Actors: Social Change and Elite Attorneys in Chicago." *American Bar Foundation Research Journal* 4 (3): 465–500.

Smigel, Erwin O. 1964. *The Wall Street Lawyer: Professional Organization Man?* New York: Free Press.

Smith, David Horton. 1994. "Determinants of Voluntary Association Participation and Volunteering: A Literature Review." *Nonprofit and Voluntary Sector Quarterly* 23 (3): 243–63.

Solomon, Rayman L. 1992. "Five Crises or One: The Concept of Legal Professionalism." In *Lawyers' Ideals/Lawyers' Practices: Transformations in the American Legal Profession*, ed. Robert L. Nelson, David M. Trubek, and Rayman L. Solomon, 144–74. Ithaca, NY: Cornell University Press.

Sommerlad, Hilary. 2016. "'A Pit to Put Women In': Professionalism, Work Intensification, Sexualisation and Work–Life Balance in the Legal Profession in England and Wales." *International Journal of the Legal Profession* 23 (1): 61–82.

———. 2002. "Women Solicitors in a Fractured Profession: Intersections of Gender and Professionalism in England and Wales." *International Journal of the Legal Profession* 9 (3): 213–34.

Sommerlad, Hilary, and Peter John Sanderson. 1998. *Gender, Choice, and Commitment: Women Solicitors in England and Wales and the Struggle for Equal Status.* London: Routledge.

Southworth, Ann. 2008. *Lawyers of the Right: Professionalizing the Conservative Coalition.* Chicago: University of Chicago Press.

Spangler, Eve. 1986. *Lawyers for Hire: Salaried Professionals at Work.* New Haven, CT: Yale University Press.

Spector, Malcolm. 1972. "The Rise and Fall of a Mobility Route." *Social Problems* 20 (2): 173–85.

Steele, Eric H., and Raymond T. Nimmer. 1976. "Lawyers, Clients, and Professional Regulation." *Law and Social Inquiry* 1 (3): 917–1019.

Sterling, Joyce S., and Nancy Reichman. 2016. "Overlooked and Undervalued: Women in Private Law Practice." *Annual Review of Law and Social Science* 12 (1): 373–93.

Stovel, Katherine, Michael Savage, and Peter Bearman. 1996. "Ascription into Achievement: Models of Career Systems at Lloyds Bank, 1890–1970." *American Journal of Sociology* 102 (2): 358–99.

Susskind, Richard. 2013. *Tomorrow's Lawyers: An Introduction to Your Future.* Oxford: Oxford University Press.

———. 2008. *The End of Lawyers? Rethinking the Nature of Legal Services.* Oxford: Oxford University Press.

Swaine, Robert T. 1946. *The Cravath Firm and Its Predecessors, 1819–1947.* New York: Ad Press.

Swidler, Ann. 2001. *Talk of Love: How Culture Matters.* Chicago: University of Chicago Press.

Tamanaha, Brian Z. 2012. *Failing Law Schools.* Chicago: University of Chicago Press.

Taylor, Aaron N. 2019. "The Marginalization of Black Aspiring Lawyers." *FIU Law Review* 13 (3): 489–511.

———. 2018. "Robin Hood in Reverse: How Law School Scholarships Compound Inequality." *Journal of Law and Education* 47 (1): 41–107.

Teles, Steven M. 2008. *The Rise of the Conservative Legal Movement.* Princeton, NJ: Princeton University Press.

Thomas, David. 2020. "The Am Law 100 Found Success in 2019: Will It Be Enough in 2020?" The American Lawyer, April 21. https://www.law.com/americanlawyer/2020/04/21/the-am -law-100-found-success-in-2019-will-it-be-enough-in-2020.

Tilly, Charles. 1998. *Durable Inequality.* Berkeley and Los Angeles: University of California Press.

Tocqueville, Alexis de. 1840/2009. *Democracy in America, Volumes 1 and 2.* Translated by Henry Reeve. Auckland: Floating Press.

Trubek, David, Helena Alviar Garcia, Diogo Coutinho, and Alvaro Santos, eds. 2013. *Law and the New Developmental State: The Brazilian Experience in Latin American Context.* New York: Cambridge University Press.

US Bureau of Labor Statistics. 2016. "Working Mothers Issue Brief." Women's Bureau Issue Brief. Washington, DC: US Department of Labor.

US Department of Justice and Federal Trade Commission. 2017. *Antitrust Guidelines for the Licensing of Intellectual Property.* January 12. https://www.ftc.gov/system/files/documents /publicstatements/1049793/ipguidelines2017.pdf.

Uzzi, Brian, and Ryon Lancaster. 2004. "Embeddedness and Price Formation in the Corporate Law Market." *American Sociological Review* 69 (3): 319–44.

Van Hoy, Jerry, ed. 2001. *Legal Professions: Work, Structure and Organization.* Sociology of Crime, Law and Deviance, vol. 3. Bingley: Emerald.

———. 1997. *Franchise Law Firms and the Transformation of Legal Services.* Westport, CT: Quorum.

———. 1995. "Selling and Processing Law: Legal Work at Franchise Law Firms." *Law and Society Review* 29 (4): 703–29.

Vickers, Jill, and Annette Isaac. 2012. *The Politics of Race: Canada, the United States, and Australia.* Toronto: University of Toronto Press.

Vilagut, Gemma, Carlos G. Forero, Gabriela Barbaglia, and Jordi Alonso. 2016. "Screening for Depression in the General Population with the Center for Epidemiologic Studies Depression (CES-D): A Systematic Review with Meta-Analysis." *PloS One* 11 (5): e015543.

von Hippel, Paul T. 2007. "Regression with Missing Ys: An Improved Strategy for Analyzing Multiply Imputed Data." *Sociological Methodology* 37 (1): 83–117.

Wald, Eli. 2010. "The Changing Professional Landscape of Large Law Firms, Glass Ceilings and Dead Ends: Professional Ideologies, Gender Stereotypes, and the Future of Women Lawyers at Large Law Firms." *Fordham Law Review* 78 (5): 2245–88.

Wallace, Jean E. 2008. "Parenthood and Commitment to the Legal Profession: Are Mothers Less Committed Than Fathers?" *Journal of Family and Economic Issues* 29 (3): 478–95.

Weiss, Debra Cassens. 2009. "Law Firm Mergers in an 'Upward Trend.'" *ABA Journal*, January 13. https://www.abajournal.com/news/article/law_firm_mergers_in_an_upward_trend.

Weisshaar, Katherine. 2018. "From Opt Out to Blocked Out: The Challenges for Labor Market Re-Entry After Family-Related Employment Lapses." *American Sociological Review* 83 (1): 34–60.

White, Ian R., Patrick Royston, and Angela M. Wood. 2011. "Multiple Imputation Using Chained Equations: Issues and Guidance for Practice." *Statistics in Medicine* 30 (4): 377–99.

Wilde, Elizabeth Ty, Lily Batchelder, and David Ellwood. 2010. "The Mommy Track Divides: The Impact of Childbearing on Wages of Women of Differing Skill Levels." Working Paper 16582. Cambridge, MA: National Bureau of Economic Research. http://www.nber.org/papers/w16582.pdf.

Wilkins, David B. 2012. "Is the In-House Counsel Movement Going Global? A Preliminary Assessment of the Role of Internal Counsel in Emerging Economies." *Wisconsin Law Review* 2012 (2): 251–305.

———. 2009. "Team of Rivals? Toward a New Model of the Corporate Attorney-Client Relationship." *Fordham Law Review* 78 (5): 2067–2136.

———. 2007. "Partner, Shmartner! *EEOC v. Sidley Austin Brown & Wood*." *Harvard Law Review* 120:1264–77.

———. 2004a. "Doing Well by Doing Good." *Houston Law Review* 41 (1): 1–92.

———. 2004b. "From 'Separate Is Inherently Unequal' to 'Diversity Is Good for Business': The Rise of Market-Based Diversity Arguments and the Fate of the Black Corporate Bar." *Harvard Law Review* 117 (5): 1548–1615.

———. 1992. "Who Should Regulate Lawyers?" *Harvard Law Review* 105 (4): 799–887.

Wilkins, David, Elizabeth Chambliss, Lisa A. Jones, and Haile Adamson. 2000. "Harvard Law School Report on the State of Black Alumni, 1869–2000." Cambridge, MA: Harvard Law School. https://clp.law.harvard.edu/knowledge-hub/reports/harvard-law-school-report-on-the-state-of-black-alumni-1869-2000.

Wilkins, David, Ronit Dinovitzer, and Rishi Batra. 2007. "Urban Law School Graduates in Large Law Firms." *Southwestern University Law Review* 36:433–507.

Wilkins, David B., and Maria J. Esteban Ferrer. 2018. "The Integration of Law into Global Business Solutions: The Rise, Transformation, and Potential Future of the Big Four Accountancy Networks in the Global Legal Services Market." *Law and Social Inquiry* 43 (3): 981–1026.

Wilkins, David B., and Bryon Fong. 2017. "Harvard Law School: Report on the State of Black Alumni II, 2000–2016." Research Paper no. 2018-2. Cambridge, MA: Harvard Law School Center.

Wilkins, David B., Bryon Fong, and Ronit Dinovitzer. 2015. "The Women and Men of Harvard Law School: The Preliminary Results from the HLS Career Study." Research Paper no. 2015-6. Cambridge, MA: Harvard Law School Center on the Legal Profession.

Wilkins, David B., and G. Mitu Gulati. 1998. "Reconceiving the Tournament of Lawyers: Tracking, Seeding, and Information Control in the Internal Labor Markets of Elite Law Firms." *Virginia Law Review* 84 (8): 1581–1681.

———. 1996. "Why Are There So Few Black Lawyers in Corporate Law Firms? An Institutional Analysis." *California Law Review* 84 (3): 493–625.

Wilkins, David B., and Young-Kyu Kim. 2016. "The Action After the Call: What General Counsels Say about the Value of Diversity in Legal Purchasing Decisions in the Years Following the 'Call to Action.'" In *Diversity in Practice: Race, Gender, and Class in Legal and Professional Careers*, ed. Spencer Headworth, Robert L. Nelson, Ronit Dinovitzer, and David B. Wilkins, 37–80. Cambridge: Cambridge University Press.

Wilkins, David B., David M. Trubek, and Bryon Fong. 2019. "Re-Gearing the Corporate Legal Eco-System in a Re-Geared World." Paper presented at the Harvard Law School, Cambridge, MA, April 15.

Williams, Joan C., Mary Blair-Loy, and Jennifer L. Berdahl. 2013. "Cultural Schemas, Social Class, and the Flexibility Stigma: Cultural Schemas and Social Class." *Journal of Social Issues* 69 (2): 209–34.

Wingfield, Adia Harvey. 2019. *Flatlining: Race, Work, and Health Care in the New Economy.* Oakland: University of California Press.

Woodson, Kevin. 2014. "Race and Rapport: Homophily and Racial Disadvantage in Large Law Firms." *Fordham Law Review* 83:2557–76.

Yoon, Albert. 2014. "Competition and the Evolution of Large Law Firms." *DePaul Law Review* 63 (2): 697–718.

Yu, Wei-hsin, and Janet Chen-Lan Kuo. 2017. "The Motherhood Wage Penalty by Work Conditions: How Do Occupational Characteristics Hinder or Empower Mothers?" *American Sociological Review* 82 (4): 744–69.

Zaloom, Caitlin. 2019. *Indebted: How Families Make College Work at Any Cost.* Princeton, NJ: Princeton University Press.

Zaloznaya, Marina, and Laura Beth Nielsen. 2011. "Mechanisms and Consequences of Professional Marginality: The Case of Poverty Lawyers Revisited." *Law and Social Inquiry* 36 (4): 919–44.

Index

Note: Page numbers followed by "t" indicate tables; page numbers followed by "f" indicate figures.

Abbott, Andrew, 21, 118

acquisitions, 17, 33–34, 35, 52

Adam (interviewee), 223, 225

Addo, Fenaba R., 262

Adjei, Jones K., 338

administrative law, 101t, 102, 103, 104, 105, 105f, 116

advancement, 63–65, 76, 78; geographic mobility and, 113–15; new avenues for, 77; opportunities for, 328, 332–33; path dependency and, 98; privilege and, 67; pro bono work and, 321; promotion-to-partnership system, 131; unequal distribution of, 64–65; women and, 115

advertising, 43, 44, 197

affirmative action programs, 266; law school admissions and, 365; legal challenges to, 39; legal profession and, 39–40

African American men: federal government careers and, 225–26; perception of law degree value and, 335; pro bono work and, 321; state government careers and, 236–37; student debt and, 260–61, 264, 270, 272

African Americans, 7–8, 12, 38, 243–59; bias and, 251–53; class and, 356–57, 358; community organizations and, 312; in corporate law firms, 52; cumulative (dis)advantage and, 260–61, 276–77; earnings and, 286; education and, 82–84; equity partnerships and, 96, 247, 248, 249, 250–51, 254–57, 259; family financial support and, 265, 275–76; financial support and, 265, 266t; first practice setting and, 88; government careers and, 10, 247; in-house legal departments and, 40; inside counsel and,

201–2; job changes and, 342; job offers and, 258–59; law firms and, 7–8, 10, 12–13, 39–40, 70, 72–73, 142, 243–59, 355; law school admissions and, 87; law school credentials and, 87; as law school movers, 114; law schools and, 38, 87, 114; leaving the firm, 244–45, 247, 248–51, 253, 254–57, 259, 355; legal services and, 247; LSAT scores and, 86; mentoring and, 251–53, 257; midcareer practice setting and, 97; in midsize firms, 72, 73; movements for social equality and, 52; nonpracticing positions and, 123–24; partnerships and, 39, 96, 247, 248, 249, 250–51, 254–57, 259, 355; perception of law degree value and, 334, 335; perceptions of tokenism and, 258–59; politics and, 304, 307; pro bono work and, 319; public defenders' offices and, 247; public interest law and, 247; race/ethnicity-based organizations and, 312; satisfaction and, 326, 330, 331; as small-firm starters, 70; as solo practitioners, 175–78; student debt and, 262, 263–73, 275–77, 356; underrepresented among bar admittees, 80; underrepresented among law school graduates, 80; underrepresented in partnerships, 40; work opportunities and, 251–53. *See also* African American men; African American women

African American women, 69, 246, 358; earnings and, 292–93, 292t; federal government careers and, 227–28; gender wage gap and, 292–93, 292t; in government careers, 74–75, 76; in law school, 38–39; in midsize law firms, 73; satisfaction and, 331; state government careers and, 233–35; student debt and, 262, 264, 270, 272, 275–76 age, nonpracticing positions and, 124

agency: in lawyers' careers, 351–66; social structure and, 10–15; structures of inequality and, 351–66

AJD Project, 12–13, 18, 23–24, 27–28, 127; Chicago studies and, 120–23, 125, 359–60 (*see also* Chicago studies); data, 127; demographic data and, 80–82, 81t; fields of practice and, 100–102, 101–2t; findings on debt, 263; findings on solo practitioners, 165; interviews, 127–30; key findings, 353–65; publications of, 246; research design and data, 353; respondents, 27–29; scope of, 49; sequence analysis, 353–54; two hemispheres thesis and, 359–60. *See also* AJD Project respondents

AJD Project respondents, 37, 38, 80; affirmative action programs and, 39; allocation of lawyers' total effort and, 106–7; business representation and, 360; capital and, 127–28; careers launched in contradictory environment, 44–45; class and, 82, 356–57; client types and, 111–13, 111f; community organizations and, 311–12, 323; diversity and, 39; earnings at wave 1 and wave 3, 109–10, 110f; education and, 82–87; entering legal profession, 32–36, 37, 43, 131–32; fields of law and, 111–13, 111f; first practice setting, 87–90; gender and, 82; job changes and, 338; large law firms and, 133–34; law schools and, 82–87; markets and, 111–13, 111f; mental health and, 345–46; Native Americans and, 94–95; nonpracticing lawyers and, 123–24; parental level of education and, 84, 86; parental nativity and, 86; parental occupation and, 82; pathways of lawyers' careers and, 54–78; politics and, 306–8, 306t; pro bono work and, 314–22; race and, 80–82, 81t, 355; relatively privileged social backgrounds of, 261; religious affiliation and, 116; responses of, 45; social characteristics of and career patterns, 79–98; specialization and, 103–4; strategies for career success, 45; student debt and, 263–73; student loans and, 33; undergraduate institutions and, 82, 83; at wave 3, 131–32. *See also specific interviewee names*

Alarie, Stacey L., 338

Alderson, Arthur S., 33

Alejandro (interviewee), 173–75, 181–82, 322

Alexander (interviewee), 223–24, 225

Alexandra (interviewee), 220–21

Alicia (interviewee), 3–5, 10, 37–38, 144, 352

allocation of lawyers' total effort, split between personal and business client sectors, 106

Allyson (interviewee), 158–60

alternative legal service providers, 43, 122

alumni associations, 310

Amanda (interviewee), 219

ambition, 128, 334–38

American Association of Law Schools, 30

American Bar Association (ABA), 23, 43–44, 310; accreditation and, 30, 31, 38; accreditation standards set by, 30, 31; diversity initiatives and, 39; founding of, 29, 30–31, 43; law firms and, 312; membership in, 313, 323; Model Rules of Professional Conduct, 313–15; pro bono work and, 323, 361–62, 373n7; reciprocal relationship between membership and partnership, 313

American Lawyer, The, 314

Amir (interviewee), 140–42

Ammerman, Colleen, 19

amount of work, control over, 122

Amuedo-Dorantes, Catalina, 288

Angela (interviewee), 208, 210–11

Annette (interviewee), 172–73, 186

antitrust law, 101t, 102, 105, 105f, 106

apprenticeship, 29, 30, 53

Arab Americans, 140–42

Armenian Americans, 175–76, 322

Asian American men, 140; earnings and, 292t, 293; gender wage gap and, 292t, 293; in government careers, 76; in in-house legal departments, 77; in midsize law firms, 73; partnerships and, 147–48; student debt and, 265, 272

Asian Americans, 12, 38, 69, 136–40; class and, 357; earnings and, 286; education and, 82–84; equity partnerships and, 96; family financial support and, 265; fields of law and, 359; financial support and, 265, 266t; inside counsel and, 201–3; in large law firms, 68; law firms and, 39, 40, 68, 70, 71, 72, 73, 246–47, 248; law school admissions and, 87; law school and, 87, 114; law school credentials and, 87; as law school movers, 114; LSAT scores and, 86; midcareer practice setting and, 97; in midsize firms, 72, 73; as midsize-firm starters, 72; nonpracticing positions and, 123–24; overrepresented among bar admittees, 80; partnerships and, 96, 147–48; perception of law degree value and, 336–37; politics and, 304, 307; race/ethnicity-based organizations and, 312; as small-firm starters, 70, 71; as solo practitioners, 179–81; student debt and, 262, 263–73, 275–76; underrepresented among law school graduates, 80; underrepresented in partnerships, 40. *See also* Asian American men; Asian American women

Asian American women, 136–40, 142–43, 297–98, 358; federal government careers and, 226–27; in government careers, 74; state government careers and, 237; student debt and, 264, 272

assignments, quality of, 132, 139. *See also* work, control over

assistant district attorneys, 234

assistant US attorney positions, 223, 224, 225, 226, 238

associates, 41, 52, 244, 247–48; associate-to-
    partner ratios, 244, 247–48; billable hours and,
    132–33; control over work and, 122; layoffs
    and, 35; need for, 53; partnership prospects of,
    244; permanent, 131; politics and, 305; race
    and, 247–48; racialized treatment of, 249–50;
    treatment of, 249–57; women as, 96; work
    satisfaction and, 44
Association of the Bar of the City of New York,
    43–44
Atlanta (Georgia), 113
attorneys general, 233–36
Audrey (interviewee), 153–54
Auerbach, Jerold S., 31
Austin (interviewee), 335–36
automobile accident cases, 42
autonomy, 50, 343; inside counsel and, 199, 205–
    6, 213–14; midsize law firms and, 122; practice
    settings and, 121–22; prestige and, 119–20;
    small firms and, 122; solo practitioners and,
    122; state government and, 122; women and,
    121–22. See also work, control over
Avvo, 42
Axiom, 122

baby boomers, 28
bankruptcy law, 101t, 102, 105f
bar, 21
bar admittees, demographic data and, 80
bar associations, 32, 43–44, 310, 364; alternative
    legal service providers and, 43; declining clout
    of, 44; diversity initiatives and, 39; local, 310;
    self-image as "noble profession," 43; state, 310;
    upstarts and, 43. See also specific associations
bar authorities, state and, 22
Barbara (interviewee), 226–27
bar exams, 31
Bartholomew (interviewee), 222
Bearak, Jonathan, 279, 282
Bearman, Peter, 55
Becker, Gary, 19–20
Berdahl, Jennifer L., 297, 298
bias, 250, 251–53. See also discrimination;
    inequality
Big Four accounting firms, 28
"big law lifers," 246
billable hours, 44, 68, 130, 297; associates and,
    132–33; large law firms and, 128–29; law firms
    and, 128–29, 132–33, 143, 146, 147, 153, 199–
    200; midsize law firms and, 146, 147; parent-
    hood and, 154–55; partnerships and, 132–33;
    pro bono work and, 319, 320, 321; women and,
    143; work/life balance and, 200
Blair (interviewee), 184–86
Blair-Loy, Mary, 54–55
Bonica, Adam, 23, 304, 305, 307

bonuses, law firms and, 133
boom-and-bust cycle, 27–28, 34
Boston (Massachusetts), 113
Bourdieu, Pierre, 15, 17, 31, 51, 128, 198, 316,
    352, 353
Bourdieusian field sociology, 15, 50–78
Bradley (interviewee), 188–89
Brooks (interviewee), 208–10
Bryce (interviewee), 191, 212
Buchmann, Claudia, 279
Budig, Michelle J., 279, 282
Bureau of Labor Statistics, 80–82, 81t
Bush, George W., 28, 306
business, financialization of, 52
business competition, in the 1970s, 52
business fields, 111–13
business generation imperative, equity partner-
    ships and, 144
business organization careers, 4–6, 10, 13, 54–56,
    87–90, 130, 186–96, 197–214; career sequences
    characterized by, 200–201; early to midcareer
    transitions and, 89t; earnings and, 110; exodus
    to, 120; first practice setting and, 88t, 89t; gender
    and, 87–90, 88t; law school ranking and, 87–90,
    89t; nonpracticing positions in, 124; race and,
    87–90, 88t; satisfaction and, 330; side door to,
    204–12; social capital in, 213; statistical profile
    of lawyers working in business, 200–202; wave 3
    practice setting and, 91–92t, 93–94; work/life
    balance and, 212. See also inside counsel
business owners, control over work and, 122. See
    also solo practitioners
business representation, 323; change and, 308;
    dominance of, 360; large law firms and, 68;
    politics and, 308–9; pro bono work and, 317t,
    318, 323; shift to, 106. See also corporate clients
business-to-business litigation, 22

California, Proposition 209, 39
Calvin (interviewee), 206–7
capital: accumulation of, 98; deployment of, 127–
    28; forms of, 57 (see also social capital); path
    dependency and, 98
career characteristics, debt-income ratio and, 265
career guidance, 132
careers: career volatility, 71 (see also job changes;
    unemployment); concept of, 55; downsides of,
    13; status-based vs. achievement-based, 55
career satisfaction. See satisfaction
career structure: gender and, 96–97; intersection-
    ality and, 96–97; race and, 96–97
career support, mentoring and, 257
career trajectories, 54, 55; access to, 128; class and,
    97, 98; education credentials and, 97; elite vs.
    nonelite, 55; first jobs and, 55; gender and, 97;
    "great divide" between, 129; individual variation

career trajectories (*cont.*)
    making up structural patterns, 353; race and,
    97; social capital and, 97, 98; social characteris-
    tics of respondents and, 79–98; systematic and
    uneven distribution of access to, 128
career transitions, 54, 63
Carl (interviewee), 227
Carlin, Jerome, 99, 165, 166–67, 186, 197
Caroline (interviewee), 230
Carrie (interviewee), 224–25, 238
Catholic lawyers, 16–17, 31, 51, 115, 116
Catholic schools, 53
celebrity trials, 27
Center for Epidemiological Studies Depression
    Scale, 345
Central Intelligence Agency (CIA), 227
chains of supervision, gender and, 121
Chambers, David L., 263
change, 14, 21–22, 32–45, 49–78, 308
charitable organizations, 310, 311, 313, 319–20,
    323
Chicago (Illinois), 113. *See also* Chicago studies
Chicago studies, 23, 51, 70, 304–5, 311, 323, 338;
    AJD Project as opportunity to revisit, 120–23;
    business representation and, 360; community
    organizations and, 311, 323; job changes and,
    338; solo practitioners and, 166, 167; two
    hemispheres thesis and, 359; two hemispheres
    thesis revisited and, 99–100, 104–5, 110, 115–
    16, 119–20, 123, 125, 127, 129
childcare, 128, 170
Chilton, Adam S., 23, 304, 305, 307
Christopher (interviewee), 222
Christopher, Warren, 310
citizen-lawyer: disappearance of, 309–12; litera-
    ture on, 310
city size, gender wage gap and, 285–86
civic organizations, 311
civil litigation, 101t, 102–3, 105f, 111, 115, 116, 118
civil right/liberties law, 101t, 105, 105f
civil rights movement, 304
Claire (interviewee), 202–3, 204
class, 11, 79–98, 129, 352; career trajectories
    and, 97, 98; debt and, 260–61; early careers
    and, 93–94; early to midcareer transitions and,
    93–94; education and, 79, 84–85; entering legal
    profession and, 80–82; family financial support
    and, 262; fields of law and, 118; first jobs and,
    79; gender and, 357–58; inequality and, 365;
    influence from law school through midcareer,
    79–98; law schools and, 79–98, 85t, 93, 357;
    midcareer practice setting and, 93–94; parental
    level of education and, 84; parental occupa-
    tion and, 356–57; partnerships and, 143–44;
    path dependency and, 98; private sector law
    and, 230; privilege and, 129; race and, 356–58;

resilience of class inequality, 355, 356–57; satis-
    faction and, 326–28; student debt and, 260–61,
    262, 264–65, 272, 275
class action law firms, 34, 42
clerkships, 218, 220–21, 223, 224, 357
clients: gaining primary responsibility for, 254–
    57; inheritance of, 132, 136, 151
client types, 16–17, 99–125, 315, 315f; corporate
    clients, 99; direct measures of total effort on,
    106–11, 109f; earnings and, 110; field prestige
    scores and, 112t; fields of law and, 104, 111f;
    personal clients, 99; politics and, 305. *See also*
    two hemispheres thesis
Clio, 36
clusters, analysis of, 57–58
colleagues, relationships with, 328
commercialism, 44, 45, 50, 51. *See also* commer-
    cial practices, prohibition of
commercial law, 101t, 102, 105f
commercial litigation, 101t, 105f, 118
commercial practices, prohibition of, 31. *See also*
    advertising
commercial real estate law, 102t, 105f
community organizations, 309–12, 322, 323; career
    benefits to involvement in, 310, 312–13; conser-
    vatism and, 311–12; gender and, 323; leadership
    positions in, 311; making partner and, 313;
    partnerships and, 323, 324; politics and, 311–12;
    practice settings and, 311–12; race/ethnicity
    and, 311–12, 323; women and, 312
community service, social capital and, 312–13
compensation. *See* earnings
competition, 334–38
Connecticut, 113
conservatism, 306t, 307, 308–9; community
    organizations and, 311–12; conservative legal
    movements, 304, 306; organization member-
    ships and, 311–12
Constance (interviewee), 3, 8–12, 22, 37, 137, 353,
    369n1 (chap. 1)
construction law, 161, 171, 172
continuity, 14, 21–22, 32–45, 49–78
contract attorneys, 52, 122
Cooper, Marianne, 297, 298
copractice, lack of, 104, 125
Cornwell, Benjamin, 55
corporate clients, 99, 106, 111–13, 125, 129, 131,
    359–60; autonomy and, 119–20; prestige and,
    119–20; shift to, 106; solo practitioners and,
    197; urban markets and, 112t, 113
corporate competition, increase in, 52
corporate counsel, diversity initiatives and, 201–2
corporate equity partners, 51
corporate hemisphere, 33, 44, 105, 131; integra-
    tion in, 39–40; legal technology and, 36. *See
    also* corporate clients

corporate law, 102, 105; as path of least resistance, 216; rejection of, 238

corporate law firms, 30; African Americans in, 52; Catholic schools and, 53; diaspora of attorneys from, 165–66; discriminatory practices of, 31–32; equity partnerships and, 357; golden age of, 51; government careers and, 30; growth in size, number, and scope, 53; law schools and, 36–37; minorities in, 52–53; new role of, 354; partnerships in, 51–52; at top of hierarchy, 51–52, 53; women in, 52–53

corporate legal sector, 16, 33; managed legal service providers, 42; 2008 global financial crisis and, 35

corporations, 35; diversity in, 40; in-house legal departments, 34–36, 40–42, 68, 72–73, 77–78, 119–20, 128–29, 131, 197–214; law firms and, 41–42; legal problems facing, 33; predominance as clients, 109; scandals and, 33. See also business organization careers

counsel, 52, 122

Cravath, Paul, 369n1 (chap. 2). See also Cravath System

Cravath Swaine and Moore, 29

Cravath System, 29–30, 31, 248, 369n1 (chap. 2); compensation and, 42; four core elements, 40–41; governance model of, 41; hiring and promotion practices, 42; professionalism and, 43; traditional hiring and promotion practices, 41, 131, 244–45, 248; up-or-out promotion policy, 131, 244–45, 248

credentials, education and, 82–87

criminal defense, 17, 359

criminal law, 101t, 102, 103, 104, 105, 105f, 106, 174, 216

criminal prosecutors, 216

crisis, 50; commentary, 14–15

cultural capital, 128, 129

cumulative (dis)advantage, 262, 276–77

Darby (interviewee), 204

Davis, John W., 310

"dead-end track," 244

debt-income ratio, 372n4 (chap. 11), 372n6; career characteristics and, 265; social characteristics of respondents and, 265. See also student debt

defense lawyers, 32, 217

DeFunis v. Odegaard, 39

deletion, 56

Democratic Party, 304–9, 306t, 322–23, 362

Department of Homeland Security, 226

Department of Justice, 225, 227; Honors Program, 226, 227

Department of Treasury, 227

depression, 344–46. See also mental health, gender and

deprofessionalization hypothesis, 120, 123

deputy attorney general positions, 234–35

deregulation, 28, 42

Dezalay, Yves, 304

Dinovitzer, Ronit, 84, 314, 316, 327–28, 331, 339, 342–43, 354

discrimination, 31, 250, 297–98, 338, 351; earnings and, 290; gender wage gap and, 295–96; at law firms, 252–53; perception of law degree value and, 334; satisfaction and, 330–31

disruption rhetorics, 28–29, 32–45, 50

district attorneys, 234

diversity, 77, 328; in corporations, 40, 201–2; failure of current commitments to, 366; inside counsel and, 201–2; law firms and, 12, 37–38; in law schools, 38–39; in legal profession, 36–40, 45; lip service to, 243; partnerships and, 40

divorce, 156, 164, 171, 172, 191–92

divorce law, Jewish lawyers and, 115, 116

Dorah (interviewee), 183–84

dot-com bubble, bursting of, 34

early careers, 93–94; advantages of early career corporate law experience, 165–66, 197; class and, 79–98; early career movers, 115; early career stayers, 115; first practice setting, 87–90, 88t, 89t, 91–92t; gender and, 79–98; large law firms and, 129, 197; Native Americans, 94–95; navigating, 90–94; race and, 79–98

early social advantage, 90

early to midcareer transitions, 93–94

earnings, 328; African Americans and, 286, 292–93, 292t; African American women and, 292–93, 292t; Asian American men and, 292t, 293; Asian Americans and, 286; bonuses, 133; childbearing and, 293–95; city size and, 285–86; client types and, 110; at corporate law firms, 52; Cravath System and, 29, 42; demographic background and, 285–86; discrimination and, 290; distribution, 282–91; equity partnerships and, 260, 289; family factors and, 290–92; fields of law and, 125; firm size and, 286–87; gender and, 279–81, 281t, 282–91, 292–95, 292t (see also gender wage gap); geographic mobility and, 115; growing inequality in, 361; growing inequality in over the course of careers, 361; inequality in, 109–10, 110f, 125; job status and, 289; large law firms and, 288–89; Latinas and, 292–93, 292t; Latinos and, 292–93, 292t; Latinx and, 286, 292–93, 292t; law firms and, 27, 41, 52, 73, 286–87, 288–89; law school tier and, 286; lockstep, 29, 41, 52; markets and, 110; mean and share of at waves 1 and 3, 110f; men and, 293–95; midsize law firms and, 73; motherhood penalty and, 279–80, 293–95, 356; Native American men and, 292t, 293; Native Americans and,

earnings (cont.)
292t, 293; Native American women and, 292t, 293; nonequity partners and, 288; normative masculinity and, 294–95; organizational settings and, 110; organizational ties and, 289–90; parental leave and, 288; parenthood and, 288, 293–95; partnerships and, 29; personal preferences and, 290; practice settings and, 110, 280–91, 281t; private sector and, 287; public interest law and, 239; public sector and, 287; race and, 292, 292t; satisfaction and, 328–29; sector and, 286–87; social characteristics of respondents and, 58–59t; solo practitioners and, 168–69; spouses earnings and, 290–91; state government careers and, 239; student debt and, 260–61, 272, 274, 276; unemployment and, 287, 288; wave 3 practice settings and, 111f; White men and, 260–61, 292–93, 292t; Whites and, 260–61, 286, 292–93, 292t; White women and, 292–93, 292t; women and, 293–95; work effort and, 289; work histories and, 287–89

"eat what you kill" model, 170

economic conservatism, 306t, 307, 309, 312

education: AJD Project cohort and, 82–87; class and, 79, 84–85; credentials and, 82–87; entering legal profession and, 82–87; gender and, 84; law school credentials and, 86–87; markets and, 113–14; politics and, 304; privilege and, 82–87; race and, 82–83; status hierarchy and, 82–87

education capital, 79, 127–28

education credentials: career trajectories and, 97; first practice setting and, 87–90, 97; gender and, 87–90; law school admissions and, 97; predictive power of, 97; race and, 87–90

education endowments, 82–87

education institutions, 87–90, 120, 121, 218; early to midcareer transitions and, 89t; earnings and, 111; elite tracks to, 219–21; first practice setting and, 88t, 89t; gender and, 87–90, 88t; law school ranking and, 87–90, 89t; race and, 87–90, 88t; satisfaction and, 329; statistical background on, 218–19; wave 3 practice setting and, 91–92t, 93–94. See also law schools

education law, solo practitioners and, 168

education opportunities, 128

education organizations, 311

elite status, pro bono work and, 318–19

Ellie (interviewee), 233–34

Ely, Robin J., 19, 288, 295, 296

Emilio (interviewee), 195–96

Emily (interviewee), 211–12

employment histories, 245

employment law, 105; for management, 101t, 102, 105f, 116; for unions, 101t, 102, 105f

England, Paula, 279, 282

entering legal profession, 80–82; class and, 80–82; education and, 82–87; entry point influence and, 79–98; gender and, 80–82; race/ethnicity and, 80–82, 81t

entrepreneurialism, 128, 173, 186, 194, 196

environmental law, 101t, 104, 105, 105f

Epstein, Cynthia Fuchs, 297

equal justice, 351

equal opportunity, commitment to, 339

equity, lip service to, 243

equity partners: in large law firms, 56–57; in midsize firms, 56–57; satisfaction and, 331

equity partnerships, 56, 65, 131–32, 143–44, 244, 260, 353; African Americans and, 96, 247, 248, 249, 250–51, 254–57, 259; Asian Americans and, 96; aspirations for, 250–51, 254–57, 259; business generation imperative and, 144; corporate law firms and, 357; earnings and, 260, 289; gender and, 354; improbability of making partner, 254; large law firms and, 164; Latinx and, 96; men and, 354; midsize law firms and, 146, 147; minorities and, 142, 247, 248, 249, 250–51, 254–57, 259; Native Americans and, 96; promotion to, 245; prospects for making, 250–51, 254–57, 259; race and, 354, 355; racial/ethnic inequality and, 133–36; unequal distribution of, 76–77; White men and, 244, 354; Whites and, 96, 244, 248, 249, 250–51, 254–57, 259, 354; women and, 77, 95–96, 136, 143, 159, 289, 354

Espeland, Wendy Nelson, 82

ethics: professional, 337–38; rules, 31

ethnicity, 16; community organizations and, 311–12; family financial support and, 262, 265–66; fields of law and, 115–16, 118, 125; financial support and, 266t; leaving firms and, 245; partnerships and, 143–44; public interest law and, 216–17; solo practitioners and, 168; student debt and, 263–64, 264t, 275, 276. See also race; and specific groups

ethnic organizations, 311

ethnoreligious groups, 16; fields of law and, 115–16, 125

Eulau, Heinz, 304

ExxonMobil, 303

family, work and, 332–33. See also work/life balance

family factors, gender wage gap and, 290

family financial support, 128, 357; African Americans and, 265, 275–76; Asian Americans and, 265; class and, 262; gender and, 262; Latinx and, 275–76; law school status and, 266; parental level of education and, 266–67; race/ethnicity and, 262, 265–66; Whites and, 260–61, 266

family law, 101t, 103, 105f, 112t, 113, 116–18, 359; gender and, 125; Jewish lawyers and, 116; law school prestige and, 119; women and, 125. *See also* divorce law, Jewish lawyers and

fatherhood, 299. *See also* parenthood

fatherhood premium, 294, 297, 356

federal government careers, 56, 70, 74, 217–18, 222–28, 238; African American men and, 225–26; African Americans and, 225–26, 227–28; African American women and, 227–28; Asian American women and, 226–27; earnings and, 110; elite law schools and, 74–75; nonpracticing positions and, 124; as path to private sector jobs, 222–23; politics and, 307; satisfaction and, 329, 330; social script for, 354; White men and, 223–24, 227; Whites and, 223–27; White women and, 224–25, 226

fellowships, 218, 219, 221

field membership, definition of, 111

field prestige scores, 111, 116–18; client types and, 112t; gender and, 116–18; law school prestige and, 118–19; law school ranking and, 112t; markets and, 112t

fields, strategies and, 20–21

field sociology, 49–78. *See also* Bourdieusian field sociology

fields of copractice, 104–5, 105f

fields of practice, 99–125, 359–60; Asian Americans and, 359; class and, 118; clients and, 104, 111–13, 111f; copractice of, 104–5, 105f; earnings and, 125; ethnicity and, 118, 125; ethnoreligious groups and, 115–16; ethnoreligious segregation and, 125; gender and, 116–18, 119, 125; Latinx and, 359; law school prestige and, 119; markets and, 111–13, 111f; race and, 116, 118, 119, 125; racial legacy and, 118; relative size of, 100–102, 106; religious affiliation and, 116; segmentation by, 125; social characteristics of respondents and, 115–19, 117t; solo practitioners and, 168; structures of, 359–60; student debt and, 274–75; time spent in at wave 3, 101–2t; women and, 116, 359

field theory, 17

financial engineering, 34

financial security, 337–38

financial support, 266t; African Americans and, 265, 266t; Asian Americans and, 265, 266t; ethnicity and, 266t; law school ranking and, 266t; Native Americans and, 266t; parental level of education and, 266t; race and, 266t; social characteristics of respondents and, 265–67, 266t; Whites and, 266t. *See also* family financial support

firm clients: gaining primary responsibility for, 254–57; inheritance of, 132, 136, 151

first jobs: as apprenticeships, 338; career trajectories and, 55; class and, 79; first practice setting, 87–90, 88t, 89t, 91–92t; in large law firms,

128–29; midcareer positions and, 79; navigating early careers and, 90–94; practice settings and, 129. *See also* first practice setting

first practice setting, 91–92t; education credentials and, 87–90, 97; gender and, 87–90, 88t, 89t; large law firms and, 97; law schools and, 87–90, 89t, 93; LSAT scores and, 89; midcareer practice setting and, 93, 97; Native Americans and, 95; parental level of education and, 89; parental nativity and, 89; race and, 87–90, 88t, 89t; relative effects of variables on, 89–90; wave 3 practice setting and, 90–93, 91–92t

fit, 156, 157, 230, 352

fixed effects, 283

Florida, 113

Floyd, George, murder of, 366

Fong, Bryon, 21, 22

fragmentation, rising, 359–60

franchise law firms, 34

Fred (interviewee), 228–29

future, prospects for, 365–66

Galanter, Marc, 131, 365, 369n1 (chap. 2)

Garth, Bryant, 84, 200, 304, 314, 316, 327–28, 331, 339, 342–43, 354

gender, 11, 45, 79–98, 129, 352; AJD Project cohort and, 82; biases, 160–62; career structure and, 96–97; career trajectories and, 97; chains of supervision and, 121; charitable organization membership and, 320; childbearing and, 293–95; class and, 357–58; community organizations and, 323; control over work and, 123; debt and, 262, 264, 265; diversity, 53, 70; early careers and, 93–94; early to midcareer transitions and, 93–94; earnings and, 279–81, 281t, 282–91, 292–95, 292t (*see also* gender wage gap); education and, 84, 87–90; entering legal profession and, 80–82; equity partnerships and, 354; family financial support and, 262; family law and, 125; field prestige scores and, 116–18; fields of law and, 116–18, 119, 125; first practice setting and, 87–90, 88t, 89t; gendered income trajectories, 279–80; gendered norms, 295–98; "gender penalty," 159; government careers and, 74, 76, 79, 216–19; household duties and, 291; inequality, 56, 246, 278–99, 351, 355, 356, 365; influence from law school through midcareer, 79–98; intersectionality and, 96–97, 245–46; job changes and, 338, 342, 344; job stability and, 55–56; law firms and, 68, 95–96, 153–63, 245–46; law school admissions and, 79, 85–86; law school credentials and, 38–39, 86–87; law students and, 38–39; LSAT scores and, 85–86, 86t; mental health and, 344–46; midcareer practice setting and, 93–94, 97–98; midsize-firm starters

gender (*cont.*)
and, 72–73; motherhood penalty and, 293–95;
norms, 298–99; partnerships and, 79, 95–96,
132–36, 143–44, 164, 352–53; path dependency and, 98; perception of value of law
degree and, 337; politics and, 304, 305, 307,
309; practice settings and, 280–81, 281t, 282–
91; private sector law and, 230; pro bono work
and, 319, 320; as proxy for race and ethnicity,
246; public interest law and, 216–17; public
service careers and, 216–17; race and, 38–39,
96–97, 245–46, 357–58; retention rates and, 97;
satisfaction and, 326, 326t, 331, 344–46, 363;
social capital and, 87; solo practitioners and,
168; STEM fields and, 116, 279; stereotypes,
118, 125, 153; traditional roles, 153–56, 164,
299; work-family narrative explanation and,
295–96, 299. *See also* gender wage gap
gender-based organizations, 312
gendered income trajectories, 279–80
gender wage gap, 279–80, 282–91; African
American women and, 292–93, 292t; age and,
285; Asian American men and, 292t, 293;
childbearing and, 281, 282; city size and, 285–
86; demographic background and, 285–86;
discrimination and, 295–96; earnings and, 288;
family factors and, 290; hegemonic masculinity
and, 356; intersectionality and, 292–98, 292t;
Latinas and, 292–93, 292t; Latinos and, 292–
93, 292t; marriage and, 279–80; motherhood
and, 282; motherhood penalty and, 279–80,
293–95, 356; Native American men and, 292t,
293; Native American women and, 292t, 293;
parenthood and, 279–80, 281, 282, 291–92,
293–95; persistence of, 285, 295–96, 356; practice settings and, 280–81, 281t, 282–91, 356;
quantile regression and, 282, 283, 284–85t;
race and, 286, 292–98, 292t, 358; White men
and, 292–93, 292t; White women and, 292–93,
292t; work-family narrative explanation for,
295–96, 299; work histories and, 287–88
general corporate law, 101t, 102, 105f
general counsels, 41–42, 44, 176
generalists, 102
general practice law, 101t, 102, 105f
Gen X, 28
Gen Z, 28
geographic mobility, career opportunity and,
113–15, 360
geography, 111–13, 112t; politics and, 305, 307
Gideon v. Wainwright, 365
Ginsburg, Ruth Bader, 299
glass ceiling, 76–77
Glick, Peter, 297, 298
global financial crisis, 14, 28, 35, 180, 189, 192.
See also Great Recession

globalization, 28, 42
golden age, nostalgia for, 28–32
Gordon, Robert, 304
governance model, 41
government attorneys, 305; politics and, 305. *See
also* federal government careers; government
careers; state government careers; US attorney
positions
government bureaucracy, 42
government careers, 8, 16, 28, 36, 51, 56, 70,
73–76, 87–90, 215–39; African Americans in,
10, 74–75, 76, 247; African American women
in, 74–75, 76; Asian American men in, 76;
Asian Americans in, 74, 76; Asian American
women in, 74; career satisfaction and, 75;
corporate law firms and, 30; early to midcareer
transitions and, 89t; elite tracks to, 238; family-
friendly nature of, 74; federal, 222–28; first
practice setting and, 88t, 89t; gender and, 74,
76, 79, 87–90, 88t, 216, 217–19; Latinas in, 74,
76; law school performance and, 216–17; law
schools and, 75–76, 87–90, 89t, 216–17; law
school status and, 87–90, 89t, 216–17; local,
228; minorities in, 79, 218–19; paths to, 217–
18; vs. private sector careers, 11–12; pro bono
work and, 323; race and, 87–90, 88t, 216–17;
scholarship on, 216; small-firm starters and,
70; state, 228–38; statistical background on,
218–19; status hierarchy and, 215; student debt
and, 274; wave 3 practice setting and, 91–92t,
93–94; White men in, 76; women in, 74, 76, 79,
217–19. *See also* federal government careers;
local government; state government careers
government law, 104
government sector, 109, 111; least populous
locales and, 112t, 113; politics and, 307–8
government service, 30
government sphere, 105
Great Recession, 135, 157, 190
Greek/Russian Orthodox lawyers, 116
Green Party, 306
Gulati, Mitu, 243

habitus, 20, 128, 198, 352
Hagan, John, 297, 344–45, 346
Haltom, William, 364–65
hard work, 334–38
Harvard Law School, 216; career study, 122
Harvard Plan, 39
health law, 101t, 103, 104, 105, 105f, 106
Heather (interviewee), 229
Heinz, John P.: AJD Project as opportunity to revisit
Chicago studies and, 120–23; business represen-
tation and, 360; Chicago studies and, 15–17, 23,
51, 70, 99–100, 103–6, 110–11, 115–23, 125, 127,
129, 166, 167, 304–5, 311, 323, 338; job changes

and, 338; nonpracticing lawyers and, 123; politics and, 304–5; on solo practitioners, 166, 167; two hemispheres thesis revisited and, 103, 106, 111, 115–18, 123, 125, 127, 129, 359
hemispheres of practice, 15–17, 99–125, 129
Henderson, William D., 33, 131
Herrera, Luz E., 169
heteronomous organizations, 120
Hewlett, Sylvia Ann, 279
hierarchies, 10, 20–21, 51, 351–66; classed, 11; continuity of, 77–78; control over work and, 121–22; gendered, 11; of legal careers, 79; operation of, 351–66; racialized, 11; reinforcement of, 40–43; reproduced in law and society, 364–65; structural, 18
hiring and promotion practices, 41; commitment to equal opportunity and, 339; Cravath System, 42; law firms and, 258–59
Hodges, Melissa J., 279, 282
"honors attorney" positions, 229
Hopwood v. Texas, 39
Houle, Jason N., 262
Houston (Texas), 113, 114
Hughes, Everett C., 99
human capital, 20, 250
hustling, 197
hybrid public-private firms, 42

IBM, 167–68
idealism, 216, 217, 238, 239
identity-based practices, solo practitioners and, 173–82
immigrants, 38; children of, 51; discrimination against, 31
Immigration and Naturalization Service, 226
immigration law, 101t, 102–6, 105f, 116–18, 174, 182–83, 186, 226, 238, 359; Asian Americans and, 125; Latinx and, 125; law school prestige and, 119
Implicit Association Test, 296
inclusion, lip service to, 243
independents, 306–8, 306t, 323
Indiana, 113, 114
individual agency, 128
individual hemisphere, 33, 34, 42; legal technology and, 36; 2008 global financial crisis and, 35
inequality, 11–12, 19–20, 166, 246; class and, 365; continuity of, 77–78; debt and, 261–62; in earnings, 125, 361 (*see also* gender wage gap); entrenched, 56; equity partnerships and, 133–36; gender and, 56, 351, 365 (*see also* gender wage gap); intersectional approaches to, 293; law school admissions and, 365; law school tier and, 56; opportunity and, 10–15; persistence of, 366; race and, 56, 351, 365; resilience of, 355; social origin and, 56; structures of, 77–78, 125, 351–66; student debt and, 261–62

inertia, 90
in-house legal departments. *See* inside counsel
Innocence Project, 27
innovation, 173; solo practitioners and, 196
insertion, 56
inside counsel, 36, 41–42, 68, 119, 120, 128, 129, 130, 131, 170, 176, 197–214; African Americans and, 40, 201–2; Asian American men and, 77; Asian Americans and, 77, 201–3; autonomy and, 199, 205–6, 213–14; becoming, 200–212; diversity and, 201–2; earnings and, 110; elite track to, 200, 201, 202–4, 213; entry to through positions in law firms, 197–98; increased prestige of, 52, 199; large law firms and, 129; Latinas and, 203, 210–11; Latinos and, 211; Latinx and, 203, 210–11; vs. law firms, 198–200; less elite track to, 200, 201, 213; minorities and, 40, 77, 201–3, 210–11; prominence of, 360–61; side door to, 204–12; statistical profile of lawyers working as, 200–202; student debt and, 205–6; White men and, 203–4, 205–7, 209–10; Whites and, 203–12; White women and, 204, 208–9, 211–12; women and, 42, 77, 201–4, 208–12; work/life balance and, 206–7, 212, 214
insurance law, 101t, 102, 105, 105f, 106
integration: in corporate hemisphere, 39–40; law firms' failure at, 245
intellectual property law, 101t, 102, 103, 105, 105f, 106, 116, 188–89, 359–60
intent to leave, 338–44, 339f, 340f, 341f. *See also* job changes
internal labor markets, 17–21, 40–43
internships, 9
intersectionality, 38–39, 245–46, 357–58; career structure and, 96–97; gender and, 96–97; gender wage gap and, 292–98, 292t; matrix of domination and, 358; race and, 96–97; social characteristics of respondents and, 96–97
invention, solo practitioners and, 186
Irish Catholic lawyers: civil litigation and, 115, 116; personal injury law and, 118
Isabel (interviewee), 233

Jackson, Robert H., 310
Jacob (interviewee), 175–76, 211, 322
James (interviewee), 3, 6–7, 11, 12, 19, 134–35, 260–61, 321, 352
JD advantage, 186
JD advantage positions, 198–99
JD-required positions, 198–99
Jewish lawyers, 16, 31, 51, 169–71, 219, 371n6; divorce law and, 115, 116; family law and, 116; law firms and, 16–17; politics and, 305
Joanna (interviewee), 235
job candidates, law firms and, 258–59

job changes, 56, 71–73, 200–201, 338–44, 339f,
    340f, 341f, 352; African Americans and, 342;
    autonomy and, 343; career stage and, 343–44;
    gender and, 338, 342, 344; intent to move vs.
    actual moves, 339–40, 339f, 343, 344, 346,
    363; Latinx and, 342; law degree rankings and,
    342–43; law school ranking and, 339–40, 340f,
    344; measuring, 373n4 (chap. 14); men and, 342;
    minorities and, 344; multivariate analysis of,
    342–44; Native Americans and, 342; networking
    and, 343; practice settings and, 340–42, 341f,
    344; race and, 342, 344; rates of, 54; satisfaction
    and, 342, 343, 346, 363; social embeddedness
    and, 343; upward mobility and, 344; women and,
    342, 344; workplace experiences and, 343, 344
job experience, 128
job market, nationalization and globalization of, 33
job offers, 245; African Americans and, 258–59;
    Whites and, 258–59
job setting satisfaction, 328
judges, control over work and, 122
judiciary, 32; paths to, 239
Juliette (interviewee), 136–37

Kahlenberg, Richard, 216
Kareem (interviewee), 179–81, 182, 336–37
Karina (interviewee), 231
Katrina (interviewee), 152–53
Kay, Fiona M., 290, 297, 338, 344–46
Kennedy, John F., 39–40
Kimmel, Jean, 288
Kornhauser, Lewis A., 263

labor law, 105
labor markets: dynamics of, 30; internal, 40–43
labor sphere, 105
Ladinsky, Jack, 99, 167
Lamont, Michèle, 335, 337
large law firms, 31, 44, 55, 87–90, 121, 134–43, 164;
    ABA membership and, 312; billable hours and,
    128–29; businesses and, 68; control over work
    and, 123; early careers and, 129, 197; early to
    midcareer transitions and, 89t; earnings and,
    110, 288–89; eclipsed in corporate fields, 360;
    equity partners in, 56–57, 164; as first jobs,
    63–70, 128–29, 354; first practice setting and,
    88t, 89t, 97; gender and, 68, 87–90, 88t; growth
    of, 63; hiring and promotion practices, 132–36,
    140; in-house legal departments and, 129; job
    changes and, 340–42; law school ranking and,
    87–90, 89t, 128–29; minorities in, 68; nonequity
    positions in, 56–57, 77; partnerships and, 56–
    57, 134–43, 164; part-time options, 77; politics
    and, 305, 307–8; privileging of White men in,
    164; pro bono work and, 314, 316–17, 317t,
    329; race and, 66–68, 87–90, 88t, 140, 288–89;

reconfigured role of, 54; rise and dominance of,
    119; satisfaction and, 329; scholarship on, 132;
    service roles and, 140; as valuable starting posi-
    tions, 52; wave 3 practice setting and, 91–92t,
    93–94; women and, 66–68, 142–43, 288–89
lateral hiring, 43, 52, 353
lateral mobility, 22
Latinas, 137; earnings and, 292–93, 292t; gender
    wage gap and, 292–93, 292t; in government ca-
    reers, 74, 76; inside counsel and, 203, 210–11;
    state government careers and, 231–33; student
    debt and, 262, 264, 270
Latinos, 69; earnings and, 292–93, 292t; gender
    wage gap and, 292–93, 292t; inside counsel
    and, 211; perception of law degree value and,
    335–36; small-firm starters, 71; student debt
    and, 265, 270, 272
Latinx, 5–6, 8–10, 12, 18, 38, 369n1 (chap. 4);
    class and, 356–57, 358; earnings and, 286; edu-
    cation and, 82–84; equity partnerships and, 96;
    family financial support and, 275–76; fields of
    law and, 359; first practice setting and, 88; het-
    erogeneity of, 372n12; immigration law and,
    125; job changes and, 342; law firms and, 39,
    40, 195, 246–47, 248; law school admissions
    and, 87; law school credentials and, 87; as law
    school movers, 114; LSAT scores and, 86;
    nonpracticing positions and, 123–24; partner-
    ships and, 96; politics and, 304, 307; pro bono
    work and, 322; race/ethnicity-based organiza-
    tions and, 312; satisfaction and, 326, 330; as
    solo practitioners, 173–75, 192–96; student debt
    and, 263–73, 275–76; underrepresented among
    bar admittees, 80; underrepresented among
    law school graduates, 80; underrepresented in
    partnerships, 40. See also Latinas; Latinos
Laumann, Edward O., 23, 103, 106, 111, 115–18,
    127; AJD Project as opportunity to revisit Chi-
    cago studies and, 120–23; business representa-
    tion and, 360; Chicago studies and, 15, 17, 23,
    51, 70, 99–100, 104–5, 110, 115–16, 119–23, 125,
    127, 129, 166–67, 304–5, 311, 323, 338, 359; job
    changes and, 338; nonpracticing lawyers and,
    123; politics and, 304–5; on solo practitioners,
    166, 167; two hemispheres thesis revisited and,
    23, 99–100, 104–5, 110, 115–16, 119–23, 125, 359
Laura (interviewee), 231
law degree: as investment, 333–34; perception of
    value of, 334–38, 363–64
law factories, 52
law firm racialization, 243–59; descriptive view of,
    246–50; lawyer selectivity and, 250–51, 253–
    57; treatment of lawyers and, 251–57
law firms, 10, 12, 130; ABA and, 312; African
    Americans and, 7–8, 10, 12, 13, 39, 40, 142,
    243–59; all-White, 247; apprenticeship and, 53;

Asian Americans and, 39, 40, 246–47, 248; attrition and, 132, 139–42, 153, 161–64, 187, 192,
195, 244–45, 247–57, 259, 338, 355–56; billable
hours and, 128–29, 132–33, 143, 153, 199–200;
bonuses and, 133; boom-and-bust cycle and,
34; career guidance and, 132; careers in, 4–7,
131–63; Catholics and, 16–17; class action, 34,
42; compensation and, 41; consolidation and
stratification of, 33; corporate, 30, 31–32, 36–37,
51–53, 165–66, 354, 357; corporations and,
41–42; in Cravath System, 29; decision to leave,
352; declaring intent to leave preemptively,
250–51; discrimination at, 252–53; diversity
and, 12, 19, 37–38; earnings and, 27; exodus
from, 120; expansion of through acquisition,
33–34; expansions in size and geographic scope
of, 22; failure to integrate, 245; fit and, 144, 156,
157; foundation-supported, 42; franchise, 34;
gender and, 95–96, 153–63, 245–46; golden age
of, 51, 54; governance model of, 41; growth in
bureaucratic structure of, 42; growth in size,
number, and scope of, 40–41, 42; as heteronomous organizations, 120; hiring and promotion
practices, 41, 132–33, 258–59, 266; as "inequality machines," 68; influence of patrons and, 132;
inheritance of firm clients and, 132, 136; vs.
inside counsel, 198–200; Jews and, 16–17; job
candidates and, 258–59; lateral hiring and, 41,
43; Latinx and, 9, 39, 40, 195, 246–47, 248; law
schools and, 34, 36–37; layoffs and, 35; mentoring and, 132, 140, 151; midsize, 43; neglect
within, 251–53; new role of, 354; nonequity
partners in, 56–57; nonpracticing positions and,
124; origination credits and, 132, 136–37, 159,
161; partnerships and, 4–8, 20, 131, 132 (see
also equity partnerships; partnerships); plaintiff,
42; politics and, 305, 307–8; pro bono work
and, 316–17, 317t, 323–24; profits of, 28, 36, 43,
44; quality of assignments and, 132, 139; racial
disparities at, 245; racial/ethnic composition
of, 8, 19, 95–96, 132–36, 243–59; racialization
of, 243–59; rainmaking and, 132; recruitment
efforts, 19; regional, 142, 159; reputation of,
34; salaries at, 27; satisfaction and, 329, 330;
segregated, 245; service roles, 140; shuttering of,
14; specialization of, 41; as stepping stones to inside counsel, 197–98; structures of opportunity
in, 20; survival of, 36; treatment of associates
by, 249–57; 2008 global financial crisis and, 35;
underlying structure of, 13; White men and,
164, 243; Whites and, 164, 243, 246–48; women
and, 3–5, 13, 19, 40, 132–36, 153–63, 187; work
policies, 132, 154–56, 159. See also large law
firms; midsize law firms; small firms
law professors, 73–76, 120, 180–81, 185–86, 215,
219; control over work and, 122; politics and, 305

law reform, 30
law school admissions, 266; affirmative action
programs and, 365; African Americans and,
87; Asian Americans and, 87; education credentials and, 97; gender and, 79, 85–86; Latinx
and, 87; LSAT scores and, 85–86; minorities
and, 79, 85–87; policies to address inequality,
365; race and, 39, 79, 85–86, 266; rankings and,
82; undergraduate grades and, 85; undergraduate institutions and, 85, 87; Whites and, 87;
women and, 79, 85–86
law school graduates: demographic data on, 80;
race and, 80
law school movers, 114
law school performance: government careers and,
216–17; public interest law and, 216–17; public
service careers and, 216–17
law schools, 29, 31, 82–87; accreditation and, 38;
accreditation standards for, 30, 31; African
Americans in, 38–39; African American
women in, 38–39; applications to, 27, 28, 36;
Asian Americans in, 38; class and, 84–85, 85t;
corporate law firms and, 36–37; diversity in,
38–39; federal government and, 74–75; financial aid and, 33; financial support for, 266t;
first practice setting and, 87–90, 89t; gender
and, 38–39; government careers and, 75–76;
graduates of in state judiciaries, 32; historically White, 38; Latinx in, 38; law firms and,
34, 36–37; minority admissions and, 38–39;
move away from vocational training, 30–31;
philanthropy and, 32; plummeting enrollments
after 2008 financial crisis, 14; prestige of, 13–
14; private, 32; public, 32, 39; race and, 38–39;
tuition and fees at, 32–33, 37, 261, 355–56;
urban, 38; vocational, 30–31; women in, 38–
39, 52–53. See also law school admissions; law
school performance; law school status
law school status, 13, 82–87, 89t, 129, 218, 370n7;
African Americans and, 87; Asian Americans
and, 87; class and, 86–87, 93, 357; education
and, 86–87; elite, 36–37, 38, 50, 51, 65–66, 69,
74–75, 128, 129, 165; family financial support
and, 266; family law and, 119; far-reaching
effects of, 365; field prestige scores and, 112t,
118–19; fields of law and, 119; financial support
and, 266t; first practice setting and, 89, 93; gender and, 86–87; geographic mobility and, 115;
government careers and, 216–17; immigration
law and, 119; inequality and, 56; job changes
and, 339–40, 340f, 342–43, 344; large law firms
and, 128–29; Latinx and, 87; lower-tier, 52, 53,
65–66, 70, 168; LSAT scores and, 86t; nonelite,
53, 69; parental level of education and, 87;
partnerships and, 132; personal client fields and,
119; personal injury law and, 119; politics and,

law school status (*cont.*)
305, 307; public interest law and, 216–17;
public service careers and, 216–17; race and,
86–87, 93; satisfaction and, 327f, 331; scholarship and, 267; securities law and, 119; social
background and, 86–87; solo practitioners and,
168; student debt and, 264–65, 270, 272, 273,
355–56; undergraduate institutions and, 86–87
lawyer conduct: rules governing, 44; state control
of, 44
lawyer effort: allocation of total, 106–19, 109f; direct measures of total on client types, 106–11,
109f; estimated distribution of (1975–2012),
107–8t
lawyers: advising and defending on ethical issues,
9; "lawyer-statesmen," 28, 31, 199, 310 (*see also*
citizen-lawyer); nonpracticing, 123–25; political orientations of, 304–6, 362–63; selectivity
of, 250–51, 254–57, 259
lawyers' careers: agency in, 351–66; collective
biography of, 128; evolution of, 90, 93; individual variation making up structural patterns
in, 353; key findings on, 353–65; narratives of,
127–30, 354–55; pathways of, 53–76; sequences
of, 353; social scripts for, 354–55; structure in,
351–66; theory and method in study of, 352–
53. *See also* pathways of lawyers' careers
lawyer-statesman, 28, 31, 199, 310. *See also*
citizen-lawyer
layoffs, 34; law firms and, 35; after tech bubble
burst, 27–28
leadership positions, 27
legal education: family financial support and,
260–62; replacing apprenticeship, 30; skyrocketing costs of, 261. *See also* law professors; law
schools
legal field. *See* legal profession
legal press, 27, 28–29
legal profession: affirmative action programs and,
39–40; African Americans and, 243–59; agency
and, 351–66; allocation of lawyers' total effort,
106–19; attractiveness of, 36; as autonomous
space, 51; boom-and-bust cycle of, 27–28;
Bourdieusian approach to, 15, 49–78; career
satisfaction and, 325–47; change in, 49–78;
changes in political economy of, 106; continuity in, 49–78; core values of, 43–44, 50–51; crisis in, 14–15, 50; critics of, 27; deep structures
of, 11; disruption rhetorics and, 28, 32–45;
diversity and, 36–40, 45; entering, 79–98, 81t;
gendered form of, 77; gendered norms in, 295–
98; golden age of, 50; hierarchies in, 77–78,
79; history of, 29; internal labor markets and,
40–43; job satisfaction, 325–47; legislation and,
29–30; living in contradictions of, 44–45; lower
hemisphere of, 51, 53, 70, 71 (*see also* personal

clients; two hemispheres thesis); as "male
establishment," 297; market-based inequalities
and, 303–4, 324; midcareer practice setting,
93–94; minorities and, 243–59; nationalization
of, 33–34; nostalgia for golden age, 28–32; organization structure and, 40–43; politics and,
304–6; power of, 45; professional norms, 43–
44; prospects for future of, 365–66; racial/eth-
nic composition of, 80–82, 81t; reality vs. narratives of, 44–45; regulatory state and, 29–30;
reinforcement of hierarchies in, 40–43; rules of
game and, 51; segmentation by field, 104, 125
(*see also* fields of practice); self-image as "noble
profession," 43, 44; as "separate and unequal,"
99; shifting structure of law jobs from entry to
midcareer, 90–91; size and concentration of,
32–36; social field of, 31; sprawling organization of, 42; stratification of, 45; structural
inequalities in, 37–38, 351–66; structures of,
45, 50; ten types of positions in, 56; theoretical
perspectives on, 50–53; upper hemisphere of,
51 (*see also* corporate clients; two hemispheres
thesis); upward mobility and, 31, 51; women
in, 37–38. *See also* lawyers' careers
legal services, 56, 218; African Americans and,
247; failure of current commitments to, 366;
inequality in provision of, 109–10; public access to, 43, 45; women in, 75–76
Legal Services Corporation (LSC), 313–14, 364
LegalZoom, 28, 36, 42
legislation, legal profession and, 29–30
Leslie (interviewee), 219
LGBTQ lawyers, 183–86, 202, 211, 372n3
liberalism, 312
Libertarians, 306
Lilly (interviewee), 219–20
litigation, 103, 106
Livingston, Robert W., 297, 298
Lloyds Bank of London, 55
loan forgiveness programs, 215–16, 221, 238,
276, 364
loan repayment assistance, 276
local government, 218, 228–38
local practices, 34
longitudinal studies, 18
Los Angeles (California), 113
LSAT scores, 86; first practice setting and, 89;
gender and, 85–86, 86t; law school admissions
and, 85–86; law school ranking and, 86t; men
and, 86; race and, 85–86, 86t
Luce, Carolyn Buck, 279
Luci (interviewee), 231–33
Lynden (interviewee), 3, 7–8, 10, 12, 142, 225, 321

macro, micro and, 54–55
managers, 41

Marcia (interviewee), 154–55, 332–33
markets, 11, 21, 111–13; cluster analysis of, 113; earnings and, 110; education and, 113–14; field prestige scores and, 112t; fields of law and, 111f; market stability through law, 29–30; social capital and, 113–14; state and, 21; urban markets, 112t, 113, 360
marriage, 76, 279–80. *See also* spouses
Marshall, Thurgood, 27
masculinity: celebrated in legal profession, 296–97; defined in opposition to femininity, 298; earnings and, 294–95; hegemonic, 278, 296–97, 298–99, 356; income inflation and, 297
maternity leave, 142–43, 159, 288
matrix of domination, intersectionality and, 358
Max (interviewee), 144–47
MBAs, 52
McCann, Michael, 364–65
McDaniel, Anne, 279
McGill, Christa, 263, 274–75
mediation, 185
men, 6–7; earnings and, 293–95; education and, 84; equity partnerships and, 354; job changes and, 342; LSAT scores and, 86; parenthood and, 294, 297; parenthood premium and, 294; partnerships and, 147–48, 152, 352; perception of value of law degree and, 337; politics and, 305; pro bono work and, 319; public interest lawyers and, 238; retention rates and, 97; satisfaction and, 326; with spouses at home, 129, 132, 134–35, 151, 280, 290–91, 299, 354, 357; student debt and, 276. *See also specific racial/ethnic groups*
Menkel-Meadow, Carrie, 118
mental health, gender and, 344–46
mentoring, 7, 8, 9, 244, 251–53, 254–57; African Americans and, 251–53, 257; importance of, 10, 257; influence of, 132; law firms and, 140, 151; partnerships and, 145; race and, 249–50; satisfaction and, 331, 363; Whites and, 251–53, 257
mergers and acquisitions, 17, 35, 52
meritocracy, 53, 56, 69, 77, 84–85, 129, 357; hierarchies of legal field and, 129; veneer of, 128, 132
micro, macro and, 54–55
midcareer positions, first jobs and, 79
midcareer practice setting, 93–94; African Americans and, 97; Asian Americans and, 97; chains of supervision and, 121; class and, 93–94; control over work and, 121–23; first practice setting and, 93, 97; gender and, 93–94, 97–98; Native Americans and, 97; race and, 93–94, 97–98
midsize law firms, 43, 72, 87–90, 121, 144–53; African Americans in, 72, 73; African American women in, 73; Asian American men in, 73; Asian Americans in, 72, 73; autonomy and, 122; billable hours and, 146, 147; compensation and, 73; early to midcareer transitions and, 89t;

earnings and, 111; equity partnerships and, 56–57, 146, 147; first practice setting and, 88t, 89t; gender and, 72–73, 87–90, 88t; hiring and promotion practices, 132–33; law school ranking and, 87–90, 89t; men in, 73, 164; midsize-firm equity cluster, 72; midsize-firm starters, 70–72; origination credits and, 146, 147; partnerships and, 144–47; politics and, 308; privileging of White men in, 164; race and, 87–90, 88t; small-firm starters, 70–72; wave 3 practice setting and, 91–92t, 93–94; Whites in, 72, 73, 164; White women in, 73; women in, 72–73
Mindy (interviewee), 226
Minneapolis (Minnesota), 113, 114
minorities, 39, 76–77, 243–59; capital value of status of, 52, 70; community organizations and, 312, 323; in corporate law firms, 52–53; departure for large law firms, 128–29; equity partnerships and, 142, 247, 248, 249, 250–51, 254–57, 259; government careers and, 79, 218–19; inside counsel and, 201–3; job changes and, 344; large law firms and, 66–68, 128–29, 288–89; law firms and, 19, 66–68, 132–36, 141–42, 192, 195, 243–45, 247–57, 259, 288–89; law school admissions and, 79, 85–86; leaving firms, 141–42, 192, 195, 244–45, 247–57, 259; LSAT scores and, 85–86; minority students, 39; movements for social equality and, 52; nonprofit careers and, 79, 218–19; partnerships and, 38, 78, 129, 136–40, 142, 164, 250–51, 254–57, 259; politics and, 307; public interest careers and, 218–19; satisfaction and, 331; as solo practitioners, 194; state government careers and, 354. *See also* ethnicity; race; *and specific groups*
misogyny, 160–62
Mitchell (interviewee), 150–52
mobility: pathways of lawyers' careers and, 53–78, 131–32; satisfaction and, 363; between sectors, 55; state government careers and, 239. *See also* geographic mobility, career opportunity and; upward mobility
Molly (interviewee), 233, 234–35
Monica (interviewee), 186–88
morality, 334–38. *See also* ethics
motherhood: delay of, 280; gender wage gap and, 282 (*see also* motherhood penalty)
motherhood penalty: earnings and, 279–80, 293–95, 356; gender wage gap and, 279–80, 293–95, 356; vs. motherhood premium, 279; partnerships and, 159; statistical modeling of, 372n2; women and, 294
municipal law, 101t, 104, 105, 105f

National Association for the Advancement of Colored People, Legal Defense and Education Fund, 34

Native American men: earnings and, 292t, 293; gender wage gap and, 292t, 293

Native Americans, 12; AJD Project cohort and, 94–95; early careers, 94–95; education and, 82–84, 94–95; equity partnerships and, 96; financial support and, 266t; first practice setting and, 95; job changes and, 342; as law school movers, 114; LSAT scores and, 86; midcareer practice setting and, 97; parental level of education and, 94–95; partnerships and, 96; race/ethnicity-based organizations and, 312; small-firm starters, 71; social characteristics of respondents and, 94–95; student debt and, 263–73; wave 3 practice setting and, 95. *See also* Native American men; Native American women

Native American women, 358; earnings and, 292t, 293; gender wage gap and, 292t, 293; in government careers, 74; student debt and, 272

Neely, Meghan Tobias, 17

Nelson, Robert L., 16, 23, 103, 106, 111, 115–18, 123, 125, 127, 304–5, 311, 323, 338, 360

networking, 170–71, 330, 343, 344

networks, 186

New Deal, 29, 33, 304

New Jersey, 113

new millennium, context of, 27–45

New York City, 113

New York State Bar Association, 43

Nicholas (interviewee), 189–91

nonequity positions, 41, 52, 56–57, 65, 131, 138–40, 159, 161, 244, 251–57; control over work and, 122; earnings and, 288; in large law firms, 77; women in, 77, 171

non-partnership track positions, women and, 96

nonpracticing positions, 123–25; age and, 124; in business organizations, 124; federal government and, 124; law firms and, 124; movement in and out of, 123; nonprofit careers and, 124; practice settings and, 124; public interest lawyers and, 124; race and, 123–24; satisfaction levels and, 124–25; social characteristics and, 123–24; state government and, 124; women and, 123; workplace authority and, 124; workplace diversity and, 125

nonprofit careers, 120, 121, 215–39; earnings and, 110, 111; elite tracks to, 219–21; minorities and, 79, 218–19; nonpracticing positions and, 124; politics and, 307; satisfaction and, 329; solo practitioners in, 168; statistical background on, 218–19; status hierarchy and, 215; White men and, 221, 222; White women and, 219, 221, 231; women and, 79, 218

nonprofit organizations, 87–90; early to midcareer transitions and, 89t; elite tracks to, 219–21; first practice setting and, 88t, 89t; gender and, 87–90, 88t; law school ranking and, 87–90, 89t;

race and, 87–90, 88t; service on boards of, 312; wave 3 practice setting and, 91–92t, 93–94. *See also* nonprofit careers

Obama, Barack, 28, 305, 306

Oklahoma, 94–95, 113, 114

Olivia (interviewee), 227–28

opportunity: geography of, 113–15; hierarchical structure of, 128; inequality and, 10–15; social capital and, 79; structures of, 20

optimal matching, 56

Oregon, 113, 114

organizational hierarchies, practice settings as, 119–25

organizational settings, 56; characteristics of, 120–23; controlled by professionals vs. non-professionals, 120; earnings and, 110

organizational theory, 17–21

organization memberships, 310–11; conservatism and, 311–12

organization size, 120–21

organization structure, legal profession and, 40–43

organized sports, 311–12

origination credits, 132, 136–37, 146, 147, 159, 161

outsourcing companies, 42

Padavic, Irene, 19, 288, 295, 296

Palay, Thomas, 131, 369n1 (chap. 2)

Palmore, Richard, 40

Pamela (interviewee), 137–40, 237, 297–98, 321–22

parental leave, 288, 338. *See also* maternity leave

parental level of education, 86, 87, 160, 177, 264, 266–67, 266t

parental nativity, 86

parental occupation, 232; class and, 356–57

parenthood, 11, 76, 153–56, 164, 203, 278–99, 334–37; billable hours and, 154–55; childcare and, 128, 170; earnings and, 288, 293–95; gender wage gap and, 279–80, 281, 282, 291–92, 293–95; men and, 294, 297; premium, 294; satisfaction and, 332–33; women and, 142–43, 293–95

parent teacher associations, 310

partners: access to and relationships with, 250; layoffs and, 35; politics and, 305; pro bono work and, 320–21; work satisfaction and, 44. *See also* equity partnerships; partnerships

partnerships, 11, 41, 52, 130; ABA membership and, 313, 323; African Americans and, 39, 96, 247, 248, 249, 250–51, 254–57, 259, 355; Asian American men and, 147–48; Asian Americans and, 96, 147–48; aspirations for, 250–51, 254–57, 259; associates and, 244; attrition and, 132; billable hours and, 132–33; class and, 143–44; community organizations and, 323, 324; compensation and, 10, 29; in corporate law firms, 51–52; in Cravath System, 29; diversity

and, 40; equity, 56, 131–32, 260; failing to
make partner, 137–43; fall in desirability of, 78;
gender and, 38, 53, 78–79, 95–96, 129, 132–36,
142–45, 147–48, 150, 152–56, 159–61, 164, 171,
187, 203, 289, 332–33, 352–53; interest in, 128;
large law firms and, 134–43, 164; lateral hiring
and, 353; Latinx and, 96; law firms and, 20; law
school ranking and, 132; low odds of making
partner, 53; making partner, 4–5, 8, 134–37,
338; men and, 132, 134–36, 143–44, 147–48,
164; mentorships and, 145; midsize law firms
and, 144–47; minorities and, 38–39, 78, 96, 129,
136–40, 142, 147–48, 164, 247–57, 259, 355;
mobility and, 52; model, 41; motherhood penalty and, 159; Native Americans and, 96; nonequity (see nonequity positions); in private law
firms, 131; pro bono work and, 321, 324; profits
and, 43, 52; prospects for making, 250–51, 254–
57, 259; race/ethnicity and, 38–39, 78–79, 95–
96, 129, 132–40, 142–44, 147–48, 164, 247–51,
254–57, 259, 355; rejection for, 352; satisfaction
and, 332–33; unequal distribution of, 76–77;
White men and, 132, 134–36, 143–44, 164;
Whites and, 96, 132, 134–36, 143–44, 164, 248,
249, 250–51, 254–57, 259, 355; women and, 38,
53, 78–79, 95–96, 129, 132–36, 142–44, 150–61,
164, 171, 187, 203, 289, 332–33
part-time employment, 287–88
paternalism, 297–98
path dependency, capital accumulation and, 98
pathways of lawyers' careers: business lawyers,
72–73; education lawyers, 73–76; government
lawyers, 73–76; large-firm starters, 63–70;
mobility and, 53–78, 131–32; nongovernment
public sector lawyers, 73–76; sequence analysis
and, 49–78; small- and midsize-firm starters,
70–72
patriarchy, 153, 160. See also sexism
Patrick (interviewee), 205–7
patronage jobs, 31
patrons, 132, 244
patterns, 55–56
Paula (interviewee), 3, 5–6, 10–12, 18–19, 38,
203, 352
Paul Weiss, 303, 307, 324
Peggy (interviewee), 208–9
Penelope (interviewee), 160–61, 295–96
performance evaluation, 328
"permanent associates," 41
personal clients, 99, 106, 111, 112t, 113, 125, 129,
359–60; autonomy and, 119–20; law school
prestige and, 119; least populous locales and,
112t, 113; prestige and, 119–20; solo practitioners and, 197
personal injury law, 27, 102, 101–2t, 103, 104,
105, 105f, 106, 116, 118, 359; advertising and,

43; Irish Catholic lawyers and, 118; law school
prestige and, 119; rise of, 31–32
personal narratives, 10
personal plight sector, 16
personal real estate law, 102, 102t, 105f
Philip (interviewee), 229–30
Pierce, Jennifer L., 297
Piper (interviewee), 156–58
plaintiff law firms, 42
plaintiffs' bar, 364–65
Plickert, Gabriele, 345, 346
political advocacy groups, 311
political economy, 21–23
political organizations, participation in, 309
political orientation, 23, 179, 304–13, 306t, 322,
323, 362–63; business representation and, 308–
9; changing stance on, 308–9; client types and,
305; community organizations and, 311–12;
descriptive patterns of, 306–8; education and,
304; gender and, 304, 305, 307, 309; geography
and, 305, 307; political party affiliation, 305–9,
306t, 311, 322–23; practice settings and, 305,
307–8; prior research on, 304–6; pro bono
work and, 319; race and, 304, 305, 307, 309;
religious affiliation and, 305
political party affiliation, 305–9, 306t, 311, 322–23
political party organizations, 311
position changes, 338
Powell, Lewis F., Jr., 39, 283
power, deep connections to, 21
practice groups, 8
practice settings, 60–62t, 99–125, 127; autonomy
and, 121–22; categories of, 88; community
organizations and, 311–12; distribution of
practitioners among, 110–11, 111f; earnings
and, 110, 280–91, 281t; first jobs and, 129; gender and, 280–91, 281t; gender wage gap and,
280–91, 281t, 356; job changes and, 340–42,
341f, 344; nonpracticing positions and, 124;
as organizational hierarchies, 119–25; politics
and, 305, 307–8; pro bono work and, 316–18,
317t, 320, 321; satisfaction and, 327–30, 328f,
363; student debt and, 270, 272, 274; wave 3
earnings and, 111f
pragmatic choice narratives, 238; operation of
gender, race, and class hierarchies in, 230–31
precarity, solo practitioners and, 169–82, 196
prestige, 56, 119–20, 299. See also law school
status
private clubs, 311–12
private interest, 44
private practices, public roles and, 22–23
private sector careers, 11–12, 42; class and, 230;
earnings and, 287; fit and, 230; gender and,
230; vs. government careers, 11–12; pro bono
work and, 317t, 318, 319; race and, 230

privilege, 128; class and, 129; education and,
    82–87; White identity and, 50, 51, 68, 129, 132,
    243, 244; White male identity and, 76–77, 78
probate law, 102, 102t, 105f; White lawyers and, 118
pro bono work, 23, 44, 50, 51, 303, 313, 315f,
    322, 364; ABA goals for and, 314–15, 361–62;
    African Americans and, 319; benefits of, 362;
    billable hours and, 319, 320, 321; business rep-
    resentation and, 323; career benefits of, 320–22,
    362; career development and, 321; charitable
    organization membership and, 319–20; com-
    pared to lawyers' total effort for clients, 315;
    defining, 373n7; as elite career strategy, 316–20;
    failure of current commitments to, 366; gender
    and, 319, 320; government careers and, 323; law
    firms and, 316–17, 317t, 323–24, 329; lifetime
    continuity of, 320; low level of effort on,
    361–62; men and, 319; opportunities for, 328;
    partners and, 320–21; partnerships and, 321,
    324; politics and, 319; practice settings and,
    316–18, 317t, 320, 321; predicting effort on,
    319f; private sector law and, 319; public sector
    and, 319; race and, 319; small firms and, 323;
    social characteristics of respondents and, 316–
    18, 317t; social conservatism and, 319; solo
    practitioners and, 317–18, 317t, 323; time spent
    on at wave 3, 315, 315f; women and, 319, 320
product liability cases, 42
professional gain, public service and, 323
professional hierarchies, 10
professional ideology, 21
professionalism, 43–44, 50, 51
professionalization, 31
professional norms, 31, 43–44
professional organizations, 309–12
professional virtue, 30
promotions. See advancement
prosecutors, 32, 217, 236–37, 239, 305
prospects for future, 365–66
Protestant lawyers, 51; politics and, 305
proxy fights, 17
public defenders, 76, 122, 216, 218, 233–37, 239,
    247, 305
public good, 44
public interest careers, 27, 28, 34, 36, 42, 56, 87–90,
    120–21, 215–39, 364–65; African Americans
    and, 247; early to midcareer transitions and,
    89t; earnings and, 110, 111, 239; elite tracks
    to, 219–21, 238; ethnicity and, 216–17; first
    practice setting and, 88t, 89t; gender and, 87–90,
    88t, 216–17; habitus of, 217; ideology and, 216,
    217; law school performance and, 216–17; law
    school status and, 87–90, 89t, 216–17; men and,
    238; minorities and, 218–19; nonelite world
    of, 221–22; nonpracticing positions and, 124;
    paths to, 217–18; race and, 87–90, 88t, 216–17;

satisfaction and, 329, 330; scholarship on,
    215–17; solo practitioners and, 168; statistical
    background on, 218–19; status hierarchy and,
    215; wave 3 practice setting and, 91–92t, 93–94;
    White men and, 221–24; Whites and, 221–24;
    White women and, 219–21; women and, 217–
    21, 238; work/life balance and, 238–39
public roles, private practices and, 22–23
public sector careers, 55; career sequences
    characterized by, 218; earnings and, 110, 287;
    nongovernment, 73–76; pro bono work and,
    317t, 318, 319; statistical background on, 218–
    19; status hierarchy and, 215
public sector law, 11–12, 42
public service, 22–23, 238, 303–24; commitment
    to, 50; professional gain and, 323
public service careers: definition of, 372n9; gen-
    der and, 216–17; law school performance and,
    216–17; law school status and, 216–17; loan
    forgiveness programs and, 215–16; race and,
    216–17; scholarship on, 215–17; student debt
    and, 274–75, 276, 277
Putnam, Robert, 309

quantile regression for panel data (QRPD), 283

race, 11, 45, 79–98, 129, 352; AJD Project cohort
    and, 80–82, 81t, 355; associates and, 247–48;
    career structure and, 96–97; career trajectories
    and, 97; class and, 356–58; community orga-
    nizations and, 311–12, 323; debt and, 260–61;
    early careers and, 93–94; early to midcareer
    transitions and, 93–94; earnings and, 292, 292t;
    education and, 82–83; education credentials
    and, 87–90; entering legal profession and, 80–
    82; equity partnerships and, 354, 355; explana-
    tions for racial disparities, 245; family financial
    support and, 262, 265–66; fields of law and,
    116, 118, 119, 125; financial support and, 266t;
    first practice setting and, 87–90, 88t, 89t; gen-
    der and, 38–39, 96–97, 245–46, 286, 292–98,
    292t, 357–58; gender wage gap and, 286, 292–
    98, 292t, 358; government careers and, 216–17;
    inequality and, 56, 351, 365; influence from
    law school through midcareer, 79–98; intersec-
    tionality and, 96–97, 245–46; job changes and,
    342, 344; job stability and, 55–56; law firms
    and, 8, 68, 95–96, 243–59; law school admis-
    sions and, 39, 79, 85–86, 266; law schools and,
    38–39, 79–80, 85–87, 93; leaving firms and,
    245; LSAT scores and, 85–86, 86t; mentoring
    and, 249–50; midcareer practice setting and,
    93–94, 97–98; nonpracticing positions and,
    123–24; partnerships and, 79, 95–96, 132–36,
    143–44, 164, 247, 355; path dependency and,
    98; perception of law degree value and, 334,

335; politics and, 304, 305, 307, 309; private sector law and, 230; pro bono work and, 319; public interest law and, 216–17; public service careers and, 216–17; racial/ethnic composition of pipeline to legal employment, 81t; racial inequality, 246, 355–56; retention rates and, 97; satisfaction and, 326, 326t, 330, 331, 363; social capital and, 87; solo practitioners and, 168; student debt and, 263–64, 264t, 272, 275, 276, 356. *See also* ethnicity; *and specific groups*
race-based organizations, 312
race-conscious admissions, 39, 266
race/ethnicity-based organizations, 311, 312
racism, 10. *See also* discrimination
rainmaking, 132
rank invariance, 283
Raymond (interviewee), 135
real estate law, 102t, 105f
recognition for work, 328
referrals, 197
Regents of California v. Bakke, 39
regulatory state, legal profession and, 29–30
Reid, Erin M., 19, 288, 295, 296
religious affiliation: fields of law and, 116; politics and, 305
religious organizations, 310, 311–12
Republican Party, 304–8, 306t, 323, 362
research design and data, 23–24, 25f
retention rates, 97
revenue generation requirements, 44
Revesz, Richard L., 263
Ricardo (interviewee), 192–95, 358
Richard (interviewee), 235
Ridgeway, Cecilia L., 299
rights revolution, 33
Rivera, Lauren A., 17, 82
Rocket Lawyer, 42
Root, Elihu, 310
Rufus (interviewee), 135–36, 336
Ryan (interviewee), 236

sales, making, 197
Samantha (interviewee), 208
Samir (interviewee), 147–48
Sandefur, Rebecca, 16, 23, 103, 106, 111, 115–18, 123, 125, 127, 304–5, 311, 314, 323, 338, 360
San Francisco Bay Area (California), 113
Sara Lee, 40
satisfaction, 68, 74, 230, 325–47, 326f, 326t, 327f, 328, 329f, 366; African Americans and, 330, 331; African American women and, 331; business careers and, 330; changing meaning of, 332; class and, 326–28; compensation and, 328–29; depression and, 344–46; descriptive results on, 325–30; discrimination and, 330–31; economic factors and, 330; effects of, 338–46;

equity partners and, 331; federal government careers and, 329, 330; gender and, 326, 326t, 331, 332–33, 344–46, 363; government careers and, 75, 329, 330; job changes and, 342, 343, 346, 363; large law firms and, 329; Latinx and, 330; law firms and, 329, 330; law school status and, 327f, 331, 363; levels, 121–23, 124–25; levels of responsibility and, 328–29; meaning of, 332–38; mental health and, 344–46; mentoring and, 331, 363; minorities and, 331; mobility and, 363; multivariate results on, 330–31; networking and, 330; nonprofit careers and, 329; parenthood and, 332–33; partnerships and, 332–33; patterns of, 325–31; perception of value of law degree and, 334–37; practice settings and, 327–30, 328f, 363; public interest careers and, 329, 330; race and, 326, 326t, 330, 331, 363; small firms and, 329, 330; solo practitioners and, 330; state government careers and, 330; student debt and, 274, 277, 330; Whites and, 330; women and, 331, 332–33, 344–46; work conditions and, 330–31; work/life balance and, 332–33, 363; workplace conditions and, 346; workplace experiences and, 363–64
Sauder, Michael, 82
Savage, Michael, 55
scholarships, need-based, 267
Scott (interviewee), 236–37
Sean (interviewee), 169–71
Sebastian (interviewee), 207
sectors, mobility between, 55
Securities and Exchange Commission (SEC), 227
securities law, 102, 102t, 103, 105, 105f, 112t, 113, 115, 116, 119, 359–60
securitization, 34, 35
selectivity, of lawyers, 250–51, 254–57, 259
self-selection, patterns driven by, 249–50
Sen, Maya, 23, 304, 305, 307
sequence analysis, 53–76, 64–65f, 79
Serena (interviewee), 221
Sergio (interviewee), 211
Seron, Carroll, 167–68, 186, 197
service organizations, 311–12
sexism, 4–5, 10, 160–63, 295–98
Shapiro, Robert, 35–36
Shearman and Sterling, 40
Sherman Act, 29
Skadden fellowships, 217, 219, 221
Skylar (interviewee), 148–50
slip-and-fall cases, 42
small-firm starters: African Americans, 70; Asian Americans, 70, 71; Latinos, 71; Native Americans, 71; Whites and, 70, 71
small law firms, 28, 36, 42, 51, 55–56, 68, 70, 87–90, 121, 144, 156, 169, 305; all-White, 247; autonomy and, 122; early to midcareer

small law firms (*cont.*)
transitions and, 89t; first practice setting and, 88t, 89t; gender and, 87–90, 88t; hiring and promotion practices, 132–33; law school ranking and, 87–90, 89t; politics and, 308; privileging of White men in, 164; pro bono work and, 323; race and, 87–90, 88t; satisfaction and, 329, 330; small- and midsize-firm starters, 70–72; wave 3 practice setting and, 91–92t, 93–94
Smigel, Erwin O., 99
social background: law school credentials and, 86–87; student debt and, 275
social capital, 17–21, 128, 129, 352, 353, 354; Bourdieusian understanding of, 57; in business organizations, 213; career outcomes and, 97; career trajectories and, 98; community service and, 312–13; gender and, 87; markets and, 113–14; opportunity and, 79; race and, 87; White identity and, 39
social capital theory, 19–20
social characteristics: career patterns and, 79–98; career trajectories and, 97; debt-income ratio and, 265; fields of law and, 116; fields of practice and, 115–19, 117t; financial support and, 265–67, 266t; intersectionality and, 96–97; nonpracticing positions and, 123–24; pro bono work and, 317t. *See also specific characteristics*
social conservatism, 306t, 307, 309, 312, 319
social construction, 11
social differentiation, shift from religion and ethnicity to gender and race, 125
social divisions, 104
social embeddedness, importance of, 343
social equality, political movements for, 52
social hierarchies, 10
social justice, 216, 219, 303–4, 324, 329
social networks, 128
social origin, inequality and, 56
Social Security Administration (SSA), 228
social structure, agency and, 10–15
social system, reproduction of, 352
social work, 219–20
solo practice: lower hemisphere of, 165–66, 169–86, 197; precarity and, 169–82, 196; as process rather than end state, 196; similarities of across hemispheres, 197; two hemispheres hierarchy and, 165–66; two hemispheres thesis and, 197; upper hemisphere of, 165–66, 186–96, 197; upward mobility and, 169–82
solo practitioners, 42, 51, 56, 68, 70, 87–90, 121, 129, 130; African Americans as, 175–78; AJD Project findings on, 165; Asian Americans as, 179–81; autonomy and, 122; continuity in career path across waves and, 168; control over work and, 122; corporate clients and, 197; defining category of, 165–66; depression and,

168; early careers in law firms and, 197; early to midcareer transitions and, 89t; earnings and, 110, 168–69; education law and, 168; entrepreneurialism and, 173, 186, 194, 196; existing scholarship on, 165, 166–68; fields of law and, 168; financial insecurity and, 167; first practice setting and, 88t, 89t; gender and, 87–90, 88t, 168, 171–73, 178–79, 183–88, 194; as heteronomous organizations, 120; identity and, 173–82; identity-based practices and, 173–82; innovation and, 196; invention and, 186–96; Latinx as, 173–75, 192–96; law school ranking and, 87–90, 89t; 168; men as, 178–79; minorities as, 194; mission- or value-driven, 182–86; networking and, 170–71; nonprofit careers and, 168; as part of lower hemisphere, 168; as part of upper hemisphere, 168; personal clients and, 197; politics and, 308; pro bono work and, 317–18, 317t, 323; public interest in, 169; public interest lawyers and, 168; quantitative portrait of, 168–69; race/ethnicity and, 87–90, 88t, 168, 173–81, 192–96; rethinking, 165–96; satisfaction and, 330; starting as associates in large law firms, 165–66; stress and, 168; student debt and, 168, 180, 184, 185–86, 193, 274; technology and, 186–88, 193–95; at wave 1, 168; at wave 3, 168; wave 3 practice setting and, 91–92t, 93–94; White men as, 178–79; women as, 168, 171–73, 183–88, 194
Sommerlad, Hilary, 297
Sophia (interviewee), 171–72
specialization, 102–4, 125, 359–60; geographic distribution of, 104; rising, 359–60; specialization index (SI), 103, 104
Spencer (interviewee), 203–4
spouses, 128, 156–60, 164, 170–75, 191–95; earnings of, 290–91; at home, 129, 132, 134–35, 151, 280, 290–91, 299, 354, 357; household duties and, 128, 291; working full-time, 290. *See also* divorce; gender
Sprague, John D., 304
staffing agencies, 43
start-up positions, 169
state, 21; bar authorities and, 22; market and, 21
state government careers, 51, 56, 70, 74, 217–18, 228–39; ABA membership and, 312; African American men and, 236–37; African Americans and, 233–35, 236–37; African American women and, 233–35; Asian Americans and, 237; Asian American women and, 237; attorneys general, 233–36; autonomy and, 122; earnings and, 110, 111, 239; fast-track positions, 228–30; gender and, 217–18, 228–37, 354; general positions, 230–33; Latinas and, 231–33; Latinx and, 231–33; men and, 228–30, 235–37; minorities and, 217–18, 231–37, 354;

mobility and, 239; nonpracticing positions, 124; politics and, 308; public defenders, 233–36; satisfaction and, 329, 330; social script for, 354; White men and, 228–30, 235–36; Whites and, 228–31, 235–36; White women and, 229, 231, 235; women and, 217–18, 229, 231–35, 237, 354; women of color and, 217–18, 233–35
state judiciaries, 32
status hierarchy: education and, 82–87; government careers and, 215; nonprofit careers and, 215; public interest careers and, 215; public sector careers and, 215
STEM fields, 116, 213, 279
Stewart (interviewee), 177–79, 181–82, 260, 335
Stimson, Henry, 310
St. Louis (Missouri), 113
Stone, Pamela, 19
Stovel, Katherine, 55
strategies, fields and, 20–21
structure, in lawyers' careers, 351–66
structures of inequality, continuity of, 77–78, 125
student debt, 13–14, 32–33, 260–77; African American men and, 260–61, 264, 270, 272; African Americans and, 260–61, 262, 263–73, 275–77, 356; African American women and, 262, 264, 270, 272, 275–76; Asian American men and, 265, 272; Asian Americans and, 262, 263–73; Asian American women and, 264, 272; career satisfaction and, 274, 277; class and, 260–61, 262, 264–65, 272, 275; consequences of, 262–63; cumulative (dis)advantage and, 262; earnings and, 260–61, 272, 274, 276; ethnicity and, 264t; fields of law and, 274–75; findings on, 263–73; gender and, 262, 264, 265; government careers and, 274; impact of, 262–63, 274–75; inequality and, 261–62; inside counsel and, 205–6; job satisfaction and, 262, 264, 270; Latinas and, 262, 264, 270; Latinos and, 265, 270, 272; Latinx and, 262, 263–73, 275–76; law schools and, 261–77, 355–56; law school status and, 264–65, 270, 272, 273, 355–56; loan forgiveness programs and, 215–16; men and, 260–61, 264, 265, 270, 272, 276; Native Americans and, 263–73; Native American women and, 272; parental level of education and, 264; practice settings and, 270, 272, 274; predicting at graduation and midcareer, 267–71, 268–69t, 271t, 273f; predicting change in over time, 272–73; public service careers and, 274–75, 276, 277; race/ethnicity and, 260–61, 263–64, 264t, 272, 275, 276, 356; racial disparities and, 275, 276; repayment of, 276; satisfaction and, 330; social background and, 275; solo practitioners and, 168, 180, 184, 185–86, 193, 274; White men and, 260–61, 265, 270, 272; Whites and, 260–61, 262, 263–73, 275–76; women and, 262, 264, 265, 270, 272, 275–76

substitution, 56
supervising attorneys, control over work and, 122
support personnel, layoffs and, 35
Supreme Court, decisions invalidating rules against advertising, 44
symbolic capital, 129, 186

talent, 128
Tara (interviewee), 155–56
tax law, 102t, 103, 105f
tech bubble, layoffs after bursting of, 27–28
tech market, 34
technology, 28; companies, 42; growth in legal, 35–36; solo practitioners and, 186–88, 193–95
Tennessee, 113, 114
terrorist attacks of 9/11, 28
Texas, 39
theoretical perspectives, 15–23; hemispheres, 15–17; internal labor markets, 17–21; organizational theory, 17–21; political economy, 21–23; social capital, 17–21
"threshold law," 170
time allocation analysis, 106, 107–8t, 109f
time-in-fields analysis. See time allocation analysis
Toby (interviewee), 182–83
Tocqueville, Alexis de, 304, 311
Todd (interviewee), 140
tokenism, perceptions of, 258–59
"training track," 244
Trevor (interviewee), 202, 204, 212
Trubek, David M., 21, 22
two hemispheres thesis, 99–125, 129, 166, 359; continued vitality of, 125; practice settings and, 119–20; revisited, 99–125, 359–60; solo practitioners and, 165–66, 197. See also corporate clients; personal clients

undergraduate grades, 85, 86
undergraduate institutions: law school admissions and, 85, 87; law school credentials and, 86–87; status hierarchy and, 82, 83, 369n6
unemployment, 56, 71, 73, 200–201, 208, 287, 288, 338
United Kingdom, 43
up-or-out promotion policy, 41, 131, 244–45
upward mobility, 130, 166; job changes and, 344; legal profession and, 31, 51; solo practitioners and, 169–82; stories of, 13–14
urban government, 51
urban markets, 112t, 113, 360
US attorney positions, 223, 224, 225, 226, 238
US News, 82, 369–70nn6–7
Utah, 113

values, 334–38, 352
Van Hoy, Jerry, 168

virtual work, 186
voluntary associations, 311

Wacquant, Loïc J. D., 31
wage stagnation, 35
Washington (D.C.), 113
wave 3 practice setting: first practice setting and, 90–93, 91–92t; Native Americans and, 95
wealth gap, 35
Wendy (interviewee), 142–43, 332, 333
Westlaw Next, 36
White Anglo-Saxon Protestant lawyers, 50, 51, 115, 116
white-collar defense, 17
White men: community organizations and, 323; earnings and, 260–61, 292–93, 292t; equity partnerships and, 244, 354; federal government careers and, 223–24, 227; gender wage gap and, 292–93, 292t; in government careers, 76; inside counsel and, 203–4, 205–7, 209–10; law firms and, 243; nonprofit careers and, 221, 222; partnerships and, 134–36, 143–44, 164; perception of law degree value and, 336; privileging of, 76–77, 78, 164, 357–58; pro bono work and, 321; public interest careers and, 221; public interest law and, 222, 223–24; as solo practitioners, 178–79; with spouses at home, 357; state government careers and, 228–30, 235–36; student debt and, 260–61, 265, 270, 272
Whites, 3–5, 6–7; class and, 357; earnings and, 286; education and, 82–84; equity partnerships and, 96, 248, 249, 250–51, 254–57, 259, 354; family financial support and, 260–61, 266; financial support and, 266t; inside counsel and, 203–9; job offers and, 258–59; job stability and, 55–56; law firms and, 246–47, 248; law school admissions and, 87; as law school movers, 114; leaving firms, 254–57; LSAT scores and, 86; mentoring and, 251–53, 257; as midsize-firm starters, 72; nonpracticing positions and, 123–24; overrepresented among bar admittees, 80; partnerships and, 96, 248, 249, 250–51, 254–57, 259, 355; perception of law degree value and, 336; politics and, 307; privileging of, 50, 51, 68, 76–78, 129, 132, 243, 244; probate law and, 118; race/ethnicity-based organizations and, 312; retention rates and, 97; satisfaction and, 330; as small-firm starters, 70, 71; social capital and, 39; student debt and, 262, 263–73, 275–76; work opportunities and, 251–53. See also White men; White women
White women, 148–50, 358; earnings and, 292–93, 292t; federal government careers and, 224–25, 226; gender wage gap and, 292–93, 292t; inside counsel and, 204, 208–9, 211–12; in midsize law firms, 73; nonprofit careers and,

219, 221, 231; public interest lawyers and, 219–21; state government careers and, 229, 231, 235
Wilkins, David B., 21, 22, 243, 310
Williams, Joan C., 297, 298
Wolfe, Tom, 27
women, 3–6, 12, 37–38, 76–77; associate positions and, 96; autonomy and, 121–22; billable hours and, 143; career opportunity and, 115; chains of supervision and, 121; charitable organization membership and, 320; childless, 296, 298, 356; community organizations and, 312, 323; in construction law, 161; in corporate law firms, 52–53; devaluation of, 296, 356; as distinctly disadvantaged in legal profession, 356; earnings and, 293–95 (see also gender wage gap); education and, 84; equity partnerships and, 77, 95–96, 136, 143, 159, 289, 354; family law and, 125; family responsibilities and, 132; fields of law and, 116, 359; first practice setting and, 88; gender wage gap and, 356; geographic mobility and, 115; government careers and, 74, 76, 79, 217–19; inside counsel and, 42, 77, 201–4; job changes and, 77, 338, 342, 344; large law firms and, 66–68, 128–29, 142–43, 288–89; law firms and, 3–5, 13, 19, 40, 66–68, 128–29, 132–36, 139–43, 153–64, 187, 288–89, 356; in law school, 52–53; law school admissions and, 79, 85–86; leaving firms, 139–40, 153, 155, 161–63, 164, 187, 356; in legal profession, 37–38; in legal services, 75–76; LSAT scores and, 85–86; mental health and, 344–46; in midsize firms, 72–73; motherhood and, 71, 74, 76, 142–43, 149, 203, 293–95, 296; motherhood penalty and, 293–95; nonequity positions and, 77, 171; non-partnership track positions and, 96; nonpracticing positions and, 123; nonprofit careers and, 79, 218; partnerships and, 53, 78–79, 95–96, 129, 132, 136, 142–44, 150–61, 164, 171, 187, 203, 289, 332–33, 352–53; part-time options and, 77; perception of value of law degree and, 337; politics and, 304, 305, 307; pro bono work and, 319, 320, 321–22; public interest law and, 217–18, 238; satisfaction and, 326, 331, 332–33, 344–46; as solo practitioners, 168, 171–73, 183–88, 194; state government careers and, 217–18, 354; student debt and, 262, 265, 276; underrepresented in legal profession, 39; underrepresented in partnerships, 38, 40; unemployment and, 77; work-family narrative explanation and, 296, 299; work/life balance and, 42. See also specific racial/ethnic groups
women of color, 246, 299; as equity partners, 354; state government careers and, 217–18, 233–35
women's movement, 52–53
word of mouth, 197
work, control over, 121–22, 328; gender and, 123; hierarchies and, 121–22; large law firms and,

123; midcareer practice setting and, 121–23; satisfaction and, 121–23. *See also* autonomy

work conditions, satisfaction and, 330–31

"work devotion schema," 297, 298

workers' compensation law, 102, 102t, 103, 104, 105, 105f, 106

work-family narrative explanation, as hegemonic, 296, 299

work histories: earnings and, 287–88; gender wage gap and, 287–88; sequential development of, 55

work/life balance, 7, 44, 68, 238–39, 328; billable hours and, 200; business careers and, 212; family and, 332–33; inside counsel and, 212, 214; satisfaction and, 332–33, 363; women and, 42

work opportunities, 251–53; African Americans and, 251–53; Whites and, 251–53

workplace authority, nonpracticing positions and, 124

workplace conditions, satisfaction and, 346

workplace diversity, 328; nonpracticing positions and, 125

workplace experiences: job changes and, 343, 344; satisfaction and, 363–64

work policies: family-friendly, 132; in law firms, 154–56, 159

work satisfaction, 44

worth, 334–38

Yoon, Albert H., 35

The Chicago Series in Law and Society
Edited by John M. Conley, Charles Epp, and Lynn Mather

Series titles, continued from front matter

The Three and a Half Minute Transaction: Boilerplate and the Limits of Contract Design
by Mitu Gulati and Robert E. Scott

This Is Not Civil Rights: Discovering Rights Talk in 1939 America
by George I. Lovell

Failing Law Schools
by Brian Z. Tamanaha

Everyday Law on the Street: City Governance in an Age of Diversity
by Mariana Valverde

Lawyers in Practice: Ethical Decision Making in Context
edited by Leslie C. Levin and Lynn Mather

Collateral Knowledge: Legal Reasoning in the Global Financial Markets
by Annelise Riles

Specializing the Courts
by Lawrence Baum

Asian Legal Revivals: Lawyers in the Shadow of Empire
by Yves Dezalay and Bryant G. Garth

The Language of Statutes: Laws and Their Interpretation
by Lawrence M. Solan

Belonging in an Adopted World: Race, Identity, and Transnational Adoption
by Barbara Yngvesson

Making Rights Real: Activists, Bureaucrats, and the Creation of the Legalistic State
by Charles R. Epp

Lawyers of the Right: Professionalizing the Conservative Coalition
by Ann Southworth

Arguing with Tradition: The Language of Law in Hopi Tribal Court
by Justin B. Richland

Speaking of Crime: The Language of Criminal Justice
by Lawrence M. Solan and Peter M. Tiersma

Human Rights and Gender Violence: Translating International Law into Local Justice
by Sally Engle Merry

Distorting the Law: Politics, Media, and the Litigation Crisis
by William Haltom and Michael McCann

Justice in the Balkans: Prosecuting War Crimes in the Hague Tribunal
by John Hagan

Rights of Inclusion: Law and Identity in the Life Stories of Americans with Disabilities
by David M. Engel and Frank W. Munger

*The Internationalization of Palace Wars: Lawyers, Economists, and the
Contest to Transform Latin American States*
by Yves Dezalay and Bryant G. Garth

*Free to Die for Their Country: The Story of the Japanese American Draft Resisters
in World War II*
by Eric L. Muller

Overseers of the Poor: Surveillance, Resistance, and the Limits of Privacy
by John Gilliom

*Pronouncing and Persevering: Gender and the Discourses of Disputing in an
African Islamic Court*
by Susan F. Hirsch

The Common Place of Law: Stories from Everyday Life
by Patricia Ewick and Susan S. Silbey

The Struggle for Water: Politics, Rationality, and Identity in the American Southwest
by Wendy Nelson Espeland

*Dealing in Virtue: International Commercial Arbitration and the
Construction of a Transnational Legal Order*
by Yves Dezalay and Bryant G. Garth

Rights at Work: Pay Equity Reform and the Politics of Legal Mobilization
by Michael W. McCann

The Language of Judges
by Lawrence M. Solan

Reproducing Rape: Domination through Talk in the Courtroom
by Gregory M. Matoesian

Getting Justice and Getting Even: Legal Consciousness among Working-Class Americans
by Sally Engle Merry

Rules versus Relationships: The Ethnography of Legal Discourse
by John M. Conley and William M. O'Barr